THE WHITE BOAR
AND THE
RED DRAGON

THE WHITE BOAR AND THE RED DRAGON

A Novel about Richard of Gloucester,
Later King Richard 111 and Henry Tudor

MARGARET W PRICE

Library of Congress Control Number:		2013901267
ISBN:	Hardcover	978-1-4797-8221-5
	Softcover	978-1-4797-8220-8
	Ebook	978-1-4797-8222-2

Rev. date: 05/24/2013

To order additional copies of this book, contact:
Xlibris Corporation
0-800-644-6988
www.xlibrispublishing.co.uk
Orders@xlibrispublishing.co.uk
305111

SYNOPSIS

A historical novel about the lives of Richard of Gloucester and Henry Tudor and the circumstances which led to them both becoming King of England, Richard, for so tragically a short time as Richard III and Henry, as founder of the Tudor Dynasty, Henry VII. Pushed by their forceful and ambitious mothers, who both had strong aspirations for their sons to ascend the throne, despite the many obstacles in the way, this story starts with their very early lives and their constant priming for kingship by their clever, determined, and obsessed mothers, Cecily, Duchess of York, and Lady Margaret Beaufort, Countess of Richmond—particularly the latter.

It is about Richard's family loyalty and the conflict of loyalties which overtook him: to the memory of his father, Richard of York, and his elder brother Edmund of Rutland, both murdered by the Lancastrians, whom he had promised his mother to avenge; to King Edward IV, his beloved eldest brother; to his mother, to his country, to his friends—and finally, to himself and his honour as a man.

His family motto was 'Loyalty binds me', and he always took this most seriously and strove to uphold it in everything he did.

Richard grew up a serious-minded, pious, and upright man, a brilliant military commander and leader, in spite of a childhood illness which threatened to cripple him, but which he fought to overcome with great determination and the resulting slightness of body which belied his strong spirit. He was a great achiever at a very early age, the favourite brother of Edward, the king, who trusted him utterly and honoured his ability with enormous responsibilities and commands.

He was adored by his wife, Anne, youngest daughter of the great Warwick the Kingmaker, who had bought Edward IV to power. He seemed ideally suited for kingship—though he never looked for it or hoped for it, until the sudden untimely death of Edward presented a set of circumstances which almost forced him to take the throne—but only for the best of reasons, which he knew were just and for the good of the country.

Far away, in South Wales, and then in Brittany and France, another young man, with no better or worse claim to the throne than Richard, was being pushed from early boyhood by his fabulously wealthy, highly intelligent, and influential mother, Lady Margaret Beaufort, descended from three royal houses, to go all out for what she insisted was his rightful claim to the throne. At first, he showed little interest—indeed, complete disbelief in the possibility of ever becoming king one day. But, as his influential mother's and Uncle Jasper's ambitions for him increased and changing circumstances showed that it was indeed a possibility, then his own ambitions became one with the driving force behind him from these two determined relatives. His mother was utterly ruthless in her methods to eliminate any possible rivals and did not hesitate to remove in any way she could, by scheming and plotting, those who got in the way of her ambition for Henry.

Each young man climbed towards the throne in different ways, neither pushed by personal ambition, but by circumstances and the influence and desires of others, particularly their mothers, both able women out of their time; both with obsessive cravings for power and the necessary determination to succeed in what they had set out to achieve.

There is a sub-plot in the story of Richard's life—his meeting and love for Katherine Mortimer in Northamptonshire; the birth of their child, who came to be known as John of Gloucester (or Pomfret) later in life, and her loss in tragic circumstances.

Richard's personal adult life was all about the loss of those he loved best and the strength of spirit which helped him deal with constant bereavements and continue in his good work for the commonweal of the people of England. He became an excellent king—but for a very short time, as he lost his life through the treachery of those he believed to be his friends at the Battle of Bosworth.

The novel is structured in a loose, episodical manner, with no chapters, but in vignettes, letters, and personal diary-like revelations and soliloquies. The writer has tried to get to the heart of each character by letting them reveal their deepest feelings themselves, often at times of great stress, trouble, or uncertainty. It is more concerned with the development of the characters and their effect upon each other than with the fighting and battles of what was later called the Wars of the Roses, though the events of this bloody and terrible period of civil war and the fast-changing political situations are inevitably reflected in the day-to-day life of the protagonists, the choices they have to make, and their eventual fates.

It is written mainly from the viewpoint of the two chief protagonists, but other important characters help to tell the story, mainly by personal comments, revelations, and letters. These include Cecily, Duchess of York, Lady Margaret Beaufort, Anne, Richard's wife, Edward IV, Francis Lovell, Richard's closest friend, George of Clarence, Harry, Duke of Buckingham, Bishop Morton, Margaret of Burgundy, Richard's sister, Kate, his sweetheart, and the two tragic boys—Edward V (later to be one of the murdered princes in the Tower) and Richard's son, Edward, Prince of Wales.

Episodes are dated accurately with place names where they occur and arranged chronologically in order, within the time scale 1460-85.

The book has been thoroughly researched in detail, with much cross-referencing done, so that the writer is confident there are no inaccuracies in places/times/events etc. Richard and Henry met only twice in this novel—possibly only once in real life—at the final battle. The first time was at Raglan Castle, Gwent, in 1470, in which were sowed the seeds of what could have been a close friendship, if they had not been on opposing sides—as the circumstances of their childhood and youth had much in common which drew them to each other and could—indeed should—have formed the basis for a natural friendship, which both desired. But conflicting loyalties to the Houses of York and Lancaster and political situations made it impossible—made them enemies instead of friends later on.

They met the second-and final time on Bosworth Field, where one was to lose his life—in that terrible bloody climax. Forced to fight the friend of his youth for his Crown and country, Richard is treacherously betrayed and cruelly slain by those he believed to be his allies and friends—and Henry Tudor becomes king—almost by default.

The writer feels that, after reading this novel, anyone who had an ambivalent attitude to Richard's supposed guilt as an evil murderer—which is the picture we see of him passed down in popular history—will have come down on his side unequivocally!

PROLOGUE 1

Richard, Micklegate Bar, York, 1460

'Vengeance is mine! saith the Lord! Remember that, boy! God will avenge men's evil deeds! We must believe that. Otherwise, how can any of us bear that-abomination?!'

Cecily Neville's voice shakes as she points upwards to the gruesome remains of the heads of my father, Duke Richard of York, and my brother, Edmund Rutland, stuck on poles above Micklegate Bar by laughing Lancastrians.

'Traitors? They are the traitors—the fiends who did that! Not only to the rightful king, my poor husband, and your seventeen-year-old brother, Richard, but to all true English people! Never forget this sight! Hold it in your mind forever, to give you the strength to do what must be done!'

She holds a hand up to her eyes, but only briefly. She has seen so many horrific sights and experienced so many terrible things in her life that she does not show her feelings easily. I know that. She has told me about them often enough, though I do not want to hear. She has never shown any weakness, even when following my father around the country on his many campaigns.

But I am a different matter, if she cares to look. My whole body is shaking, as if with an ague. I can smell the rotting flesh above me, even taste the miasma of it in my mouth, and my eyes are brimming with bitter tears, which I try hard to hold back, as my mother is constantly telling me how one must be self-controlled, even in dreadful situations. Her words ring in my head—as she intends them to—repeating themselves over and over, like a death knell.

'Vengeance is mine, saith the Lord! Hold this in your mind forever—to do what has to be done! Vengeance! Vengeance!'

Prologue 2

Henry Tudor, Pembroke Castle, South Wales, 1461

'Uncle Jasper, Uncle Jasper! What is happening? What are you doing? Where are you going? Can I come too?' I pull hard at my uncle's reins, quite distraught. I do not understand what is going on—all the grim, set faces around me and the frantic preparations to depart. I only know that I am not to be included. And no one is speaking. No one is telling me anything. I am not used to being ignored.

My nurse takes hold of my arm firmly, but not unkindly.

'Come, Henry, come with me! Your Uncle Jasper has no time to talk to you now, whatever! Get away from the horses' hoofs! You will be trampled on!'

I shake myself free, annoyed with Nurse Bethan's efforts to restrain me. I will find out what is going on. I will! 'Uncle, where are you going in such a hurry? And why aren't you taking me?!' I grab hold of my uncle's left boot and yank at it as hard as I can, determined not to be ignored. I am almost in tears with frustration.

'Because you're too young at only four years old, Nephew. I can only take men with me. There's a great Yorkist army coming here, and if they catch me, they'll kill me! I have to get away fast and go into hiding in the mountains!'

He bends his huge frame down and pats me on the head encouragingly. 'But I'll be back soon, never fear! As soon as it's safe to do so! You must be good now, boyo, and do as your nurse tells you!'

'Will you write to me, Uncle? I shall miss you so much!'

'And I you, lad! I will find time somehow to write. You will be safe enough here. They won't harm you or the servants. It's me they want! I hope to see you before too long, God willing!'

He turns his great horse's head round towards the gateway, waves once more to me, now crying uncontrollably, and rides out of the courtyard at the head of a small company of soldiers, who are his bodyguard and go everywhere with him.

I am now quite inconsolable and my tears fall freely as I watch my dear uncle's departure. I do not know when he will return and I feel so lonely already.

'Now, Henry, young gentlemen do not cry! Be brave! That is what your Uncle Jasper would want, and you must behave in a fitting manner! I am sure your uncle will get away safely and be back soon to see you again!'

Just then, Gwen, the little maid from the kitchen, comes up to me and pushes a big plate full of newly baked laver bread in front of my nose.

'Cheer up, little one! I have cooked this especially for your tea! I know how you love it so! It is your favourite, so come in now with me and enjoy it! Put away those tears! Your uncle would not like to see you cry so!'

'I couldn't tell the lad the truth now, could I? That the likelihood of my coming back is very slim?'

'No, my lord. He is just too young to understand. Better to leave him in ignorance of the true situation!'

'That my castle and lands have been appropriated by this usurping King Edward and myself attainted as a traitor? I could lose all, even my life! Everyone knows what happens to those judged traitors! If I am caught, I shall die the most horrible of deaths! My nephew must not be told of this, if it should happen, God forbid.'

'It will not happen, my lord! My men and I will make sure of that!'

'I know that you will protect me with your lives and are loyal to me unto death, and I am grateful for it. You do not know how I depend upon you!'

'Aye, my lord. We will willingly die first before they touch a hair of your head!'

'But I am worried that they may abduct Henry as a hostage or even kill him—though I assured him he would be safe in Pembroke Castle with the servants! After all, he has a claim to the throne! I know it is a distant one—but it exists!'

'Surely they would not stoop so low as to harm so young and innocent a child? Lancastrian or not?'

'Who knows?'

'You must pray that even they would not be tempted to such an evil deed!'

'Aye, what have little children got to do with this endless bloody struggle between Lancastrians and Yorkists which has gone on far too long already? But it is Henry's ancestry which puts him in such deadly danger!'

'Put it out of your mind, my lord. Concentrate on saving yourself. That is the urgent matter now! The quicker we get to the mountains of North Wales, the better. They will never find you in those fastnesses!'

'You are right. I know them like the back of my hand! And all the best hiding places where I can hole myself up for as long as I need to!'

Earl Jasper turns round one last time to gaze regretfully at his castle—where his beloved nephew, Henry Tudor, will be safe, hopefully, until he returns—if he ever does. He shakes his head and turns determinedly northwards.

Nurse Bethan also shakes her head as she goes to follow her charge into the castle and up the stone steps to the nursery quarters which Henry still occupies. She does not truly believe her reassurances to the little boy, nor Earl Jasper's, that he will return soon. She knows the true situation—which must be kept from Henry at all costs. He must have hope kept alive in him. It is her job to keep him healthy and happy—even if it means not being truthful to him.

Her thoughts give her no peace while she watches Henry go up to enjoy his tea, his tears soon forgotten.

A castle guard, her friend, stops to inquire at her long face.

'Cheer up, Bethan! There is nothing you can do about the situation, whatever, except protect the boy as well as you can!'

'But if something awful does happen to the earl, the child will be inconsolable! And it would be my job to break it to him! I dread that.'

'Well, you will have to deal with that if and when it happens! No good moping about it now! The earl can look after himself and has a good bodyguard.'

'Yes, but the little one would be devastated! Henry is self-willed and difficult to control at the best of times, and he adores his uncle! He would run wild completely, I am sure, if the worst comes to the worst!'

'But think, he would have you to comfort and console him!'

'At least, I suppose, I will have him to myself now, at least for a while—perhaps he will listen to me more and do as he is told, instead of constantly running off to find his uncle. The earl has been too easy on the boy. He needs discipline.'

'I expect he is sorry for the child, having no mother or father, and tries to take their place as much as he can by lavishing love and attention on him constantly!'

'That is true. But I am sure he is still better off without that awful Lady Margaret Beaufort! She could not have cared for him much, running off like that last year to marry the Earl of Stafford—but then the king would not let her have her child, and she was a good disciplinarian—unlike Lord Jasper!'

At that moment, Henry comes running down the stairs again, calling, 'Nurse Bethan! Aren't you coming to have some of this laver bread? It's lovely!'

He suddenly wraps his arms around her and buries his head in her ample bosom.

'I love you too, Nurse Bethan. You won't go away and leave me as well, will you, as Mother and Uncle Jasper have? I miss Mother too, though she was not so kind to me as Uncle and you. Why does everyone I care about go away and leave me?'

He bursts into tears again, soaking the front of her kirtle. She smiles ruefully over the child's head at her friend and hugs the little boy tight.

'No, I will not leave you, Henry! I will care for you as long as you need me!'

Middleham Castle, Yorkshire, Late Summer, 1461

Cecily, Duchess of York, was watching her two sons, George and Richard, on the green before Middleham Castle, training in martial arts with their friends, Francis Lovell and Robert Percy. All four boys were under the mentorship of the Earl of Warwick here at the castle, learning to be knights.

She observed them through a large window in the Solar in a rather detached fashion, as she was really more interested in her companion. This was her handsome nephew, Richard Neville, the earl, who was watching the boys with her and calling out encouragement to the youngest one, Richard, every now and then. The boy was fighting valiantly and with much determination for one so young.

Tall and athletic, his body strong and supple, Neville was everything a man in his prime should be.

She bit her lip as she looked at her youngest son, Richard—such a contrast.

She had always had an eye for a handsome man. Her husband, Richard, Duke of York, whom she had loved devotedly until he was murdered by the Lancastrians, was one such. She had never left his side, even on campaigns—even when she was heavily pregnant.

She sighed and shook her head doubtfully. 'What is to become of him? However long or hard he trains, he will never grow big enough or strong enough to be a knight!'

'Don't you believe it, Aunt. He is very ambitious and cannot wait to grow up and go into battle against the Lancastrians! He is always talking about it, you know! Sometimes, I believe he thinks of little else! He badly wants to avenge his father's and Edmund's deaths! In that small frame burns a most determined spirit!'

'Really? Well I fear his ambitions are doomed not to be realised, though seeing the heads of my poor husband and Edmund on the Micklegate did affect him deeply, I know. The desire may be there—which is commendable—but as for him actually being able to do anything about it, that is very doubtful. However hard we may wish for something, it does not necessarily come to pass. One learns that bitter fact soon in life. I have been praying for years—nay willing—the Lancastrians' downfall! And especially since this King, Henry VI, has proved so ineffectual—even pathetic! He is completely under the thumb of that French bitch, Queen Margaret, who seems to make all the decisions, and he gives in to her every whim—just for a quiet life, it seems! A weakling for a king, pah! Now my husband would have been splendid as king, if only he had got the chance. He was meant to be!'

'I agree about Henry. He is really quite inadequate, in body, mind, and character! He seems to hate most usual male pastimes, except hunting occasionally, and prefers to spend his time praying and studying theology with his priests. I think he would have been far happier as a monk than as a king! He is certainly more at ease with a book in his hand than a sword!'

'There is nothing wrong with devotion to God and his Word, nephew. I have always tried to live by God's Commandments, to instil awareness of him in my children and to bring them up in fear of him! It is a mother's duty to lead her children in the right Christian way. But I doubt if they have listened to half I have said. They are all self-willed and self-centred—especially Edward! Their church attendance is only lip service most of the time, I feel.'

'Richard, Aunt, is most devout, though I cannot say the same about George, I am afraid! The lad seems to really enjoy the chapel services here and attends Mass at least twice on Sundays and at least once every weekday—even when you are not here. He is also physically determined and active. I am sure he will grow into a fine man you can be proud of, in spite of his frailty of which you despair and his poor health as an infant!'

As if to back up his words, there was a gleeful shout from Richard down below, as a particularly strong blow of his knocked his elder brother George's wooden sword right out of his hand! Anne Neville, the Earl's youngest daughter, who had been running round and round cheering Richard during the mock fight, clapped loudly. She was Richard's shadow, being quite devoted to him—and he to her.

'A point for me, I think, sirrah!' exulted Richard, wiping his hand across his brow where the sweat dripped continually into his eyes despite his efforts. It was an exceptionally hot day—even for August.

A young page ran forward with a tray on which were several beakers of small ale chilled in the castle cellars. Richard grabbed one, downed it in one go, then started on another, drinking in long, deep swallows, almost without a breath.

'That's better!' he cried. 'Now I'll take you on, Francis!' He brandished his small sword and advanced towards his best friend with determination, his face screwed up against the sun and with his effort.

Richard Neville leant through the large Solar window and called, 'No, boys. I think that is enough for today. Come indoors. It is cool here and you must rest. Anne, you come too. You will get ill if you become overheated!'

Richard groaned but resigned himself to Warwick's command and walked in slowly with the others, dragging his sword by his side as they climbed the stairs breathlessly. A few moments later, they all stood before the Duchess Cecily and Neville, covered in dust and sweat but excited and happy.

'I won, Mother. I beat George! I would have beaten Francis and Robert too if you had let me go on!'

'As Lord Neville said, Richard, that is quite enough for today! Your face is purple, boy! Don't you know when enough is enough? Go now, all of you, and wash and change.'

At her words, an old maidservant, the Neville children's nurse from babyhood, whom they rather resented now, feeling themselves too old for her ministrations, no doubt, came forward and shepherded the children out of the Solar.

'You see what I mean about determination and ambition, Aunt? He will not give up easily and likes to beat everyone! Surely he will succeed in life, at whatever he makes up his mind to do?'

'You may have convinced me a little!' Cecily nodded, smiling one of her rare, tight smiles, so brief they seemed grudging. 'But we shall see. I think he may overtax his strength trying to prove he is as good as everyone else.'

'Not only as good as, Aunt, but better than! I agree though. We should not let him overdo things! I know all about delicate children, none better. Both Isabel and Anne have been so from birth, no one knows why, for I have a strong constitution, my wife likewise.'

They had good cause to worry, for by that evening, Richard had lost his bravura; wanted nothing to eat, and was running a high fever. He still objected to being made to go to bed early, even though he ached all over. By morning, his nose was running and he sneezed continually. His throat was so closed up and painful he could hardly swallow and his body felt on fire.

"Tis only another of his summer colds, my lady, I am sure. Nothing to be afraid about!' the old nurse assured Duchess Cecily.

But in a day or two, their mild anxiety turned to real concern. The boy was unable to get out of bed and was having great difficulty breathing.

'My right shoulder and arm won't work,' he croaked. 'They feel dead!'

'It's all right, lad,' comforted the nurse. 'You just overdid the sword-fighting the other day in all that heat. 'Tis exhaustion. You'll be fine in a day or so!'

But Richard was not. Nor for many days and weeks afterwards.

The best doctors were summoned, even the king's own physician, Dr Hobbes, whom he trusted implicitly. Hobbes came all the way from London at once when summoned by Lord Neville. King Edward also sent urgent messages asking to be informed of Richard's daily condition. He loved his young brother dearly; no one could deny that. He wished he was able to leave affairs of state and come up to Yorkshire at once to be by Richard's bedside.

The doctors just shook their heads in consternation after examining him many times. They took samples of his urine, bled him daily, and also obtained samples of faeces, which they pondered over and discussed lengthily. They made him stick out his tongue whilst they observed it from all angles and peered down his throat inquiringly. They poked and prodded his arms and legs and moved them around in different directions until he cried out with pain. But it was obvious they were completely baffled by his illness.

'It is a mystery to us,' Dr Hobbes hesitantly confided at last, not wanting to admit their inadequacy in the situation, but forced to. 'The sore throat and the streaming cold seem to have abated, and he can now breathe almost normally—God be praised—but the paralysis—it may persist!'

The other doctors nodded sagely, afraid to impart this grave news but impelled to and feeling foolish, no doubt in the duchess's rather forbidding presence.

'His shoulder, arm, and leg may never properly recover, if at all! We think he has had a rare case of what is known as infantile paralysis. He has, in fact, escaped lightly, Madam, if it is that dreaded childhood disease!'

'He will certainly live now, of that we can be sure! Most die of it. I have heard of cases in Italy recently where death has occurred quickly, because the chest muscles were affected so badly the patients could not breathe—'

'Yes, yes!' interrupted the Duchess impatiently. 'Are you trying to tell me that he is to be a cripple then?' she cried horrified. 'Is there nothing more you can do for him?'

'Nothing, my lady, we freely admit it. His recovery is in God's hands now. We can only pray. We advise you to do likewise.'

They withdrew, rubbing their hands together and shaking their heads in a futile fashion.

But Richard did improve, slowly, it was true, for he had made up his mind to recover completely. This was not going to beat him! He could not wait to get outside and start his training again to be a knight. His whole being was focused on just that.

His mother prayed daily for him in Middleham Castle Chapel, as did Lord Neville and his entire family, and the villagers prayed in the local church. Richard was popular with them, always engaging them in conversation when he was well; asking about their work, their families, and their problems.

Lord Neville came to see him every day as well, to cheer and encourage him, as did Francis Lovell and Robert Percy, his friends, also Anne, Isabel, and Lord Neville's wife, the Lady Ann. Little Anne in particular was always by his side. She seemed to spend most of her time with him, chattering away and plumping up his pillows—also dosing him with the obnoxious mixtures the doctors had prescribed to build up his strength again. He much preferred her company to the fussy old nurse, though he knew she tried to do her best to care for him.

'If it weren't for you, Anne, I would go mad stuck in this room! Only you, your family, Francis, and Robert come to visit me. George has been only twice, and then I know he could not wait to get away again as quickly as possible! He made that obvious by wrinkling up his nose when he came in! That hurt! I suppose sickrooms do get stuffy and smelly, but I can't help it and he did not bother to hide how he felt. But that's George—selfish through and through! I love him but I often don't like him much!

And then there's Mother! She has only visited me once, as far as I know! I was asleep and woke to see her standing at the bottom of my bed gazing silently down at me, and the look on her face, I could not make it out. There was pity there, but something else too, something which struck cold deep inside me. I can only describe it as loathing! But she is my mother! Does she loath me so now that I have become a cripple?

Does that make me unacceptable as her son?

She prays for me, oh yes. I know she spends long hours in the chapel praying for me. Doing her Christian duty, I suppose! But what I want is for her to visit me, keep me company, try to cheer me up with kind words as the rest of you do! Why does she keep away from me? Why do I appal her so?'

'She is a very religious lady. Maybe she thinks she can do you more good by praying to God for your full recovery constantly than by spending time here?'

'But I am her son! Mothers should love and support their sons! She adores Edward, George too! I'm beginning to think that she does not want to come near me any more, because she cannot bear to see me the way I am now! She has always been strict and severe with me, and I never seemed able to please her, whatever I did—but now—I am sure she hates me!'

'Richard, I am sure your mother does love you. Perhaps she finds it hard to show her feelings. Some people are not easily affectionate, even to their nearest and dearest.'

'Edward and George have always been her favourites—Edmund before them too. None of them could do any wrong in her eyes, and I was forever in trouble with her at Fotheringhay, even as a tiny boy! She has always picked on me with constant criticism! I do not think she ever cared much for me, because I was not big and strong like the other boys, and now I am a cripple, she despises me!'

Francis Lovell, Richard's closest friend, came in at that moment.

'I heard that, Richard! Stop feeling sorry for yourself! You are not a cripple! Look how much you have improved lately! It may be slow, but every day, you are a little better! And of course your mother does not hate you! Mothers do not hate their children. They love and support them, whatever they are like, whatever they become, whatever they do!'

'I have only improved because of what you have done—you and Anne! Mother does not bother, whatever you say. Robert and Lord Neville come quite a lot and try to cheer me up with jokes and snippets of scandal from around the castle! But Edward, the brother I love most and who has always loved me and been concerned for me, cannot come here at all because he is always away fighting or busy being king in London and with important affairs of state! It isn't fair!'

'Richard, you know he would come if he could. It is a very long way, hundreds of miles! Does he write to you?'

'Oh yes, often. However busy he is, he has always found time for me. When we came back from exile in Brugge and were under house arrest in London, he would come every day to see me. George as well, of course, but it was me he always seemed most pleased to see!'

'There you are then,' Francis assured him. 'Lots of people care about you! And the Duchess Cecily does too, I am sure!'

'I will show her! When I am better I will train harder than ever! Exercise improves the body and my muscles need a lot of help! You and Robert must help me with lots of work-outs. When I grow up, I will be the bravest, strongest knight in the country and make Mother proud of me!'

'Of course you will. You know you can do it!' cried Anne. 'Now it is time for your exercises around the room. Then we will rub your shoulder, arm, and leg with that special oil Francis got from the old herbalist in Middleham village. It is good, isn't it, Francis?'

'Very good. Earl Neville said that when he strained his leg in that fall while he was hunting, he rubbed it in daily and it worked like magic! The old woman said that if we rubbed it in every day and moved your shoulder, arm, and leg up and down a lot, you would get better more quickly, as the muscles need to build up again. You must not lie in bed any more but try to keep moving and exercising as much as you can.'

'I will, I will! Let's start right now!'

Richard heaved himself off the bed and hobbled slowly and painfully around the room, leaning on Anne and Francis for support. The effort made him grimace with pain, but he kept at it.

And he went on working at his exercises, grimly determined to show everybody—especially his mother—that he would never be a cripple. Anne, Francis, or Robert came each day to help him, and he improved quickly—until the day came when he was allowed to leave his room and climb down the steep steps into the Solar, or the Great Hall, even to go out for short walks in the autumn sunshine.

One day, early in December, when the weather was too bitterly cold to venture outdoors, he was sitting on a wooden settle in the Solar by a roaring log fire, feeling rather depressed because he could not go out. He hated being shut indoors, even in winter. Also, Lord Neville, Lady Ann, his wife, Francis and Robert, and Isobel, Anne's elder sister, had set off a week ago for Warwick Castle, the earl's most important residence, where he would hold Christmas Court for Edward the King and numerous relatives, friends, and foreign dignitaries. There was much to prepare for in advance at the great castle for the Christmas celebrations. The weather had been dreadful when they left, with intermittent snow and freezing fog, and it would take twice as long in such weather to complete the journey. So he had been left alone, apart from the Duchess Cecily, Anne, and just a few servants, as most of the household had accompanied Lord Neville, with many carts full of stores, furniture, bedding and other articles the Earl considered essential to take with them to Warwick Castle for his stay there with his family for Christmas and New Year. With so many guests to accommodate, they would need them all.

But Anne had insisted on staying. Dear Anne. If it hadn't been for her constant companionship and care over these last few difficult months, cheering and encouraging him with the exercises, and when the pain became too much, forcing him to continue anyway, he knew he would not have got better so quickly, in spite of her telling him it was his own determination which had done it, for her insistence that he kept to the regular exercises and massage had worked! He was almost back to normal, except for a little weakness still on the side which had been paralysed. This made him limp a bit at times, when he was tired; that was all. Anne had been an excellent nurse, though still so young! He was very grateful to her.

She had refused outright to go to Warwick Castle yet with her parents and the others, insisting that Richard needed her so much she must stay with him.

She knew he would only have his austere mother and the selfish George for company otherwise—if they chose to give it at all, that is.

'Richard! Tomorrow you will accompany George and I to Warwick Castle! The Lady Anne will also be in my care on the journey. I do hope that Edward will definitely be able to join us for the Christmas festivities. We have not seen him for so long. But of course, he may be called away any time to deal with yet another Lancastrian uprising somewhere! Who knows?'

Duchess Cecily was standing by his side, making one of her rare appearances. These days, she seemed to spend most of her time in prayer and had expressed an interest in following the Benedictine Rule. Somehow, Richard could not see her as a nun. She was too self-willed, too self-opinionated. Nuns were humble, self-effacing creatures, which his proud mother certainly was not!

Richard had grown rather sullen and bitter since his long illness because of her neglect of him and made no answer.

'Did you hear me, boy? Are you deaf as well as deformed? I feel you are sufficiently recovered now to make the journey, though a litter may be advisable.'

'Never, Mother! I can ride! I am sure I can do that perfectly well!' he shot out, angered by her cold words. It was as if she had slapped him hard in the face, and her icy tone seemed to confirm what he suspected about her present attitude to him. He was now just a liability, to be dealt with as best as may be. He turned his head away and stared morosely into the flames.

'I am glad of that, as Earl Neville has told me you may resume your knightly training after the New Year.'

'Good! And I shall work even harder to catch up and prove to you that I am no cripple, nor deformed!

Everyone else believes in me and cares what happens to me. Why is it that you, my own mother, has no faith in me? Once you laid a great task on my head at Micklegate Bar! Do you not remember? Because I do and am determined to carry it out one day. Avenge my father and brother, you said. That I will do! When, I cannot be sure, but I made a vow!'

Cecily's eyebrows rose somewhat at his words, and her mouth pursed a little. Then she turned abruptly away.

'I will instruct your pages to pack your things. We leave at dawn!' And she was gone.

Against his will, Richard felt his eyes prickling with tears and hastily shook them away. She would not make him cry, she would not! He would show her. He would show them all!

Pembroke Castle, South Wales, 30 September 1462

The young Henry Tudor, now almost six years old, looked up from his primer in a state of excited animation at the sound of horses' hoofs in the castle courtyard below. He turned to Lady Anne Devereux, his face all lit up in a way she had never seen before. He looked almost happy for once!

'It's Uncle Jasper. It must be! He's come back at last!'

Avoiding the restraining arm of his tutor, he ran to the window and gazed down. But what he saw there made him draw back, uncertain and afraid.

A troop of mounted and armed soldiers had surged through the open portcullis, headed by a large, bearded figure in full armour, who was covered in dust and mud, as indeed the whole party were. Henry could almost smell the sweat from the hot, tired men and the lathered, winded horses. He backed away from the window and ran back to Lady Anne.

"Tis the Yorkists come to take me away! Perhaps they have caught Uncle Jasper and now they want me! He said they would not hurt me, but I have heard such terrible tales about what they do . . . !' he trailed off, shaking.

'What tales are these, boy? Who has been frightening you?'

'Why, the castle servants tell me. Nurse Bethan said—'

'Whatever she said, she had no right to! She is here to protect you, not to terrify you! I will speak to her shortly!'

'No, my lady, please don't be angry with her. She is kind and good and looks after me well. Who are these men, then? They look as if they have just ridden fast from a battleground!'

'Which indeed they may have! Though I see no blood upon them. It is my lord husband, Lord Herbert! It is so long since you met him you have forgotten what he looks like! The king has granted him The Lordship of Pembroke for his outstanding services to the Crown and for fighting so well in the Battle of Towton last year! He is lord now, not only of this castle, but of all the lands and towns of Pembroke, and everyone must be loyal to him and swear their allegiance—!'

'No, that cannot be!'

She was cut off in mid-sentence by a desperate cry from Henry, who jumped away from her in great distress.

'No, it is not possible! Uncle Jasper is lord here! He is Lord of Pembroke! He will come back soon, when the fighting is over, to claim his rights and to look after me again! I don't understand!'

He dissolved into tears, shaking his head as he rubbed his eyes with the backs of his hands. He was always being told that boys must be brave and never cry, but it was hard not to sometimes, very hard. Lady Herbert drew him to her and wiped his eyes with her kerchief. 'There now, little one. None of us understands this terrible war which has gone on for so long and torn our countries and its peoples apart!

How could a small boy be expected to? The Yorkists have a White Rose as emblem, and the Lancastrians have a Red Rose, but roses are beautiful things and smell so sweetly, and all there has been for years is the smell of death . . . !' She trailed off, no doubt remembering that it was a vulnerable child she was talking to, who must be protected from such knowledge.

'Is my Uncle Jasper dead then, if Lord Herbert's been given this castle? He must be dead!'

'No, I am sure we would have heard. Lord Herbert was made Lord of Pembroke in July, two months ago. A messenger came to tell me in August and also informed me that your uncle was hiding in the northern mountains somewhere. I am sure he is safe!'

'And no one thought to tell me this news before? And every day, I have prayed for his return, not knowing whether he was alive or dead . . .'

'We thought it best to keep this news from you as long as possible. We knew it would upset you! Children should be shielded from life's unhappy events!'

'Not this one! Not any more! I am not a baby. I want to know everything that is going on, especially if it has to do with my Uncle Jasper!'

'I know you love him dearly, boy, and miss him sorely. But I have done my best for you since we came here. We all have. We try to keep you as happy as possible in the circumstances.'

'And I thank you for it, my lady. But I beg you, do not shield me any more. I need to know about things.'

'Very well, Henry. I promise that from now on, you shall hear all the news like the rest of us, good or bad! But come, my lord husband will be waiting in the Great Hall below! I am sure he is most anxious to meet you!'

She took Henry's hand and beckoned to her daughter, Maude, who had been sitting quietly by their tutor, Master Scotus, writing out some latin verses, for she shared Henry's lessons with him, and his love of learning. She was a girl of few words, but very intelligent, like Henry, and they competed to see who could earn the most praise from this eminent Oxford scholar who taught them every day. She was a year or two older than Henry, but they had become great friends and were always in each other's company.

'Master Scotus, I am sure that you will excuse the children from their lessons for the rest of today, as my lord husband has come home? Tonight there will be a great feast in honour of his homecoming and success in the last battle. Why do you not take this opportunity to rest or take the air down by the sea? It is a lovely day. If I had not so much to do, I would be out at work in the fresh air myself, tending my herb garden! We use so many different herbs for medicines and ointments that I take especial care of them! Now I must go and order hot water for my lord's bath and check that the cooks have everything in hand for tonight! I have invited many guests to celebrate with us!'

The tutor nodded briefly, glad of the unexpected break from his teaching routine, although he found both children—especially Henry, most stimulating to teach. The boy had a razor-sharp and very enquiring mind in spite of his tender years, and his constant questioning about everything he was taught kept Master Andreas Scotus very busy attending to his demands! He was also in charge of the education of Maude's brothers and sisters, but they were younger and were taught at a separate time, as they could not possibly keep up with Henry and Maude.

As they descended the great stone stairway, Henry's mind continued seething with the unfairness of it all. It should be Uncle Jasper's homecoming they were going to be celebrating that night, not Lord Herbert's. He had just taken over everything that belonged to his uncle! How could that be right? Wasn't it stealing? The Bible said that taking someone else's property was breaking one of the Ten Commandments!

How could the king give away something which belonged to another man? Confused and unhappy, Henry followed Lady Anne and Maude downstairs.

As they entered the Great Hall below, which was overflowing with crowds of Lord Herbert's men and servants carrying in boxes and bags, he saw the tall figure of Lord Herbert advancing towards them. After greeting his wife and Maude affectionately, he turned and looked down at the small boy in front of him.

'Well, young Henry, I hope I find you healthy and happy? I know that my Lady wife has cared for you well and that you want for nothing!'

'I am most grateful to her, my lord. She knows that. But I still miss my Uncle Jasper!'

'Of course you do, boy. That is only natural! I am sure you will see him again one day! Now I must bathe and get ready for the great feast which I know is being prepared! I will talk longer with you tomorrow!'

He turned away and began to stride towards the spiral stone staircase which led up to his private apartments, followed by his wife.

Henry just stood, glowering, unable to utter a word, though inside he seethed. He desperately wanted to throw a tantrum like he used to when he was tiny and Nurse Bethan would not let him have something he wanted; to scream and shout and roll around on the floor to relieve his feelings! But he kept his mouth clamped shut. He knew that if he said anything, anything at all, the floodgates would burst open and the restraint he had been showing would break down in a moment!

He was grateful now for the training in behaviour he had received from Master Scotus, apart from the book learning.

At the feast, which he knew he was bound to attend, though in no mood for rejoicing, all he had to do was to be polite and say as little as possible and he would get through the evening somehow.

Pembroke Castle, The Feast, 30 September 1462

The feast was at its height. Many important guests had already eaten their way through the first course, which consisted of various shellfish—mussels, prawns, shrimps, lobsters, crabs, and also sea bream, salmon from the rivers, along with an amazing array of other rare and strange fish. These included conger eel, sea crayfish, and even sea mammals such as porpoises and seals.

Ale flowed freely and was consumed by the gallon, also mead and wine. Many of the guests were already very merry.

Great dishes full of a large variety of fruits were arrayed along the centre of the long trestle tables: apples, pears, quinces, even grapes from France, for ships from French ports frequently docked in Pembroke Harbour, full of exotic goods, along with the fishing boats owned by the local people. There had been a bumper harvest that year, with so much fruit—and a lot still to be picked—that what was not eaten, if properly stored in cool places, would last through winter right into next spring.

But Henry hardly noticed the great array. His thoughts were elsewhere, with Uncle Jasper in the mountains of North Wales, where he was supposed to be hiding out.

'What is wrong, Henry? Are you feeling ill? You usually enjoy your food!'

The concerned questioner was Maude, who sat next to him, happily devouring a dish of steamed salmon with relish.

'I'm just not hungry, that's all,' he answered absent-mindedly.

'But you must eat! And there's so much to choose from. The next course includes swan and peacock. Are you waiting for those?'

'No, I'm just not interested in food today, that's all. I've other things on my mind!'

Henry knew that Maude was only asking because she cared about him. She was a kind girl, and being a little older in years, tended to mother him rather as girls will small boys and always stood up for him when his mother or their eminent tutor, Andreas Scotus, found fault with him over something he had done or had omitted to do. Mature and wise for her years, Maude seemed to have an intuitive understanding of what he was going through that day.

'Try not to be resentful of my father, Henry. He is a good man and kind and will always look after you as if you were one of his own sons and keep you safe.'

'But I don't want him to! It's my Uncle Jasper I want to care for me. He should be here. This feast should be for him!'

'Well, he isn't, and it's not! It's sad for you, and I can imagine how you must feel so upset at the moment, Henry. I would too if I had lost all those closest to me as you have: your father killed before you were born, your mother going away when she remarried, and now your beloved uncle having to go into hiding in fear of his life! But try to be thankful that at least you are safe here, with a kind family to look after you!'

Henry knew that Maude was fond of him, as he was of her. He did not want to hurt her by criticising her father. His black mood dominated his whole mind at the moment, however.

'But your father should not even be here! He should not be Lord of Pembroke! This is my uncle's castle, my uncle's lands! One should not take what belongs to others. It's one of the Ten Commandments! Lord Herbert is a thief!'

There was a sudden shocked silence at his vehement outburst, and all eyes turned towards this high-born young lad who could not control his feelings, or his mouth.

'Sssh! Henry! You must not say such things!' cried Maude, putting a finger on his lips. 'Be not so bitter! How could my father have refused the king's gift? It would have made King Edward angry, and one does not make kings angry deliberately. It is not safe!'

'I don't care! The king was wrong to give away Uncle Jasper's castle! He had no right to do it! And your father is wrong to accept it!'

By this time, the whole hall was silent, staring open-mouthed at this loud-mouthed young upstart. Young he may be, their faces said, but wild and wilful and very unwise! By now, if he had been an adult, he would have been put under arrest and dragged off to prison, accused as a traitor, to await the king's punishment, but Henry had completely lost all his earlier self-control. He felt as if his head was bursting with misery. It was all just too much for him to cope with, and in spite of Maude trying to hold him down in his seat on the bench, he jumped up, threw down the apple, he had been nibbling, and flung himself out of the hall.

He ran and ran, under the open portcullis, straight out of the main gate and along the lowered drawbridge—luckily left like that for the evening so that any of the important guests might come and go at will.

The strong, salty wind from the west battered his face and filled his nose and lungs with blessed fresh air. After the smoky, stifling atmosphere of the

Great Hall, where scents of food mixed with strong body odours had made him feel he could not breathe, as he already felt stifled by his raging anger and misery, he breathed deeply of it as he ran, the great gulps of sea air flushing away the bitterness and heartbreak.

He came to a stop on the quayside, his chest heaving convulsively, and found himself teetering right on the edge, gazing down into the inky blackness of the harbour water.

Gradually, his breathing slowed and steadied, and he became calmer, but he still stood there, peering into the dark water. It drew him like a magnet, mirroring his dark thoughts.

'Come along, young master. They are all so worried about you up at the castle, whatever! Lady Anne sent me to find you and bring you home!'

It was the lean figure of Davydd ap Llewellyn, his friend, son of the castle horse master, who stood by him now, his arm on Henry's shoulder. He was about ten years old, strong and wiry, but small for his age. He helped his father break in horses in the fields behind the castle and train them to have no fear when carrying men in full armour into battle. He had taught Henry to ride last year, and Henry liked him a lot. They were friends. He was proud of his friendship with Davydd, though the Herbert children and Andreas Scotus frowned on it. Strangely enough, Lady Anne encouraged it, realising, no doubt, that Henry needed all the friends he could get, even if they were of low birth. Davydd was down-to-earth and sensible and helped to keep the somewhat wilful smaller boy in line.

'Home? Is that what it is? It doesn't feel like my home any longer! I feel like an outcast in that castle now!'

'Well, boyo, there is nothing you can do about the situation whatever! May as well accept it! As my father says, "What can't be cured must be endured!" At least you have a good home, food, and clothes to keep you warm. And people who care about you! I know many round about here who have none of those things! So you must be grateful for what you have got!'

'Count my blessings? Is that it? Forget about my Uncle Jasper? Forget that Lord Herbert has stolen his castle and lands?'

'No, of course not. But you must realise that it is the king who has caused all this! He gave Lord Herbert your uncle's castle and lands because he is a loyal Yorkist and supports him. Your uncle is a Lancastrian and hates the king! That is why he has been stripped of his rights. He is the king's enemy! Do you not see, boyo? There is nothing to be done here but accept your lot! You are too young to fight King Edward's will!'

'Maybe, but one day, when I grow old enough and become a knight, I will fight him! One day, I will make sure that my uncle's birthright is returned to him!'

'For now, lad, you must accompany me back to the castle and make your apologies to Lord Herbert! There is no other way. He may not treat you so kindly in the future if he thinks that you openly hate him and defy him! Learn to accept his will—you will be happier for it!'

The solid good sense of the older boy, his good friend, at last permeated Henry's self-centred black mood, and he allowed himself to be escorted back into the castle by him, agreeing to trust his advice. That day, he had learnt a lesson in survival—that one must dissemble when it was in one's own interests.

'Now you must go and apologise to Lord Herbert and Lady Anne, Henry boyo! You are their guest and they will no doubt be angry at what you said and how you behaved in front of all his other guests!'

'I don't care. It isn't fair!'

'Life isn't fair, but you have it better than most—think about what I said down by the dock! Go in now and find his lordship!'

Davydd gave Henry a shove in the direction of the Great Hall, from which the sound of merriment and minstrels' music issued, though the music was almost drowned by laughing and loud voices. Very reluctantly, but knowing that what Davydd had said made sense, Henry walked slowly to the hall, with dragging steps, expecting a severe reprimand and punishment for his unacceptable behaviour earlier.

But when he appeared in the archway, there was an immediate hush, and then Lord Herbert put down his flagon of wine, strode towards the boy, picked him up, and held him high above his head.

'Here he is, the recalcitrant youth! But we all forgive him for his outburst, don't we? He is only very young, after all!'

He let out a great laugh and swung Henry round and round in the air until he was dizzy, then deposited him by Lady Anne, who put her arms around him, pulling him on to her lap. In that moment, he realised he had better make the best of things. After all, these people cared about him, even though he was not of their family, and he must respect Lord Herbert from now on and try to obey his will. He was already fond of Lady Anne, as she had shown great kindness to him, being like a second mother really, and Maude and the other children were all friendly to him too. He had expected recriminations and a beating, but was getting nothing but kindness. They understood how he felt!

Lady Anne picked up a piece of roast swan and held it to his lips. 'Come, Henry, you must eat! Try this—just for me. Yes?'

Henry took the meat and put it into his mouth, chewed it, and found it very good. Suddenly, with his change in mood, he realised that his appetite had returned! He slid down off Lady Anne's lap, bowed to her in thanks, then stood humbly before Lord Herbert.

'I apologise, my lord, for what I said and for running out so rudely from your table. But I was so upset . . . !'

'I know, my boy. Forget it and enjoy the rest of the feasting!'

When he returned to his seat beside Maude rather shame-facedly, she smiled gently at him and offered him a portion of fruit tart, which he ate with relish.

Lord Herbert then stood, held up his arms to get attention, and addressed the assembled guests.

'I thank you all for celebrating with me my good fortune in acquiring this great castle and all the estates and towns surrounding it from our lord, King Edward!

But my family's real home is at Raglan Castle, in Gwent. We will be returning there in a week or so, when I have seen that this castle is properly garrisoned and fortified against attack by the Lancastrian armies during my absence!

I will try to be a fair and just Lord of Pembroke and will always hear your grievances and try to right wrongs which may have been done to you. If you have any disputes or grievances for me to deal with before I depart for Raglan, I shall be available to receive them from tomorrow morning!

Now I ask you to try this wonderful new wine I brought back with me after the French wars, several dozen barrels in fact! It is from Gascony and is of the highest quality, matured for years in deep, cool cellars. If there is one thing the French can do, and they have many faults, it is make excellent wine!'

The guests cheered and applauded as a group of pages began to distribute pitchers of the new wine, and very soon, the whole company were overcome by its effects, as it was much stronger than their usual wines. After the huge amount of food they had consumed, it rendered many comatose on the floor amongst the rushes, where they dozed happily, unaware of hounds sniffing round their heads, nosing for scraps from the feast tables. Gentry and chief townspeople who had intended returning home spent the night where they had fallen; others managed to stagger to stone windowsills or wooden benches along the side of the hall, where they stretched out, dead to the world.

Outside, in the castle yard, the many waiting horses were taken to the stables, and when these were full, were let out in the fields behind the castle for their owners to find next morning when they had recovered!

Henry, having come to terms with the arrival of this new Lord of Pembroke, now realised he had no choice but to accept that he would soon have to leave Pembroke Castle altogether—the only home he had ever known, and travel to another, alien place to live. He assumed he would be going with the Herbert family to Gwent, as Lord Herbert was his guardian.

Why did he lose everyone and everything he loved? His mother had abandoned him; his Uncle Jasper had been forced to flee and leave him behind, and now he had to leave his beloved castle. Would Nurse Bethan come too? Would his tutor, Andreas Scotus, accompany the family? And what about his best friend, Davydd ap Thomas?

He was bewildered and apprehensive and, at that moment, felt he would much rather be a simple farm boy in the hills of Wales, living all his life in one place, but having his family all around him. He might be poor, but he would have what mattered most—a mother and father, brothers and sisters, and a secure home.

Shene Palace, Richmond, New Year's Day, 1463

'Sire, there is a most insistent supplicant to see you. He will not go away! He has his daughter with him, a young girl not more than twelve. She is weeping, Sire, and—'

'Yes, yes, man, get on with it! What are you trying to say?'

King Edward was slumped on his throne, very inebriated. His head ached abominably and he was certainly in no mood to deal with supplicants today. But it was a tradition that anyone, high or low, could approach the king on New Year's Day with a plea and he would be seen.

Until a few moments ago, Edward had been happy enough, in spite of his hangover. He had all his family around him: his brothers, George of Clarence and Richard of Gloucester, his mother, the Duchess Cecily, his sister Margaret, and his dearest sister Elizabeth enjoying a quiet day after the frantic festivities of the Christmas week.

Last night had been particularly memorable, in more than one way, or should he say in more than one bed? He couldn't seem to think straight. He just remembered far too much wine and several willing wenches.

'Sire, he is a poor man, and he has waited since dawn, determined to put his case to you!' the steward announced.

'Oh, very well. You'd better bring him in, I suppose!' Edward sighed, yawning. 'But it had better be something worth disturbing me for today!'

A tall, painfully thin middle-aged man, his face worn with care and his hands with hard work, led in a young girl, certainly no more than twelve and small for her age too, except for her belly, which protruded in an almost obscene manner, it seemed, to Richard of Gloucester. She was not much older than him, and it was obvious she had been cruelly misused.

'I come to seek justice, Sire, for my poor daughter! Only yesterday did I manage to get out of her the name of the brute who got her in this way, against her will, she insists, when I threatened to beat the truth out of her, child or no child! She admitted she had been too terrified to tell the truth before! She had been threatened that if she did not keep her mouth shut, he would have it shut for her permanently and all my family turned out of our home!'

'And who is this brute?' drawled Edward, not really interested.

'The Lord Hastings, Sire, your Chamberlain and best friend! We live on his land. We have a small farm near—'

'Yes, yes, that is enough! Have you any proof of what you are telling me? How do I know that this is not just some story conveniently concocted because the real culprit—mayhap a farm labourer with a taste for young flesh—won't admit his responsibilities and marry her?'

'Nay, nay, Sire. I am a God-fearing man! And an honest one! What I say is the plain truth. Lord Hastings raped her and this is the result!'

'Well, what do you expect me to do about it? This kind of thing happens every day! Am I expected to make restitution for every bastard?'

The girl's father winced, and Richard did not blame him. Edward was being very callous about this affair, but William Hastings was his best friend, and today was not the best day to ask him to deal with it. Richard knew his elder brother was very tired after the Christmas festivities and other private activities and that he had a bad headache.

'Sire, he should be punished! I am not asking for anything except that he acknowledges the child as his and provides for its upbringing! That is only justice, surely?'

Edward drew several gold pieces from his pouch. 'Here, you will have to be satisfied with these and be thankful I take you at your word! I could have sent you away empty-handed! I hear so many sad, trumped-up stories and receive so many begging letters. If I believed them all and paid up every time, I would soon be a beggar myself, eh?'

He slapped his hands on his thighs and roared with laughter, calling for wine. 'What was it they said? The hair of the dog . . .'

'I thank you for my daughter, Sire. You are very generous. But what of Lord Hastings?'

'What of him? Do you expect me to send for him this minute and tell him off just to satisfy your so-called sense of justice? Go now. This interview is at an end!'

Edward clapped his hands, and the steward ushered them both out firmly, the girl crying quietly and the father shaking his head. Richard turned to watch them go. He was full of pity, especially for the young girl. And his heart went out to her father too, bewildered by the fact that he had not received the King's Justice, which, he suspected, was probably of more worth to him than the gold.

———

So they were true then, the stories he had heard about Lord Hastings—that he preferred very young girls and if he could not get them willingly, then he just forced them? It was horrible, horrible!

'Cheer up, Dickon! It's about time you knew the ways of the world! At least I helped them! Do you think badly of me then for giving them short shrift?'

King Edward had got up, swaying slightly, and put his arm round Richard's shoulders, the big, protective brother. 'The look on your face, Dickon! Anyone would think you had witnessed murder!'

'I have not witnessed justice—real justice! The man was right. Lord Hastings should be punished!'

'But he's my friend, Dickon, and one does not put one's friends on trial!'

'Not even if they deserve it and are obviously guilty of what they have been accused?'

'How can you know that? Do you really think I believed the man's story? I only gave him the gold to get rid of him! For all we know, he had abused the girl himself—it happens! And I'm just too tired today to be bothered with such things!'

'So will you speak to Lord Hastings about it and find out if it's true?'

The king laughed and slapped Richard's back. Then he sat down heavily on his throne again and rubbed his temples peevishly with the tips of his fingers.

'Enough of this, Dickon. Let it go! Take pity on your poor brother's head!'

'I do, Edward, but I do not admire my King's so-called Justice!'

He turned his back on the king, went to the window, and watched the snowflakes falling. He felt their icy cold without touching them. They matched the feeling inside him.

'The trouble with you, Dickon, is that you're an idealist! You'll soon grow out of it—at least I hope you will!' cried George. 'Or you're going to have a very miserable time! The world is a hard place, and if a man gets any kind of justice in these times, he can count himself lucky!'

Big and bluff and golden-haired like Edward, George thought himself, at fifteen, very much the man of the world; very worldly-wise. He knew how to use his charm with devastating effect on everyone, usually getting his own way.

And then that day, he was an adult! Last night, Edward had initiated him into the pleasures of bedding a girl!

He could not wait until tonight for more!

But the one girl he really wanted seemed out of his reach—like the Pole Star. That was Isabel Neville, Lord Neville's eldest daughter—he who was now known as The Kingmaker, since he had helped Edward to the throne. Without him, Edward would never have managed it on his own, he thought enviously.

But Warwick was a proud man, the greatest and richest landowner in the kingdom—far richer than the king himself. He seemed to own more of everything than anyone else, and George knew he had set his sights on Isabel marrying at least a king! And she probably would do too, with the enormous dowry in gold and estates to bring to the husband who was chosen for her! And that was the heart of the matter. He did not think Warwick would accept him as his son-in-law. He knew Isabel was as fond of him as he of her, though they had only met circumspectly at Middleham Castle when he and Richard were in training there as knights, under Warwick's mentorship.

When the time came for her to be married, she would have no choice in the matter. Love would never enter into it, sadly.

Meanwhile, there could be plenty of diversions.

The Duchess Cecily, who up to then had said little, came up to Richard where he stood looking out of the window.

'Richard, I applaud your sense of justice! It is admirable! You will grow up to be a wise and fair man, I feel! That is very much to your advantage and to the advantage of the House of York—for you have a great task ahead of you!'

'What do you mean, Mother? I am not sure I understand you.'

'I know you remember what I said to you at the Micklegate in York about the need for revenge! Your father was the next rightful king when he was murdered! And your brother Edmund—innocent of sin—killed at just seventeen years old!'

'How could I forget?' Richard's face crumpled at the memory. 'I made up my mind then to avenge them, and one day I will! Just you wait and see! I do not forget the vow I made then and many times since!'

'I believe you, boy. I see now that you have inner strengths. Edward may be king and George may be much older than you, but I feel that you will be the one to get ultimate revenge on Queen Margaret! George is too idle and overmuch concerned with enjoying life and Edward is too busy being king!

I despaired of you after your illness, but I realise now that, though you may be small and not so well-endowed physically as your brothers, you have a most capable brain in that head of yours and compassion in your heart for poor men. That will stand you in good stead as you grow into adulthood! Lord Neville was right! He said you would turn out well in spite of your physical disadvantages! I did not believe him then, but I do now, for it is not how a man appears, but what he is like inside that determines his worth!'

She moved away, back to where Elizabeth and Margaret sat, leaving Richard almost open-mouthed with amazement. His mother had hardly ever seemed to speak to him unless really necessary for as long as he could remember! She had always adored his elder brothers and indulged them, whereas she had invariably been hard on him. He had frequently felt rejected; unloved. Now she had actually admitted to admiring something he had done; declaring that he was worthy in her eyes!

It made him feel good again. He must think of more ways to earn her praise!

Middleham Castle, Yorkshire, Early Spring, 1463

The brothers Richard of Gloucester and George of Clarence, with Richard's friends Robert Percy and Francis Lovell, were seated at their studies on a fine, bright March morning. Outside, a, sharp frost was just beginning to thaw in the slowly strengthening sun, but the boys were snug and warm in the library, near a roaring log fire.

George was frankly bored stiff, as that day, they studied law with their tutor, which George found dry as dust and completely irrelevant, as everyone knew that the King's Justice had broken down under the incompetent, mentally ill Henry VI and that now men did more or less as they pleased, especially if they were powerful and rich. So what was the point? His elder brother Edward IV had begun to institute new laws in Parliament, but it would take a long time to build up a proper system to enforce them again.

Richard, however, was completely engrossed in the work given to him to study. Their tutor had gone for his afternoon break and the boys were taking the opportunity to relax a little, even though they had been set work to get on with and knew they would be questioned closely on it as soon as Master Gardner returned, all except Richard, who was so completely engrossed that he hardly noticed when the tutor had gone or that the others had stopped work. 'Richard, anyone would think that boring old tome had pictures of nude women in it! You have not lifted your eyes from it this past hour!' Robert remarked amused.

'He's serious-minded, my little brother!' retorted George. 'Too serious-minded for his own good! Eleven years old and he's an old man's head on his young shoulders! You need to lighten up a bit, lad!'

He got up and leant indolently on Richard's chair back, peering over his shoulder to see just what it was that absorbed the younger boy's attention so utterly.

'"Immunity from punishment by virtue of position." That looks very interesting, I must say! Not exactly guaranteed to stir the mind, let alone the senses! Forget that rubbish, Dickon, and look at this!'

He produced a small book of hand-painted pictures on vellum from his scrip. '"Images From the Saracens' Harems!" Now that's more like it!' He slammed shut Richard's great book and thrust the book of pictures under the boy's nose. It showed a naked couple sexually entwined in various positions, most looking very uncomfortable. Richard pushed it away, disinterested.

'You're just not natural, boy! Are you of the other persuasion, like the Greek men and boys we've been studying?' George bantered.

'Don't needle him. He's just a bit young yet, that's all! You're three years older than him, remember! He'll get interested eventually!' laughed Francis Lovell.

'Well, he's a slow starter then. You're only a few months older than him, and you find them fascinating like Rob and I! I hope he wakes up soon, or he's going to be such a bore to drag around!' retorted George scowling.

'Leave him alone, George! Just because what he's reading is boring to you! Richard has the best mind of us all. Master Gardner has said so more than once!'

Richard quietly opened his great book of law again and recommenced reading, completely unruffled by the banter going on about him. He was used to it and did not even bother to answer George's remarks. In fact, he had not opened his mouth at all. The look on his face gave the impression to George that he was above it all, and that infuriated his elder brother. Little prig! Thought his superior intelligence set him above other mere mortals, did he? He needed teaching a lesson! He would think of some way to bring him down a peg or two!

Richard had learnt long ago that the best way to deal with George when he was in that kind of mood was to ignore him. He knew that it made his elder brother angry, but he didn't care. His best defence was silence, as, all his life, comments had been made, directly or indirectly, about his inadequacies, physical and otherwise. He just didn't respond, and it amused him to see that this attitude could drive those making the remarks into a fury of frustration when he didn't rise to their bait.

'I asked you a question, Dickon! Have I got a queer for a brother then?'

Richard deliberately pretended not to understand and feinted the question. He was bored with George's stupid remarks.

'If it's queer to want to get on with the work I've been set, then I suppose I am. Now go away and get on with your own work!' He understood perfectly what George had meant about the Greeks; he just did not choose to answer; that was all.

'George has got a point you know, Dickon! That book does look rather heavy for you to take so deep an interest in at your age!' commented Francis, 'And why this particular part of the law? It looks like you're learning it by heart!'

Richard looked up, meeting his enquiring gaze with a smile. Francis was his best friend, and he loved him like a brother—more than a brother—certainly more than the irritating George. He must be honest with him.

'It's been on my mind ever since New Year that Lord Hastings could get away with no punishment at all after such an evil deed.'

'Oh, you mean the pregnant twelve-year-old girl, I suppose?' interrupted George.

'But Edward dealt with the situation fairly—he gave her father a lot of gold!'

'But that wasn't justice! That just wasn't enough! He should have had Hastings arrested, tried, and punished! And he got away scot-free, as Edward has done nothing about it, because William is his friend! What Hastings did would have been bad enough with a woman—but to do it to an innocent child!'

'Forget it, Richard! Edward told you to at the time! He's the king, so he's the one who dispenses justice and decides whether to punish offenders—not you! Why should it concern you so?' George sneered, yawning. 'Get your mind on something worthwhile!'

'It is worthwhile! What could be more worthwhile than a proper system of unbiased justice for all men, rich or poor, without fear or favour? That is what I understand the King's Justice to be! Edward must do something to reform the law! It is his duty as king to see that the system which got so lax under Henry VI is put right! People knew that he wouldn't—or couldn't—do anything to control their behaviour, so they took advantage wholesale. They are still taking it! But Edward is strong and clear-minded. He is well-loved and respected. Surely he should be able to do this, if he puts his mind to it?'

'So speaks the infant lawyer! If it's the king's business, then leave it to him, and take an interest in boys' more normal pursuits!' George grinned and slapped Richard's back.

'How about joining us tonight? We're riding into York to see what we can find to amuse ourselves! Understand? All this wretched, boring study! What's it for? I enjoy the weapon and horse-training and the music, singing, and dancing lessons even, but all this mathematics, religion, latin, and law—well, I find them quite pointless. What use are they? When we are knights, we will spend our days fighting, no doubt, feasting and drinking in the evening and f***ing at night! The rest is irrelevant!'

George shut his own book on Roman Law with a loud bang and mooched impatiently towards the window, where he moodily stared down.

'You would not dare to speak so if Master Gardner were here!' commented Robert Percy. 'You know he is always telling us that we need informed, cultured minds in our position! Studying these things is supposed to achieve this!'

'Who cares? It's boring, boring! I'm practical and realistic. I know exactly how I will spend my time when I am of age—and it will not be poring over books or having deep discussions about religion or the law!'

George looked out of the window again, trying to find something, anything, to ease his boredom.

'Ah, now there's someone interesting!' He pointed down below. 'Come and look!'

Francis and Robert stopped what they were doing and joined him, but Richard acted as if he had not heard.

'Who is it?' asked Robert. 'Where?'

'Isabel Neville and her sister Anne.'

At these words, even Richard left what he was doing and joined the other boys. He was very fond of Anne. Next to Francis, she was the one closest to him as friend and dear companion. George looked down at the girl he wanted more than any other. She was tall, stately, and gentle in manner. And he knew she felt the same way about him as he did about her.

'I have asked Lord Neville point-blank whether he would consider our betrothal, expecting an immediate refusal. But he seems quite amenable to the idea, after all. It is Edward, Edward, who says no! Why? What can he have against us being wed? She would agree, I know it! For her, I'd pull myself together, follow the straight and narrow! I'd drink less, give up whoring, and try to be a good husband. But it does not look as if I'm to be given the chance! Why should Edward decide my personal life for me? He decides everything else! I mean to have it out with him, once and for all!'

'Be careful, George. Don't get the king's back up, or he'll put his foot down more than ever!' warned Francis. 'You know how he likes his own way in everything—even more so since he became king!'

'But I just don't see what he objects to in the match! If he'd explain, I'd try to understand—not that I'd accept it! I'm determined to wed Isabel, whatever he says!'

'It is strange. After all, her father has helped him so much. You'd think he'd be grateful and welcome such an alliance! Two great families uniting!' said Robert.

'Perhaps Ned has other reasons for objecting,' intervened Richard. 'I know he has become rather resentful of Lord Neville lately, feeling he interferes too much now Ned is king. He no longer requires his help in making important decisions, but still Warwick insists on trying to guide him in everything!'

'You may have a point, young Dickon. But I like my own way too and will not be put off, whatever Ned feels about Warwick now! Isabel is the only one who can keep me steady. I know I take the easy way too often—she would be an incentive to discipline myself! I can have any girl I want—and frequently do—I have plenty of money, large estates, but none of it means anything without Isabel!'

The two girls, arm-in-arm and chattering quietly, quite unaware they were being watched and talked about, disappeared around the edge of a tower, and George gave up his frustrated musings. Sighing, he picked up his set book on Roman Law, and all of them had only just settled back to work when Master Gardner could be heard returning.

Raglan Castle, Gwent, South Wales, June 1464

'Not far from thence. A famous castle fine, that Raggland hight, stands moated almost round—The stately tower that looks on pond and poole. That fountain trim, that runs both day and night, Doth yeeld in showe, a rare and noble sight!' (fifteenth century poem).

'Hundred rooms filled with festive care, its hundred towers, parlours and doors, its hundred heaped-up fires of long-dried fuel, its hundred chimneys for men of high degree' (Daffyd Lywyd, fifteenth century).

Henry Tudor was in the central courtyard of Raglan Castle with Maude and Anne Herbert. They were seated under the White Horse fountain, which was the coolest place to be on that baking hot June day, as they felt the intermittent spray ejecting from the fountain top, which made the heat bearable. Also, there was a little shade where they were, cast by the tall tower above them with its crenellated battlements.

Maude was teaching him how to play chess, and Anne, who had never been able to take to it, watched them both in amazement. Henry was so quick to learn that he was soon checkmating Maude, who had been taught by her father and had been playing for several years. She was a very good player, but Henry's fast-developing skill with the pieces was soon putting her to shame.

The children had been told to keep out of the way, as the castle was being prepared for the annual Bardic Celebrations, or Gorsedd, which started on Midsummer's Day, 24 June, that day.

This great palace of a castle, which William's father had started building, he had continued, extended, and furnished so lavishly that it was, in effect, the Court of Wales, today played host to bards from all over Wales on this important occasion, who came to perform their great epic poems to an assembled audience of most of the nobility of Wales. Lord William was a patron of the arts and literature and had a wonderful collection of priceless manuscripts of the Welsh bards and the even earlier Druid religion in the Welsh language. These were kept in the Great Library. Some of them he had shown to Henry, who had been much interested in them, and who, William knew, was highly intelligent. Lord Herbert's favourite, and one of the most rare and valuable, was an exceptionally beautiful, illuminated manuscript called 'The Hours of the Blessed Virgin Mary', written about 1440, especially for him.

This Great Library would be the focal point of the opening celebrations that evening. Famous musicians would be coming to entertain the guests too. Celebrated harpists had arrived already and had struggled up the stairs to the library to tune their instruments in readiness for the evening's entertainment, for it was already late afternoon. Bands of minstrels would also sing and play lutes and rebecs in between the bards' declamations. At the end of the evening, there would be dancing for the guests.

'You may listen to the poems and the songs and music for as long as you like,' Lady Anne Devereux had told them, 'but I think that by halfway through, you will be ready for your beds. Some of the bards' poems are very long!'

The cooks had been very busy all day long getting ready refreshments for the expected guests. Some would have been travelling several days to get there, and in that heat, lots of cool ale, which had been kept in the underground store cellars, would be served along with chilled wine.

But there was only one guest whom Henry was interested in—his mother, Lady Margaret Beaufort, had been invited and was travelling all the way from her home in Woking, Surrey, to be there. He did not know whether to be glad or sad that at long last he was to see the mother whom he had last said goodbye to at Pembroke Castle when he was only four. And he couldn't even remember what she looked like, except that she was small, very small.

But she was, to be fair, always writing to him with advice and guidance, reminding him how he should behave and also of his royal blood. She went on forever about that and addressed him as the Earl of Richmond, not that it had much significance for him, but it obviously had to her! He did know that Edward the King had given the estates and title of Richmond in North Yorkshire to George of Clarence, his brother, so that did not make much sense to him. She always signed herself Margaret, Countess of Richmond too, most scrupulously. He had a box full of her letters to him, all signed in this way, some of them really long and full of hard words, so that he had been obliged to get his tutor at Raglan, Master Edward Haseley, a most eminent Oxford scholar, to read and interpret them for him. He knew he shouldn't, but he only felt mildly excited even though she was his mother. If it had been Uncle Jasper coming, then he would have been wild with joy!

She had had to get special permission to visit him too—from King Edward—so he supposed he should be grateful she was coming.

Raglan Castle, Gwent, Night, 24 June 1464

Henry lay shivering in bed, though the night was stifling hot. He was very tired and thought that maybe he was getting ill with a fever, as his head was bursting with images and thoughts which chased round and round like a hare maddened by the hunt.

So much had happened that evening: He had marvelled at the minstrels, with their singing and playing; delighted in the harpists' mournful tunes, their fingers stroking the strings which made sounds which seemed to him like Welsh mountain streams in full flood; but most of all, he had been enchanted, mesmerised even, by the bards with their strange incantations. Their poems had been endlessly long and mostly quite incomprehensible to him, not because of the language—he knew Welsh, though the Herbert family spoke mainly English—but by the strangeness of their utterings. They had flowed over him, into him, filling him with a strange exultation.

He had expected to be bored; the other children were very soon nodding and were taken off to bed by their nurse, but he had wanted to stay. It was as if he had been drugged with poppy juice and couldn't move—and he was still in the dream they had created of gallant knights, ancient battles, and splendid deeds.

He could not sleep due to his turbulent mind, even though his body ached with tiredness.

And then, of course, there was the disappointment—his mother, Lady Margaret Beaufort, had not come. True, a messenger had arrived on an exhausted, sweating horse that had been ridden too fast and too far on such a hot day with the news that her carriage wheels had got stuck in a dry rut in a narrow country lane just thirty miles away and that the wheel had broken when they had tried to get it out by urging the horses to strain to their limit.

She had been forced to take refuge for the night in a poor country inn nearby, while the wheel was repaired by the local wheelwright, but she would arrive some time the next day. Henry was used to being let down by the mother he hardly knew, had never seen since he was an infant. He had grown accustomed to being without the members of his family he was supposed to be closest to. But this time, he had really looked forward to seeing her after such a long time.

The moonlight, streaming into his chamber through the large windows overlooking the Fountain Courtyard, silvered everything about him. It looked cool, even though the night was so intensely hot. He tossed and turned, feeling unable to breathe. What he wanted, needed, was fresh air.

He found himself descending the grand staircase from the state apartments, which led directly down to the Fountain Courtyard.

In the middle of the fountain, the great White Horse statue stood, the moonlight glistening on its streaming mane and tail and reflected in the gushing water issuing from its open mouth. It looked almost real in the eerie light, and Henry fancied that at any minute, its rearing front legs would descend and crush him. He stepped back, even though he knew he must be imagining things, and it was at that moment that he felt he was not alone.

On the other side of the White Horse fountain bowl an old man sat, clad in long white flowing robes. He seemed to be staring at Henry intently, his deep-set eyes as blue as mountain gentians, his long white beard and shaggy eyebrows frosted silver by the moonlight. Henry was not frightened but intrigued, for he recognised the old man. He was one of the ancient bards who had held him spellbound with their stories and poems of old.

'Henry of Richmond, heed my words—Beware the White Horse, or die by the sword!'

The boy shivered uncontrollably at these strange words. They seemed to issue from the old man, yet his mouth had not moved.

'What do you mean?' he whispered, almost unable to speak. His tongue seemed frozen in his mouth. He was not often scared by anything, but now his back was crawling and he felt the hairs rising on the back of his neck with fear.

'Henry of Richmond, heed my words—Beware the White Boar, or die by the sword!'

Dazzled by the moonlight shining directly into his eyes, dazed by the cryptic words which seemed to be emitting from the empty air all around him and not from any human source, he closed his eyes, but only for a moment. When he opened them again, the old bard had gone. He looked around everywhere, but there was no sign of him. The courtyard was empty. The only movement was the continuous gushing of the silvered water from the White Horse fountain. Henry shook himself, believing he must be in a waking dream and desperate to break out of it into reality.

Westminster Palace, London, September 1464

King Edward IV, his entire court assembled, lolled at ease and somewhat the worse for drink on the red satin cushions of his chair of state, his golden-haired wife, Elizabeth, proudly upright beside him, the wife he loved to near distraction, whom he wanted constantly, but whose very existence, it seemed, was to cause him endless trouble.

Already, half the nobles of England had expressed their disapproval of his clandestine, and what they considered his most unwise, marriage. Married for love? Their eyebrows had gone up in disbelief in the Great Council at his recent announcement that he had married Elizabeth Woodville in secret. Kings married for expediency and for political gain—what was he thinking? She was quite unfit, not even of royal blood!

He had dealt with their expostulations calmly, determined not to let them rile him.

He was king after all, and kings did not have to justify their actions; to ask permission to act as they saw fit!

But he dreaded dealing with the one whom he expected at any moment now; the one who had helped him to power, without whose actions he would have achieved little.

'His Lordship Richard Neville, Earl of Warwick!' his Chamberlain, William Hastings, announced, 'and his Lady Wife Ann. Also his youngest daughter, Lady Anne!'

Warwick the Kingmaker! For that was what he was called by all and sundry! His great friend and most loyal supporter—up to now. The richest and most powerful noble in England! But what was his reaction going to be to his new queen? He soon knew!

'My Lord King!' Neville bowed low, and his wife and daughter curtsied. The king lifted his hand to acknowledge his important visitors. Lady Neville and Anne then quietly withdrew and joined the other court ladies. What was to come was men's business, and they knew how Warwick felt; how he was boiling with rage inside, whilst outwardly calm.

Warwick barely acknowledged the new queen, and she, very aware of the snub, drew herself up in determination and laid her heavily bejewelled hand on Edward's arm in a gesture of possessiveness. He patted her hand with his free one and then caressed it lovingly. None of this was lost on Warwick. He sniffed loudly and lifted his chin before speaking.

'My lord, you will live to regret your actions, believe me! They are the height of folly! The French alliance, it was all set up. Now 'twill be gone like a puff of wind! For 'tis a serious snub to the king of France after I had arranged your betrothal to the French princess!'

'After you arranged! You cannot arrange every aspect of my life, especially not the personal side!'

Edward smiled dotingly on Elizabeth, who laid her cheek on his shoulder briefly. 'What care I for the French king? He will no doubt have little trouble in finding another suitor for his princess—if she is half as beautiful as my Bess here!'

'That is not the point, Sire. There is far more at stake than your personal happiness! There is the whole future of England to consider! The people are tired of war. This alliance could have ended the wars with France for good and all!'

'Well, what's done is done and cannot be undone—even if I wanted it—which I most certainly do not! Learn to live with it, Richard! I am very grateful for your past support and help in getting me to the throne—you know that—but now I am king, I will be a king with a will of my own!'

'And that is it? That's all the thanks I get for risking my life and those of my men again and again to gain you the throne? Now I am to be made to look a fool in front of the whole of Europe just to satisfy your lust?'

'Have a care, Richard. I am an amiable and easy-going man and have always been your friend, but if we are to remain friends, remember to whom you speak now!'

'How could I forget, since I was the one who made you what you are!' flashed Warwick bitterly.

'I think you must agree with me, Richard, that this interview is best ended, before I lose my temper with your attitude! Amiable I may be, but you know my anger can know no bounds when stirred up! As king, I cannot condone your words, so I am telling you now as a friend to go away before I am forced to do something I may regret!'

'Something else? Don't try to threaten me, Edward! When you have had time to think, you will realise that I am right and that you have made the biggest mistake of your life! It is one which could lead to calamity for the House of York! Come, my dears, we are leaving!' Warwick gestured to his wife and daughter, who immediately left the other ladies and came to his side meekly, but not before Anne had cast a covert glance at Richard of Gloucester, smiling shyly up at him as she caught his eye. He returned her smile, thinking how beautiful she had grown lately.

After Warwick and his ladies had gone, the Earl breathing heavily and hard put to it to contain his temper, Richard's attention was immediately back on Edward, who was also furious and now lost his temper. He was stamping angrily around the room, even kicking at the furniture.

'How dare he? Who does he think he is? I've a good mind to have him arrested for speaking so to his king!'

'Why don't you, my love? He is about to cause you big trouble, I am sure!' the queen wheedled. She hated Warwick and hoped he had gone too far this time and Edward might take her advice. It would be a thorn out of her side, certainly, if Warwick were eliminated.

'He fears for the future of the realm, Ned!' Richard quietly intervened, defusing his elder brother's anger. 'He can foresee repercussions, which perhaps, on reflection, you may realise too. I think that is all he meant by his words. Kings do not normally marry out of the royal blood!'

'Dickon, dear brother, are you against me too?'

'Not against you, Ned, but fearful for you, as no doubt Warwick is!'

Richard did not miss the look of pure hatred thrown his way by Elizabeth. They had taken an instant, if silent, dislike to each other the moment she had been brought to court by her doting husband. He could see right through her—and she knew it—to her shallow, avaricious, and vicious nature, and she realised immediately that here was a rival for her new husband's love. Richard was his favourite brother and they had always been very close. Edward listened to and acted upon Richard's advice, though he was ten years younger.

She knew she was in the presence of a superior mind in Richard, who was far and away beyond the intellectual capability of her golden boy of a king, in spite of his extreme youth. She also resented the fact that Edward constantly rewarded his ability. He had already bestowed great powers upon the boy, apart from estates. The king had made him Constable of England and only lately had put him at the head of his armies who went to quell the Lancastrian uprising and fighting in Northumberland.

She knew—and was glad—that this had also gained him the enmity of George of Clarence, who was now bitterly jealous of Richard because of what he perceived as the constant favouritism bestowed on this brother who was three years younger than him.

George may have derided Richard earlier for what he considered his lack of normal interest in the pursuits of young men, but now he feared his mental capacity. Edward's constant preferment of Richard had caused an ever-widening rift between all three brothers, which did not bode well for the future.

Middleham Castle, Yorkshire, Early Spring, 1465

Lord Neville, Earl of Warwick, strode out to the tilting grounds where Richard of Gloucester was matched against Robert Percy at the quintain. His face was set and very red, and his anger, suppressed in front of the king's messenger, burst forth now as he reached the boys.

'There is a message come from the king, Richard! He wants you back at Westminster forthwith! No explanation, but I know why. It is obvious! I am in his disfavour, so he wants you away from my influence! Apart from anything else, it is a great pity, for you have not finished your training yet. But what His Majesty decrees must be obeyed! So you had better get your pages to help you pack. You must start at dawn—it is a long journey!'

Warwick could not contain the bitterness in his voice, no more than he could quell that in his mind. The rift with Edward had probably widened irrevocably now, as the king no longer trusted Richard to his care.

'But why should Ned send for me now? If he disapproved of your influence over me, why did he let me come back here at all after your disagreement at Westminster last September? I am sure you are wrong, my lord, and he requires me for some special work or mission.'

'He will probably use that as an excuse for recalling you to court, but I know better! I know how his mind works, and he can be very devious! He will never come out with it in a straightforward way!'

Richard was very downcast at the thought of leaving Middleham Castle, which he had grown to love, as he loved his gruff mentor, though Warwick was a hard taskmaster. He was very fond of the whole Neville family: John, the earl's younger brother, who was an excellent trainer in the knightly arts, Isabel, Warwick's stately elder daughter, his wife, the Countess Ann—and of course, Anne, his youngest daughter—especially Anne. It would upset him greatly to leave Anne, and he knew she would feel the same about his sudden enforced departure. He must find her before going to do the earl's bidding and try to explain.

'My lord, I am very sad to leave. You have all treated me with such kindness and made me feel part of your family life. You have been like a father to me—and I never really knew my own . . .' he trailed off, at a loss what else to say. He did not want to leave this secure and happy family nor face the court with its undercurrents of jealousy and backbiting, especially among the queen's many family members and adherents. Her presence at court made it an unpleasant place to be those days.

'We have done our best, lad, to make you happy here and shall miss you too—especially my younger daughter Anne, I think! Here she comes now. I will leave you two young people to say your goodbyes privately. I know it will be a big wrench for you to part from one another!'

Neville was well aware of the close friendship between Richard and Anne and hoped—as he felt sure they did—that one day something more would come of it.

'Oh, Richard, I overheard the messenger telling father and came at once! Do you really have to go? What does the king want?'

'I do not know yet, Anne. But he has trusted me already with some great tasks which George really wanted. For some reason, Edward is convinced that I can carry them out better.'

'Which I am sure you can! You're far more responsible than George, and the king knows that and honours your ability!'

'Lord Warwick thinks he's calling me back to court out of spite! But Edward is a kind man and his friend. I'm sure he would not act so!'

'You always think the best of people, Richard. And you won't have a word said against the king. I know he is your brother and you love him, but . . .'

'He has always been kindness itself to me, especially when I was very small—and he is open-hearted and generous. It would be unlike him to act in this way for the reasons Warwick believes!'

'Everyone has their faults, Richard. Even the king! But come, let us have a last walk together before supper. The time is so short, and I don't know how I'll bear it when you've gone.'

Anne's voice broke and she dashed away what looked suspiciously like a tear.

Richard put his arm round her and pulled her to him, and she put her head on his shoulder—and in wiping away her tears, which were coming thick and fast now he found some comfort for himself.

Westminster, London, May 1465

'But, Edward, you cannot banish your own mother from the court! She is old and maybe sick. Think what terrible things have happened to her in life. She does not know what she is saying!'

'Richard, you of all people should not defend her. She has always treated you harshly and made George and I her favourites when we were young. You were ever the one on the outside.'

'I know, but I cannot believe she is saying these things and still in her right mind! She was shocked and angry when you married Elizabeth Woodville. Indeed, we all were. But she accepted it then like the rest of us. Why should she suddenly come out now with these shocking revelations, as she calls them? Why not then? Nobody will believe what she is saying, anyway. They will call it the ramblings of a sick old woman.'

'Whether people believe it or not is not the point—the words have been said, for all the world to hear!'

'That the king is a bastard? It is nonsense. George and you both look alike, and Edmund was tall, fair, and handsome too. If any of us could have a finger pointed at us, it's me. I am small and dark.'

'But father was dark too, remember? And slighter in build. You take after him.'

'And who was this archer she claims was your real father—Blaybourne, was it? Can you imagine our upright, strictly religious mother straying from the path of wifely duty with an archer? Even when she was young? Besides, she adored Father!'

'Anyone can be tempted . . .'

'Don't judge others by your own experiences, Edward. We all know you can't resist a pretty face when it comes to women!'

'But she had been alone in Rouen a long time, while Father was away fighting.'

'No, it's impossible! Our proud mother, so aware of her royal blood, going with an archer? It's just not true. I will never believe it! I will visit her at Fotheringhay and beg her to retract her words.'

'But whether she does or not, I cannot have her here any more. That would be like accepting what she said as the truth. She must never come to court again! Anyway, she was quite happy to go. She said she no longer wished to live in a "den of iniquity" and that Elizabeth's coronation was the last straw!'

'Give out a proclamation saying that the Duchess Cecily is taken with a fever of the brain and that her words were wild ramblings in her delirium. How are the people to know any different? They will believe what they are told. Say that she has been sent to her old home in the country to rest and recover her senses. Meanwhile, I must in all haste to Fotheringhay!'

Fotheringhay Castle, Northants, June 1465

'But, Mother, surely you can see that what you have said will cause Edward a great deal of trouble?'

'That is what I intended. He has been wayward and self-willed all his life, going his own way in spite of the wisest advice. He lives in an immoral, selfish way and is not fit to be king. I have loved him dearly, but I no longer approve of him! I have kept this knowledge to myself all these years, as I never wished to hurt your father, who loved me as much as I did him. But now I feel compelled to tell the truth!'

'But what about your reputation? And the honour of the House of York?'

'At my age, there are more important things than my reputation. And it is because of the honour of the House of York that I have revealed my long-kept secret!'

'I do not understand. This can hardly do it any good?'

'I want you to be king, my son! You are the only one worthy. Edmund was good, but unreliable. George is not fit in any sense, and Edward, as I have said, cannot rule his own passions. How can he be fit to govern?'

'He is the first-born, which makes him king by divine right. Also, he is a human being, with a human being's faults and failings. He cannot be a paragon of virtue, because you will it so! You must accept him as he is. There is little you can do about it anyway, now he is king.'

'You think not? Then you do not know me, my son. You always did stand up for him.'

'He has always been so good to me. And there is something else. You may not have heard, being so far away from the court now, but it is rumoured—though not confirmed—that the queen is with child.'

'Perhaps God will be good to us and it will die!'

'Mother, how can you say such things? I am sure you do not mean it.'

'It would solve a lot of problems! If she were barren—which it seems she is not—or the child was stillborn, it would be easy to get Edward to put her aside and marry a princess who would bear him an heir of royal blood! That is necessary for the continuation of the House!'

'But he loves her to desperation. He would never put her aside.'

'That is not love, not real love, but lust. He has been lusting all his life—why should this be different? He soon grows tired of his women. He only married her because she put a spell on him. That mother of hers, Jacquetta, the French whore, is a witch! One of the queen's maids of the bedchamber told me in confidence that Elizabeth would never sleep with him—on the advice of Jacquetta. She gave her daughter love potions to put in his wine at night to make him so mad with lust that he would agree to anything—even marriage! That is how it came about. This maid also said that one night she saw Elizabeth put a dagger to her own throat and threaten to slit it herself—if he tried to force her! Now, what do you think of that? The king is in the grip of witchcraft!'

'I do not believe in witchcraft, Mother, and I am amazed that you, as a God-fearing and devout woman, would believe in it either.'

'Where God is, the devil is also, seeking to undo God's good works!'

'Mother, I suggested to Edward that he issue a proclamation saying that you were sick and that that was the reason for your sudden revelations, made in your delirium. It is better that your unwise words are glossed over and that you issue a denial of them.'

'Never! They are the truth, and the truth will always out. Let the people make of it what they will!'

'So you will not retract your words?'

'Not in any circumstances.'

'Very well, I will inform Edward. But it does mean that he may never forgive you and that you will be estranged for the rest of your lives.'

'That may happen, but if it does, I still know that I have done the right thing.'

'All you have done, Mother, is to relieve your guilty conscience!'

'And start to clear the way for you. You remember your task in life—to honour your father's memory and to avenge his death! One day, I know you will do this—with my help. You have a great future ahead of you, Richard. You are an able and an upright boy. All you have to do is to make up your mind to do the right thing and take your chances as they present themselves!'

'You speak in riddles, Mother. I do not understand you.'

'One day, you will, believe me. Now please go, for I am very tired. I find daily life stressful these days and prefer to be quiet and at my devotions.'

Raglan Castle, Gwent, 28 January 1466

Woking Old Hall,
Surrey,
20 January 1466.

My Dear Henry,

I am writing to you hoping that you will receive this letter of congratulations in good time for your ninth birthday on 28 January. I only wish I could have been with you for your birthday, but it is such a long way to Raglan from here, especially in mid-winter! And you know that I do not enjoy good health.

When I came last June to visit you and for the Eisteddfod, which Lord Herbert had invited me to, the terrible heat on the journey made me feel ill, especially when my carriage broke down and I could not get to you in time for the opening ceremony concert. I know you were very disappointed and probably thought I was not coming at all! But I did arrive eventually, didn't I? And we spent a pleasant week together. It was good to see you after so long. I could not believe how you had grown!

You know that it is the king who has kept us apart all these years? He would never allow me to have the care of you; otherwise, I would have you here, now.

He lets me live freely only under sufferance because my good husband, Lord Stafford, supports him. King Edward knows my Lancastrian persuasions and fears the influence I have as one of the wealthiest women in Britain, with so many important connections, most of whom are opposed to his rule! I suppose I am lucky that he allows me to keep my estates at all—which will one day be yours. I am writing to send you my good wishes for your birthday, but also to remind you of your obligations and expectations.

I have constantly urged King Edward to restore your rightful title of Earl of Richmond to you and the North Yorkshire estates belonging to it, appropriated by that grasping younger brother of his, George of Clarence! But so far, my pleadings have had no effect. I will never give up though, and maybe one day soon, my importunity will change his mind and he may give in—just to get rid of me! So do not give up hope of coming into your own eventually!

You are, I must remind you again, of royal blood and the last surviving heir to the claims of the House of Lancaster. You could be king one day! The only other real claimants are Richard of Gloucester and George of Clarence, but they certainly have no better claim than you!

Richard has been given great responsibilities lately by the king, although he is only in his fourteenth year. To give him his due, he has apparently carried out these duties in an exemplary fashion. But all this power at such a young age must have made him very arrogant and self-important! Pride comes before a fall, so they say, and good King Henry will soon humble the lad again, no doubt, when he returns to power, which I pray will be soon!

Now, my son, you see what can be done with the right connections? You too could have such a great future if you make up your mind to fight for it in a few years' time!

The first step is to get King Edward to acknowledge your claim to the Richmond inheritance, and I will do all in my power to see that he does that! I work for nothing else at present—though later on, I intend to work for even higher aspirations on your behalf. I am devoted to your cause! However, as a woman, I can only do so much, in spite of my wealth, power, and influence. Soon you will be old enough to fight for yourself! Uncle Jasper will aid you in this—he is a seasoned campaigner and has always been determined that you should get what is rightfully yours. You are also receiving a thorough training in the knightly arts at Raglan, which will help you give a good account of yourself when it comes to battles!

Once again, Henry, I send you my congratulations, and there are surprise presents from me which you will receive on that happy day soon, presents which I know you will treasure and which will serve you well!

Your devoted mother,
Margaret Beaufort,
Countess of Richmond

Raglan Castle, 28 January 1466

Henry read and reread this birthday letter from his mother, feeling rather overawed by what she expected of him. It had never even entered his head that there was a possibility of him becoming king one day. He was not sure that he had any desire to be. But he was also rather excited to think that his future could be a great and glorious one, if he only worked for it, as his mother so obviously did! That seemed to be the one thing on her mind!

He would have liked to show the letter to his closest companion and confidante, Maude, but as the Herbert family were all committed Lancastrians, he felt he was unable to confide his mother's great ambitions for him expressed in the letter. But he could tell her what his mother had said about the birthday presents and about Richard of Gloucester's amazing achievements! He sought her out in the Solar, where she was contentedly playing with her new Welsh Corgi puppy, received for Christmas, in front of an enormous fire of mountain ash logs. The puppy alternately nipped the ball she rolled for it and an old slipper of hers she had found for him and then transferred its attentions to Henry's ankles and legs as he came towards her. He yelped as the sharp little teeth embedded themselves in his left calf.

'Sorry, Henry. He doesn't yet realise that his play bites actually hurt! I'm afraid Corgis are known for their nipping habits! It's bred into them I suppose, as they are often used as sheepdogs by the hill farmers! Let me see—has Evan drawn blood?'

'No, but I shall remember to wear thick breeches when I come near him in future!'

'By the way, Happy Birthday, Henry! Did you get my present? I asked your body servant Ivor to leave it on the bottom of your bed so you'd find it first thing!'

'Yes, I needed a pair of tough leather gauntlets. They will be very useful when training my new hunting falcon. I had a long letter from my Lady mother today. She says there are some presents coming for me later on which I am sure to treasure! I wonder what they can be? She is very religious, so I suppose one of them will be an illustrated book of Psalms or Devotions, or some such. I shall have to be grateful, whatever they are!'

'Have you no idea what they can be, Henry? Maybe you will be pleasantly surprised!'

'Who knows! No, I have no idea. I will have to curb my impatience until they do arrive! But the letter was also full of the exploits of Richard of Gloucester. He is only five years older than me but already commanding armies and being given posts of huge responsibility by the king!'

'Perhaps he can't find anyone else he trusts enough to do these things!' said Maude, picking up Evan, who had started on Henry's ankles again.

'But he has another brother, George, who is three years older than Richard, and he does not honour him so!'

'Perhaps he is untrustworthy—or a fool? Just because he is royal does not mean he is responsible!'

'I suppose you're right. But hearing about Richard makes me feel very inadequate, especially as my mother keeps harping on about the great deeds I shall do when I am old enough and the high positions I shall occupy! She can think of nothing else, it seems!'

'Mothers are always very ambitious for their sons, especially only sons like you!'

'I hope I can come up to her expectations! She says Richard's success is all because he has the "right connections"—King Edward, I think she must mean. What other boy his age could be offered such incredible opportunities? But he is the king's favourite brother!'

'Exactly! So stop fretting—you are but nine years old today! Who knows what great feats you may achieve in the future? Give yourself time! Richard is an exceptional case, after all!'

'Will I ever be able to match up to my Lady mother's expectations though? Will I make her proud of me one day? She works so hard on my behalf.'

'Perhaps she feels guilty for neglecting you all these years! That could be the reason she writes so frequently now and supports you so strongly, though she knows the king is wary of your very existence and could punish her at any time for her attachment to you!'

'Why is he wary of my existence? What could I possibly do to harm him?'

'It is not what you could do now—but in the future! Or what your mother and your Uncle Jasper could do for the Lancastrian cause in your name! Don't you see? You are a threat to him, though you do not feel it! My father explained it all to me long since. That is why you are kept here. If she had you with her, she could raise a rebellion in your name possibly.'

'I did not intend to tell you this—but she says that I may be king one day—that I have the blood royal in my veins and that she is working ceaselessly towards that day. Her plans must all be made in secret though, as her husband is a Yorkist, and if the king found out what she was doing, he would surely strip her of all her estates and possessions and throw her in prison!'

'There you are then! That is exactly what I mean. Here, now, and being so young, you could do little on your own, but you are a figurehead to the Lancastrians—she is probably only awaiting the first chance to push you forward when they decide to challenge King Edward again!'

'I do not like being a pawn in a political game of chess! It makes me feel very uncomfortable—and rather afraid.'

'Well, you are! That is why you are kept here, quietly, out of the public eye. If you lived in London, things would be very different! And the king knows it!'

'You are very wise, Maude. I am glad to have you for my friend. You explain things that worry me so well too! I wish I could meet this heroic Richard of Gloucester—he is what I aspire to! He is very able and achieves much! And I am sure it is not just because his brother is the king. If he were not clever, he would not be able to carry out these great tasks, but would fail miserably! It is a pity we are on opposing sides, a great pity!'

'I can hear horses trotting into the main courtyard below! Perhaps it is the messengers with your mother's presents! Shall I come down with you?'

'Yes, and call the others too. I want everyone to see that my mother has not forgotten me on my birthday!

In the last year, she has actually been remembering my existence! When I was tiny, I was convinced she cared nothing for me and had abandoned me entirely! Now I know it was the king's will that I was left with your family—which has become my family, and you are all very dear to me now!'

'As you are to us! She was just waiting until you grew old enough to understand that you are a person of some importance in the scheme of things before she started communicating with you so frequently! But all these years, she has obviously not forgotten you and has been pinning her ambitious schemes on you! She knows that soon you will be old enough to become a real threat to the Yorkists!'

Westminster Palace, London, February 1466

'Your Majesty, the queen is safely delivered of a healthy child and both are doing well!' The maidservant, having run all the way from the birthing chamber in the queen's apartments, was beaming as she breathlessly came out with the news they had all been waiting for. King Edward smiled broadly and stood up in expectation.

'And now I have an heir, no one can question my right to reign, not even my embittered mother! I will come at once to see the boy!'

The maid took a step back, hesitantly. 'The baby—it's—she's a girl, Sire!' She looked afraid, as if she expected the king to be angry, as everyone knew that kings wanted their firstborn child to be a son. But she need not have worried. If the king was at all taken aback, he did not show it.

'Rejoice with me, everyone! I have a daughter!' he announced proudly to the assembled court, which included many of the queen's Woodville relatives, and he slapped Lord Rivers, Elizabeth's father, on the back jovially.

'Come with me to see them, my lord! Two proud fathers together!' The other Woodvilles started to follow him too, but he motioned them back.

'Later, later! Give her a chance to recover. You must not crowd the queen or the baby! But, Richard, you can come now too, if you like.'

He took Richard's arm and, with his other arm around Lord River's shoulder, the trio set off along the corridor, the king laughing all the way.

The remaining Woodvilles, looked at each other, aggrieved and affronted. They had been waiting there for days for the imminent birth, and now that they had been excluded, they felt it bitterly.

Lord Richard Grey, the queen's youngest son by her first marriage, voiced their feelings volubly. 'We all know how Richard of Gloucester hates and despises my mother, and yet Edward favours him above us! It is not to be borne. You would think that, loving Elizabeth to distraction as he does, he would not allow anyone who is her enemy anywhere near her—especially at this time!'

'Perhaps the king does not recognise the hatred between them? Richard never shows his feelings towards her when Edward is around!' mused Thomas, Marquess of Dorset, his elder brother.

'He must know. But of course, Richard is his favourite brother. He can forgive him anything, it seems!'

Just then, George of Clarence came hurrying into the chamber as they grumbled among themselves, and they immediately hushed their voices. But it was too late—he had heard their last comments.

'Don't let me interrupt you. You're only voicing what I've been feeling for a long time now! Richard's always been his favourite, right from when he and I were little together. Our big elder brother wrote to him far more frequently when we had to go into exile and flee to Brugge. He received letters all the time from Edward—and I had hardly any at all! And when we were later under house arrest back in London, he came nearly every day, but it was Richard he came to see, Richard he embraced! I felt left out then, I can tell you!

And now he prefers him over me when bestowing missions and the command of men! Surely, by virtue of my age, I should receive these? I am three years older than Richard, after all!'

Thomas nodded. 'Aye, but he has hardly any estates to speak of! You are far better off in that respect—and you are wealthier too! Isn't that worth more in the end than anything else? The king has always been generous with gifts to you!'

'And what I have, I will hold! My dear brother will never get his hands on any of my estates, as well as Edward's affection!' He sat down heavily on the nearest seat, which happened to be the chair of state—and was sitting like that with a brooding scowl on his face, chin in hand, elbow leaning heavily on an arm-rest, when the king returned a short time later, flanked by Richard and Lord Rivers. Edward's expression of beaming bonhomie was immediately replaced by one of extreme annoyance as he caught sight of George.

'And what's this then? Hankering after my seat, George? As long as you're not hankering after the position that goes with it, huh?' His laughter boomed out, as George got up hurriedly, rather shamefaced, and bowed low to Edward.

'I hear that congratulations are in order, brother? Now that you have every happiness—a beautiful, loving wife, a new child, and the kingship too—would you not consider acceding to my request for Isabel Warwick and I to be betrothed? I have brought up this matter with you more than once lately.'

The king, caught off guard, but not unaware of George's deliberate timing in asking him yet again, whilst he was in a good mood, what he had refused him outright several times already, slapped George heartily on the shoulder and laughed again.

'Now, now, George, don't push my patience too far. You are always wheedling for something or the other, it seems—every time I see you, you are at it again! And you have so much. When you are a little older, we will come to the matter of your betrothal!'

'You mean you are agreeing to it in principle, and it's only because you think I am too young for marriage at present that you are holding out on me?'

'That is not what I inferred. I meant that, when the time comes, a suitable match will be found for you. I am sure that there are plenty of pretty European princesses who would be only too glad to marry such a well set-up and wealthy young man!'

'You are playing games with me, brother! You know it is only Isabel I want. You have no right to do that!'

'I have every right!' Edward thundered, his mood changing suddenly, as it was wont to do, especially when he was crossed. 'Lately, you have become like an annoying gnat buzzing round me with your constant begging for this favour or that! You may be sixteen, but sometimes you act like a spoilt little child! Richard here is far more mature for his years, and he is not yet fourteen!'

'Of course, dear Richard can do no wrong, can he?' George began, but got no further.

'Out of my sight, George! You would try the patience of a saint! This was a very happy time for me until a short while ago. Then you came and spoilt it all! Now go, before I lose my temper with you altogether!'

George took the hint, turned, and retreated hastily from the room. Edward impatiently waved the rest of the assembled company out too. When they had gone, Richard sat down beside him on a footstool.

'You are very hard on him, Edward. He does have a point—you are somewhat grudging to him, whereas you are always so generous and open-hearted to me. Who can blame him for getting envious? Remember the northern command you gave me? He was very bitter about that, being so much older than me, and I'm afraid his jealousy and bitterness could cause much trouble for us all in the future!'

'He has to be kept in his place. Lately, he is far too full of himself. And I did not give you that command out of favouritism, but because you were more fitted to it than George! You are far more able, even if younger! You are the cleverest of us all—I may be king, but I envy you your capable, clear mind!'

'I thank you for the trust you place in me, brother, and I hope I may never give you cause to rue it. Loyalty binds me! It has always been my motto, and you have my loyal allegiance until death! But, to go back to George—'

Edward groaned, 'Do we have to?'

'What is your real objection to his betrothal to Isabel Neville? It would be a good match—think of the enormous estates she will inherit! Richard Neville is the richest man in England! And he is far richer than you, even though you are king!'

'And don't I know it! That's another one who needs taking down a peg or two! I fear he is becoming a threat to us, Richard! He is full of resentment since I sent him packing last spring and powerful enough to do us real damage if he'd a mind to! Do you think I want our two families united by marriage, given the strained relations between us?'

'But surely it would bring you together again? You were the best of friends until you decided to marry Elizabeth without telling anyone!'

'No, he would think I was giving him permission to rule and guide me again, and I won't have that any more! It is best if I keep him at arm's length. I don't want him to think I have put aside my anger at his attitude to my marriage!'

Richard shook his head. 'I hope you will not regret this decision in the future, Edward. I know Richard Neville well—remember, he was my mentor and friend too! I grew to care for him and for all his family. Basically, he is a good man. It is a great pity we cannot go back to being friends once more!'

'And you care for one of his family in particular, I believe, Richard? Young Lovell, your friend, told me how you and Anne were always together.'

Richard felt his face grow hot. He hoped he was not blushing. 'We have always been good friends, that's all!'

'Well I'm glad of that! I had thought that maybe you were also thinking to the future and perhaps hoping that you and Anne would be betrothed! One brother hankering after a Neville girl he cannot have is enough for me to deal with at the moment, thank you!'

Richard felt an inward moment of fear. If Edward really knew how he felt about Anne . . . but he was not about to tell him at that moment—that would have to wait.

Raglan Castle, Gwent, 1468

Woking Old Hall,
Surrey
September 1468

My Dear Henry,

Your Uncle Jasper has lately suffered another defeat at Harlech Castle, in spite of fighting with his men to defend it. It is the last of our great castles to fall to the Yorkists when they besieged it and has held out for seven years! Unfortunately, your uncle just did not have enough soldiers with him to overcome the Yorkist force, led by Lord Herbert, your guardian, who was victorious. It will make you very angry—and sad—to hear that King Edward has rewarded Lord Herbert with the Earldom of Pembroke now, having stripped Jasper entirely of his title and lands in revenge. I do not know if he will ever have them back, unless King Henry is restored to power soon. Uncle Jasper has been pursued by Lord Herbert's men but is not easily caught, especially in his own country, which he knows well.

The King of France encouraged Uncle Jasper's foray into Wales, gave him ships and men and money, but it was not enough. You may wonder why Louis did this? Not out of the kindness of his heart, you may be sure, but because he was piqued that Edward had chosen to make an alliance with Burgundy instead of France! So Uncle Jasper was used as a pawn in a revenge attack, just to get back at Edward! Your Uncle Jasper is always most unfortunate in his confrontations with the Yorkists, but at least he has escaped unscathed each time—he is as slippery as an eel!

Take heart, Henry! Although this is depressing news, your uncle will soon bounce back and find another way to cause King Edward more trouble! However, there is little chance that you will see him again until King Henry VI is restored, which God grant may be soon! Jasper is nothing if not determined and always has your future interests at heart, whatever setbacks he encounters, and they have been constant! He and I both believe that the Lancastrian cause will triumph in the end over this usurper, as Henry is the true king by divine right, and so God must be on our side!

But poor King Henry continues to languish in the Tower of London where Edward keeps him prisoner, and he spends all day at his studies and devotions, for he is most pious. His mind is not what it was, and he often retreats into himself and will speak with no one. It is very sad, and Queen Margaret's domineering nature has not helped, though he has often been glad to sit back and let her run things. She has a will of steel, and if anyone can get her husband back into power, she will! Though she's exiled, she has even gone into battle herself to fight for the cause! He cannot fight for himself any more, even if he is freed, because of his affliction of the mind. There have just been too many troubles for him and they have affected him badly.

Edward's sister Margaret was married in July in a very ostentatious ceremony in Burgundy to Charles the Bold. Edward no doubt wished to cement his position and avert war by getting the Duke of Burgundy as an ally against the French. He does not trust Louis—who would? He is devious and unpleasant—also obnoxious in the extreme in his personal habits, from what I hear. Much good may the alliance do Edward!

But it will not last—foreigners are not to be trusted and are often underhand in their dealings. No doubt Edward thinks he is assured of a large army from Burgundy if the need should arise, now he and the duke are brothers-in-law! But any promises are sure to be broken, so we need not worry too much about that!

Richard of Gloucester continues to go from strength to strength! He is only five years older than you, and Edward heaps even more positions and responsibilities on him! Only lately, he has commanded an army in the north to put down Lancastrian rebels there!

No doubt Lord Herbert—now Earl William Herbert—will be returning to Raglan Castle soon, full of himself and his exploits, and there will be great rejoicing and celebrations! If you are unhappy at his success—and good Uncle Jasper's defeat—as surely you must be, you must continue to dissemble, as you have learnt how to do over the years, and say nothing of your true feelings to keep the peace, for his family have been good to you in spite of everything. Just remember, it will surely not be for much longer.

Right will triumph in the end! Hang on to that thought when you are low in spirits! And remember your great destiny—which I know in my heart will surely come to pass!

Your loving mother,
Margaret Beaufort,
Countess of Richmond

Cecily, Duchess of York, Fotheringhay Castle, Northamptonshire, October 1468

My Dear Richard,

I am writing to congratulate you on your recent achievements in subduing the Lancastrian rebels in Northumberland! You showed great courage and ability for one so young, and in his first command!

Your dear father would have been so proud of you! You have inherited his campaigning capabilities! Edward is a brave and clever knight too, but he is ten years older than you! You show great promise. One day, I feel sure that you will succeed in the greatest command of all!

And I am determined that your ability will be recognised by everyone. I dare to prophesy that in the not-so-distant future, you may be king of this great country! You certainly deserve to be, and I will do all in my power to help you achieve this. I do not know yet just how it will come to pass. I'm just certain that it will! You may call it a mother's intuition! When I think how I used to despair of you physically as a small boy, especially after your bout of infantile paralysis! But you worked even harder at your training then and left the other boys at Middleham far behind, not only in the knightly arts, but in your studies!

My son, I feel nothing but regret that I did not recognise your true worth when you were very young and judged you but outwardly. How wrong I was!

The fortunes of the house of York have turned again for the best, with the recapture of Harlech Castle this summer and the defeat of Jasper Earl of Pembroke there—now earl no more, as Edward has seen fit to give the earldom to Lord William Herbert, who led the attack on Harlech. Jasper somehow escaped again, as he always does—into his impenetrable mountains! Of course, Lord Herbert is the guardian of the last possible Lancastrian claimant to the throne when King Henry dies—and he is not in the best of health—after the Prince of Wales, that is. Henry Tudor is his name, some five years younger than you, and the only child of Margaret Beaufort.

He was left in the care of his uncle, Jasper, at Pembroke Castle from the age of four, when his mother married the Earl of Stafford. He has seen her only once since then, I believe, when she visited Raglan Castle, the Herbert family seat in Gwent. This was after they moved back there from Pembroke Castle, which Lord William had taken over when Jasper fled in 1461. One has to be sorry for the boy. He lost his father in battle, as you did, then his mother deserted him, and his Uncle Jasper had to flee, leaving him in the care of strangers. At least you have brothers and sisters—and myself, of course. He has no one. But he is a royal prince and could be a rival of yours, if you ever do make a move to take the throne!

Well, Richard, I continue to be very quiet here at Fotheringhay and do not envy you having to put up with the intrigues of the court! It is not for me any more, since Edward's unwise marriage, though I did relent a little and agreed to be the baby Elizabeth's godmother—I have no quarrel with an innocent babe!

I was so sorry I could not make the long journey from here to Burgundy in July for the marriage of your sister Margaret to the duke. I hear it was a very grand affair indeed, and the cost must have been enormous! I wonder whether Edward had to pay for any of it, or Burgundy emptied its coffers instead?

Edward is very generous, but I don't think he realises that he actually does not have the money for all his extravagances! The queen has probably had nearly all Edward's gold by now—she and that mother of hers, Jacquetta, are both very fond of French fripperies!

It is time now for my evening prayers, so I must put down my pen and say goodnight to you. I will remember you in them as always. I pray every day that your chance will come to avenge your father and brother—and in what better capacity could you do that than as king? Then you could grind the Lancastrians under your heels!

Your loving mother,
Cecily, Duchess of York
Westminster Palace

10 June 1469

London

My Dear Richard,

When you receive this note, I hope that you will join your brother George and I at my London residence tomorrow in the morning.

I wish to discuss something very important with you both, which it is better we do face to face than by letter.

We will be here at ten of the clock. Please inform my man yea or nay—he knows to come straight back to me with your answer.

Richard Neville

The messenger who had arrived with it a short time before hastily withdrew, as Richard looked up from the note at him and inclined his head briefly.

Within a few moments, the man had run down to the palace yard and was galloping away.

'Whatever it is, it must be urgent!' Richard thought, a little puzzled. He wondered what all the haste and secrecy was about? Warwick often wrote to him since his rather premature departure from Middleham.

Often, he would enclose a letter from Anne, but there was nothing from her today, as she was still in Yorkshire.

How he missed her—and the quiet of Middleham, surrounded by the rolling hills of Wensleydale. He sighed, then sniffed, trying to smell the good clean air of Yorkshire, if only in his imagination—but the smells of London, filtering in through the open window, defeated him. It was very near the River Thames here, and its particularly rancid smells drifted up to him—which seemed to consist of a mixture of stagnant water, urine, and dead cats, especially as the tide was out and the stinking mud flats exposed all kinds of unspeakable flotsam and jetsam.

The next morning, he presented himself promptly at 10 a.m. at the imposing Neville townhouse called the Herber to be admitted by Warwick himself—there was no sign of any servants.

"Tis best we speak privily. I have sent the servants to the fair on Bankside. I only keep a skeleton staff anyway, as I am more in Warwick or Middleham than here. They were pleased to be free for the day. I expect they think I'm entertaining a lady! If only it were so—but far more weighty matters occupy my mind. Ah, here is George!'

He had ushered Richard into the library, an imposing room full of priceless manuscripts and books—none of which Warwick ever touched, as he was a man of action and had no time for reading or studying.

George was waiting by the window, idly playing with some pocket dice, but he turned as they entered and put them away.

'Good day, my lord! And brother mine. Has Warwick told you of our business?'

'Not yet, but all the haste and secrecy has me intrigued!'

'And well you may be, young man. If one word of what we are about to discuss gets to the wrong ears—and thence to the king—we could all find ourselves accused of treason!' Warwick stated.

'Treason? I do not like what you say, my lord! No thoughts of treason have ever entered my head, nor will they in any circumstances, so I have no wish to stay! What I do not hear I know not of.'

'Let his lordship speak, Dickon! Do him that courtesy, even if you don't like what you hear. You don't have to agree with his plans.'

'Plans? What plans are these?' Richard ventured cautiously.

'To be blunt, Richard, Edward has driven me first to anger, then to despair, and now to resolve—to put another in his place! He has proved, by his many unwise actions, that he is not fit for kingship!'

'In whose opinion?'

'In my opinion and in that of many others who were his loyal supporters before his marriage, Richard. I put him where he is, and I can depose him!'

'What has he done that you should even think of such a thing—let alone plan to do it?'

'Ponder, Richard. First, that unwise and hasty marriage, saddling us not only with his unfit queen, but all her ambitious, grasping Woodville relatives as well—the court is crawling with them. Wherever you turn, you stumble over one, usually begging some new favour or other from Edward—and they don't ask small favours! Between them, they have acquired by marriage nearly all the greatest estates in England—except mine of course—not to say all the great heirs and heiresses—whose estates will come into their possession in the future!

Then there is a King of France mortally offended that Edward rejected the French princess in favour of a commoner—as I knew he would be! That was very poor statesmanship on Edward's part. We need to keep in with France—but Edward does not seem to care less! Perhaps he doesn't understand what poor judgement he showed? If Elizabeth Woodville were a pleasant person, it might perhaps be bearable, from a personal point of view, but she is vicious, unbelievably haughty, and vindictive in the extreme! Look how she finds ways to pay back people who even slightly or unwittingly offend her? And she has Edward just where she wants him! He is so besotted he can see no wrong in her. He is like a big boy playing at king under her influence! The people hate her and all her relatives—especially that father of hers, the acquisitive Lord

Rivers and her mother Jacquetta, they call the witch! It is bad for England, all of it, and must somehow be stopped!'

'And you propose to stop it?' asked Richard quietly. 'I have no love for the queen either. I knew what she was the moment she showed her face at court. But if we hurt her, we hurt Edward! I have vowed to be loyal to him always, and I will not break that vow for anyone, or anything, or for any reason! Now, I think I had better go. I will forget this conversation—it will be as if I never heard your words, Lord Warwick.' Richard turned on his heel to go, sickened by Warwick's proposed betrayal.

'Loyalty binds me, eh, Richard?' sneered George. 'You always did put ideals and principles before common sense! Well, I've agreed to go along with Richard here! Our Edward has grown too big for his boots, and I'll be glad to see him deposed!'

'And I suppose you think you're going to step into his boots, George? Is that what you have been promised for offering your support then?'

'First, Lord Warwick is going to arrange for Isabel and I to marry. We've waited Edward's pleasure long enough! We are already secretly betrothed and will be married in Calais shortly. As it is out of Edward's domain, there is no way he can stop it, even if he finds out beforehand. So, if your good conscience and loyalty compel you to tell him, it won't make any difference!'

'What about the dispensation from the Pope? That could take months—you are first cousins!'

'And for that reason, we are not bothering to wait for it. We are just going ahead! Why should Edward or the Pope have yea and nay on our personal happiness? They do on everything else! And Edward took his happiness without telling anyone, anyone at all!'

'But he is the king!'

'And the king can do no wrong! Or if he does, he can get away with it! Oh, grow up, Dickon! It is an accident of birth, merely, that he has ascendancy over us! And then there was that business when Mother swore he was a bastard anyway! Who knows? Well, I've had enough! And if Warwick here decides to try and put me in his place—I am next in line to the throne—I shall not be averse!'

'You're are a misguided fool, George. I promise that you will regret your decision to challenge Edward. He is not perfect, but the people love him in spite of his mistakes, and he is a good king in other ways, whatever you say. Do you not fear the traitor's death for treason, if all your plans fall through?'

'The traitor's death? But Edward and I are brothers—he would not dare to do that to me . . .'

George's voice betrayed a slight hesitancy, ' . . . would he?'

'He may not have any choice—a traitor is a traitor after all, brother or not, and would have to suffer a traitor's death! Think well on what I have said, George, and change your mind before it is too late. Against my inclinations, I shall say nothing of what I know about your plans to Edward, to give you time to reconsider!'

Richard turned sadly to Lord Neville. 'All my life you have been like the father I never had, and I have always loved and admired you. But what you ask of me now is too much. Surely you can see that? If you carry out your intentions, it is possible we shall never meet again, sadly, for I cannot split my allegiance!'

'And I, Richard, would find that very sad too. But I have made up my mind, whatever the consequences. I truly believe it will be best for England if Edward is replaced!'

'Then there is no more to say but goodbye, my lord. I cannot believe it has come to this!'

Richard shook his head and turned his back on his lifelong friend and mentor and the brother he despaired of as a poor, wayward, misguided creature, whom he loved but could never trust again.

Something in the back of his mind was warning him that perhaps he was saying goodbye forever to the possibility of Warwick's daughter Anne becoming more to him than just a dear friend in the future—but he determinedly pushed it away and resolved not to let it influence his decision to have nothing to do with possible traitors to the brother who was so dear to him.

Westminster Palace, 18 June 1469

The veins in King Edward's neck swelled into knots and his face turned purple as he clenched his fists convulsively, screwing the message he had just received from France into a tight ball, which he then threw in Richard's general direction.

'Read that. How dare he!'

The messenger hastily bowed and withdrew as Edward rose and began to pace around the chamber. He was breathing fast and furiously, his temper about to erupt in full force. Richard quietly retrieved the screwed-up missive by his feet and smoothed it out to read as Edward fumed. He felt he knew what it was in advance. He had been expecting it for days.

'My lord husband, what has happened?' cried the queen. 'Whatever it is, it is surely not worthy of an apoplexy?'

For once, the king ignored her and stopped by Richard, stabbing at the paper in his hand.

'Warwick! Who does he think he is? I can hardly believe it. He has declared himself in opposition to me and is gathering an army to challenge my right to the throne! The devious, underhand devil!'

Suddenly, his temper seemed to subside and he flopped down like a deflated bladder on the throne. 'And to think he was my friend . . .' he trailed off. 'What have I done that he is about to take arms against me and mine?'

'He is a traitor, my lord husband, and must be caught and dealt the harshest punishment. Think of all his estates and money you can then appropriate!' Elizabeth's topaz eyes glittered like a reptile's in anticipation. 'Hanging, drawing, and quartering will be too good for him!'

The king shook his head. 'Do not talk of it. I cannot bear it. I should be hating him, and yes, I am angry, but I do not want it to come to that! He must be placated, brought round, persuaded to give up this foolishness—he cannot win. The people love me and will flock to fight for me.'

'Placated? Arrested quickly and executed, you mean!' flashed Elizabeth. 'You could never trust him again if you let him live.'

'What say you, Dickon? What shall I do? I am not often in a quandary. I would appreciate your wise council.'

'You have little choice, Ned. If he has gone so far as to start gathering an army against you, then you must gather one too.'

'But I do not wish to fight him. Surely there must be a way of settling this amicably without going to war and without losing face? And I will not have you to help me, as you are getting ready to go into Wales to settle the Lancastrian risings there.'

'But this is more important. Wales can surely wait for a while? Warwick's defection has to be dealt with without delay!'

William Hastings, the Lord Chamberlain and Edward's closest friend and confidant, came rushing into the room suddenly and threw himself on his knees before the king.

'My Lord King, there is urgent news!'

'More?' groaned Edward. 'We are already trying to deal with Warwick's defection!'

'Your brother, the Duke of Clarence, has turned traitor too and joined Warwick in France. They plan to invade and wrest the throne from you by force! And Warwick has already gathered a mighty force in the Midlands before going to France to recruit more—King Louis has promised to help him!'

Edward looked weary. 'I always knew George was weak and stupid. And what, I wonder, has Warwick been forced to promise Louis in return?'

'His daughter, my lord. He has agreed to marry his daughter to Queen Marguerite's son, Edouard.'

'The fair Isabel?'

'No, his younger daughter, Anne Neville. His daughters have gone with Warwick to France—and Isabel is to be married in a few days time to George in Calais. She is his reward, it seems, for his joining forces with Warwick against you!'

At these words, Richard's heart seemed to stop. A leaden stone filled his chest instead. Disbelief, anger, and an almost unbelievable sense of loss filled him. And at that moment, hearing that he had probably lost her, he realised that he loved Anne. He hardly heard the news about Isabel and George, except to register vaguely in his mind that George had got his own way once again, as always.

Edward was on his feet once more. 'I expressly forbad that marriage! Can I do anything to stop the wedding? Can I make George see reason? Can I get him to forget all this nonsense about being Warwick's supporter and just come home? I'll forgive him. I don't want war. There have been too many battles already, too many good men killed. The people want peace and so do I. Aren't the Lancastrians enough to deal with without those closest to one turning traitor?'

'My lord, he is out of your jurisdiction in France, even though we occupy Calais. And the wedding is not important now anyway. You have greater things to deal with!' Hastings asserted, leading Edward back to the throne, where he sat down heavily, dejection showing in every part of him.

'Dickon, dear brother, it seems that you are right, and we shall have to fight. I do not have the heart for it, I must admit, but there seems no other way.'

Richard shook himself from his dark thoughts. Action, urgent action was needed now. Perhaps it would make him forget?

'I fear there is not. I will to horse at once and rally the troops. Do not fear, Edward. Warwick will not prevail!'

Richard bowed to the king and was gone.

Edward looked down at himself and laughed. 'Maybe the forced riding ahead of me will help get rid of some of this excess weight of mine. It is at times like this, I must admit, that I wish I did not enjoy drinking—and eating—so much!'

'My love, do you have to go yourself?' Elizabeth complained. 'You are the king. Can you not deputise? You know you have not been too well of late.'

'It is my duty to lead my men—where they go, I must go. And all that is wrong with me is too much high living—and loving, my dear!' He patted her on the chin. 'Maybe a rest from both will do me good, huh?'

Laughing, he put his arm round Hastings and they went together to get out some maps from an alcove.

'We must plan strategies, my good Hastings! There is no time to lose!'

Warwick Castle, 30-31 July 1469

'You cannot keep me here as a prisoner—I am your anointed king! You are going against God's laws and making your own. You always did have delusions of grandeur and an ambition to become ruler—I knew that, although you made me actual king. What has happened to you, Warwick? We used to be such good friends.'

'It is more what has happened to you, Edward. Since you made this unwise marriage, you have changed and are no longer fit to be king.'

'In whose opinion? Just yours?'

'In the opinion of many who used to be your loyal supporters. That is the reason you could get so few to support your cause at the Battle of Edgecote, why so many deserted, and why your soldiers were hopelessly outnumbered by my men!'

'The people will not stand for it. They love me. You will have to release me. It is not to be borne!'

'For the moment, you stay here as my guest, while we decide what should be done.'

'Your guest? Guests should be treated honourably—not kept against their will! When Richard hears of this, he will bring a force to release me, I know it. I can trust Richard with my life. He is utterly loyal. And the queen's father, Earl Rivers, will raise another army to rescue me when he is informed of this!'

'Do not be too sure of that, Edward. Lord Rivers is dead.'

'Dead? But he was not even injured in the battle. What happened?'

'He was executed, along with the queen's brother, John, and the Earls of Devon and Pembroke, after the battle.'

'On your orders?'

'Yes, on my orders! Rivers was the head of this troublesome Woodville family—all scroungers—and had been dealing unscrupulously with some of his retainers. He was best removed. Now he can cause no more trouble. John and the two earls looked to get in the way of my plans too—so they had to go.'

'He was my good friend—and John, her brother—Bess will be devastated—she loved him dearly.' Edward fell silent, but only for a moment. 'And these plans of yours? I suppose they are to make yourself king? "Kingmaker" was once an honourable title you bore. You were held in awe and admired for your ability, not just your status. But not any more. Not by me and certainly not by the people when they hear of your actions. Shame on you, Richard Neville! You cannot hope to get away with this!'

'See that this gets to my brother, Duke Richard of Gloucester, and you will be most handsomely rewarded! As soon as he arrives here with an army to rescue me, you will have the entire contents of this pouch. On that you have my word as your king! And to show you that I can honour that promise, here are five gold nobles at once to speed you on your way!'

Edward opened up the pouch, which swung on a belt at his side and extracted five gold coins, putting them in the groom's hoary hand. Then he let the man peer into the still almost-full purse.

'You will be a poor man no longer. Look here—there are fifty more where those in your hand came from!'

With eyes glinting avariciously after gazing upon more gold than he had ever dreamt could be his and not believing his luck, the groom hastened to bow and assure Edward of his good faith.

'My Lord King, your bidding shall be done—and fast! I will leave shortly, when all are asleep, and go on Lord Warwick's swiftest horse! It will not take me long to get to York, where your brother the duke lies. Then I shall be back for my reward!'

'Which you will have nobly earned by serving your king, who is in dire straits! Now make haste to the stables and ready your horse for its long journey. The Duke must get my message as soon as humanly possible!'

'Ah, my lord, we have decided that you will be more secure at Middleham Castle in Yorkshire, and you will be conveyed thence later this day.'

Warwick had come into the king's bedchamber with this news early that morning. Edward had been deprived of the freedom of the castle for the last few days, ever since he had sent the groom on his mission. He began to think now that perhaps they had been overheard, because of the delay, but doubted it, as their conversation had taken place in the open air with no possible places of concealment for Warwick's spies.

Edward anxiously scanned the rolling approaches to the mighty castle from the windows of his prison room and wondered whether the groom taking the urgent message to Richard had arrived? Richard would surely set out the moment he heard of his predicament. And what of the messenger? Edward had made a promise to him and had every intention of keeping it—after all, the groom might be very useful to him again if he could be so easily bribed to work against his own master—Edward had seen the greed in the man's eyes and knew he would keep his side of the bargain just to obtain the gold.

It was now late in the afternoon, nearly four of the clock, and Edward had grown ever more anxious as the hours went by and nothing happened. Nobody had come to his room since a servant had brought him bread, meat, and wine about midday.

Then he saw a cloud of dust in the distance, mixing with the haze of heat. Neville's men coming to escort him to Middleham? No, it was a lone rider!

A half-dead-looking horse bearing a dusty, sweat-soaked rider was trotting up the castle drive—Edward leant as far forward as he could into the deep window embrasure, willing the man to, look up and see him waving frantically. But the man was too far gone in exhaustion to notice anything, his head hung down like his mount's and he turned the horse to the right, towards the stable area.

Five o'clock came and went, and the king was in a fever of frustration. Why was nothing happening? Where was Richard? Had the groom brought him any message back from Richard? How would he get it to him? Didn't he want his reward? Why the delay?

Just then, there was a rattling of keys outside, and the chamber door swung open. Two of Neville's burly henchmen strode in, caught Edward by the arms, and propelled him out of the room and down the stairs. 'Time to go, Your Majesty! You're leaving for Middleham at once. Come along now. Don't give us any trouble then!' one of them snarled as Edward tried to shake off his restraining hands.

'Take your hands off me! I will not attempt to escape, and remember, I am your anointed king, so show some respect! Or when I am restored—which I am sure will be in a short while—you will find I recall well those who are my friends and those who are not!'

The men looked at each other, slightly abashed.

'No offence, Sire, just following orders, that's all!'

They led him outside to where four more armed guards waited on horseback, then went back into the castle. A groom came forward to help the king mount a horse which he led by the reins. It was him! As the groom cupped his hands for Edward to mount, the king whispered, 'Tell Duke Richard I go to Middleham!' and pressed the pouch into the man's palms as he bent to adjust a strap. The soldiers on horseback noticed nothing, being too busy watching a very comely serving maid walking across the courtyard with a basket of eggs, especially as she made a point of sending a seductive smile in their direction.

'He will reward you well!' he added, his own eyes on the girl. Even in his present situation, he appreciated a pretty face. The man turned briefly, walked towards the girl, whom he engaged in conversation, and then they were both gone. Edward wondered whether she had been deliberately employed by the groom as a diversion.

At that moment, Earl Warwick appeared, splendidly dressed, on a great white horse to accompany Edward. He rode next to the king as they set out. The horse was far more splendidly caparisoned than Edward's, and the king knew a moment of anger. This was so deliberate, so obviously meant to make a statement—already Warwick was setting himself up as the greater of the two of them!

'And so to Middleham, my lord!' Warwick asserted, 'with your own personal escort!'

Middleham Castle, Yorkshire, August 1469

The ancient walls of Middleham Castle came into view at last as Richard and his tired party of nobles approached. They had been hastily assembled when the news came of the king's plight—how he had been captured at Olney, taken to Warwick Castle, where he had been kept a few days, and was now imprisoned in the Earl of Warwick's Castle, Middleham, in Wensleydale, which was far enough from London to make Warwick think it secure.

The messenger had ridden non-stop to York, without break, changing horses several times on the way, and arrived in a state of collapse in the Duke of Gloucester's presence. He had been handsomely rewarded by Richard, as the king had promised, given time only for a short rest and refreshment at the inn where Gloucester had been staying, then sent on his way back to Warwick Castle without delay, to put King Edward out of his uncertainty whether rescue would come before Warwick had him moved again or perhaps even executed.

With Richard were all the greatest nobles in the land sympathetic to the Yorkist cause, including Richard's closest friend, Lord Francis Lovell, and King Edward's best friend and Chamberlain, Lord William Hastings, the latter furious with the Earl of Warwick for having imprisoned his king. Messengers had been sent far and wide to assemble this influential body of men who meant to show Warwick that his behaviour was unacceptable and also to the queen in London, who immediately went into sanctuary with her child, fearing for all their lives.

As they approached the main gateway, they were surprised that no one had come out to challenge them. In fact, the constable came to the gate, recognised the Duke of Gloucester immediately, and ordered the portcullis raised at once.

'My Lord of Warwick is away today but has given me no orders to prevent your entrance.'

'Because he had no idea that we would be coming!' Richard interrupted in a peremptory fashion. 'Take me to King Edward at once. He is here, I believe? He is expecting me!'

Completely taken aback, the constable bowed, turned, and led the way to where Edward sat in the Great Hall, guarded by three burly henchmen. The king seemed quite relaxed, however, was even playing cards with one of them at a side table. At the sight of Richard and his company, he jumped up, scattering the pack in all directions, and hugged his younger brother in delight.

'I knew you would not delay! You cannot guess how glad I am to see you! And you, Hastings—indeed, every one of you!' He acknowledged the various nobles as they knelt and kissed his coronation ring. 'The messenger was honourable after all—I felt he would not betray me but made sure by making him richer than he ever dreamed—with the promise of more where that came from!'

'He was also rewarded by me, so he is well set up for life for a few days' hard work. But of course, he will never dare to return to Warwick Castle, or Neville will have his hide!' Richard replied smiling. They all laughed.

'We have come to remove you from danger here, my lord, and accompany you back to London,' Lord Hastings said, bowing low. 'What Warwick has done is illegal. Somehow news of your captivity has already got to London and there is uproar among the commoners.'

'I knew the people would not stand for it. They still love me well, though some have grumbled lately about the tax rises.'

Just then, the heavy wooden doors of the hall flew open with such force that it slammed back against the stone walls with a loud thud.

Richard Neville, Earl of Warwick, strode in, his face contorted and livid with fury. 'What is the meaning of this?' he shouted. 'What is going on here?' Then he caught sight of Richard on one side of the king and Hastings on the other.

'My brother has come to escort me back to London—and I think he has plenty of support in the matter. Do you not agree?' Edward replied calmly, looking pointedly at the assembled lords. 'And if you do not, no matter, because we shall be departing thence anyway, whether it pleases you or no—'

'I am master here, and I will say if and when you can go. You are my prisoner!'

'Until we arrived, that may have been so, my lord,' said Richard. 'But not any more, I would say. By virtue of greater numbers alone, we have the upper hand here now, I think you will find!'

So angry he could barely contain himself, Warwick, now purple in the face, looked round for something, or someone, to vent his spleen on. The unfortunate constable of the castle hovering in the doorway took the full force.

'Have you no sense at all? What were you thinking of, letting them in?'

'My lord, I could hardly stop them. And you gave me no orders to. I had no idea what they had come for!' he stammered.

'Fool! Can you not think for yourself for once? Show a little initiative? Get out—now!' He slammed the door with such force in the constable's face that the wooden rafters in the vaulted ceiling of the Great Hall shook.

'If this were a game of chess, I would say that you had been well and truly checkmated, Neville!' Lord Hastings remarked, highly amused. There was a loud guffaw from Edward, in which they all joined heartily, pleased to see this great lord's discomfort and his overweening arrogance and pride brought low for once. There was not one of them there who had not felt envious of all he represented—not only his enormous estates and wealth, but the power he wielded. They had all been subjected to his high-handedness at least once in their lives. His attitude to those in lesser positions than himself had always caused seething resentment. It gave them great satisfaction to see him so powerless for once.

But he recovered his composure and confidence very quickly. 'Well, Edward, you seem to have outwitted me this time, but it will not always be so—you will see. I have enormous resources, as you all know, and other plans which I can put into effect very soon with no trouble at all!'

With these cryptic words, he swung out of the hall another way and could be heard stamping up the great stone staircase to the upper floor to his state apartments, where his wife, Lady Ann, was awaiting him in the Solar with some trepidation.

'I fear he will not be easily thwarted in his plans, brother,' said Richard. 'He is a most determined and arrogant man and has always been used to getting his own way in all things.'

'So have I, Richard, as you know! And I also have one big advantage over him, powerful as he is—I am king!' Edward retorted. 'And with all you good and loyal gentlemen as my supporters and the people on my side also, who could ask for more?'

Raglan Castle, Gwent, South Wales, September 1469

Woking Old Hall,
Surrey,
29 September 1469

My Dear Henry,

Much has happened since I wrote to you last. I wonder if you get news at all until long after things have happened, being so far away!

The Earl of Warwick, the greatest and richest baron in the land, has rebelled against the king! Now the cracks begin to appear in the great alliance. This cannot but do our cause great good. And, would you believe it, the king's brother, George, Duke of Clarence, has thrown in his lot with the earl. No doubt he hopes to be king next, with Warwick's help!

The earl has helped him to get his wish to marry his elder daughter Isabel, which everyone thought could not take place, for it needed the dispensation of the Pope, as they are first cousins. Also, the king had forbidden the marriage—so George is openly defying his brother!

The king was captured by Warwick after the Battle of Edgecote, on 26 July, near Banbury, and he and George kept him prisoner, first at Warwick Castle, the earl's great fortress in the Midlands, then at Middleham, his Yorkshire castle. No doubt Neville thought that he would be safer there, as it is so far away. But with the aid of his loyal brother, Richard of Gloucester, he has escaped!

Now he is back in London and Warwick is probably gnashing his teeth in impotent frustration after seeing all his well-laid plans to depose Edward and take over the country come to naught!

Let them fight it out among themselves—the more they disagree, the better for the Lancastrian cause!

Your day is getting nearer, my son. I promise you, it will come! The Yorkists are digging their own graves by so much disagreement. Warwick even executed Earl Rivers, the queen's father, and John, her brother, after the battle, at a whim. That will cause a rift between that Woodville woman and His Majesty, no doubt.

The one to watch is Richard of Gloucester. With George out of the running, for turning traitor to his brother (he was next in line to the throne), there is only Gloucester left to inherit, if the king should die young! He has remained loyal to Edward through thick and thin, so he is now the one in direct opposition to you.

I know you may think it impossible that what I predict could ever come to pass, but, with the Yorkists checkmating and eliminating each other, they themselves are unwittingly bringing that day ever nearer!

I hope you are keeping well, my son, and are in good spirits? Practice your sword skills regularly, so that, when the time comes, your skill will serve you well!

Your loving mother,
Margaret Beaufort,
Countess of Richmond

Kate of Northamptonshire, In the Forest, Late September 1469

Kate reined in her frightened horse with difficulty and listened, staring all round in the gathering gloom, but seeing nothing to account for her mare's nervousness. There was only the familiar gnarled, moss-covered trunks of ancient oaks and elms, the smell of the first fall of leaves underfoot—already rotting, as it had been a dry summer and leaves had started dropping very early—and the small rustlings of shy woodland creatures in the bracken undergrowth. A rook flew by, squawking, up on to its night perch in a mighty elm to join its fellows, all pushing and shoving for space. But that was all. Nothing out of the ordinary.

She lifted the reins to continue the last mile or so back to Appleby Hall, and then she smelt it, the rank stink of an unwashed male body.

Before she had a chance to urge the horse on, he was upon her from a branch above, pulling her off the horse, straddling her on her back in the rotting leaves and trying to rip open her bodice. The filthy smell of his breath and rotting teeth so close to her face made her retch with disgust; his frantic efforts to probe her mouth with his tongue and push his hand up her kirtle set off a desperate reaction in her. She struggled violently, kneeing him in the groin with all her strength, hitting out at the sides of his head with her clenched fists, even biting his ear in a determined attempt to get him to roll off her. But he just laughed, undeterred, and with one hand untied the front of his ragged, dirty breeches—he seemed to be excited by her terror-filled struggle—it increased his determination.

In all her sixteen years, Kate had never felt fear—and now it dominated her whole being. She felt she was fighting not just for her honour, but for her life.

Now he had one of his disgusting hands kneading her breast and digging his nails into the nipples, the other in her groin, twisting his fingers into her most private places. Then they were roughly retracted, and he began to thrust his erect member where they had been. She screamed as the penetrating pain began—and then he screamed—one long, agonised screech as the knife went into the side of his throat! Then came a thick, gurgling sound—and he rolled off her. There was silence. She dared to open her eyes. There was blood shooting out from the severed artery in his neck, which he clutched fruitlessly with one hand—his last terrified action—to no effect. It sprayed the trees and bushes all around.

And then she did vomit, turning on her side and retching out all the anguish and horror.

Now she became aware of her rescuer. He was bending, wiping the dagger which had saved her from disgrace on the bracken and then putting it away in a small ornate scabbard on his jewel-encrusted belt. Then he turned towards her, knelt, and gently pulled down her kirtle to cover her.

'Can you walk? I will get you away from—this.' He pointed at the dead man. 'Your horse is just over there. I will help you mount her. Then I will escort you and make sure you get home safely.'

He bent and lifted her easily and began to carry her towards the mare. He was obviously strong, in spite of his small stature.

'Thank you, but I can walk. I am unharmed, thanks to your timely aid!'

'Did he . . . ?'

Still shuddering with shock, Kate said, 'No. I was lucky. Another minute or two, and he would have had his way. I thought he would kill me after.'

'He no doubt would have, so that you could tell no tales. He was probably a deserter from one of the armies, fleeing from the fighting. If he had let you go, he would have been more easily caught when you reported his whereabouts and hanged for his desertion.'

'He is not one of my father's men,' Kate retorted. 'None of them would have dared to treat me so!'

By then, he had helped her back upon her horse and mounted his own, prepared to escort her home. 'How did you manage to appear like a guardian angel at just the right moment to save me from that villain?' Kate ventured, looking properly at him, now that her fear had abated. She felt no fear with him. He was a young man—not much older than herself—and he exuded kindness and concern. He was obviously very high-born. His clothes alone—the rich velvets and silks, the lynx fur around the collar of his cloak, and the precious jewels which studded his doublet and weaponry—told her that. But it was mainly his proud bearing, cultured voice, and well-sculptured face with its pale skin and high cheekbones. His eyes were a melting dark brown, like liquid amber. Though he was of the nobility, there was not a trace of arrogance in his voice or attitude—which was unusual. It made her warm to him.

'I heard you screaming as I rode along the track a short way hence.' He pointed in the direction of the main forest thoroughfare nearby. 'And I could not leave a lady in trouble!'

'May I know the name of the brave knight who rescued me? It is like something from the tales of King Arthur, when knights saved damsels in distress!'

'Well, you were certainly that! And I am a knight. I am Richard of Gloucester.'

'Duke Richard? The king's brother?'

'Yes. At your service! And I was on my way to Fotheringhay Castle to see my mother, the Duchess Cecily. She will be anxious, thinking that I have been in the thick of the Battle at Edgecote, when in fact, I was nowhere near it! I have been in Yorkshire rescuing my elder brother Edward, the king, who was imprisoned in Middleham Castle by Richard Neville, Earl of Warwick, after the battle.'

'My father and brother went to fight there late in July,' Kate stopped, confused. She had been about to tell this proud Yorkist that her family were Lancastrians.

'I hope, for your sake, they were neither killed or injured,' answered Richard, looking into her beautiful golden-flecked eyes and noticing the proud tilt of her chin and the shining red hair which tumbled over her shoulders in waves like molten copper. She tossed it every now and then, like a horse's mane, as it fell over her forehead and blew across her eyes in the evening breeze.

'So far, they have been lucky,' she said, aware of his admiring glances. 'But whenever they go off to fight yet another battle, my mother and I cannot wait for their safe return. And if these wretched wars do not stop soon, there may come a time when they do not come back at all—and that would kill my mother. I know it would.'

'What is your name? You have not told me,' he said, perhaps trying to change the distressing subject.

'I am Katharine Mortimer of Appleby Hall near here. My father is Sir Reginald Mortimer and my elder brother is Henry Mortimer,' she answered, proud of her heritage. 'I am usually just called Kate, though,' she added as an afterthought.

He laughed. 'Well, Kate, Mortimer is a name to be proud of—a very old and distinguished family! What were you doing riding alone so late in the forest anyway? It is almost dusk.'

'I have my freedom and go where I will. I have never been afraid of attack, by day or in darkness. My father's tenants would not dare to touch a hair of my head. They would have his fury to contend with if they did—and that can be fearsome!'

'He sounds very formidable!' laughed Richard again.

'He is, but he is a good man, in spite of his temper. My mother and my old maid, Ruth, they do not like me riding out alone, true. But there has never been anything—or anyone—to fear before.'

'In these uncertain times, there are all sorts of strange men, landless and vicious—often deserters—roaming around after the battles. I beg you, Kate, to ride with a companion from now on. You may not be so lucky next time, and I should hate to think what may happen to you, if you do not heed my warning.' He smiled at her again, and as their eyes met, a shaft of feeling like nothing she had ever experienced before engulfed her, so that she felt it almost as a pain. His smile seemed to bathe her in a glow of well-being. She seemed to melt under his gaze.

By then, they had reached the gates of Appleby Hall, and the long drive stretched ahead, empty, like the days before her would be, without him.

As he turned his horse to make his way back to the road and continue to Fotheringhay Castle, she had never felt so bereft.

'I will return betimes to see how you are,' he said suddenly. 'Just as soon as I have reassured my Lady mother of my safety.'

Her heart leapt, filled with a joyous expectancy.

'My lord, I thank you again for all your help to me today, and I will expect you with great anticipation. You will be a welcome guest!'

The words seemed lame and hardly gave an inkling of the tumultuous emotions filling her. As she waved goodbye to him, she was filled with a great sense of loss. Loneliness had been an alien feeling to her before that. She had always been happiest alone. Now, as he disappeared into the trees, it tore her apart.

'Kate, Kate! Where are you, girl? These days, always dreaming, always in a world of your own! Ah, there you are! Where have you been?'

Kate's mother's voice permeated her consciousness at last. Her mother was right. Since Richard's departure a week ago, she had not been able to concentrate on a single thing. All she could think of was when he would be back. He had said he would come, and somehow, she knew he meant it, at the time. But how long would it be?

'I am very sorry, Mother. I did not hear you.'

'I need you in the still room at once, girl. What has got into you?'

Her mind had been in a turmoil ever since that evening in the forest. Not because of the attempted rape, but because something else had affected her far more—Richard. She could not forget his smile and the feeling which had coursed through her as he looked at her was with her still. All night, she dreamt of him, and by day, her mind kept straying inevitably to him too, so that she found herself daydreaming and constantly annoying her mother.

She believed that he would come, as his sincerity had been obvious, and yet her common sense told her that he had far more important things to occupy his time, such as affairs of state. She knew that he was the king's favourite brother and his strong right arm; everybody did. He had many important duties to attend to. And what would he be doing taking a real interest in her when he could consort with princesses and earls' daughters? Perhaps he was just being kind, because he must have seen the look on her face as he turned to go. She had never been any good at hiding her feelings; wearing her heart on her sleeve.

'We must get on with the bottling, Kate. There are so many late fruits this year that we must all help to get them bottled and put away for the winter. 'Twould be a pity to waste any, so we have to hurry before any go bad. Pick over that basket of blackberries, will you? Then I want you to wash the plums over there and find the candle ends to melt the jar sealings.'

Kate automatically got on with the various necessary tasks, as her mother had a very sharp tongue when not obeyed at once, especially when she was worried, as till then her father and brother had still not come home.

Later that night, in bed, she listened to the wind soughing in the elms around the house, and imagined herself with him, alone, here; how she would settle down in his arms and lay her cheek against the black glossiness of his hair; how he would put up a hand and turn her face to his—how he would press his lips to her eager ones—she shook herself. She must stop these stupid dreams. It could never happen—how could it? He was far above her—a prince of the royal blood, brother of the king!

She might attempt to stop these wishful thoughts when awake, but she had no control over her dreams when asleep. He came to her then and she awoke in the mornings with a terrible sense of loss. How could she feel this way, when she had never owned his love in reality?

Kate, October 1469

It was one of those glorious gusty October days when the sun, in between scudding clouds, shone as hot as in Summer for one or two hours in the middle of the day, and Kate could not bear being cooped up in the house any longer. It had been a month since their first meeting, and Richard had not returned. She was filled with a mixture of anxiety and frustration and needed to wash them away in the best way that she knew—with a long gallop on Honey, her mare. The horse enjoyed a good gallop as much as her mistress, and as they set out to ride around Kate's father's estates, the mare tossed her golden mane almost in an imitation of Kate's habit.

They skirted the forest—she would no longer ride in there alone because of her new fear of the wickedness of men—and anger was added to her feelings at this. She loved autumn in the forest, and now the gold, brown, and red leaves were being blown in a swirling dance at the wind's will, heaping them up in dry piles in the root hollows of the great oaks and elms. She longed to be riding in there, hearing the crunch of leaves underfoot, watching the squirrels, red as the leaves they scratched through, busy collecting nuts and storing their winter larders; smelling the mossy, peaty earth kicked up by her horse's hoofs.

The mare was very sure-footed, but even she could not be aware of every rut and pothole hidden under the gathering carpet of leaves. It had been a very wet spring earlier on, followed by a hot, dry summer, and the holes and ruts had become rock-hard. When Honey's front hoof caught in one, it stuck fast, and the horse came to an abrupt halt, catapulting Kate over her head and into the middle of a bush.

She got up, quite unhurt, and brushed the leaves from her kirtle and out of her hair, then bent to examine Honey's front right hoof, for she was holding it up as if in pain. There was no obvious injury, but Kate felt she should let the horse take it easy for a while in case she went lame, so she began to lead her along the track to Appleby Village. It was a good five-mile walk home, though Kate did not worry about that. She was more concerned about Honey. It was her selfish fault that the mare was hurt, galloping her along in a place she knew to be hazardous because of the ruts. When she got home, she would ask Harold, the chief groom, to examine the horse's leg and hoof properly, and if there was any damage suspected, to administer one of his strong horse liniments, which would probably do the trick.

As they moved slowly along, she heard the thunder of hoofs at a distance behind her, and soon, a cloud of dust appeared on the horizon. She stopped to see who it was riding at such an urgent pace and moved the mare out of the way to the side of the track.

It was a lone rider in blue and gold livery, a young man, his horse and himself covered in dust. He stopped by Kate as he came up to her, and she could see that he looked anxious.

'How far is it to the next village? I must get help for my lord, who has fallen off his horse a short way back when the horse stumbled over some stones in the road. We were going to Appleby Hall. He said he knew someone there. Have you any idea where it is?'

'I live there. I am Kate Mortimer, daughter of Sir Reginald Mortimer, the squire. Who is your master? Maybe I can send some of our estate men to help him?'

'He is the Duke of Gloucester. He has twisted his ankle badly and cannot walk.'

Kate's heart jumped uncontrollably. He had been coming to see her! And now he needed help.

'My horse may be injured too. So I cannot ride her at present. But if you ride on to Appleby Village not far ahead, they will tell you where the hall is. It is about five miles from here, only two from the village. When you get there, tell my mother what help is needed, and she will send men to carry him thither on a litter, if he cannot ride at all. Meanwhile, I will go to your master to see if I can help him in any way. It was me that he was coming to see at Appleby Hall, so it is the least I can do!'

Kate's whole body seemed to be buzzing with feeling as she tied Honey to the nearest tree and began to walk back along the track. He had been coming to her—that was all she could think of—he had kept his promise!

Meeting and Parting, Late October 1469

Richard eased himself up into a more comfortable position and smiled at his nurse companion. He had been in Appleby Hall for a week now, nursing a badly twisted, though luckily not broken, ankle. Kate's mother had treated it daily with her cold compresses of witch hazel, and the swelling and pain had all but gone, though the bruising was still very evident. Kate had kept him company and tried to cheer him when he worried about the commitments he was neglecting.

'There is nothing you can do but rest for the moment and let it heal, so forget the great world outside and concentrate on getting better,' she asserted.

'That I am quite happy to do in your soothing company,' he said. 'I suppose my herald will have got to Northampton and sent a relay of messengers to London as I instructed him, so that the king does not wonder too long at my absence?'

'If he as reliable as you say, then of course he will have done it. Now forget London and the king—you are here now. For the moment anyhow—with me.' She had not meant to add the last bit, but the words had just slipped out somehow. The last week had been the happiest of her life, but she knew that any time now he would be up and away and probably out of her life, leaving her desolate again.

'Apart from this accursed ankle, I have enjoyed my stay in your father's house.' He lifted her hand, which he had been gently stroking, and lifted it to his lips.

'Truly?' she whispered, her pulses racing at his touch.

'Most truly. Apart from being a most beautiful girl, you are a wonderful companion!'

Kate laughed. 'Surely you flatter me, sir? You must meet so many lovely ladies at the court?'

'But none like you, Kate. Your fresh earnestness, your kindness, your innocence are like a breath of fresh spring air to me. The ladies of the court are of another breed—hard, vain, avaricious, and self-seeking, like the queen—I dislike them and have very little to do with them if I can help it! You are so different.'

'But you will go back to court nevertheless and be with them when you are better—which will be very soon,' Kate said brokenly, tears coming unbidden and coursing down her cheeks. 'They will have your company, even if you dislike them—and I will not—who . . .' She turned away, wiping her eyes with her long sleeve.

'Who what, Kate?' he inquired, gently taking her in his arms and kissing away the tears. 'Who what?'

'Who loves you, my lord!' Kate burst out. Then a paroxysm of sobbing claimed her, and she pulled herself up and out of his arms, running from the room to her own, where she threw herself on the bed and lay sobbing quietly, until sleep overtook her at last, calming her troubled heart.

Her mother found her late in the afternoon, coming to see why she was not helping her in the dairy.

'Do you ail, girl?' she enquired, sitting on the edge of the bed and feeling Kate's forehead.

'No, Mother, but I am very tired,' Kate said. 'I am sorry I have neglected my duties in the dairy. I will come now and help you.'

'The young duke is asking for you. Please go and see what he wants.'

Very hesitantly, feeling that she had revealed too much—far more than she intended—about her feelings for Richard and made a fool of herself, Kate went to his room. He smiled with real pleasure as she entered.

'Why did you run away, Kate? Are you afraid of me?'

'No, my lord. But I said too much.'

'You only said what I wanted to hear. I prompted you to it when you were distressed. I am sorry if I upset you.'

'I was upset because I knew I loved you and that you would soon be going away.'

'Did you not believe that I could love you too?'

'Oh, my lord, how can that be possible? I am not a great lady.'

'I told you that I do not like "great ladies"! It is you I like, you I want—you I love! Kate, come to me, here!' He held out his arms and she ran into them. It was like coming come after a long journey far away.

For both of them, it was a magical time—discovering each other—forgetting the existence of everything except their love—there seemed to be nothing else that mattered.

But it could not last. Kate knew that. It was an impossible dream. Sooner or later, the outside world would intrude—wrench them apart.

The messenger, who Richard knew was inevitable, arrived at the end of October. He had been questioned repeatedly by the king, when he took the original message to him about his brother's whereabouts, using a relay of horses. When he at last admitted that Richard was 'with a lady', Edward laughed heartily and commented, 'Let him enjoy her while he may! I am glad he has discovered the charms of ladies at last!' Being a great womaniser himself from an early age, he had often worried that the boy seemed to be a very late developer where the ladies were concerned.

But now Richard was needed urgently to go to Wales and quell the new Lancastrian uprisings in Cardiganshire and Carmarthenshire.

'The king demands your presence at court as soon as may be and told me to ride like the wind. I've worn out several horses doing it!' the messenger asserted breathlessly, holding out a letter with the king's unbroken seal upon it. Richard thanked him, then Kate told the man to go down to the kitchens for some refreshment, then to the stables for a strong, fresh mount before departing.

In the message, Edward informed him that he had appointed him Constable of England and Constable of North Wales.

'The king really appreciates you, Richard!' said Kate in admiration. 'Such important positions! Do such great responsibilities not intimidate you?'

'Sometimes. A little,' Richard admitted. 'But he has no one else that he can trust. He knows that I am bound in loyalty to him. What really does upset me is the realisation that I must leave you—though I was expecting the summons any time. The king must be obeyed. And he needs me.'

'I need you too,' said Kate quietly.

'I know, my love, but there is no help for it. I must leave immediately!'

'Will you return?'

'Of course. Just as soon as I have sorted out this Welsh crisis.'

'But that could take weeks—even months!'

'But I have no choice, Kate. You do see that, do you not? I am the king's right hand. He depends on me for so much—always has.'

Kate sighed and nodded. 'I understand. But it will be so very hard to lose you when we have only just found each other.'

'You are not going to lose me—ever. I will write as often as I can. But I do not know how long the letters will take or how long I will be. Wales is a long way away.'

And so he departed, with Kate trying very hard to hold back her tears—and wondering how her life, utterly changed since their meeting, could now be borne alone.

Raglan Castle, Gwent, 28 January 1470

Woking Old Hall,
Surrey
20 January 1470

My Dear Henry,

I send you fondest wishes for your thirteenth birthday on 28 January. This is a very important birthday, as you are entering your teenage years and are really no longer a child, but a young man!

This should reach you by then, even allowing for the terrible conditions of the roads at this time of year.

The presents I am sending you this year are very special indeed, to mark the fact that you are growing up fast! I know that you will be thrilled with them! When they come, you will see why I am now asking you to treasure them and use them well—for they will be very useful to you, hopefully for years!

If only your birthday did not fall in mid-winter, which always makes it quite impossible for me to journey all that way in bad weather to see you. It is sad, but I am just not in good enough health to attempt it. I always seem to be making excuses for not being there for you, as a mother should be, but you at least understand now why we could never be together when you were very small. King Edward willed it so, God rot him!

I long for the time when this usurper will be ousted and Henry, the rightful king, is back in power. Then you will be able to come and live with me openly and with no fear.

I will be thinking of you on your birthday and sharing your excitement in spirit as you receive your special presents!

Let me know as soon as you can how you are and how you spent your birthday, although I can guess already what you will be doing immediately you get your exciting presents!

Your loving mother,
Margaret Beaufort,
Countess of Richmond

Henry put down this latest letter from his mother with his head whirling in anticipation. It had taken a week to arrive, and this day was his birthday. He could hardly wait to see what these special presents were! She had been sending him presents every birthday for some years, but they had never been very exciting, though he had dutifully thanked her for all of them, of course.

But these sounded different, exciting, to be treasured and used well for many years! What could they be?

Raglan Castle, Gwent, 28 January 1470

Woking Old Hall,
Surrey
22 January 1470

My Dear Henry,

By now, you will have received your special birthday presents, if you are reading this note which accompanied them.

Do you see what I meant when I said that you would treasure them and should use them well?

Again, best wishes for your birthday, my son. I wish that I could be there to see you receive the presents, for I know that they will mean much to you. You are no longer a child, so I have chosen them bearing in mind your approaching manhood. I know you will appreciate that.

Enjoy them—but also learn to master them both so that they will give you good service for many years.

Your loving mother,
Margaret Beaufort,
Countess of Richmond

Henry read this note the messenger had put into his hand very quickly, as the man had produced a long, leather-wrapped package. He bowed and handed it to Henry, who unrolled it expectantly and then shouted with delight.

'Maude, Anne! Come and see what Mother has sent me for my birthday—isn't it splendid?'

And indeed it was, a small but perfect sword of shining steel, its hilt gleaming with jewels, the scabbard inlaid with intricate patterns of gold and more precious stones. He pulled it proudly from the scabbard and waved it around in the air, then pretended to fight an adversary, lunging and feinting as he dodged from side to side, the two younger Herbert children watching excitedly, clapping in admiration.

'You look like a knight, Henry!' cried Anne.

Maude nodded. 'One day, you'll be doing this for real!' she said.

The messenger spoke again, stopping Henry as he swung the sword round and round. 'And that is not all, my young lord. Here is your other present!'

At his words, a young groom came forward leading a magnificent Arabian stallion. It was docile enough, but its muscles rippled with latent strength and it tossed its head proudly.

Henry ran straight to the beautiful creature and began to caress its soft nose and stroke the glossy back. He had no fear of horses; his friend Davydd had taught him to ride at Pembroke Castle when he was only five. But none of the horses there—or here—had ever been his alone.

'I shall call him Owen, after Owen Glendower, my brave ancestor! I have heard about him and read his exploits many times. This is the most splendid horse I have ever seen! I want to ride him at once. Please to help me up!'

The young stallion had a new saddle and reins of superbly wrought Spanish leather; the saddle was embossed with the coat of arms of the House of Richmond, and the stirrups were of solid silver.

The groom held his hands interlocked for Henry to vault up on to the horse's back, which he did in a moment.

'Now give me my sword back!' he ordered the messenger, who had taken it for him while he mounted. Henry then held it up triumphantly with his right hand while manoeuvring the reins easily with his left, urging the eager horse into a trot, then into a lively canter round and round the courtyard.

The messenger who had brought the horse to Raglan stepped forward and held up a hand. 'Have a care, my young lord. Do not ride him too fast. He is but recently broken in and does not know you as his master yet. Ride him gently at first and let him get used to you on his back, then he will do your bidding for life. He is gentle, but very strong and lively and could throw you if you push him too much at the moment.'

Henry nodded and slowed a little, but not much. He was lost in his own world of knights and battles. He was King Arthur, Sir Launcelot, Owen Glendower, and Alexander the Great on Bucephalus—all rolled into one.

He slowed down at last, leapt off, slid his new sword into its shining scabbard at his side, patted Owen and declared, 'These are the most wonderful presents anyone could have! Please tell my Lady mother I am thrilled with them, when you return, and that I will care for both of them and use them well, as she asked me to.

When I grow up and become a man, I will ride to war with my knights and if—when—I become king, I will ride Owen at the head of my armies—he will be the bravest warhorse ever!'

The two men turned to each other, eyebrows raised, wondering who had put such big ideas into the little lord's head.

Gwent, South Wales, February 1470

Richard of Gloucester and Francis Lovell rode side by side on their tired and mud-splattered horses, letting them amble at will along the narrow hillside track which served as a road in those parts. It would be impossible to move any faster anyway, as the thick mud underfoot and the many deep water-filled ruts made it dangerous going, not to mention the everlasting rain.

His new position of Constable of South Wales, recently bestowed by the generosity of King Edward, had made this journey necessary. He had to show himself to the people. This he had also tried to do in North Wales in November, after being appointed Constable of that region, with the same difficulties as now—the appalling weather.

Richard took his new duties seriously and was determined to carry them out to the best of his ability. He missed Kate and thought of her often—but his duty came first. He had just been at Pembroke Castle, which came under his administration, as Earl William Herbert was dead.

And now they were out of Pembrokeshire and about to leave Breconshire and go into Gwent, for they were on their way to Raglan, the Herbert's castle, to see Anne Devereux, Herbert's widow. Richard wished to thank her personally for her husband's part in capturing Harlech Castle from the Lancastrians in 1468 and for his great bravery at the Battle of Edgecote last July, after which he had been captured by the Earl of Warwick, the victor, and executed. Also, he wished to extend his sympathies to her in her widowhood.

He was not bound to do this, but felt that, as he was in South Wales, he must.

'How far are we from Raglan, my lord?' enquired Francis, wiping the streaming rain from his eyes for the hundredth time. 'Have you any idea?'

'At this rate, in this weather, who knows? As the crow flies, it is not far, according to the maps available, but they are very unreliable, and these endless winding mountain tracks will make it twice the distance.'

He looked around briefly to where the rest of his men rode disconsolately in single file, stretching back as far as his eyes could see on their even more miserable horses.

'What a country!' grumbled Lovell. 'I don't think there's been one dry day since we arrived here three weeks ago!'

'It is February, Francis. What can you expect? Soon we will be entering the Great Forest, and it should be more sheltered there. We are very exposed on these open mountain sides.'

'They are called the Brecon Beacons, I believe? I'm sure it is beautiful here in summer, but in mid-winter . . .'

'A month ago, we would have had to contend with heavy snow. At least it's all thawed now! Cheer up, Francis. We cannot be far from shelter. The first farm we come to, we will beg a night under cover—a large, cosy barn would be ideal. Tomorrow, we will press on through the forest, down into the valley of the River Usk, and follow its course to Abergavenny. After that, the distance is short. We should be at Raglan Castle in a few days, barring catastrophe.'

'And after Raglan, what then?'

'That I have yet to decide. Possibly to Chepstow Castle, as Earl Herbert's son, William, inherited the castle on his father's death and is now residing there. I feel I should meet him too. Or we may divert to Monmouth and stay at Monmouth Castle first. It is one of the most important towns of the region, and I should make myself known to its chief townspeople.'

'And so we will be here for some time yet, I assume? A pity it is a miserable climate. I long for the comforts of home.'

'So do I, Francis, my friend! But I assure you, just as soon as I feel I have done my duty to the people here as their overlord, we will make for the Severn Estuary below and take ship from Newport to London. I do not fancy making the long journey home the way we came over land on horseback!' Richard laughed, rubbing his nether regions.

After another hour or so, they began to descend into the vale of the Usk, and all along the ridge, for what looked like miles and miles, stretched the great Forest of Gwent, called Wentwood, or, in Welsh, Coed Gwent. Far away, the silver ribbon of the Severn Estuary glittered, and beyond that—out of sight then in the misty rain—the sea.

'After we have crossed the River Usk, we shall be in the forest proper, but we will leave that for tomorrow. Now, what we need is rest and refuge—and a good meal!' Richard said. 'Keep your eyes open for any possible shelter.'

He had hardly uttered the words when they heard voices speaking fast in the Welsh way. They could not understand what was being said, but it was easy to tell that a furious argument was going on from the continual loud outbursts in a language which was usually so lilting and musical-sounding.

A group of four or five men appeared, leading another, whose wrists were tightly bound in front of him, and he was shouting at his captors and struggling to free himself at the same time. They all stopped dead as Richard and Francis drew level with them, staring at the newcomers, obviously assessing their high status by their rich furs and velvets, though they were dripping wet.

'What is happening here?' demanded Richard, hoping that they also understood English but knowing it was unlikely in these parts.

'My lord,' the captive cried, throwing himself at Richard's feet. 'I am falsely accused!' He spoke not only in English, but in a cultured voice. 'I have ancient rights in this forest, from my father, grandfather, and back to the Conqueror. And these men challenge them. I see you are a man of great importance and perhaps you can help me, for I know of no other who will here.'

'What is disputed? What do they accuse you of?'

The man pointed to one of his captors, who held a highly polished longbow fashioned in yew. 'That is mine and I was simply walking through the forest hoping to track a fine deer, when I was set upon by these ruffians who say that I do not have the right to hunt here any more. By whose authority? I own this land. I inherited it from my father. It has been owned by my family for generations!'

'Back to William the Conqueror, as you said,' Richard answered dryly. 'And where are they taking you?'

'Back to my manor about a mile away for the night, and then tomorrow, they plan to take me to the Forester's Court in the middle of Wentworth Forest to be tried. They say there is a new overlord of all this land and that he has forbidden all hunting on pain of death. There are two ancient oaks there where men are hanged . . .' He shuddered visibly.

'Do any of these men speak English so that they can tell me their version of this affair?' Richard enquired.

'Nay, my lord. They are but henchmen of this new overlord. They say he is Lord William Herbert of Chepstow Castle. His father died a few months ago after the Battle of Edgecote, and he, as the heir, has just taken over the castle and imposed these new restrictions, so they say.' He pointed with disgust at his captors, shaking his head.

'I knew his father, a brave man, loyal to the king unto death. The Earl of Pembroke, Lord Herbert, died for my brother.'

'Your brother, my lord? You mean King Edward? Then you must be—'

'You are in the presence of His Lordship, Richard, Duke of Gloucester!' Francis interposed proudly.

'My lord, I had no idea who you were! Forgive me for imposing on you with my troubles.'

'If justice needs to be done, I am at your service. We will attend your trial tomorrow in Wentwood Forest, and I promise you I will get to the bottom of this issue, if not tomorrow, then certainly very soon. I plan to visit Lord William at Chepstow Castle on my tour of duty as Constable of South Wales after Raglan Castle, whither we are bound now, and will raise it with him. Meanwhile, may I beg shelter and food for my men and myself for the night? As you can see, we are sorely in need of it.'

'Any time, my lord. I will be proud to accommodate you! And my lady wife will be in such transports of delight to have such honoured guests!'

'You had better tell your captors what has been said here, who I am, and what has been agreed between us,' said Richard, amused at the man's obsequious enthusiasm.

'My lord, I will, I will. I do not know how to thank you for what you propose to do for me.'

'Save your thanks until I have done it!' laughed Richard. 'On the morrow, you will still have to face trial. I cannot just put a stop to it altogether, without having all the facts of the case.'

'But if all goes well, you can order Lord William Herbert to release me?' the anxious man asked, taken aback by the doubt in Richard's voice.

'If you are indeed innocent of the crime of which they accuse you, then you will go free, that I can promise you. The laws of Britain became very lax under King Henry VI and urgently need reform, now that men seem to be making their own and taking the law into their own hands for their own convenience! I believe all men should be treated equally, both high and low, and that a man should be assumed innocent until he is proven guilty!'

Wentwood Forest, Gwent, The Foresters' Oaks, February 1470

'My lord, why are you concerning yourself with this trivial issue when you have so many really important things to do and so far to travel yet before returning home?'

'It is important, Francis. I truly believe that justice is for all. How could I live with my conscience if I left that man to his captors to do what they like with him without fair trial?'

'But he is getting a trial today—in the Forest Court.'

'I suspect that the whole thing is a tissue of lies and that the case against him, such as it is, is a trumped-up charge. Men are making their own laws in these troubled times. I must investigate the truth—or otherwise—of it. Surely that is part of my position here—to see that men deal fairly with each other? There is so much corruption around. The court is bad enough—that is one reason I hate to go there, with the Woodvilles jockeying for position by fair means or foul. The queen's mother, Jacquetta, is one of the chief instigators of such behaviour. Look how she appropriated that wonderful tapestry belonging to Sir Thomas Cook! He would not sell it to her at the ridiculous price that she set, so she got him arrested on a trivial charge, then had men steal the tapestry from his house in London. Then the queen insisted that he pay an outrageous fine of eight hundred marks to her as "queen's gold". And he had just been fined £8,000 by the courts! No wonder the ordinary folk of this country think that they can try it on too. The court hardly sets an example of just and acceptable behaviour!'

'I see what you mean, Richard, and your earnest wish to help all, rich and poor, is typical of your kind nature, but you cannot put right all the ills of man.'

'No, but I can do my best for those I am able to help.'

'You are a good young man, Richard, and that is why I am so privileged to call you my friend—but you are an idealist and I fear that you will take on more than you can possibly deal with.'

'That is my problem. I may be of royal blood, but surely I can empathise with the common man?'

'Richard, without meaning to sound traitorous to King Edward, I think you would make a great king, if ever the opportunity presented itself to you.'

'It is hardly likely to. Edward is sure to have many sons. But I thank you for your loyalty. You have always been a good friend. No one could have better.'

They had been getting nearer and nearer to the centre of the forest, where the two great oaks, known as the Foresters' Oaks, were situated. This spot had been used since time immemorial for impromptu courts, where men were judged by their peers on any kind of offence, trivial or otherwise, from the theft of a horse to murder. The local people had always accepted the decisions made here as fair and just—until the outbreak of lawlessness and violence upon people and property all over the kingdom lately, because of the lax laws.

Evan ap Thomas was very nervous, in spite of Richard's reassurances that he would make sure that justice was done and that, if he were innocent of any crime, he would be discharged.

A crowd of locals had congregated below the great oaks to observe the proceedings, and more and more were approaching the court clearing. About a hundred yards away from the place, Richard stopped his horse and signalled to Francis and the group of men they had brought with them to do the same.

'I will be watching, and observing everything that happens,' he assured Evan, 'but I will not let myself be seen until I know how things are going.'

'Suppose they decide to hang me out of hand?' Evan cried.

'Trust me. I will be close by. Nothing is going to happen to you.'

Evan and his captors started going forward to the clearing under the great oaks, where there were about a dozen of his neighbours sitting on fallen logs or standing around, who would be the jury this day. He knew most of them, and these were his friends and acquaintances. But there were a few whom he knew had grievances against him, particularly one man who had been trying to get his hands on some of his lands for years and was wealthy enough to have bribed all and sundry to find Evan guilty. And this was the one he feared most, knowing him to be unscrupulous and ruthless, even though he felt himself to be innocent. At the worst, he had committed a crime of omission—not knowing the new law—if indeed it existed at all. But was it not said that ignorance of the law was no excuse and no defence?

'My Lord of Gloucester, I beg you to take careful note of the man with the staff. He is an old enemy of mine and has been trying to get his hands on some of my inherited lands for years. He says that they were wrongly appropriated by my father in a boundary dispute and that they are rightfully his. But I know this is a lie. My father would have told me of it. I would not put it past this neighbour, Hugh ap Davies, to have fabricated the whole affair and bribed whoever he had to, to get his own way. He is rich enough and certainly ruthless enough to do it!'

'I will watch and listen to him carefully, have no fear, and I will watch the chosen jury for signs of guilt.'

The proceedings began. The one chosen to be judge for this trial rose and began to speak. He spoke in Welsh, and then in English, for the benefit of those who knew no Welsh.

'Evan ap Thomas, you are charged with hunting in the forests of the Earl of Pembroke, William Herbert, which is against the new law. How do you plead?'

'Not guilty. I was not on any land but my own, which I inherited from my father, and which he inherited from my grandfather. How can that be unlawful?'

'You were caught with a bow of best yew in your hands. You were tracking a deer. And there is no question that the earl is lord over the whole of the forest, so whether the land is actually yours or not, you are still subject to the earl's decisions. And he had decided to put a stop to hunting in this area, as it is his hunting ground.'

'But my great-great-great-grandfather was given this land by William the Conqueror! I have the original deeds to prove it. He was of Welsh blood and married a Norman noblewoman. Surely I have rights by inheritance? My ancestors have hunted on the land for four hundred years!'

The man with the staff, Hugh ap Davies, moved forward and faced the crowd. Then he hit the ground three times with the staff to get attention and held up his other arm.

'Just because Evan ap Thomas states that this new law is not known to him does not mean that he is less guilty. We of this jury all know of it, do we not? Was it not made two months or so ago, around Christmas Tide?' He waited for the other jurors, who nodded and murmured their assent to his words, though a few looked uncomfortable and fidgeted with their belts or daggers.

'Then this man is guilty as charged. Is there any man here would dispute that?' The other jurors shook their heads, but some of them kept their eyes on the ground and shuffled their feet uneasily.

'In that case, it is up to the elected judge to pronounce him guilty and to state the appropriate punishment. I will call upon him now to do that.' He stepped back, and the elected judge came forward to pronounce the sentence.

'Evan ap Thomas, you have been found guilty by your peers and will receive the due punishment for this offence. But I ask also before pronouncing sentence, is there any man here that does not agree that he is guilty as charged?'

'I do not,' said Richard quietly as he stepped forward into the clearing, and a hush descended on the crowd who had been eager for the verdict. All eyes were upon this commanding figure. They looked at each other, wondering who it was, so young but with such authority. He was obviously a proud noble, by his luxurious furs and velvets, but most of these people had never been far outside their villages and had no idea who he was.

'I am the king's brother, the Duke of Gloucester.'

'And what do you do here this day, my lord, at out humble court?' the judge asked, puzzled.

'I come to administer justice, where I feel it is doubtfully administered.'

'What do you mean, my lord? We have all agreed that this man is guilty. Where is the fault?'

'The fault is in the fact that I believe this so-called "jury" has been coerced beforehand by unscrupulous men of wealth and influence for their own ends.'

'How can you believe that, my lord? We are all honest men here.'

'I believe that most of you are, but some who would otherwise have supported their neighbour have probably been bribed or threatened beforehand to agree with the guilty verdict. It was a foregone conclusion.'

'My lord, this is a terrible accusation to make. How do you justify it?'

'Because I happen to know that one of the jurors here has his own axe to grind and would do very well from a guilty verdict, as he can then appropriate some of the lands of the accused!'

'Where do you get such information, my lord? And of whom do you speak?'

'Let us say from a source I trust. And these proceedings will now go no further, as I am using my superior authority to put a stop to them, until certain jurors have been questioned and investigated. But that will be done not only by me, but by Earl William Herbert himself, whom I am about to visit at Chepstow Castle. If this new law did originate from him, then he will confirm the fact. In the meantime, I will take the prisoner in charge with me, and I wish to take your jury member with the staff also, Hugh ap Davies, I believe his name is? No other juror will leave this village until given permission to do so, as some will have to be investigated by Earl William's men. Before I leave here, I want a list of all those other eleven men's names.'

There was a stunned silence after these words, and nobody moved or spoke as they took them in. Then, as Hugh ap Davies was taken into custody by two of Richard's men, who put him on a horse, leaving his hands free so that he could use the reins, but with each of his arms tied to one of theirs, so that he could not make a dash to escape if he had a mind to, a babble of voices broke out, both in Welsh and English.

Richard and Francis had Evan ap Thomas ride at the head of the column, well away from his adversary and accuser, who was to ride along in the middle of it, making it even more impossible for him to escape. But, before he was led away, Hugh managed to shoot a look of venomous hatred at Evan, which was full of menace. Richard and Francis saw it and drew their own conclusions.

Then, after Richard had been handed the hastily drawn-up list of names by the judge, they proceeded on their way to Chepstow Castle.

Raglan Castle, Gwent, Late February 1470

'My lord, that was a very good deed you did for the Welshman,' cried Francis Lovell, riding by the side, as always, of his master and friend, Richard, Duke of Gloucester. 'It gave joy to my heart to see him ride away home, a free man, because of your intervention. If you had done nothing, he could very well have been hung in Wentwood Forest.'

'I am only glad that the new Lord William of Chepstow has the same ideas about what true justice is as I have. His father was an honest and good man and had obviously instilled the same virtues in his eldest son. I liked him, Francis—did you?'

'Very much. And he will rule this part of the country well, though he is so young. He seems just and caring about the common man—as you are Richard. The way he dealt with the other one—what was his name?—these Welsh names are so confusing—was exemplary. As you suspected, the man proved to be corrupt and willing to go to any lengths—including bribery, coercion by threats, and a lot more besides, I am sure—to get his hands on Evan's boundary land. He was bribing jurors and threatening them with violence—and their families—if they did not do his will!'

'If we all work together to stamp out injustice—those of us who have the authority to do it—then the House of York will build up a reputation for fair and honest dealing and the people will love us for it. Perjury and corruption must be eradicated, and fair-dealing for all must take its place!'

'I told you before, Richard, that you are an idealist. But there is nothing wrong with having such ambitions for one's country. The problem is that human nature can be utterly base when a man sees an opportunity for gain. Only a few will be moral enough to resist the chance for advancement or material benefit, by fair means or foul, even if it involves terrible injustice to others in a weaker position.'

'Do not be so pessimistic, Francis. I truly believe that there is some good in all men, somewhere—if only one can find it. One has to encourage it by providing a system of law which gives all men an equal chance. The bad will be punished and the innocent will be exonerated. Good laws are surely an effective deterrent to would-be wrong-doers?'

'But how can they be enforced properly? Especially in out-of-the-way places like this? If a man is determined enough and there is no one in authority to actually stop him, he will go ahead anyway and do whatever he wills, lawful or unlawful—it has always been so.'

'Then we must establish a system with a body of professional judges and proper courts of law in every town in the land! After what I have seen, I shall encourage Edward to initiate this.'

'I wish you luck in your endeavours, my friend! As I have already told you, I believe you would make an excellent king. You have the right idea for the commonweal of the country.'

'And as I have told you, Francis, that is most unlikely ever to happen! Only if some calamitous event occurs which wipes out Edward, his children, and my brother George of Clarence. I am well down the line of inheritance!'

'But you are in direct line, Richard. I wish—'

'Now you are beginning to sound a little traitorous, Francis! I know you have no ill will towards Edward and mean him no harm, but if you were overheard saying such things, what would people think? They might even believe that I, as the king's brother—and your closest friend—felt this way. You know that I do not, but others don't!'

'I am sorry. I did not think. Forgive me, my lord.'

'Freely, Francis. Now we are approaching Raglan Castle, where we will meet not only Lord William Herbert's widow—who is also the mother of young Earl William of Chepstow Castle, the Lady Anne Devereux—but one who has intrigued me greatly for some years, one who also has a claim to the throne, if somewhat ephemeral—like mine! He is but a boy of some thirteen years—Henry Tudor—the last hope of the Lancastrians!'

The First Meeting, Raglan Castle, Gwent, Late February 1470

Henry Tudor, now a strong, well-grown boy of thirteen years, was out riding his well-trained horse, the birthday gift from his always-absent mother, Margaret Beaufort, whom he had named Owen, after his famous ancestor, Owen Glendower.

He had reached the summit of a steep hill about a mile away from Raglan Castle and was now surveying the surrounding country, which was mostly level, with few hills, so he had an excellent view for a very long way in all directions, in spite of the seasonal mist, which that day was mixed with the usual steady drizzle. He and his horse were taking a short rest after the arduous climb through rough, rocky scrubland and stunted bushes. Up there, the remnants of the winter snows still lingered in the dips and crannies between the rocky outcrops. It was bitterly cold, but Henry did not feel it, as his attention was caught by something in the distance—something unusual. He strained his eyes to make out the moving objects—for there were many of them—yes, a long line of slowly moving horsemen. At the head of the cavalcade rode a lone horseman holding up an easily recognisable banner. No one could fail to recognise its significance—the White Boar—the banner of Richard, Duke of Gloucester! It was quite plain to see even at this distance, held proudly upright, fixed in its special holder to the side of the saddle.

Henry's heart began to pound even faster! Richard, Duke of Gloucester! The one he had heard so much about! At last he was about to see him in the flesh! The great commander, the king's favourite brother! And him only five years older than Henry! Everyone knew how Richard was favoured by the king over his elder brother George when it came to acquiring positions and commands. And George was known to be bitterly jealous of this favouritism shown to his younger brother! Richard was probably en route with his men to Raglan Castle! Henry had heard from his mother in one of her recent letters—she was always writing long, encouraging letters to him—that Richard was touring South Wales in his new position as Lord Lieutenant of South Wales, showing himself to the people and meeting the chief townspeople and noble families in each district. There had also been a messenger a day or two ago—probably sent on ahead by Richard—to give Lady Anne Herbert notice of his imminent arrival, so that she would not be caught unawares by so eminent a visitor! And there he was!

Quickly, Henry jumped back up on to Owen's back and was away down the steep slopes at a gallop. Owen was very sure footed and never faltered. He covered the ground back to the castle quickly, reaching the great gate just as the first horseman arrived at the end of the drawbridge, lifting high the White Boar banner in both hands. Henry stopped and held his panting horse reined in tightly to watch the duke and his soldiers cross the drawbridge into the great castle. The gateman had already raised the portcullis when he realised who these illustrious newcomers were. At the head of the column, just behind the banner man, rode two figures, who, though very wet and muddy from their long journey, wore clothes of the finest velvets and furs against the cold. One of them must be Richard, Duke of Gloucester. But which one?

As Henry had never seen him, he had no means of knowing. The one with glossy black hair, rather shorter than his companion, wore a black velvet hat bedecked with jewels—that must be the duke! Henry had heard that he was rather short in stature and not very strong-looking, following a childhood illness. But that this was more than made up for by his distinctive personality and great abilities. And by his authoritative voice! And at that moment, a strong, commanding voice rang out as the cavalcade drew to a halt.

'Well, Francis, Raglan Castle at last! A long and arduous journey here in appalling weather, but I can see why this castle is nicknamed the "Royal Palace of Wales"! It is magnificent! Look at those crenellated battlements! Quite splendid—all of it!'

'Indeed it is! Lord Herbert's family did well for themselves! I believe his father only started to build it in 1433. And Lord Herbert has finished it.'

'With every embellishment possible to the outside—it looks more like those French castles and chateaux than the usual Welsh castles built by Edward the First! I look forward to seeing the splendours within I have heard so much about—particularly the wonderful library! It holds manuscripts so rare as to make them priceless, a veritable Alexandrian library in our times! What a pity our loyal Lord Herbert did not live long enough to really enjoy his marvellous home! It has been a bad outcome for him—executed after the Battle of Towton by that traitor Warwick!

Now only his widow and children can enjoy this palace—only they are left to dwell in these grand halls! It is a terrible thing when faithful and loyal men are murdered by traitors! That is why I have felt the need to make this special visit to see Lady Herbert, so that she will know how much the king—and I—appreciated her husband's loyalty. And how much we bemoan his untimely and brutal death!'

'And that boy, my lord, the Lancastrian boy who some say has an equally good claim to the throne of England as any of the York royal family, he is here! Soon we shall meet him. Henry Tudor!'

'Perhaps his claim is better! His mother, the formidable Margaret Beaufort, is in direct line from John of Gaunt, though on the bastard side, from his late marriage to his long-time mistress Katharine Swynburne!

Soon we shall see this boy, as you say—this Henry Tudor! His ancestor was the great Owen Glendower, who led the Welsh in the last revolt against their English overlords! He later married Henry V's widow—the delectable Katharine of France! From his seed comes this boy—the last hope of the Lancastrians! All other possible claimants to the throne on their side are dead, after that bloody Battle of Towton!'

Henry badly wanted to shout out at once who he was. He wanted to call out, 'He is here, my lord! I am Henry Tudor!' proudly from where he sat so uprightly on Owen, but he managed to stifle the almost overwhelming urge. His training and upbringing told him instinctively that this was not the time—this was not the place.

The nobles caught sight of him sitting quietly there and eyed him up and down, possibly wondering who he was. He was in rough riding clothes and was unidentifiable from a dozen other boys. Possibly, they thought him a page, as he quietly watched them, for now Francis Lovell addressed him.

'Lad, we are expected, I am sure, but there is no one to receive us here. Please go to my Lady Herbert and inform her of our arrival! Say that the Duke of Gloucester and his retinue have arrived at last, somewhat the worse for wear from this eternally wet Welsh weather, and beg her indulgence in the urgent matter of lodging and sustenance!'

Henry bowed as low as he could in the saddle, first to the duke, then to his companion and friend, Francis Lovell, still longing to say at once who he really was and that he was not some errand boy! But something held him back. Later on, there would be a proper meeting, with proper introductions, when he had bathed and dressed in his best clothes. Then, Lady Herbert would present him to the duke, after he and his men had been duly welcomed by Lady Herbert and their immediate needs seen to. Hot baths, a roaring fire, and mulled wine would surely be their first requirements! They all looked soaked and frozen! He knew how to behave in the circumstances—he had been drilled in etiquette for all occasions as well as trained in the knightly arts. And his first duty was to his royal visitor—the rules of simple hospitality to guests required that. His own needs must wait the appropriate moment.

'My lords, I hasten to carry out your commands at once! My Lady Herbert will no doubt be in her Solar, whence I will hurry with news of your arrival! I know that preparations have been going on for days since your messenger came and all is in readiness for you! Please to make your way through the great gate into the courtyard, and I will also send messages for grooms to attend to your exhausted horses!'

He bowed again in the saddle, turned Owen round, and was away through the great gate before the duke or Lovell could utter another word.

'Well, my lord, it seems we are expected in spite of the lack of proper reception! The messenger informed Lady Herbert of your imminent arrival after all. I suggest we do as the lad said and get inside to warmth and comfort as soon as possible!'

'Aye, Francis, and of course they would not have known the exact hour to expect us. I anticipate a most comfortable stay in this most splendid palace of a castle! I must admit that this eternal wet weather is a trial and I cannot wait to get into some dry clothes. And oh, think of it—the comfort of a roaring fire and dry beds which surely await us!'

'And good food and good wine too, my lord!'

'But we must also be sure that the men are housed comfortably and are fed well! They have had a long and miserable ride, I fear!'

Duke Richard laughed and urged his men forward with a wave of his arm as he and Lovell crossed the great wooden drawbridge, passed under the raised portcullis, through the great gate, and into the courtyard, Richard idly remarking, 'That boy was seated on a magnificent horse! Far too grand for a page boy! I wonder . . .'

'My lord, I count myself honoured that you should come all this way especially to see me! I know my husband held the king, your brother, and yourself in such high regard that he considered the personal risk he was taking in fighting for you worth it!'

'It is a great sadness to the king and I that he died in such terrible circumstances after the battle. And after all he had risked! That is why I was determined to come here myself to offer you my condolences. And, I must admit, I was curious about this wonderful castle of yours—having heard how it is named "The Palace Court of Wales"! And the description is indeed apt. I would believe myself to be in some grand French chateau, not a castle in the wilds of Wales, if I did not know otherwise!'

'Aye, my lord. His father spared no expense in the building of it and my husband spared none in the decorations and furnishings.'

'It is the wonderful library I am most anxious to see. Your husband was a man of culture and taste, and I believe made a collection of rare and wonderful manuscripts?'

'Indeed he did. I know little of these things myself, but I do know that some of them are quite priceless!

Would you care to see it now, my lord? Sadly, I must tell you that the only other inhabitant of Raglan who shows much interest in it is our young Lord Henry Tudor, who has dwelt with us since the age of four—first in Pembroke Castle and then here, ever since my husband was made his guardian by the king. He is now thirteen years old and as much given to study and book learning as to the usual knightly pursuits—at which he excels!'

'I believe he has been lucky enough to be taught by good tutors?'

'Yes, Master Scotus schooled him well, and now another eminent Oxford scholar my husband engaged imbues him with a love of learning also. When he is not out training or riding his lovely Arabian horse Owen, given to him as a thirteenth birthday present by his mother, Lady Margaret Beaufort, he is most frequently to be found in the library, working his way through the hundreds of manuscripts in my husband's great collection!

He is a good boy, and I have become very fond of him—as my husband was—indeed he is as much part of the family as if he had been my own son!

His own mother has hardly seen him over the years, though she does write to him often. I believe he regards me as more of a mother than her though.'

'That is surely inevitable—as you are the one who has been there for him!'

'Yes, but to be fair, the king did not allow Lady Margaret the care of her only child. She was made to leave him under my husband's guardianship when she went away to remarry the Duke of Stafford! But she has never lost touch with the boy—and, as I told you, writes frequently to him.'

'It was probably the political situation that made Edward decide to make over his guardianship to your husband! After all, Henry is of Lancastrian descent and is now the last possible claimant to the throne on their side! It is well that his training has been in the hands of one so capable as my lord Herbert!'

'Yes, but the lad still hankers after his much-loved Uncle Jasper! It is somewhat cruel, in my estimation, that one so young should have been deprived of his mother and his beloved uncle because of a political situation he was too young to comprehend! That is why my husband and I have tried to be good substitute parents to him, and not just guardians. We have loved him—and I know he returned our love and appreciated our care! Our children love him too—and Maude, our eldest girl, particularly so. We had hoped there might be a match between young Henry and Maude in the future!'

'Unfortunately, his Uncle Jasper is a rebel and a traitor to my brother, the king! He is always stirring up trouble against us and has spent most of his life in hiding or in exile!'

'The boy does understand this now. But he must still be full of resentment at being deprived of those who should have been his nearest and dearest—for whatever reasons!'

'Well, it is sad that he has been a political pawn all his life. But that is the way with those born into high positions! I am all eagerness to meet young Henry—although I feel I may have done so already!'

'Where, when, my lord?'

'On our arrival, there was a sturdy young lad sitting on a magnificent Arabian horse by the drawbridge as we arrived. My friend, Lord Francis Lovell, assumed he was a page and sent him on an errand to tell you of our arrival. But I knew no page boy would be riding such a horse!'

'Aye, my lord, that was young Henry! And that was his beloved Arabian horse, Owen, given to him by his mother on his thirteenth birthday in January! He worships that horse!'

'I am not surprised! It is a beautiful and high-bred creature!'

'She gave him another gift too—a jewel-studded sword and scabbard of great value! He is always practising with the sword and has become a most proficient swordsman and rider for his age!'

'No doubt he will make a great knight in the near future!' laughed Richard.

'That is his greatest desire, my lord. He thinks of little else!'

'And I expect it is for the Lancastrians he aspires to fight?'

'I am sure that is inevitable, my lord. He knows his ancestry—and is proud of it! But he is never boastful of his intentions—though I am sure his mother urges him on in her many letters! She is a proud, ambitious woman and is sure to have inspired him with notions of possible kingship, as he is the only one in direct line to the throne on the Lancastrian side who has some claim—however small—to the throne!'

'I grow more and more desirous of a meeting with this young man! Who knows what hidden hopes and desires may stir in his mind? But I fear he is doomed to disappointment if he has dreams of the throne! My brother is young, strong, and able! He will surely occupy his position for a great many years yet! And Elizabeth, the queen, is also strong and fertile and will surely give him many sons! So young Henry has little chance of realising any ambitions on that score, which may have been put into his head by his ambitious mother!'

'I am sure you are right, my lord! Now, shall I find a page to direct you to my husband's library, as you expressed such a strong desire to see it and marvel at its contents?!'

'That would be a great pleasure to me, my lady!'

'I will call a boy directly to take you to it. Who knows? Young Henry may be there. It is a very wet and miserable day, and it may have put even such a keen horseman as he off riding for today!'

Henry was busy looking for his guardian's most prized manuscript, *The Book of Hours of the Virgin Mary*—which Lord Herbert had kept locked away, as it was so rare and precious. Henry knew that Duke Richard appreciated rare manuscripts, as he and his mentor, Lord Herbert, had, and he wanted to have it in readiness to show this illustrious visitor to Raglan. He had only ever been allowed access to it twice—when Lord Herbert had chosen to show him it, but he had no idea where it was stored away. Lord Herbert's death meant that he could not ask him and would just have to search diligently among the hundreds of precious manuscripts which filled the shelves all around. They came from many countries and were written in many languages, though the religious ones were mainly in Latin, which Henry had been well-schooled in. But there were some languages he could not identify, let alone read. He could recognise Arabic and Sanskrit and Hebrew. There were even ancient Egyptian hieroglyphic scrolls made of papyrus—which were a complete mystery to him—though he longed to be able to decipher the strange picture-language.

This place held the utmost fascination for him, and he had spent many happy hours here browsing, both with his much-missed guardian and his daughter Maude—his constant companion, who loved learning for its own sake as he did—and on his own.

Henry knew that the special manuscript was kept in a silver box which Lord Herbert had carefully locked and then pocketed the small key after showing the manuscript to him last. Even if he found the box, how would he open it? He had no idea where the key might be. Maybe Lady Ann might know? Surely she would have access to her husband's keys now that he was dead? But first to find the silver box . . .

He was reaching up, searching carefully along a high, deep shelf, with little success, when the library door opened and in strode Duke Richard.

'Aha! So Lady Herbert was right. She thought I might find you here—and that you could show me Lord Herbert's rare manuscripts, which I know he so highly prized. He was a great collector!' Richard said this as he gazed round the huge room, not only a library, but used in the summer for concerts—such as the Eisteddfod.

'My lord!' said Henry, hastily climbing down and bowing low to his royal visitor. 'I was even now searching for the most precious manuscript of all to show you. I fear I have had little success as yet.'

'You mean *The Book of Hours of the Virgin Mary*? You see, I heard about this rarity from Lord Herbert when he was at Westminster. He and I shared a common interest in such things. I believe it was especially made for him?'

'Yes. In 1440, I believe, my lord.'

'I should dearly love to see it!'

'You shall, my lord, if only I can find it,' answered Henry, ruefully shaking his head as he continued his fruitless search along the high, deep shelf.

'If it is that precious, surely he kept it in a special place apart from all the other manuscripts here?' said Richard. 'Perhaps my Lady Herbert will know where?'

'I doubt it, my lord, as she very rarely came here and does not have the same interest in the manuscripts as Lord Herbert did.'

'Never mind. I am going to stay here for a few days, so I am sure it will turn up before I have to depart! Tell me about your beautiful Arabian horse. I hear he was a gift from your mother?'

'Yes, and he is my most precious possession! He is so sure-footed on these hills around and completely obedient. My Lady mother gave him to me for my birthday. His name is Owen.'

'After your famous ancestor, Owen Glendower, no doubt?'

'Yes. He married Henry Vth's widow, Katharine of France. So I am descended from royalty! My mother tells me not to forget that!'

'It is something to be proud of, lad, but do not let it give you any false hopes!'

'I do not, my lord, not really. My Lady mother continually tells me that I may be king one day and to prepare myself for it—but I do not see how that can possibly be.'

'Your mother has great ambitions for her only son—which is only natural—but they can never be achieved. I think you are a sensible and down-to-earth lad. Do not waste your time on impossible dreams. You could no more be king than I could!'

'My lord, I am sure you are right. But she is always writing to me, urging me on, saying things like, "My time will come!".'

'It will, lad, but not in the way she supposes. You will, no doubt, become a great knight in good time and achieve great things. But take no notice of a fond mother's dreams!'

'I cannot pretend to understand what the continual conflict between the House of York and the House of Lancaster—from which I am descended—is all about. My Uncle Jasper, whom I love dearly—and never see—is on the wrong side, as far as I am concerned. If he was for the House of York, then I would see him more often.'

'That is true, Henry, but a man can only act on his deepest-held beliefs. Your uncle has been misled in these, and that is why he is a fugitive from the king's law and so often in exile.'

'I have not seen him since I was tiny, but I know he is a good man, even if he supports the Lancastrian side. He was very good to me. I miss him. I loved him dearly.'

'It is a sad thing when families are split up in this way through differing loyalties. But you are very young yet—do not let the constant strife concern you until it has to. By the time you are a man, no doubt all the differences between the two opposing sides will be settled, and England will be at peace. I pray so! Too many good men have died needlessly in this endless conflict.'

'I was very sad when Lord Herbert was killed. When I was small, I hated him and resented him being given my Uncle Jasper's castle at Pembroke by the king. But he was always so good to me and forgave me for my feelings against him at the time. He seemed to understand how I felt. I had come to regard him as a father—having none of my own. My real father died young, and I never knew him.'

'We have a link in common there, lad. My father too died young—he was murdered when I was only eight by Queen Margaret's soldiers. My elder brother Edmund also. I felt great hatred and resentment against all

Lancastrians because of this. My mother has continually urged me to seek revenge for those murders. Like you, I never really knew my father. He was always away on campaigns—which my mother followed him in—and I was left at Fotheringhay Castle in the care of stewards and tutors. Our childhoods have been rather alike in many ways. Except that I had brothers and sisters, of course, and you were an only child.'

'The Herberts have been my real family. My mother left me at Pembroke with them when I was very small, when she remarried. Soon after, my Uncle Jasper had to flee. I was a most unhappy small boy for a long time—until I came to realise that these were good people I was with, who treated me like a son. My mother writes endless letters to me from her home in Woking, but she has never been there for me as the Herberts have.'

'You have indeed been fortunate in living with them! And I am sure your mother does care for you really—it is just that circumstances forced her to give you up into the care of others.'

'I know that. And I am sorry for her, really—and for myself—as she has such high expectations of me, which I do not think I will ever achieve!'

'Mothers are like that with their sons—especially only sons! My mother too urges me on to achieve more and more. She is very like yours in that respect.'

'But, my lord, you have achieved amazing things already! I have followed your exploits with much interest. My mother has kept me informed of your various commands and achievements. When I think you are only five years older than me, I wonder how I can ever achieve anything at all!'

'But remember that I am the favourite brother of the king. He started giving me great responsibilities when I was barely older than you. He trusts me entirely, you see. He knows that I am utterly faithful to him. Sometimes, my spirit quails at the heavy weight of responsibility he thrusts upon me—but—I do my best!'

'Are you going back to Westminster now that you have visited Raglan and offered your condolences to Lady Anne?'

'Soon, soon—I have to. But I have yet to visit Monmouth, and then we will be on our way to Newport to take ship for London. I do not fancy riding all that long way home again. Your Welsh weather tends to spoil what should have been a pleasant tour of South Wales!'

'My lord, in summer, it is glorious here! It is a pity you had to come here during the most miserable month of the year. I am looking forward to riding for miles on Owen, when the weather improves.'

'I envy you that horse! Perhaps tomorrow we could go riding together, and you could show me his paces?!'

'I would be greatly honoured, my lord. Let us hope the rain clears and I will show you the castle estates.'

'And perhaps introduce me to some of its inhabitants?'

'If that is your wish, my lord. Some of the tenant farmers would really appreciate a visit from you.'

Richard laughed. 'And I would be greatly interested to meet them! Come now, let us find Lady Herbert again. Forget your search for the valuable manuscript for the moment. We can always ask her if she has any idea where Lord Herbert kept it. It is possible he kept it privily away from here.'

'All I know is that it was in a silver inlaid box—and I have not come across that yet.'

'Maybe Lord Herbert kept it in the state apartments? We can only ask her. If she does not know, then we will search again. Also there are many other wonderful manuscripts here I long to peruse!'

The next few days were like a wonderful dream for Henry. From the moment of their meeting, he felt that Richard and he understood each other. He felt strongly drawn to the young duke, who gave of his time unstintingly and his friendship openly. It was as if they had always known each other. The difference in ages was of little account. The box was found, also the key, as Lady Herbert knew of a secret cupboard in Lord Herbert's bedroom, and Henry and Richard spent several happy hours poring over the rare manuscript and many others. Henry found that, like himself, Duke Richard had been well-schooled in languages, religion, mathematics, and the arts of music, singing, and dancing, as well as the knightly arts of horsemanship and weaponry. They rode together up into the hills around Raglan. Often, Lord Francis Lovell accompanied them—and the weather cleared enough for them to avoid a thorough soaking every time they ventured out. A royal hunt was arranged and Henry spent the whole day by Richard and Francis's side, marvelling at their true aim in the hunt. That night—the last before Richard had to leave—a great feast was given in his honour, and the catch of the day provided the main courses. There was venison and hare, partridge and pheasant, and much else besides.

At Richard's final departure the next day, Henry felt bereft. Never would he have believed that he could come so close to someone else in so short a time. They were like old friends—like brothers even—after only five days! The duke promised to write and keep in touch with Henry, who promised likewise. The fact that they belonged to opposing sides was entirely forgotten—did not seem to matter in the least. No differences ever arose. The differences were those created by others. They were just two young men who felt a strong friendly attraction for each other and, if circumstances had been different, Richard knew he would have liked to take young Henry back to court and present him to the king as his friend. But that, of course, was impossible!

As the cavalcade wound out of sight on a blustery, but dry, early March day, Henry sighed. Everyone he cared for or admired always went out of his life. Why was this? Would he see Richard again soon? Somehow he did not believe it would happen. He was old enough to appreciate the political forces which would make it impossible—unless the duke came to Raglan again. Henry could never visit him in London. That he understood.

'Well, my lord,' said Francis Lovell, as they rode towards Monmouth, thence to Newport and a ship for London, 'I think you have made a big impression on that young man. Hero worship shone out of his eyes from the moment he met you!'

'Aye, Francis—if things were different, I would have brought him back with us to court. He and I have many things in common. But alas, that cannot be. The stupidity of war and opposing factions will keep him from my side—where I would have liked to have him. I wonder what his future will be? I am sure he will grow into a good and upright man. He cares for people, as I do. When we visited the tenant farmers, they were all obviously fond of him for his straightforward and friendly attitude to them. It is very sad to me that circumstances will mean it is unlikely that we will meet again—at least for a very long time—unless of course, this eternal war can be brought to a satisfactory and swift conclusion!'

'Realistically, Richard, is that likely?'

'No, Francis, I do not think it is, much as I would like it to happen. I fear many more good men will die needlessly while King Henry's vicious Queen Margaret is determined to continue the endless power struggle! The man is not fit to rule, physically or mentally. But while he lives, his supporters will continue to fight to put him back on the throne and oust Edward! Where it will all end I do not know.'

Appleby Hall, Northamptonshire, March 1470

'But, Mother, I truly believe he will come to me again! He was so sincere. We really love each other!'

'What is love to a young girl is rarely anything but a passing fancy to a man! That is a bitter fact we women learn early! And someone in his position! Do you truly think he has given you any more thought since October last? Have you received letters from him?'

'No, but he is so busy, Mother—he has such great responsibilities. He had to travel into Wales—no doubt he is there still! He would be too occupied to write. But I know he will come soon!'

'Have you written to him and told him of the coming child?'

'No, how could I? I have no idea where to send the letters!'

'How about to Middleham or even to the king's court in London? They would get to him eventually, no doubt. And if he really cares about you, as you insist, he should come here to you at once—if he has any decency in him! But I doubt it!'

'He is the most decent man I have ever met, Mother! I believe he is truly a good person and would do right by me!'

'Perhaps set you up in a house of your own in London and give you money for the child's upbringing. But he would never marry you! He is the king's brother! When he does marry, it will be to some princess or great landed heiress, at least! Do not hold out any hopes on that score, my girl! Even if he loves you, he would never offer you marriage—you would be nothing more than a kept mistress. Is that the kind of life you want? You have been brought up in a moral home. Your father will be mad with anger if ever he finds out about this pregnancy. You will have to go away, Kate, to have the baby. Your father will be home any day now—you know I had that letter from him only last week! Have you told your brother of this matter?'

'No, he has been so ill after that dreadful wound in his thigh. And I hardly show yet anyway. I did not want to worry him!'

'Thank God you are so slim. Five months gone and your waist has hardly thickened yet! But I dare not let you stay here for when your Father returns—if he should guess. He loves you, but I know he would probably take a whip to you! And he would swear to kill your lover—king's brother or not!'

'Where can I go? And suppose Richard comes whilst I am away having the baby?'

'I would tell him where you are and hope he makes his way to you at once! There is your cousin Joanna in Northampton. She has several little ones now and may be persuaded to take you in until the baby is born. But you could never bring the child back here afterwards. Your father would never allow it! The best thing you could do really would be to have the child adopted. It is far too late now for you to get rid of it.'

'Abort Richard's child? Never! It is the fruit of our love! And if he never should return—though I cannot believe that could possibly happen—it will be all I have left of him . . .' Kate trailed off miserably.

'I will write a letter for you to take with you to Joanna's. She may be glad of your company and help with her little ones. Since her husband died so recently in battle, she has no support and only one servant to help her. It may all work out very well—I can think of nothing else. Why did you leave it so late to tell me, girl—with your father expected at any moment?! It is difficult to make proper plans now!'

'I am sorry, Mother, but I had thought Richard would have come by now and taken me away with him!'

'You truly believed that this would happen? I feel you are very deluded, girl! Now you had better go and pack your most necessary belongings quickly. I will tell Robert to have the litter ready for you first thing in the morning to take you to Northampton to Joanna's. There is no question of you riding in your condition—it could be dangerous—but then, if you should lose this baby, it may be for the best in the end.'

'Mother! I am sure you do not really mean that! You love babies! How could you wish harm on a little innocent?'

'No, I suppose not, but it would solve a lot of problems, you cannot deny!'

'I will be all right—I know it! Richard will come! And when he does, you must direct him straight to Joanna's house and tell him what has happened!'

'And he will probably ride off in the opposite direction! I know I sound harsh, girl, but I am aware of the ways of the world better than you! Noblemen do not want to be saddled with the bastards they so easily father! They want the pleasure without the consequences—it is an accepted fact!'

'Not this nobleman, Mother. Richard is different—he is caring and considerate—he would never abandon me!'

'Well, we shall see! Now, go and pack—you will have to start out early tomorrow morning! And I will compose the letter to Joanna.'

Northampton, Late August 1470

'It is no good, Joanna. I know I am more trouble than I am worth to you! It was very good of you to take me in, but it is not really working, is it? I just want to go to London to find Richard. I can think of nothing else!

'Mother says he has not come there. I must find him. Something must be wrong, or I am sure he would have come and Mother would have directed him here! And my mind is not on helping you—not really. You have helped me so much, especially when the baby came. I could never have coped without you. And Ruth—she is a tower of strength!'

'She may be getting on in years, but she knows all about babies and will stand by you, whatever happens!'

'She is more than a maid—she has become my friend! I could not manage without her now!'

'I have heard that Duke Richard has only just left Wales,' said Joanna. 'So he could not come to you—maybe he has not even received your letters yet, as he has been in Wales so long? You directed them to Westminster and Fotheringhay Castle, did you not? He has probably been touring all round South

Wales, visiting the chief towns and meeting the nobles and most important townspeople in each district. He took ship from Newport to London, so it is not likely that he will come here until he has had your letters—if he comes at all!'

'You are just like my mother! You think he has forgotten me. But I know him. He is not like that!'

'You are very young and trusting, Kate—did not your mother tell you how fickle men are once they have got what they want from a girl? Do not hold out too many hopes of his ever coming to you again—the odds are against it!'

'I trust him, Joanna. I know he loved me as much as I loved him.'

'Even if he does want, or intend, to come to you, many important things have happened while he has been in Wales to occupy his attention,' answered Joanna. 'Warwick and Clarence rebelled again in February, but later, the king forgave Clarence when he came begging forgiveness and even promised him Warwick's lands. The king is easily duped, methinks!'

'Richard told me how much the king loves Clarence—as well as himself. He wants to believe there is good in Clarence!'

'There was another terrible battle called Loosecote Field in March, and King Edward dispersed the rebels. In May, Warwick and Clarence fled to France in fear of their lives. That Duke of Clarence is a turncoat of the worst kind—he is sure to come to a bad end—king's brother or not! It is said that on 26 July, Warwick made a deal with the wicked Queen Margaret in France. He has betrothed his younger daughter, Anne Neville, to Edouard the French prince, Margaret's son, the Dauphin. The news is also that Duke Richard is to become Warden of the West Marches towards Scotland.'

'Once he gets there, I will never see him! I must get to London to see him before he goes. I cannot wait any longer.'

'Will you tell him about his baby? He should provide for him, even if he does not intend to continue with your affair.'

'It was far more than an affair, Joanna, as I keep telling you. And I just do not know whether I will tell him. It depends on how he behaves towards me when we do meet. I know I cannot go home, as my father is there and would be furiously angry with me—and Richard, if he found out about the baby. I would not put it past him to go after Richard and try to kill him! And I do not belong here—whatever you say, I am a burden to you. Tomorrow, Ruth and I will leave with the baby—for London.'

'What will you do? Where will you stay?'

'I do not know yet. But I will find work and somewhere to stay. Ruth can look after John while I am working. There should be no problem—and in my free time, I can try to make contact with Richard when I hear he is back. I must be nearer to him. It is too far from London here!'

'I cannot help but think that you are very foolish to go on your own to London—you have no idea of its dangers! A woman alone is just not safe in so large a city which is known to be full of wickedness.'

'But I will not be alone—I will have Ruth,' insisted Kate. 'She will look after us both!'

'Well, I cannot stop you—but I wish you would listen to reason. Young people always think they know best and never listen to advice!'

'Stop worrying, Joanna. I will be fine! Perhaps you could write to Mother for me and tell her where I have gone? The letter will reach her more quickly from here than from London. I will pack tonight and tomorrow we will be on our way to London. I must admit I am very excited by the prospect. I have never been there, and I have heard there is so much going on that one would never have a dull moment!'

'Maybe so, but there are many evil men there, and a young girl is easy prey to their dissembling and wicked ways!'

'I promise I shall take great care, Joanna—the only man I want anything to do with is Richard.'

'Very well, but I am not happy about it—you were entrusted to my care, remember.'

Raglan Castle, Gwent, 18 October 1470

Woking Old Hall,
Surrey,
10 October 1470

My Dear Son,

Such wonderful news! At last the tide has turned in our favour!

You have no doubt heard that God has seen fit to look at us favourably again after all these years. The Lancastrians are in the ascendant again. And your time draws ever nearer.

As you know, your Uncle Jasper has been in France until September, in the service of King Louis. He hoped to obtain his aid in supplying forces to supplement those he can gather in Wales and the parts of England which support the Lancastrians to fight the Yorkists once more. All of it takes a lot of time, effort, and money. But Uncle Jasper is dauntless and determined in your service and, it seems, never lacking in new energy after so many setbacks. He is an admirable man!

As he can now return to Wales, he can come and see you, Henry, without hindrance. King Henry VI has been reinstated by his great ally, the brave and resourceful Earl of Warwick, and is now back in his rightful place on the throne at Westminster Palace.

That usurper, Edward, has fled in fear into the Low Countries with nothing but the clothes he stands up in. And it serves him right! Pray that he never returns. Warwick, who made him king, is now his sworn enemy and is firmly on the Lancastrian side. This can only be to our advantage. He is a very powerful man with enormous resources—the richest man in England. Queen Margaret and the earl have made an agreement between them for Warwick's younger daughter, Anne, to marry her elder son, the Crown Prince Edouard, which will certainly cement the alliance. The queen will be returning to England soon with a large French force to support her husband. She is a strong and determined woman and fights like a lion. The king does need her—she has always been the strong one. He has always relied on her indomitable strength and courage, especially since his breakdown and sickness of the mind have incapacitated him so greatly, poor man.

When your uncle has visited you, he has to depart again almost at once to gather his forces, but we have arranged for you to stay with Sir Richard Corbet for a short while. He will bring you very soon to visit me and then take you to your uncle in London, when he is ready to have you by his side again permanently. After that, I believe he intends to take you to Harlech Castle, in North Wales.

No doubt you will be sad in many ways to leave the Herbert household. I know you have been happy there and that it is the only real home you have ever known. You can blame the usurper Edward for keeping you apart from me all your childhood. It was not my choice, I am sure you realise that now. But living with the Herberts in the wilds of Wales has been a kind of exile for you nevertheless—from now on, you will occupy your rightful position in high places. Now you will be the Earl of Richmond and spend much of your time at court. You will be given lands and houses—hopefully those belonging to the House of Richmond, which Clarence, that acquisitive brother of the erstwhile king, appropriated. He has held on to them tooth and nail, in spite of all my pleas. However, his position has weakened greatly, now that his brother has fled the country, and he may be more easily coerced into relinquishing what was rightfully yours from birth.

I look forward to our meeting again, my son, after so long, and to your stay at Woking Old Hall in the near future. How wonderful that you can now show yourself in public, unafraid, and come to London! I am sure Edward would have had you killed without compunction if you had dared to emerge from your Welsh backwater before now. You have always been a threat to him with regard to the rightful ownership of the throne of England! Keeping out of the public eye in the quietness of Raglan was the right thing for you in the circumstances.

Expect your Uncle Jasper any time now. What a joyful reunion that will be—followed by another very soon, with me—your absent, but ever-concerned mother! You always loved and admired your uncle as a small boy, before he was forced to leave you, and I am sure that love, trust, and admiration for him is still in your heart, despite the long separation. He has waited and suffered over the years with just one aim and ambition—to see you take your proper place in the scheme of things.

Your arrival here is awaited with great anticipation not only by myself, but by my entire household. I live quietly—not being in the best of health; otherwise, great entertainment would have been planned for you. I am sure you will understand that I must have peace—whoever my guests are. Also that, for health reasons, I am unable to come and get you myself. The journey is just too long and arduous for me.

Your very loving mother,
Margaret Beaufort,
Countess of Richmond

Henry read this latest missive from his mother, disbelieving what he read. It had been so long, nearly ten years, since he had set eyes on his beloved Uncle Jasper and nearly five since he had seen his mother. He had to think hard to picture either of them in his mind. Indeed, he would be very sad to leave Raglan Castle, especially Maude, and Anne Devereux, who had been like a true mother to him since his own had deserted him as a tiny boy. Also, he would greatly miss his horse, Owen.

But already a great excitement was bubbling up inside him, taking over his whole being. London! He had never been there!

Maybe he would meet the king? But a sadness also lay at the back of his mind—he would not see Richard, who had become his great friend in so short a time, and whom he had missed so much since the duke's visit to Raglan in late February. Richard was in Burgundy with his brother Edward, maybe in exile for always. 'What a pity he is on the other side,' he thought for the hundredth time—a Yorkist—and so far away.

But Henry stirred himself at the initial excitement caused by the imminent big changes in his life, turned, and ran indoors to find Anne and her family, flourishing this most exciting letter—which he knew would have the same effect on them—excitement and sadness at his leaving. He felt secure in their affection—they had been his real—his only—family.

Would these changes, exciting as they were, be for the better? For the first time, he began to give some credence to his mother's certainty—and steady assurance—of great things being ahead of him in the future.

Kate, Southwark, London, October 1470

Kate was leaning out of the overhanging tavern window, pushed and jostled by other tavern employees and customers who had found their way upstairs to the staff quarters to try and get a better view of the procession—this unexpected, this grand, but rather pathetic sight of the confused, half-crazy Henry VI on parade through the streets of London after his sudden readeption. He was propped up by cushions, but he sagged forward like a doll losing its sawdust, in spite of two strong men on either side of him. At the same time, he looked uncomprehendingly all around him—as if not connecting the waving, cheering crowds with himself.

As she gazed on this pseudo-triumphant sight, Kate's brain hammered the words on everyone's lips, 'King Edward and Richard of Gloucester have fled the country—proclaimed usurper and traitor by the great Earl of Warwick!' They were even now crossing the Channel in haste, into exile in Belgium, hotly pursued by the earl's men.

The horror of the situation left her in disbelief, mingled with the pity she felt, also being shown by the equally confused people for the poor, befuddled creature being paraded for them—their rightful king, returned to his proper place of authority by the victorious Earl of Warwick—but a pure figurehead, no less. He had never been much. His wife, Margaret of Anjou, had ruled effectively in his stead. But she was in France. And now he was as nothing. He blinked at them from eyes dazzled by the light of day after the gloom and dusty darkness of the tower . . . It seemed that Warwick, unable to rule his protégé Edward, had effectively disposed of him and, using this poor, feeble-minded 'king', was determined to rule the country himself—if not in name, certainly in effect.

And what would this appalling turnabout in royal fortunes mean to Kate? She hardly dared to think about it.

She had only been in London a month or so and had not succeeded in contacting Richard up to then, as he had been in the north. And now this! He had fled to the Continent and she had no idea where! He was in danger of his life! Could he ever return while Henry and Warwick lived? He seemed lost to her. Would she ever see him again and tell him about the son of whose existence he knew nothing?

Kate turned away from the window and pushed and shoved her way out of the crowd, still watching the procession. She fled up the narrow wooden stairs and along the corridor leading to her small room under the eaves, which she shared with Ruth and baby John. Tears were blinding her as she pushed open the door and threw herself on her pallet in a paroxysm of despair, feeling as if her heart would break.

The one thing that had kept her going—the hope of meeting Richard once again—was gone. She felt utterly alone now, abandoned, and dreadfully homesick. If it had not been for baby John, whom she now gathered into her arms and strained to her heart for their mutual comfort, almost smothering him with the strength of her feelings while Ruth looked on sadly, content to let her mistress's anguish take its course before attempting to talk to her, she would have just packed up her few possessions then and there, hired a horse, and made for home—her home was her only security now. She had hoped to find it in Richard, but the realisation of his involvement in a political world in which she had no place, which had taken him away from her perhaps forever, bore cruelly down on her then. And it was quite impracticable for her to go home—for the same reasons as she had gone to Joanna's in the first place—her father. He would be consumed with anger against her and her lover. He hated the Yorkists, in any case, being a committed Lancastrian. He would never accept her, knowing who the baby's father was. She had made her bed and now she must lie on it. There was no way out.

'Oh, Ruth, what have I done?' she sobbed. 'And what shall I do?'

"Tis always the woman who suffers, girl. The men get away scot free, be they rich or poor. 'Tis a fact of life. You loved him—you lay with him—and now you must bear the consequences. It has always been the same. But you young girls go on giving in to their false words and tender embraces. You deluded yourself. Even if he hadn't had to go into exile, he would never have come to you again!'

'No, Ruth, I will never believe that! He loves me as I love him!'

'Where women feel love, men only feel lust—and women believe it is the real thing! We would be better making for home and putting up with your father's ire than staying here. He is a good man—he would get over it in time. He loves you. You are in real danger here from the lustful rakes of the city—Joanna and your mother warned you! Most of the girls in this inn are whores—you are not—but you soon will be if you remain here! Mayhap just to survive!'

'Never! Never, Ruth. I would rather starve! I belong to Richard!'

'You probably will then. And what will he care? Tell me that?'

Kate was silent. She had no answer. She still trusted in Richard. But she felt so alone.

'King Edward will return soon, girl. The people love him. They will not want that evil Margaret of Anjou back, and her husband, this poor Henry, is but the Lord Warwick's puppet. He cannot last long. And with Edward will come Richard of Gloucester. If he then seeks you out, you will know he was in earnest. If not . . . Meanwhile, I advise you to go home before you come face to face with the wicked and lustful men here! It will happen sooner or later, I promise you!'

'I cannot, Ruth, I cannot!' A fresh burst of tears engulfed her. But they soon subsided as the good sense of Ruth's words sunk in. Her maid was wise and full of common sense. She was comforting and strong. How much worse it would be if she were alone with the baby and did not have Ruth's comforting presence! She threw her arms around Ruth and kissed her.

'You are a tower of strength, Ruth! What would I do without you? I could not manage at all! Who would look after the baby while I worked?'

Indeed, she could not have come this far without her faithful maid's help. She had been lucky to find a job almost at once in this tavern in Southwark, 'The Prince of Wales'. The tavern keeper had no doubt been attracted by her striking appearance and offered her work immediately—probably seeing her as a draw to his customers—though his wife was not so certain, maybe seeing Kate as a threat initially, as her husband was known for his dallying. But she had treated Kate well, nevertheless, giving her this room for herself and not objecting to the baby and Ruth. The pay was not much, but her board and food were free and there was plenty of good food. There were drawbacks, of course. She did not like the clientele at all—they were mostly coarse, rough men, working men, over-familiar, who leered at her drunkenly and never missed an opportunity to grab at her thighs or buttocks, some even sliding their dirty hands up her skirt to fondle her. The bolder ones squeezed her breasts as she leant over them bringing tankards of ale or clearing the tables. They just laughed when she objected and did it all the more, so she had learnt to laugh off their attentions light-heartedly and to avoid them when she could. No real harm had come to her yet from their good-natured attentions anyway. The tavern keeper's wife had told her shortly, when she first complained, that it was all part of the job unfortunately. If she didn't like it, she knew what she could do. The men propositioned her too, frequently, but, unlike the other girls, she always refused, though the extra money would have been very useful. She had discovered that babies were expensive and felt guilty that she had not been able to pay Ruth for her help and companionship yet. Not that Ruth minded. She was happier here than if she had been left behind at Appleby Hall with Kate's rather short-tempered and irritable mother as her mistress. And she loved Kate and baby John.

Other types came there occasionally—and these she was very wary of, especially the noblemen of the court, who sometimes came to drink and whore—on the prowl for willing girls to spend the night with. They paid well, but many were known to be perverted and depraved in their desires. The tavern keeper's wife told her to avoid them, if possible. In their search for new thrills to titillate their jaded appetites, they were capable of anything. One of her girls had been taken away by a group of them not long ago and subjected to torture and gang rape—then left for dead down on the towpath by Westminster Bridge. They regarded themselves as above the law and were never caught. Even those who were identified in these cases avoided punishment by their ability to pay bribes to lawyers and judges. It was a shameful situation, but the laws had all broken down under Henry VI's inadequate rule, and now he was back. Edward and Richard's attempts to enforce them and bring in effective new ones would surely lapse again.

Kate was determined never to resort to getting money by this means—with rich or poor. She could just about manage on what she earned—and the tips helped.

But her resolution was put severely to the test a few nights after Henry's procession. And things changed for her from then on. Her new security—such as it was—was completely undermined. She knew terror again—the kind she had felt in the wood with the vicious army deserter determined to have his way with her.

Two noblemen, obviously of very high degree by their sumptuous clothes, came tavern-crawling to the 'Prince of Wales'. And Kate's whole new fragile world was turned upside down, destroyed utterly. The look in these men's eyes, far gone in drink, as they gazed at her was exactly the same as that in the eyes of the filthy would-be-rapist encountered in the Appleby woods. It was predatory, determined, completely without compassion, cold and fixed, like that of a poisonous snake about to strike. They took their time—waiting patiently whilst the tavern gradually emptied, intent on their prey. They said nothing—but she knew what they were about. She shuddered and sweated, not from the heat in the crowded inn, but from naked fear—which she was forced to hide, as she went mechanically about her duties all evening. The two followed her round with their eyes, meanwhile drinking huge quantities of wine, as if priming themselves for what they planned to do later on. At midnight, when the tavern was due to close and most of the other stragglers had drifted away home or been ejected, they got up from their seats in a corner, somewhat unsteadily, but very determined on their course of action. It was time to show their hand—and Kate knew it. She tried to appear unconcerned as they approached her. One produced a bag of silver and tried to give it to the innkeeper, indicating what they wanted for their money. Luckily, he shook his head. He did not sell his girls—it was up to them what they did after hours, she heard him remark acidly and turn away. Kate shuddered in utter horror as he left the taproom to go to his quarters, leaving her to deal with these two she knew to be all evil—it emanated from them like an animal scent. She tried to sidle in an unconcerned way towards the door behind which the steep stairs lay—her way to safety. The door was shut. She hoped they did not realise what she was about. But they were only too aware. One took her wrist, while the other dangled the bag of silver under her nose. She only knew she must not show fear, but like a trapped animal, she shuddered inwardly as they smiled ingratiatingly at her—perhaps trying to dissemble. She decided to challenge their hand. She smiled back and tossed her curls, taking the bag of silver and putting it down her bodice. Then she jerked her head, as if in invitation towards the stairs door. She was taking a terrible chance. But what they did not know was that there was a strong bar behind the door. If only she could get through the door and slam it in their faces and throw the bar before they realised and could follow! They had consumed enormous quantities of wine that evening—her reactions were surely better than theirs—even in her terrified state.

They followed her somewhat unsteadily, but still very intently, as she moved towards the door and opened it a little. They must not see the bar on the back of it, or she was lost! She turned, beckoning and smiling, and they came, all unsuspecting. At the last moment, she lunged backwards into them, knocking at least one of them half off his feet and was through the small aperture and wrenching the bar across to lock the door. Drunk they may have been—but they were not stupid. And they were stronger than her. They pushed furiously at the door with their combined weight and made it impossible to fix the bar in place. She abandoned the attempt and ran like the wind up the narrow stairs and along the corridor, up another flight of stairs, and stumbled gasping for breath into her little room, slamming the door and barring it, just as they stumbled to the top of the second flight. At last, the huge amount they had drunk was telling on them. But in a moment, they were hammering and banging angrily on her door, shouting to be admitted. Luckily, she had thrown the bag of silver down outside the door, and after a while, she heard the rattle of it as they picked it up and, abandoning their futile quest, moved away, stumbling in an erratic fashion down to the taproom and yelling to the landlord that his girls were nothing but teasing sluts and needed a good beating. Luckily, they were not answered and must have found their own way out after throwing a few chairs and tables round in their drunken fury. Then there was silence. Ruth, holding the baby fast, turned to her where she stood leaning against a wall trying to get her breath.

'I told you this would happen! And it will happen again! Next time, you may not be so lucky!'

Westminster Palace, London, November 1470

Henry VI sat staring vaguely at the courtiers that milled around him. He did not seem able to focus properly. It was almost as if he did not know what was going on. If only Margaret were here to support him. She was on her way here—he knew that—but without her, he was lost. He did what he was told. If Richard Neville, Earl of Warwick, or his other councillors said, 'Stay here,' he stayed. If they said, 'Go there,' he obeyed likewise. But it was all too much. How he wished he was back in his room in the Tower of London! It may have been imprisonment—but there he felt safe. There was no stress.

Nothing was expected of him. Whereas here—he understood enough in his confused state to realise that the unwanted burdens of kingship had been heaped again on his unwilling head.

He had once more been thrust into the centre of things, much against his will, when he much preferred observing life from the fringes. How would he cope? If only he had not been born into this—for him—unnatural existence! His natural inclinations had always been towards the quiet life, complete withdrawal even. He would have been so happy as a monk, a priest, or a scholar. Books were his life. And prayer . . . He felt like a fish out of water, gasping for breath.

His great father, Henry V, had always denigrated him, made him feel utterly inadequate, when he was alive—and he still felt the same—though his father was long gone.

'Sire, your visitors have arrived from Wales! Will you be so gracious as to receive them now?' The king's Chamberlain was on his knee in front of him, looking excited about something.

'Visitors? From Wales?' he murmured, confused.

'Yes, Sire, the Earl of Pembroke, Earl Jasper, and young Henry Tudor, his nephew! You'll remember the boy's mother, Lady Margaret Beaufort, wrote to you, telling you that they were coming? The boy is now thirteen years of age, and Earl Jasper and Lady Margaret are most anxious for him to meet you. As the boy is also!'

'Ah, yes, I remember now. You did tell me they were coming.' His befuddled mind could not register a reason *why* they were coming though. But he nodded patiently and waved the Chamberlain away. If only everyone would leave him alone! He did not want visitors. For the thousandth time, he wished his queen were here. She kept writing that she was on her way but never arrived. She would know how to receive these visitors—whoever they were? For the life of him, he could not understand why he had to receive them, why they were so important?

Ah, yes, the boy Henry was the last of the Lancastrians—a future king perhaps? Descended from his own mother, Katherine de Valois, who had married Owen Glendower, the Welsh groom she had fallen in love with, after his great father's early death from dysentery in the French Wars. Did he want his blessing? What did he want? What was he supposed to say to the boy?' He shook his head, utterly perplexed.

There was a loud blare of trumpets! The Chamberlain was on his knee in front of him again. What now?

'My lord, it is Richard Neville, Earl of Warwick, who awaits your pleasure! Will you receive him now? He says it is very urgent! I am sure the Welsh lord and his protégé will understand and wait. Anyway, Lord Warwick takes precedence.'

Richard Neville—ah, yes, the one who had hoisted him back on to this throne, where he had no real wish to be, but who was his steadfast supporter and who was taking all the real burden of rule off his shoulders. He supposed he ought to be grateful, but somehow he wasn't.

'Of course, announce him at once and bring him straight to me!'

The Chamberlain bowed low and backed from Henry's presence. A moment later, the great Kingmaker—so-called—Earl Richard Neville stood before him. Henry held out his hand, and Richard Neville knelt and kissed his coronation ring.

'Sire, Edward the usurper has fled to Burgundy, to cast himself on the uncertain mercies of his brother-in-law Charles, Duke of Burgundy, his sister Margaret's husband. He is only accompanied by his brother, Richard of Gloucester, William Hastings, his Chamberlain, Lord Rivers, his brother-in-law, and a few guards! He took nothing with him in his haste. All he has in the world are the clothes he stands up in! He is a spent force, utterly dependent on the Burgundians' good will. He is gone for good! I feel I can assure you of that. You are safe—and in your rightful place, from which you should never have been ousted! And I am your most faithful and devoted servant unto my life's end.'

'You are a good man, Richard, and have great strength of body and mind—both of which I envy you! I trust you utterly to do the right thing by this great country of ours, which has suffered interminably for many years through the enmity between the Houses of Lancaster and York! I pray every day that peace will come soon and that all men will live in harmony, which is surely God's will?'

'Sire, I feel sure that now is the time to reinforce the peace by reinstating the Lancastrian lords with their estates which were attainted by Edward! Will you allow this?'

'Of course. I will do whatever you think necessary and proper to bring peace to this troubled land of ours. That is what I pray for chiefly! It is men's vaunting desire for power and position which causes all this strife in the first place. Why cannot men accept the lot which God has allotted them—rich or poor?'

'My lord, I fear it is in the nature of nearly all men to desire more than they have! Only the saintly ones—such as yourself—have little or no ambition to better themselves! But then you are the king—what higher position could you crave?'

'I am no saint, Richard, I assure you! Every day, I prostrate myself in prayer to the Good Lord to cleanse me of all sin and impure thoughts and desires! I had no wish to be king—it was thrust upon me! I am quite unfit for its burdens! Without you and Margaret, my good queen—may she return soon—I admit I would be quite lost!'

'You denigrate yourself, Sire! It is only because of your sickness that you feel this way! Now you are reinstated and all the stress has ceased, you will recover quickly and regain your strength of body—and mind!'

'I thank you for your faith in me, Richard! But I know myself better than anyone! Sick or well, I am unsuited to this position in every way.'

'Sire, take heart! Relax and leave the problems and burdens to me! And now, I believe that Jasper, Earl of Pembroke, awaits outside with his young nephew, Henry Tudor, and the boy's mother, the formidable Lady Margaret Beaufort! No doubt they come to petition you for the boy's lands and title of Earl of Richmond. I do know that his mother frequently begged King Edward to restore them, after they had been appropriated by George, Duke of Clarence. I beg you to give these petitioners a fair hearing—they have waited many years for reinstatement!'

'I will, of course. That goes without saying. Send them in now,' Henry sighed.

'Uncle Jasper, isn't that the great Earl of Warwick?' whispered Henry as a heavily bejewelled, commanding figure emerged from the king's throne room. Earl Jasper nodded.

'Aye, boy. To be honest, he is the king now in all but name!' he whispered this last back, knowing that his words could be interpreted as treasonable if overheard by the wrong ears.

'What do you mean, sir?'

'He commands the king! Without Richard Neville, King Henry is a broken reed. But come, I must say no more. The king's Chamberlain approaches us. Now is our best chance to beg the king for your rightful inheritance! So show great deference and respect to His Majesty—even if he is but a figurehead. Only he can make the decision to reinstate you!'

The boy nodded and following the Chamberlain behind his uncle and mother, approached the throne and knelt humbly with the others at Henry's feet.

'Rise, all of you! I believe you have waited a long time to see me? And even longer for the wrongs done against you to be righted? I am sorry for your long wait today, but the earl brought me urgent news which demanded my immediate attention! Luckily, it was good news! How can I help you now?'

Henry's mother approached first eagerly, curtseying low to the king.

'Your Majesty, I am glad that you have just received some happy news—whatever that may be! Perhaps, now that you have regained your rightful place and things are going well again for the House of Lancaster, you may consider doing a great service to my son here? He is the rightful Earl of Richmond. But Edward, the usurper, gave all the boy's estates and his title to George, Duke of Clarence, that grasping brother of his! It is in your power to strip him of what is not rightfully his and return them to their rightful owner by descent—my son Henry Tudor here—your loyal and faithful servant, as indeed we are all your faithful servants!'

Earl Jasper and Henry both nodded vehemently and bowed low again at these words. King Henry was staring fixedly into the face of his young namesake with a very strange look—it was very intense and yet had a faraway quality too.

'Young man, something tells me that you have a great future ahead of you! Of course I willingly return your title and estates to you—but one day, you will rise far higher! I'm convinced of it! Maybe you will even rule this great land of ours!'

'What makes you think that, Your Majesty?' broke in Lady Margaret eagerly, moving several steps forward up the dais. Jasper and young Henry raised their eyebrows at each other, the earl certainly mystified by the strange words, though not Henry, having heard his mother predict the same thing so many times before.

'I do not know. It is a conviction that is come upon me, and it is growing stronger every minute! The future, after all, is in the hands of the young—and this young man has something in his face and bearing which speaks to me of future greatness! I cannot explain it—I just know it!' The king fell back in his chair, his brief animation abandoning him suddenly as if it had never existed, leaving him the same sad-faced, pathetic wraith of a man he had been before the boy had appeared.

'Oh, Sire, if only this could come to pass, it would be the fulfilment of all my hopes and dreams for him! For years, I've also believed he would achieve great things and is destined for higher position—even the throne—as you have intimated! But,' Lady Margaret laughed, 'not for many years yet, Your Majesty! And it is a mystery that this chance could possibly come to him—seeing as your son, the Prince of Wales, lives and thrives!'

'Yes, Lady, it is a mystery to me too—but your son is very young yet, and it may be, as you say, many years ahead, this great position which I feel he will rise to! My son will surely succeed me—but the strange conviction within me when I gaze upon this boy here will not be denied!'

'The king may suffer from his nerves and be weak in body and mind, so it is said, but I think he is no fool if he can see what I have seen plainly all these years,' commented Lady Margaret to Earl Jasper as they left the audience chamber and entered the ante-room, where they could not be easily overheard.

'And what he has just said increases my determination a thousandfold—if that be possible—to see young Henry here king in very truth one day! I have worked, and will work to my utmost, to achieve this for him! I will take any risks and undertake any necessary actions to see him on the throne, which will be his rightful place!'

'Have a care, my lady! Remember that the king is known not to be in possession of his full wits—this could just be the ramblings of a mentally sick man! Do not set too much store upon his words—nor you, Nephew!' asserted Earl Jasper, shaking his head. 'I too have worked all my life to get young Henry here his rightful position and estates back. Now I think we have achieved that at last, it is best not to go chasing after the moon as well!'

'Pshaw! Believe, Jasper! The king's words—and his strange conviction—are surely a message from God! A confirmation of what I have always felt and known in my heart!'

Court of Burgundy, Christmas, 1470

'Dickon, who could have imagined we could fall so low is such a short time! It is Christmas Day, and the most miserable I've ever spent! I have a son and heir, born on November the twenty-second, whom I have never seen—and poor Elizabeth is still in sanctuary in that draughty, miserable place! It must be so unhealthy for the baby too! Supposing he sickens and dies? Babies succumb so quickly to any disease going around. A simple cold can kill. Disease is no respecter of persons—not even the Prince of Wales!'

'Stop worrying, Edward. He comes of strong stock—I'm sure that he is thriving!'

'But I have not even received one letter from Elizabeth. Surely she must have written to me? I have written to her a dozen times!'

'I expect the letters are not getting through, either way. Warwick will have seen to that! He rules with a rod of iron at present. Henry is but a poor pawn in his game. This situation cannot last long though! The people still support you, and you have many followers gathering here who will fight to help you regain your throne when the time is right!'

'That wretched turncoat Warwick! And my own brother George is supporting him now for his own ends. These are two men I loved well, Dickon, in spite of everything. Now they have gone too far. When I return, I will have no alternative but to condemn them both to death for their evil deeds against their rightful king—no more sentiment!'

'That's the spirit, Ned! Now we must put on happy faces and join the celebrations, whether we feel like it or not! Charles of Burgundy is your best hope of assistance in regaining your rightful place on the English throne. We must persuade him, by every means, to provide funds to enable us to gather a strong army to return to England and defeat Warwick. You can forget about Henry—he is but a figurehead!'

'What about Margaret of Anjou? She returned to England in November with her son, Edward, and she is no mean force to deal with. Having her at his side, as well as Warwick, Henry could prevail!'

'Never! Believe me! Warwick will overstep the mark sooner or later. He will overreach himself. It is inevitable. His overriding ambition will be his downfall. Just be patient, Ned.'

'I long to believe you. You have wisdom far beyond your years, Dickon.'

'Come, Ned, put away your miserable thoughts, and let us join the duke and his court in the great Feast of the Nativity. You always did enjoy drinking—and French wines are the best in the world, and the most potent!'

'And French women are fascinating and very beautiful. Who knows, I may make a conquest here to divert me!' answered Edward. 'You are right, Dickon, as always. What would I do without you?'

Richard, though his brother was ten years older, felt the elder of the two as he put his arm round Edward and led him towards the Great Hall where the sound of music and merriment could be heard.

Raglan Castle, Gwent, 28 January 1471

Woking Old Hall,
Surrey,
20 January 1471

My Dear Henry,

I am writing to you hoping you will receive this letter of good wishes in time for your fourteenth birthday on the 28 January. I have paid highly for the fastest messengers to convey this—and your presents, which follow—as it is such a long way, so you had better receive all by then, or I shall have something to say to them!

I only wish I could have visited you in Wales, but it is not possible. However, I will be with you in spirit, if not in body. I am not strong, as you know, or in good enough health to undertake such a journey in mid-winter. I hope you will understand.

As I have told you before several times, I would have had you here with me long since, if I could. But King Edward—now ousted in October last and away in exile in Burgundy with his brother, the Duke of Gloucester, thank goodness—was always adamant that you stay there under the Yorkist guardianship of Lord Herbert, made Earl of Pembroke in 1468, who was executed after fighting in the Battle of Edgecote in July last year. This would have been, I know, very unhappy news for you, and you must have felt very sad, for, after all, he was also a good man and you must mourn him—if misled in his Yorkist affiliations—and he and his family always looked after you kindly and well. I expect you came to regard him as your father, as you never knew your own. That was inevitable.

The new political situation means that, at long last, what you have waited for so long will happen soon—your Uncle Jasper will be able to take entire responsibility for you again! It will no doubt be a big wrench for you, though, leaving Raglan Castle after all these years and going to live with your Uncle Jasper in Harlech Castle, which he recaptured from the Yorkists, and which I know he is keeping well-defended, in case they try to get it back!

Now that God's Anointed, King Henry VI, is back in his rightful place on the throne, I shall continue to importune him to restore to you your rightful title of Earl of Richmond and the many estates in Yorkshire belonging to it, appropriated by George of Clarence, Edward's younger brother. When Edward was king, he could deny George nothing, it seems, and allowed him to hold on to what was never rightfully his, in spite of my constant pleadings on your behalf! Henry did promise me, when we visited him at Westminster last November, that he would reinstate you and would authorise it, but nothing has happened yet. I fear his befuddled brain and the strong influence of the Earl of Warwick and Queen Margaret have persuaded him against it or he has just forgotten all about it, no doubt, so sick is he in his poor head.

But because you are, as I have told you before, of royal blood and have a good, if not the only true, claim to the throne directly in line from Prince Edward, poor Henry's son, I am determined to get the king to act on your behalf in the matter of your title and rightful estates, of which you were wrongfully deprived. They are your entitlement, your birthright. It is quite inconceivable that Clarence should continue to hold on to them now, even though he is in close cooperation with the Earl of Warwick, the real king in effect, if not in name. Not so long ago, there were many between you and what I know in my heart to be your ultimate inheritance—the throne. Now there is only one sick man and his only son, who has resided in France with his mother Margaret D'Anjou for so long that he is, I am sure, almost wholly French in character. He is said to have a very unpleasant and cruel nature—not ideal material for kingship. Who knows, something may happen to prevent him ever attaining kingship? So you have a definite chance. Henry is old and sick in mind and body, so I do not expect he will live long, even if Margaret returns to support him.

On the Yorkist side—if they ever return to power, God forbid—there are only George of Clarence and Richard of Gloucester, Edward's brothers, who have any real claim to the throne after Edward—but it is certainly no better than yours!

As you know, Richard was sent into Wales in November 1469 to restore order there after the Lancastrian rebellions in Cardiganshire and Carmarthenshire. He was only seventeen then, and was made a leader of hundreds of soldiers, and he was only four years older than you at the time! He was given so much power by Edward, his elder brother, and so many influential positions, right up to the time last October when they had to flee into exile in Burgundy, that I imagine his head must have swollen to twice its normal size! But all that has changed now, of course! Think of it, Constable of England and Chief Justice for Wales whilst still nothing but a boy of seventeen! Apparently, being so able a commander, he carried out his duties excellently. I suppose Edward had no one else he could trust to take on such important work, except this young and able brother of his—known to be his favourite. And now they are both landless and powerless exiles, stripped of everything! They say that King Edward and Richard escaped only in the nick of time from Warwick's pursuit, with just the clothes they stood up in! How are the mighty fallen!

You too could have a really great future and important responsibilities like Richard by the time you are his age. Uncle Jasper will help you, I know. I am sure that you will be happy to be with him again after all these years you have been separated from him and living at Raglan Castle with the Herbert family.

My dear son, enjoy your birthday and think on your glittering future—which may not be so far off, now that the Lancastrians are supported by the great Earl of Warwick. He is very powerful and influential. He exerts his will to accomplish great things! King Henry is lucky to have him as a supporter, especially as Queen Margaret has been so far away in France for so long and he himself is so weak and sick. He must depend on him greatly.

Write soon and let me know how you are. There will be some presents arriving for you on your birthday, as usual, as I mentioned, which I know you will like!

Your loving mother,
Margaret,
Countess of Richmond

Henry read his birthday letter, as always feeling that his mother expected too much for him—and from him—but also excited by her predictions for his future. That seemed to be the one thing that constantly obsessed her mind.

He was very intrigued and impressed, as always, by Richard of Gloucester's achievements. News had filtered regularly into Raglan about Richard's success as a commander of men and as a tactician in campaigns, for the Welsh supporters of the Lancastrian cause had been well and truly routed by this capable young duke and his men. He must be very able indeed, or he could not possibly have carried out such feats!

Would he, Henry, ever be able to achieve so much in the world? Would he ever be able to impress his mother with such achievements? He wished that he could meet this clever Richard of Gloucester again! But that did not seem very likely, given the political situation.

He sighed as he folded his letter. Then a thought struck him. If this long drawn-out war was still going on in a few years, then who knew, he may meet Richard in battle?!

He knew he would be sad to leave the Herbert family permanently, as his departure now seemed imminent. He had grown to love the gentle Ann Devereux. She was more of a real mother to him than his own had ever been, and he had cried with her and her children when the terrible news came of her husband's execution after the battle of Edgecote. Nobody deserved to die like that after fighting so bravely, whichever side he was on.

He would miss Maude greatly, and he knew she was devoted to him, and that her father had wished them to marry later on—he had even expressed that desire in his will.

But in spite of all this, he found excitement welling up in him at the thought of being reunited with his beloved Uncle Jasper. And at Harlech Castle! He had never been to North Wales. Apart from his brief trip to London to see the king last November, he had never been anywhere much really. It was an exciting prospect!

Southwark, London, Late March/April 1471

Kate was beside herself with joy! A letter from Richard—at last! True, it had been redirected by her mother from Northamptonshire and had been sent at the end of November—but what did that matter? He still cared. He worried about her. Little did he know about her true circumstances! And if he did know, what could he do, exiled in Burgundy with the king?

Warwick still seemed to reign supreme—ruling the poor puppet king Henry with ease. Surely he would go too far soon? For all his arrogance and power, he was not really king. His popularity with the people was waning dramatically. They were sick of the situation—and poor ineffectual Henry—and wanted their true king, Edward, their golden boy, back! Surely Edward must know their mood by now—even so far away at the Burgundy Court in Brugge? And when he decided to act—then Richard would be at his side—Richard would come back! Her heart turned over with the thought of it. And at that moment, she decided to answer him and tell him where she was. But to tell him of his son? Of that she was not so sure. She knew he would be proud of the beautiful boy, and she was sure he would accept the child as his, but what could he do for him—or her—until his brother was restored to power? And this, she felt sure, could not be long delayed. The taproom in the evenings was full of resentful mutterings against Warwick—and more than mutterings—downright anger!

But the anger turned to excitement a few days later. The news spread like wildfire through the city.

Edward had returned—he had landed in the north by the Humber about the middle of March and had been working his way southwards ever since with men, money, and arms given him by Charles, Duke of Burgundy, and was now on the very outskirts of London. He was coming to reclaim his throne! And Richard would be with him! Edward had declared himself king again and sent orders for the mayor and magistrates, telling them to arrest Henry and open the gates of the capital to their rightful king.

But they had also received orders from Warwick adjuring them to hold firm against 'this usurper, Edward'. They were in a quandary and had not known what to do for the best. But self-interest won the day, as those who had loans outstanding from Edward decided it was best to concur with his wishes or they might never see their money again!

And there was more very frightening news which turned the people's stomachs with fear, so that their joy at the news of Edward's imminent arrival was soured—Margaret of Anjou, that she-devil queen, was on her way from France equipped with a large force supplied by King Louis to join Warwick, whom she had reluctantly allied with earlier in 1470, after his persuasive promises to put her husband Henry back on the throne. This he had done, but could he keep him there? Also, he had promised on his honour to be loyal to her son Edward, Prince of Wales, as the next king.

All this could only mean one thing—which no one wanted, having had more than enough of it—war!

And Kate's joy turned to anguish at the thought that if there were battles soon, which seemed inevitable, Richard might be badly injured—even killed—and never know he had a son. And she would never see him again. The thought was so unbearable that she threw herself into her work with such a vengeance during the next week or two that she could barely crawl up the stairs to bed each night well after twelve when she had finished the clearing up after the tavern closed. It was the only way to blot out her acute trepidation and concern about what the future might hold for herself and the child if there was no Richard any more. But she kept her ears open for every scrap of news that the tavern patrons tossed about each evening.

The long days went by and then the news was joyous! At least for the Yorkists. Kate knew that she should feel the opposite way at the news of the Yorkists' overwhelming success. After all, her father and brother had fought on the Lancastrian side for a long time. But she could only feel thankfulness and joy that Richard was safe—at court with his brother, the king, and very near! She had written him that letter telling him she was in London. Surely he had received it by now and must come soon? Edward was reinstated as king at last! There had been a terrible Battle at Barnet, and the Earl of Warwick had been killed! Also, Queen Margaret's son, Edward, Prince of Wales, had been murdered after the battle—so now Edward had no one to oppose him! Queen Margaret was a spent force, so it was said—in terrible grief over the murder of her dear son, the Prince of Wales—her last hope for the Lancastrians.

It was very late one night when nearly all the regulars had gone and she had already started to clear up but found herself stopping and standing near to listen to a pair of Yorkist courtiers who were far gone in drink and whose tongues were very loose, when one of them, larger and rather older than the other, turning and seeing her there, eyed her up and down in such a lascivious way she felt her flesh crawl.

'Want to join us, pretty one?' he drawled, leering drunkenly.

She hastily moved away and started collecting tankards again, but too late—their interest was aroused. It was the last thing she wanted to happen. She usually tried to keep as unobtrusive as possible, but her curiosity had led her into this trap. Was there to be a repeat of that night when she had only just escaped by running upstairs and locking her door? And these men were noblemen—used to having their own way—in everything.

'Lost your tongue, my lovely?' the other one chided. He turned to his companion and elbowed him, pointing at Kate. 'Bit of sport here to end the evening nicely—don't you think?'

They both laughed and began to rise—very unsteadily, it was true—but with a horrible kind of determination. She hastily put down the tray of tankards and made for the stairs door. But the first one to notice her—not nearly as drunk as his companion—was there first. He stood with his back against the door, barring her way.

'Not so fast, sweetheart. Do you know who I am? I assure you I usually have my own way when I want something—especially if it's a woman! That's right, Richard, isn't it?'

They laughed coarsely again and the younger man, thinner but dressed very richly in a foppish fashion, nodded his head, 'True, my lord Dorset—you always get your way!'

Kate realised she knew who this man breathing wine fumes into her face was as he pulled her towards him and began to fiddle with the drawstrings of her bodice. She tried to pull away, her mind working furiously at the same time. This was the queen's eldest son by her first marriage, the Marquess of Dorset—known widely for his degenerate and lusty lifestyle at court and away from it. No girl was safe from him! And the other one he had addressed must be Lord Richard Grey, his brother—another notorious rake! And she had fallen into their clutches!

And of course, Richard had mentioned their close association with Lord William Hastings, the king's Chamberlain and best friend—also his boon companion in many a debauched night. He had bewailed the fact that his dear brother Edward, the king, was so influenced by him and these other depraved ones. Edward was very fond of whoring also—as well as drinking—but Richard would have nothing said against him, for he loved him so dearly!

If only Richard were here! He would soon stop their evil intentions—but he wasn't! What could she do?

Suddenly, she thought she had the answer!

'I am spoken for, my lord! By someone at court who would not take kindly to what you have in mind!'

Lord Dorset stopped for a moment, withdrawing his hand from her now-open bodice, where he had been fondling her breasts and biting at the nipples. He raised his head. 'Oh yes, and who could a serving wench like you possibly know at court?' They both laughed again. 'Is it the king? I somehow doubt it! Come along, my dear, enough of this. Have you a room here? If not, then you are coming with us!'

'No, it is not the king, but someone else in very high office! You touch me and I have only to inform him and—'

'And what? What could he do to me? Whoever he is or isn't? I am one of the king's closest friends. Whoever this mystery man is you say protects you cannot prevail against the king, who is always loyal to his friends—whatever they do! Admit that you are lying! Come now! I cannot wait a moment longer to sample your charms—neither of us can!'

Kate squirmed in horror. What was this—they both planned to take her? She had to speak!

'It is Richard, Duke of Gloucester, the king's favourite brother!'

'Little Dickon? So he's found out what it's all about at last, has he? Began to wonder if he ever would! You should hear his brother George of Clarence on the subject! Even Edward—at times! Worried about him, they were! And where did Dickon meet you then, my sweeting—and more to the point—when? He's been in exile in Brugge quite a while and only returned a few weeks ago!'

'It was in Northampton, where my father's manor is. I helped him when he had a fall from his horse on the road nearby and injured his ankle,' she stopped. She feared she had said too much already. After all, this man was no friend of Richard's.

She wished she had never had to mention him. But there was no other way to extricate herself from the dreadful predicament. Surely Richard would not mind?

'Ha, so that's it! That was when young Dickon discovered the fun to be had with a pretty woman? Which you undoubtedly are, my dear! Edward will love this! Seem to remember he mentioned something about Dickon's stay in Northampton last autumn. I cannot wait to tell him! And I am sure Dickon won't mind sharing you. He has good taste!'

They both laughed uproariously, and Kate, her one defence—so she had thought—proved useless, felt hard put to it not to cry. They were deriding Richard—they had no fear of him or his position. She was lost!

'But—you say your father is a landowner. So what in the name of God are you doing here? Come. Admit it's all a pack of lies, girl!'

'It is all true—but I came here because . . .' she stopped, biting her lip. She had nearly gone too far and mentioned the child.

'Well, why? Following Richard, was it? Couldn't do without him?' They laughed again. 'Imagine—love-sick over sickly little Dickon!' Dorset sneered.

'Who cares about Dickon? We're here now and he's not! Let's get on with it. What he doesn't see, he'll never know about. She certainly won't tell him what we do!' Grey laughed.

'You're right, Richard! He wouldn't touch her with a bargepole—afterwards!' Laughing coarsely, Dorset grabbed her arm and began to drag her towards one of the long wooden settles.

'We'd all be more comfortable in your room, wench—but if needs must, this will have to do!'

As the two of them determinedly pushed her down on the wooden bench and began to pull up her skirts and petticoats, Kate screamed repeatedly, hopelessly. 'God, help me! Help me!'

Suddenly, the stairs door flew open and the big, burly landlord and his wife burst into the room.

'My lords, leave her alone, I beg you! Kate is a barmaid only—she works here just to support her baby! She does not go with the patrons. I told her many times she could make more money that way—working after hours, like, but she wouldn't have any of it. There are plenty of other girls here will only be too happy to satisfy your wishes. Let me call them and you can take your pick!'

Dorset and Grey had let Kate go at his words, an incredulous look on both their faces.

'Her baby? Now there's a bit of news to titillate the king!'

He looked at Kate. 'Is it Dickon's then?' Kate was silent, her head drooping, busy rearranging her clothes.

'It is, by God! It must be! Dickon's little bastard! He's got one at last! About time he joined the club! I cannot wait to tell Edward! You, my dear, will keep for another time,' Dorset directed at Kate. 'Maybe you'll be more amenable then. Could be to your advantage, you know. We pay well!'

'I don't want your money. I'd rather starve!' Kate retorted, spitting directly at his face.

'Hoity-toity! So Dickon's your one and only then? You should find out what a real man can do for you! Come on, Richard, to court! This bit of news cannot wait! Edward will lap it up! What a turn-up for the books! Dickon's got a woman at last!' Lord Dorset planted a kiss on Kate's bosom, and the two of them left—both laughing. Kate shuddered thinking of what could have happened. Maybe the very mention of Richard had protected her after all—even though they both seemed to despise him as a man.

Westminster Palace, May 1471

'Well, my Lord Richard, I do admire your taste! But I deplore how you provide for your sweet mistress—or rather, do not!'

William Hastings, Lord Chancellor to the king, laughed uproariously, slapping Richard on the back in his hearty fashion. 'A Southwark tavern? Can you do no better for her? I know you are frequently strapped for cash and bewail the fact that you are not often solvent without your dear brother Edward's help, but surely you have enough ready money to set her up in a decent lodging? I assume you must visit her there?'

Richard turned, puzzled, towards the speaker.

'What do you mean? I have no idea what you are talking about!'

'Why, the succulent Kate, of course! You are most fortunate—especially as she keeps her favours solely for you, it seems!'

'I am at a loss, Lord Hastings, to understand to whom you refer. I know no woman in Southwark!'

'Well, she certainly knows you, Dickon! Didn't seem to think you would be too pleased if she pleasured others too!'

'Pleasured? Who?'

'Why, my lord, the Marquess of Dorset and his brother—the queen's sons. Said you would be quite put out if she gave in to their demands!' He laughed again.

William Hastings rubbed the side of his nose with one finger, exchanging a glance of amusement with the king, who was rocking with laughter as they teased Richard. 'Or maybe you just don't want to admit you've discovered girls at last!'

'Come on, Dickon! Tell all!' Edward urged, getting up and putting his arm round his favourite younger brother. 'I must say, for a while, we thought you would never make a start! No interest at all! But maybe you've just been a dark horse—as William here suggests! And better late than never!'

'I swear I am hiding nothing! I do not have any woman in Southwark!'

'Well, she did say you met in Northampton . . .' Hastings began.

Richard shook himself free of the king's arm and turned away thoughtfully. 'Kate? His Kate—in Southwark? So near?' He had received a letter from her,

---

sent from Northampton—in November—but nothing since. Had she come to London then? But why? And without telling him?

Edward's mood suddenly changed as he became contrite at the look on Richard's face.

'Sorry for teasing you, Dickon. But you must admit you've never shown much interest in women up to now! But I can see you are serious about this one. The Marquess here tells me she is very beautiful.'

'That is not her only attribute,' said Richard quietly. 'She is good and virtuous—'

'Not so virtuous as to reject your advances, lad!' grinned Hastings. 'There's the baby to show for it!'

Richard swung round to face Hastings. 'Baby?'

'Yes, if she's telling the truth and you are her one and only love—then it must be yours!'

'I know nothing about any baby! She wrote to me in November and I only got the letter recently when we returned from exile in Brugge, but there was no mention of her having had a child!'

'So you didn't even know you have a son then?' Edward said. 'Apparently, the innkeeper told Richard Grey and the Marquess of Dorset that the baby was a boy! A bastard certainly, but every man needs sons—bastards or not!'

Richard made up his mind then and there. He must go and seek out Kate—at once. He could not leave her in such a place!

'It is true, Sire, that I love her—and she me, but we have not seen each other for so long that I had no idea she was in London even—and as for the baby! I intend to go immediately to this Southwark inn and find her—rescue her from such a place. It is not to be borne! What has happened to her that she left her father's manor and works as a drudge there?'

'Perhaps her family disowned her when they found out about the baby—and who the father was?' said Hastings.

'It is possible, I suppose—I believe her father is of the Lancastrian persuasion.'

'Did you know that when you took up with her?' enquired the king. 'Hardly a suitable paramour! And all these lovely court ladies at your disposal on our side! And I thought you had a penchant for Anne Neville? Though that is surely out of the question now that her father has turned against us?'

'I am not interested in the court women, Edward—you know that. They are shallow, vain, and conceited—also avaricious in the extreme. I could never go with one, let alone love her! As for Anne—that was just a childhood friendship—we were thrown together so much at Middleham . . .'

'Then this Kate must be a rare mortal to come up to your high moral standards, lad,' Edward said, teasing again. 'I should like to meet her one day.'

'Never!' said Richard rather too hastily.

'Think I might seduce her from under your nose, then?'

'Edward, you are known far and wide for your amours—but Kate is not such a one to be picked up and dropped lightly—even by the king!'

'Well, lad, go to her. Go to your virtuous woman. After all, it says in the Bible that such a one is a pearl of great price—so rare is it!' Hastings and Edward could not help sniggering again at these words—it was obvious to Richard they neither of them believed what he had told them of Kate's character. Perhaps they had never been lucky enough to meet such a truly good girl?

'Go on—bring her to court if you want! I promise to leave her alone. I am intrigued by this paragon of virtue. Luckily Lord Dorset discovered her for you, hiding away there, wasn't it? She could hardly come to court looking for you!' laughed Edward.

Richard bowed to the king but ignored the Marquess of Dorset as he hurried out, intent on the rescue of Kate.

Baynard's Castle, London, May 1471

'You should be perfectly safe here, my love!' Richard murmured, taking Kate's face between his hands and kissing her fondly. 'And the little one! And you have Ruth to care for you. I will engage a nursemaid too, if you like! My mother, the Duchess Cecily, owns this mansion, but is rarely in London. I will tell her I have put you here for your own safety after what has happened, and I am sure she will not mind. There are just one or two servants to look after you and to keep the house in good order, so you should be very comfortable! I will come as often as I can to see you both! Why did you not tell me about the child as soon as you knew you were pregnant? Did you think I would not support you?'

'I'm sorry. I just did not want to burden you. You lead such a busy life in the king's service, and I was afraid to stay at home and incur my father's wrath when he discovered my condition and that you were my lover! He is an ardent Lancastrian!'

'And you—do you not have split loyalties?'

'No, I was never interested in politics, like most women—but now I am all for York! How could I be otherwise! All that concerns me is that my dear love is here and has promised to protect me and the babe! Your world is wide, Richard, but mine is simply concerned with caring for my child and being safe from those court creatures!'

'Bringing you here by night will ensure that they have no idea where you are. You need not worry. They will soon find other women to pursue. It is their mission in life, I fear! Richard Grey and the Marquess of Dorset will soon seek other conquests when they find you gone!'

'They are not good friends for the king, surely? They must lead him into bad ways?'

'He is easily led and weak when it comes to women, Kate. It is not all his friends' fault! I love him whatever his faults of character. No one is perfect, for he is strong in other ways and has always supported me unwaveringly.'

'He does not deserve your loyalty! You are a far better man than he is! If he had any strength of character, he would dismiss Dorset from the court and bar Lord Grey too!'

'Maybe, but it is not up to us to decide how the king behaves—however we feel about his associates! Let us talk of happier things! The boy, now! He will be known as John of Gloucester—if you agree? And I will support him, educate him, and provide him with possessions and estates as befits my son. I will acknowledge him to the world and keep him near me. When he is old enough, he will be given positions befitting his rank. He is my beloved son—born of a beloved mother!'

'And to think that my mother and my aunt Joanna both thought you would just treat me as a light-o'-love—and would never return to me—even discard me! I trusted you and knew better, Richard, my dear one. I know you will never be able to marry me. They will find some high-born princess or duchess for you—no doubt foreign—but I feel I will always have a great part of your heart!'

'You will indeed, sweeting! And John also. Never fear—I will not desert you, whatever happens. I would marry you if I could—but I know and you know that it will never be possible.'

'Will you acknowledge me and stand by me even if your future wife objects?'

'Even then—she will have to accept you and the child's existence!'

'You are such a good man, Richard. Your loyalty never wavers to those you love.'

'Loyalty binds me! That is my motto and I will never depart from it!'

Westminster Palace, London, 22 May 1471

'So that's it, then. Crazed King Harry is gone! His melancholy finished him off at last! They say the news of his only son Edward's death—murdered after Tewkesbury—had him beating his head on his cell walls in the Tower until he knocked himself unconscious—never to wake up! The gaoler heard him at it late last night. They found him this morning in a pool of blood!'

'I don't believe it! It's too convenient! Coming at just this time! He's been done away with! Now Edward is king in truth, there cannot be another one living at the same time—crazy or not! To die on the same day as Edward returns? His death is too much of a coincidence to be anything else but deliberate!'

'Agreed. I'll lay odds of a hundred to one that Edward ordered it to be done!'

'But who would do such a thing—even for the king?'

'Lots of people—if the price was right! Maybe his own brother—Richard?'

'Hardly! Royals don't do their own dirty work! There's always someone willing to help them out—if they pay a high enough price! But hush—the king comes! It would not do for him to overhear what we are surmising!'

The two throne room footmen hurriedly closed their conversation and bowed as Edward entered, a frown disfiguring his normally happy demeanour.

'Wine! Get me wine—several bottles! I have a mind to get roaring drunk! This whole thing reflects very badly on me and mine, even though I had nothing to do with the old fool's death!'

The two footmen, eyebrows raised at each other, hurried away to do the king's bidding.

'My love, do not let it get you down! He obviously brought about his own death, as it is said! His only son's death was one blow too many for his faltering mind!' Queen Elizabeth murmured, stroking the king's arm.

'But everyone will say I ordered it—it's almost as if he deliberately killed himself as a last desperate attempt to blacken my name! And he has probably succeeded!' Head in hands, he shook off his wife's consoling hand.

'Richard! Where is Richard? I need him now!'

The horrifying news was all round London in a short time. Kate heard it from the servants late in the afternoon and could only think of Richard and how it could affect him, being the brother of the king—who would surely be incriminated in Henry's death. It was an unfortunate start to what should have been a triumphal beginning to Edward's reign following the conclusive victory at Tewkesbury for the House of York.

The Lancastrian cause was all but dead. Only one possible claimant to the throne now existed for them—the young Henry Tudor, far away in Wales. Richard had told her of his meeting with the boy and how they had got on so well. What a pity that now they would become bitter enemies on opposing sides—it was inevitable! But the boy was only about fourteen, far too young to raise an army to oppose Edward at this stage—Edward was now really secure as king. The death of Henry—by whatever means—made it certain that all Lancastrian opposition was dead. Even Queen Margaret could do nothing now. She was a broken woman, having lost her only son, the Prince of Wales, and now her husband, whom she had fought for with such determination. She was also safely imprisoned in the Tower—probably to be executed in the near future. Kate shivered. Such was the fate of those on the losing side.

Henry Tudor, Off Tenby Harbour, Pembrokeshire, Late May 1471

Henry Tudor gazed at the fast-receding bay of Tenby, Pembrokeshire. He was leaving his land, his beloved Wales—for how long? Forever, possibly. Going into exile in France was not a pleasing prospect—but he had no alternative. His life probably depended on it now.

His Uncle Jasper, his lifelong protector, was by his side and smiled ruefully down at the youth, as Henry commented, 'Where are all my Lady mother's grand dreams and aspirations for me now, then? The Lancastrian cause is surely finished forever after that terrible Battle of Tewkesbury? All the Lancastrian nobles of any importance have been killed, and Edward sits more firmly on the throne than ever!'

'Not all, boyo—there is you! They forgot about you away in Wales—the Yorkists—but will remember you now! Many great Lancastrian nobles fled into exile in France long since—when they saw how things were going. You will be among friends. And I will keep you safe and protect you, as I have always done, whether near or far! And King Louis will protect you also until another opportunity presents itself to forward your interests. You are the last hope of the Lancastrians—so a very precious charge for me!'

'My mother has dreamt of the throne for me all these years! I am sure she is obsessed with grandiose ideas, and now the possibility of achieving her ambitions for me are as far away as they can possibly get surely?'

'When all seems lost, there is always hope, my boy! Do not give up yet! I have picked myself up and carried on after endless disappointments and defeats! It's the only way! As I said, you still have strong support—though it is scattered—in France many exiled Lancastrians will fight on your behalf when the time is ripe!'

'But Edward is a young man. He will probably live for many years! He also has a strong young wife! She will surely bear him many sons to succeed him, even if his life is cut short. I would rather give up all idea of becoming king and live a normal, settled life! I yearn to return to the quiet peace of Raglan. I miss Maude Herbert and my horse Owen more than I can say! I know Maude misses me too—her letters tell me so. Her father wished us to be affianced in good time and we were both willing, but ...'

'But events catch up with us, boyo! You have been precipitated from a quiet backwater on to the world stage! There is no escaping it!'

'Well, this is no life, being pushed and pulled from pillar to post! I wish sometimes I had been born a commoner!'

'Well, lad, unfortunately, you were not! It was your misfortune, if you like, to be born into the highest rank! A chess piece you may be in the political game, but your high birth ensured that you have no choice but to accept it!'

'So I must just be a prey to all the winds that blow, like a rudderless ship, for good or evil—tossed hither and thither with no hope of a settled, happy life?'

'As, I said, Henry, there is always hope. I still believe that circumstances could change dramatically once more and present another opportunity for the Lancastrians to be in the ascendancy again. And you would be the kingpin of any attempt to regain the throne!'

'But maybe I do not *want* to be king! I am sure I would be happier doing other things! I don't care much for the thought of being on the throne! I am in the grip of my Lady mother's and your ambitions for me and maybe I do not want to know any more!' Henry turned away angrily, his face dark with frustration.

'You will have to accept your destiny, boyo. You have no choice! If an opportunity arises for you to become king, you must take it! Too much depends on you—the lives and safety of thousands of people, perhaps!'

'I wish it didn't! Am I to have no freedom of choice in anything?'

'If you do become king, you will be all-powerful and capable of enormously important decisions which every king has to take! That is called power! Then, no man will gainsay you! Think about that, lad! It is surely not something to sniff at if given the opportunity to rule. Most men would aspire to it, if only they had the chance!'

'Well, I do not! But I suppose I will do my duty if asked to! The need for that has always been drummed into me!'

'High position, great estates, and riches bring responsibilities too! There is no escaping that fact! Now I think we must put our minds to more immediate problems. The wind has got up sharply, you may have noticed, and those black clouds look very ominous. I am sure we are in for a storm shortly!'

Woking Old Hall, Surrey, Summer, 1471

My Dear Henry,
Remember I assured you when you were small that your time would surely come?

———

Well, you have now become the most important member of the Lancastrians! And I know you have many loyal supporters there in Brittany with you already. And now those that escaped from the battle and found their way to safety after Tewkesbury have also joined you. The king cannot be very happy about that. He keeps telling me to bring you back—that he will not harm you—but I distrust him absolutely!

For now, you are safe at the court of Duke Francis. I know you were in low spirits when you had to escape there across the channel with Uncle Jasper. And that terrible storm must have been terrifying! Thank God you arrived safely on land, even if you were making for France in the first place and were blown off course.

Your escape into exile was absolutely necessary after King Edward came back into power after the battle of Tewkesbury, as you are now the next—and only—legitimate Lancastrian candidate by bloodline to the kingship. And King Henry himself—poor soul—murdered at Edward's orders, to be sure—prophesied that you would one day sit on the throne! He may have been mad, but he had foresight.

Edward is an usurper. And usurpers are sure to come to a bad end! God will punish him. His own mother, the Duchess Cecily, admitted he was a bastard in 1464. She revealed he was the son of an archer, Blaybourne! He is just the fruit of her lust for a common archer while she was lonely in France because her husband Richard, Duke of York, was always away fighting and left her on her own too much. I believe that she spoke the truth. She is not the kind of woman to speak lightly. And she was driven to it by Edward's secret marriage to that awful woman, Grey—and she just a commoner! Also, by Edward's increasingly degenerate lifestyle. She does not regard her own son as fit to be king because of this—apart from his lowly birth. And that means that if he is a bastard—an imposter—then his children have absolutely no rights of succession after him at all. You have! You are descended from pure royal blood. John of Gaunt was your ancestor, remember that!

I continue to work on your behalf here as much as I can, though a woman's powers—even mine—are limited and depend on the goodwill of men. I often wish I had been born a man. I have every bit as much ability and intelligence as any man in power! But then, of course, I would not have had you, my son.

Be as happy as you can and wait patiently. I am sure that, when you do return, your circumstances will have changed immeasurably.

I just know it. I have always known that you were destined for great things!

Don't ask me how. I just do. Poor King Henry felt it too.

I am sure you miss Raglan, the Herbert family, and your life there. But you must bear it as best you may. You must bide your time and enjoy Duke Francis's hospitality—which is very generous, you must admit!

Your loving Mother,
Margaret,
Countess of Richmond

Westminster Palace, Summer, 1471

'I worry about this renegade Jasper and his nephew, Henry Tudor, Richard! He was so quick off the mark getting him away to Brittany! What did he think I would do? Have him killed on the spot for being a very distant future threat to my security on the throne?'

Edward IV rubs his eyes wearily. After yet another night drinking heavily and servicing Mistress Shore, he is not at his best—especially for political matters.

'Henry Tudor is young, Edward, and completely ignorant of the ways of men! He has lived in Welsh backwaters all his life! He knows nothing of fighting, warfare, tactics, or politics. He is surely not a real threat at all, even with his uncle's support and protection? Jasper has never been successful in any of his campaigns or endeavours! He is a loser! He's spent most of his life on the run!'

'Yes, Richard, but neither of them are short of supporters, even in exile. I should think that anyone who is anybody left on the Lancastrian side has fled to Duke Francis's court, either before—when they saw how badly things were going for them—and certainly after Tewkesbury! And Jasper will be teaching him everything he knows, as a seasoned campaigner, about warfare and tactics! He will be sure to prime him well to take his chances when he is old enough. You may be sure of that!'

'You know, I met him at Raglan? I got to know him quite well in the few days I stayed there. He is an unassuming boy, totally without arrogance and certainly not ambitious, to my mind. He is quiet and studious like Lord Herbert, who was his guardian. They both shared a love of rare manuscripts. It is his mother, the formidable Lady Margaret Beaufort, who poses the real threat, I think. She is obsessively ambitious for him. He bewailed the fact to me!'

'That woman! If she were a man, I would have had her executed long since for treason! She is openly of the Lancastrian persuasion. It is only because her second husband, Stafford, is such a loyal Yorkist and promised to keep her in line that I have spared her up to now. She defies me still, I know it, and is in contact with her son regularly. And with her enormous wealth and influence, she could do a lot of damage. She can also ensure strong support for her dear son. If anyone can fill him with the desire to try for my throne—and provide the resources to back him up—it is her! While that boy lives—and grows up—he is a thorn in my backside, which I am sure will become ever more painful if it is not pulled out and got rid of! And all the time support will grow for him amongst the Lancastrian exiles. I am trying to persuade Francis of Brittany to give him up to me. I have promised him our firm support against Louis of France if he does this. And he cannot turn his nose up at that! He needs us to succeed in his desire to become King of Brittany in his own right, with Brittany an independent state. Louis wants Brittany merged into France and all under his thumb! I have also tried bribing Louis into sending out men into Brittany to capture Henry Tudor and his pesky uncle and send them back to me in custody—with the same incentives (bribes if you like)—of help from England in the event of war with Brittany!'

'And have either of them shown any willingness to do this?'

'Not Francis. But I think Louis could be worked on. He is a devious devil. I believe he would go a long way to capture the boy to make a good deal with me!'

'I wouldn't trust that one further than I could throw him! Forget Louis. Continue to work on Francis. After all, he actually has Henry at his court! But I still think the boy is harmless.'

'On his own, perhaps. But his supporters will push him to assert his possible right to the throne, slender though that may be. If not soon, then some time in the future! I know it!'

'I got quite friendly with him when I visited Raglan Castle as I told you. If he had been a Yorkist, I would even have liked him by my side. I would have invited him to be one of my squires.'

'You mean, you would actually have desired him as a friend?'

'Yes, we got on very well, have similar backgrounds in many ways—and similar tastes. It is a pity he is on the wrong side. It is a friendship which could go nowhere.'

'Well now, more urgent matters have to be dealt with! King James of Scotland is becoming a nuisance again, and his brother, the Duke of Albany, even more so. I wish they would be satisfied with keeping on their own side of the border! Scotland is a big enough country. But no, there are constant raids into our northern lands. I want you there, Richard, as one of proven military ability, to deal with the unending troubles on the Scottish border. Scarcely do we seem to get them settled, when it all breaks out once more!'

'You are sending me north again?'

'Yes, you know and love the north country anyway. I am restoring to you the posts of Constable and Admiral of England, held by Warwick until his death, and also you will be Steward of the Duchy of Lancaster-beyond-Trent. So you now have all the lands of the north to command, which formerly belonged to that traitor, Warwick!'

'I thank you, my lord! You have made me a very happy man! You know I do not really like living in London or being at court much.'

'No, you are a man of the wide open spaces and a lover of your freezing moorland air!' Edward shuddered. 'You are the ideal man for the job! So you shall have the castles of Sheriff Hutton and Middleham, which, I know, is your favourite place to be.'

'It is my heart's home, Sire! I always loved it, from the moment I arrived there to train under the Earl of Warwick in the knightly arts.'

'Well, now it is yours. You will also have authority over the Earl of Northumberland!'

'He will not like that. He has always been used to having his own way!'

'The Percys need taking down a peg or two! They are far too big for their boots, always have been. So now, you are Lord of the North, my dear and most trusty brother. I wish you Godspeed and success in your endeavours!'

Anne, Westminster, Late 1471

So Richard has been given Middleham by the king, my old home. And his, when he was a boy in training there. I know he loves it, as I do, so I have no resentment at him inheriting it. All my inheritance was forfeit anyway, because of my father's disaffection. And my sister Isabel's. George of Clarence has managed to get his hands on a large portion of it. I know he is working to get it all. He is an avaricious, self-seeking man. My mother was immediately stripped of all her estates after father was killed at Barnet. She has nothing now.

She is existing on the goodwill of her friends. Perhaps Isabel and I will end up with nothing too—though I do not think so, somehow. Richard will see that I am looked after anyway. He will persuade the king to be kind to me, I know that. I trust him. He has always cared for me, as I do for him. I wish I could go back to Middleham to live too. With Richard. I hate London and the court. The filthy, polluted air of London makes me cough. I seem to have a cough on and off most of the time now. I long for the clear air of Wensleydale.

I saw Richard again when I came to London for King Edward's triumphal procession to Westminster in May.

I had to take part in the procession, and Richard was just ahead of me. He looked very grand on his great white horse. He always did prefer white horses. It was splendidly caparisoned—like its master. It is a very young stallion, and he loves it dearly. Richard has named it White Surrey.

He turned to smile at me several times. He does not include me in his anger at what my father did. He loved my father once—very much, looked up to him as if he were his father, as he never knew his own. But I suppose he hates the Earl of Warwick's memory now. It is not surprising. Father was always headstrong, wilful, and vaunting in his ambitions He had a power-mania. Mother used to warn him this would lead to his downfall, but he only laughed at her. I know he was wrong to do what he did, but I miss him. I loved him very much too, in spite of all.

I am not well, and it is so stifling in the city. I am afraid, particularly of George of Clarence. I know he plans to use me somehow to achieve his own ends. Perhaps he will even have me secretly killed while Richard is away and cannot protect me. I feel so vulnerable. Edward, the king, treats me with respect and care, but I do not think he realises how utterly ruthless George is. With his charm and his handsome face, he gets away with everything. The king has good reason to distrust him too, after he sided with my father, but he forgave him it all! He must love him a great deal to forgive so readily every time he goes against him. But I know he loves Richard best. Richard has always been his favourite brother. And George resents this—greatly. I think he even hates Richard now. Brothers should not hate each other. But George's nature is ruled by jealousy of Richard's place in the king's heart and by his avariciousness. I try to avoid him, but he is now trying to persuade the king to let him be my protector—while he angles his way to get hold of the rest of my inheritance. My protector?! I would not trust him an inch. He is a wolf in sheep's clothing! An utterly untrustworthy man. The complete opposite to Richard. I would trust him with my life! I wish he were here, all the time. Particularly now.

George says he loves Isabel. She is his wife, so he should. She loves him too, though what she sees in him is anybody's guess. I tried to warn her against him from the start. But she was set on marrying him, even though she probably realised he was marrying her to get his hands on her estates. She would not listen to reason. Even mother could not persuade her. She was completely taken in by his charm and handsomeness.

They even went against the king to get married! He would not allow it, but off they went to Calais and did it anyway—even without waiting for the Pope's dispensation, as they were cousins!

I do not mourn my so-called husband, Edouard. He was murdered after the battle of Tewkesbury. My father engineered that marriage by humbling himself to the she-wolf Queen Marguerite and pretending to side with her to get her support when he tried to overthrow Edward. He needed her armies to help. The only one who ever loved Edouard was his mother. They had twin natures. I hated and despised him. He was loathsome.

My father really hated Queen Marguerite, and she hated him, venomously. The only reason she agreed to help him was to get her poor husband Henry VI reinstated with my father's help. They managed it too—for a short while. And she took out her feelings on me. She was always cold and belittled me constantly. Her son was as vicious as she, and perverted. He liked to watch men beheaded for fun, even when he was a child! I was terrified of him and repulsed by him too. Luckily, he did not touch me—not even in the marriage bed. I think he was other ways inclined. Thank God for that! So I am still intact for the man I hope to marry, the man I love, have always loved—Richard. God bring him back safely from the borders soon!

Westminster Palace, September 1471

'But where is she then, George? You say she is gone from your home, of her own volition? Why would she do that? As her so-called protector, you did not guard her very well!'

'No one knows, Richard, not even Isabel. One morning recently, she was just not there. Isabel was with her the night before and she said not a word about going away. It is a complete mystery! We searched high and low in the house and grounds, but there was no sign of her! And the servants knew nothing when questioned!'

'I do not believe you, George! Edward, Sire, do you not agree with me that George is surely lying? The look in his eyes, which I know so well, says so. He has secreted Anne away to keep her from me! I know it! I wish to marry her. And of course, he does not want that. Then his chances of securing the entire Warwick inheritance is gone forever!'

'My dear Richard, calm yourself! She will be found, 'tis certain! And if George has her hidden somewhere, then he will be made to reveal her whereabouts, you may be sure!'

'I tell you, Sire, I know nothing of where she may be. I swear it! Richard here cannot prove a thing against me!'

'We will see about that, Brother dear. In this, you will never have your way! I love Anne and plan to marry her. I will search ceaselessly until she is found. If you can bribe or threaten your servants and retainers into silence, then I can use stronger threats—to their very lives—to break that silence. They may fear you, but they will fear me more!'

'Now, Richard, I am sure it will not come to that! A search must be instigated at once. I myself will provide the men to help you. I am sure George here will not mind—if he is as guiltless, as he says—if you start with his various properties? If she is at any of those, she will surely be found quickly?'

'It will be a waste of time and your resources, Sire! I tell you, she will not be found on any of my estates!'

'Strangely enough, George, I believe you! You are too devious to hide her in such obvious locations where she could so easily be found. Sire, his own words convince me she is somewhere quite near, but in a place no one would even think to look. Well, I will have every house, tavern, and shop in this great city searched until she is located. And if I find that you were behind it, George, you had better not be anywhere near me when I do!'

Kate, Fotheringhay Castle, Northants, October 1471

The nightmare came again to me last night—Richard arrived, but too late. They got here first.

Baynard's Castle, London

I am sitting here, with some tapestry work, but I do not touch it, have not touched it all evening. I am far too pent-up!

Ruth is in bed and asleep long since, baby John too. I sent the servants to their quarters at 10 p.m. They must be up so early. I can let him in myself.

I am convinced he will come tonight! My recent note has been answered! Richard is back in court and I have written to him several times. At last, he has answered! I know he will come to me soon—probably tonight, as the note came this afternoon!

So I must wait up, though it gets so very late—in the certainty that he will be with me at last!

I cannot understand why he has not come here before this. I heard he arrived back at Westminster in September from the Scots border. What has he been doing?

I am in a fever of expectancy to see him! I cannot go on like this.

I hate this huge, gloomy palace. I want to get away and get John into the country. It is unhealthy here for him, right by the river. The smells that arise from it are not to be borne and the diseases that come with them, I am sure are all around—a vulnerable baby could not resist them. The city is a fetid, disease-ridden place.

If Richard were here all the time, it would not be so bad. I would risk everything to be with him. But of course, he cannot be. But he must move me elsewhere. I will not stay here.

There is a clanging sound. It echoes through the hall, shaking me from my half-sleep—the doorbell! But of course, it must be Richard—at last!

I rush along the hall to the great door. It is very difficult to open, with many bolts and locks. I have never done it before. It is very heavy, but as I unlock the last bolt, it swings open inwards without me having to pull it—It is Richard, as anxious to see me as I am him!

'My love . . .' but my words freeze on my lips, my heart seems to stop as I stare at those sardonic, leering faces. I hastily try to push the door closed again, but it is just too heavy for me. And there are two of them. Their strength and determination to get in soon outwits me.

I am running down the great hall in a terrified rush, but they are easily overtaking me. They are laughing—with the thrill of the chase, no doubt.

I stand panting, like a hare at bay—they are too strong for me, too determined!

I know what they intend to do—and it is like looking on the necessity of instant death.

'We intercepted one of your notes, my dear! And answered it!' Lord Dorset says. He is red-faced, panting, but looks like a hunter mad with blood-lust—'Very convenient! We have been searching for you for a long time! Ever since he took you away from that whore's den in Southwark! You should be flattered! I never forget a pretty face—especially one I want to bed! We knew Richard had you hidden away somewhere! But he's too busy now looking for another lady-love to come at your request! But we are eager enough!' He laughs loudly again. They both do.

'Looking for whom?' I cry out, grasping the back of a chair to steady me.

Their gaze is predatory—like two serpents about to strike.

'Why, the Lady Anne Warwick, of course, his intended bride! George of Clarence has hidden her away somewhere for his own ends, but Richard will find her eventually! He is searching the whole of London! She was not at any of Clarence's estates, but then, he is too cunning to hide her there, but Richard had to be sure, I suppose!

No time for you, my dear! It may take him months! And he is most determined! As are we! We are here, my dear, far more attentive than your supposed lover! Face it, he has forgotten you now! The thought of Anne's vast estates, which he will get his hands on when he marries her, has quite eradicated you from his mind!'

'Never! Richard loves me. We have a child together!' I blurt out.

'So what? I have dozens of bastards—many I have never even heard of, I suspect! And Lord Grey here too, I expect. We've long forgotten their mothers too! Nice at the time—but then, there are plenty more fish in the sea, as they say!' They both snigger, sickeningly.

'But we are wasting time! This time, you will not outwit us, pretty one! You may as well accept it! You will probably enjoy our attentions—most women do!'

Then, with more laughter, they come at me, approaching from two different sides. My physical horror is echoed by the horror and hurt in my heart and mind—Richard is not here to save me this time from these vicious would-be rapists—and worse—Richard loves another.

Richard, Westminster Palace, November 1471

'Dorset, you vicious degenerate! Sire, this creature—whom you call friend, and Lord Grey, his equally depraved brother, have committed a most terrible act upon the innocent woman whom I love—who bore me my beloved son, John! What are you going to do about it? Neither of them are fit to be your closest friends, the queen's sons or not! I have felt this for years. Now this act of pure evil has prompted me to speak my mind at last! They have always been a bad influence on you!'

'Dickon, my dear young brother, what is this girl to you anyway, really? You are to marry the Lady Anne at Eastertide, the one you have truly loved for years, I know. And she is the greatest heiress in the land! Why should you care so much about a passing mistress who bore you a bastard? Bastards are two a penny! Like Lord Hastings here and Lord Dorset and his brother, I am sure I have dozens I do not even know the existence of! And you have looked after this Kate, have you not? Even taken her to our dear mother's safe-keeping at Fotheringhay Castle, as she is ill? What more can you do?'

'It is you, Edward, as king, I wish to do something! To punish this rapist here and his vile brother! How can you take it so lightly, Sire? She loves me and trusts me. I could not be there when she needed me, as I was searching for Anne, whom our dear brother George had abducted! I was not there when Kate needed me, and these—things—took advantage and deliberately intercepted her message to me and tricked her into thinking it was I who was coming to see her that night at Baynard's Castle! And all the time, they were planning to get in and rape her! They tried before, you know. That is why I took her there to what I imagined was a safe place! I had not reckoned with the deadly and ruthless determination of your "friends" to get their own way with her! They should be severely punished. They do exactly what they like, presuming on your friendship to back them up and get away with everything!'

'What would you have me do, Dickon? Behead them? For something which is happening dozens of times every day in all walks of life?'

'Edward, you have known many women—have you actually ever raped one? I don't think you have, in spite of your excesses, which are well-known. You have the decency to draw the line somewhere, at least. But these—these dissolutes—who dare to call themselves friends of the king, have done it many times in their lives! And you seem to regard it as an act of no importance whatever!'

'In the scheme of things, Dickon, it is not! And I admit, I have never needed to rape any woman—they always come to me more than willingly, thank goodness! And I do prefer to have a compliant mate! My advice to you, dear little brother, is to forget it! And think instead of the woman you are to wed soon! She is the important one! You have done what you can for this Kate of yours, as I said before. Now leave her to our good mother's care! Make provision for the boy, if you feel the need to, but then let it go—the whole affair! This is the best advice I can give you!'

'I cannot believe that you dismiss it out of hand without a second thought! I have loved you well, Edward, as my brother and as my king, but I feel I do not know you any more—that I have never really known you properly! It was bad enough you also did nothing to George for having poor Anne abducted and subjected to two months of hell in that dreadful kitchen! I also remember, as a boy, being so shocked that you would not punish Hastings here when he raped that twelve-year-old girl, who came to court heavily pregnant with her distraught father to demand justice! What did you do? You gave the old man gold, I remember, and called it justice!

Now there is no morality left in this great kingdom of ours, let alone justice! I will not forget this and if you, as the king, will do nothing to punish them, then, one day, I promise you, on my most sacred honour, that I will find a way to see they get what they deserve! They will not escape my wrath, either of them!'

Anne, St Martin-Le-Grande Sanctuary, London, Late 1471

At last I am safe! Safe from George of Clarence in particular! Richard searched a long time, but he found me in the end and rescued me from that dreadful place! I knew George wished me ill, especially on that awful morning when two of his henchmen dragged me from my room at dawn and bundled me into a closed litter, one with a hand tight over my mouth so that I could not scream for help! I was terrified. They answered not a word, however hard I pleaded during the journey, but one just put a gag in my mouth to silence me and continued, plodding on deep into the stinking back streets of the city.

Before I knew it, I was taken from the litter and propelled down several flights of steep stairs to what I can only describe as a hell-hole! So confused and distraught was I by that time that it could have been hell, for all I knew.

The roaring fires, the stink of roasting carcasses, and the almost unbreathable hot air filled with fumes and spitting hot fat, the raucous shouts and laughs emitting from the place, which I soon saw was a large and busy basement kitchen, made it very like what I imagined hell to be.

They deposited me and left at once, again without a word.

There, for two whole months, I was made to work hard, like any common skivvy, ignored or laughed at when I protested, as I frequently did—at the beginning—that my being there was all some terrible mistake! I was even threatened with a whipping by the head cook if I did not do as I was told and give up whining! I could not believe that this had really happened to me so unexpectedly and irrevocably. But I knew George of Clarence was behind it somewhere, when I overheard the landlord of the cook-house tell one of the pastry cooks that he had once worked for Clarence and that this business he now ran was a perk given to him for 'services rendered' to his master in the past!

But it is all over now—thanks be to God! And Richard has placed me here in sanctuary, where I am safe until we are married.

Yes, we are to be wed in the spring, at Eastertide! My heart's desire has come true! King Edward has given his consent, and scheming George cannot touch me again, ever.

Richard vows he will find some way to punish George severely for his actions—he will not get away with what he did to me! He arrested the landlord and his wife and threw them into prison without trial. That is unlike Richard, but he was so very angry. But they were probably forced or bribed by George to do what they did. The landlord's wife did treat me as well as she could, in the circumstances, I suppose. I tried to get Richard to let her off, but he would not listen.

The two henchmen who abducted me were also gaoled at once.

Isabel comes to visit me here. She is shocked by what George did to me, but not surprised. She is starting to realise how ruthless her charming husband can be when faced by anyone who thwarts his desires!

Richard has had to go away again for a short while. Some more trouble in the north, I suppose. He did not say why he had to go. But he has promised to be home for Christmas for sure, when he will take me to the court at Westminster for the great holy feast.

After New Year's Day, preparations will start for our wedding at Easter. I cannot believe how my fortunes have changed in such a short time, from hopelessness to joy! Richard is a truly good man, and I am a lucky woman to have him. I have known him all my life and trust him entirely. He will be a devoted husband, I know that. I love him deeply and I am completely certain that he loves me—has always loved me—as I have him!

Henry Tudor, Brittany, Late 1471

I feel confused and unhappy, in spite of being given every comfort here by Duke Francis at his court in Brittany. Uncle Jasper and I are treated like honoured guests, and we have many friends and supporters with us, Lancastrian exiles who fled from the Yorkist rule, especially after Tewkesbury.

I am kept constantly entertained with hunting, hawking, tournaments, feasts, and pretty girls of the court who flock around me, and I am given plenty of money to spend as I wish. But I miss Maude. We would have been contracted to marry soon. Lord Herbert wanted it. Maude wanted it and I wanted it. There was an understanding between us. I miss the whole Herbert family—and I miss my homeland, Wales. This place seems alien to me. It is very beautiful, especially the wonderful coastline. But I keep thinking of Pembrokeshire—not too far away across the Channel—and Gwent, where my beloved horse Owen must be missing me as much as I miss him.

I wish I were not so important a pawn to the Lancastrians, for that is all I am. They are keeping me safe here to checkmate the House of York 'whenever the opportunity presents itself', according to my Lady mother. Whenever that may be! I just had another letter from her recently going on about the same thing, always harping on my possible wonderful future! But I am more concerned with now. Meanwhile, I am forced to live in exile from all I love and know. I admit, I am homesick, very homesick.

The regular letters from my mother do not help at all. She is so obsessed with my future she does not realise how I hate my present life. I have been shunted around from pillar to post most of my short life, and just when I felt settled—at Raglan—Henry VI is briefly restored to power, and I am taken to London to see him by Uncle Jasper and my mother. His strange prophecy I did not believe at all. After all, everybody knew he was mad, anyway. His words could be given no credence. And then, when Edward was restored, stronger than ever, and poor Henry VI was murdered in the Tower that same night, Edward rode in triumph into London to claim his throne. Every other noble of any importance had been killed at Tewkesbury and, I was bundled off here in haste by Uncle Jasper. To be honest, we set out for France, actually, but got blown off course in a terrible storm and landed in Brittany instead, lucky to be alive! It would not have mattered which ruler welcomed me—they only do it because I may be useful to them anyway as a bargaining tool! King Louis would probably have treated me as well as Duke Francis does, for his own ends. I am old enough to realise that. King Edward wants me back, my mother wants me back too, I know, but advises I remain here for the present. I am very wary, and so is Uncle Jasper. Circumstances have made us so. Who knows? Edward may have me killed if I return. He is not to be trusted, not one whit. He has even promised my mother to give me lands and estates—but it is just an empty promise to get me back into his clutches. And anyway, the Duke of Clarence still owns my real inheritance—the Earldom of Richmond and all the estates that go with it and will not give it up. He is a greedy, avaricious, and untrustworthy man. Even the king cannot trust him—his own brother! Especially since he allied with the Earl of Warwick against Edward earlier on—though he is reconciled with the king now. Edward always forgives him everything! The king will not make him give up my lands, however much my mother begs on my behalf. She has been doing it for years. King Henry promised to let me have them back, at his brief readeption—but of course, nothing came of it, as he did not last long!

Before, I was not really very important. Now it seems I am. But all I want is to go to Raglan and see Maude and Owen. I want what I know and love. Isn't that a natural thing to desire? I am sure it might be very grand to be king one day, and Uncle Jasper keeps telling me about the absolute power it brings and the wonderful palaces, jewels, and clothes. But I am not ambitious like him and my Lady mother. They assure me that I will become so when I am old enough to realise what it would all mean. Meanwhile, I suppose I have to make the best of things as they are. What else can I do?

Fotheringhay Castle, Northamptonshire, Late December 1471

My Dear Richard,

Your mother extends her greetings for the Holy Feast of Christmas to you, also her congratulations on your forthcoming marriage to the Lady Anne Neville. You have chosen well to marry her, especially as her great estates will fall into your keeping! And of course, I know you have always loved her, since you were brought up together at Middleham Castle.

I like the girl, but she does not look very strong to me, and you do need a wife to bear you lusty sons in your position!

I fear I now have unsettling news for you about Kate, whom you left in my care. The boy John flourishes and grows apace, but I feel his mother is far from well. After her terrible ordeal which you told me of, at the hands of that appalling Dorset and his brother—God rot those two vicious dissolutes!—it is not surprising, I suppose. However, she should have shown some recovery by now, but does not. Physically and emotionally, she is at a very low ebb. She insists it is not because of your betrothal to Anne, though that would be cause enough to give her great sadness, as she loves you well. That is obvious. She says she realises it had to happen sooner or later—that you could never marry her. It is something more. She cannot eat and does not even try. She is often sick. She says nothing of it, but I know. I fear indeed that she may be pregnant from that terrible double rape. She talks of going home all the time and that she would find the help she needs there. She is very thankful to me for my care of her but obviously wants her own mother. She is even willing to dare the terrible anger of her father when she goes home with John, your son. And I feel I must let her go, for her own peace of mind, if nothing else. If she is pregnant, then her own mother is the right one to care for her. I am sure you agree. I love the child, John. He makes me feel young again. But he too should be near his maternal grandmother, if Kate goes.

Try to come and visit the poor girl—indeed, visit us both, as soon as you can after Christmas here, if she remains, or go to Appleby Hall, her home, to see her and come to me either before or after. Fotheringhay is not far away from her home, thank goodness, so you can easily do it.

She is determined to go to Appleby Hall for Christmas. I shall provide her with an escort to protect her on the journey.

I agree with you that morality no longer exists in this poor benighted country of ours and deplore Edward's lack of it, as you know, and especially now his unwillingness to punish these depraved friends of his, who have led him astray all his life—along with Hastings, that other degenerate—for this despicable deed. I think Edward may have sunk so low into depravity under Hastings's influence that he no longer has a conscience! A good king should have a conscience!

I feel so sorry for Kate. She did not deserve this treatment from the hands of such vile men.

May God bless you and keep you safe, my dear and most upright son! You are the best of my sons!

How I neglected you as a child! I pray to God every day for forgiveness for that, along with my many other sins. You have grown into a man to respect and admire. Pray God you will one day be in the position to put your deeply held ideals of justice and morality into practice for the good of our country! Edward, sadly, is on the downward slope. George also. I pray for them both daily too, that the good God will turn their hearts away from immorality! Your time will come, Richard, as I have assured you many times before. And the sooner, the better!

Your loving mother,
Cecily, Dowager Countess of York

Kate, Appleby Manor, Northamptonshire, January 1472

I was so very happy when I was here last. In this bed, my bed, I knew the most blissful time in my life. With Richard. Here, I discovered real love and pledged myself to my dear one for life and he to me. Now that I am sick unto death in the same bed, I can hardly bear to remember. Any of it. It is all finished for me now—I know it.

I did not tell my parents about that terrible rape at first, though I realised I was pregnant from it, against my will. I just had to get here and rest, though I knew what I intended to do. It was enough to put up with my father's rage over John, which I had anticipated, but he has calmed down now and is charmed by the boy, as most people are. But he still swears he will make Richard pay if he ever gets the chance. Now that I am ill, he is so worried about my condition that he forgets his initial anger.

I knew there was an old woman on the outskirts of Appleby Village skilled at helping girls in my condition. And she did. I try not to dwell on the horrors of that morning—it was something I would never willingly experience again. But it was afterwards the real trouble began for me. A few hours later, I began to haemorrhage badly. I had been warned that this could happen, so I just took to my bed and rested, hoping it would gradually stop and told my mother that my stomach was upset. But the heavy blood loss persisted. Now, two weeks later, I still bleed constantly. I had to tell my mother the truth in the end about the rape and the abortion, as I needed her help so badly. But she could do little, nor the village doctor, though they both tried every remedy they knew, to no avail. They think I have been damaged internally. I daily grow weaker, as the life blood ebbs from me. I cannot rise from my bed. Indeed, I can barely lift a hand to drink or eat, not that I want to. Ruth does her best too, trying to get me to take nourishing beef broths and cordials. They all minister to me constantly, even my father, but I just want to be left alone—to sleep. It is the only escape.

If I die, which I am likely to do—and soon, I feel—so what? My life is over without Richard anyway. He loves another and is to marry her—a great lady—just as I knew would happen. I pretended that I did not care about it—but the hurt was terrible inside—more so than the damage to me caused by the rape and that terrible abortion.

My love will never come to me again—even if he wants to—he will not be able to. So what does it matter what becomes of me now? Mother will care for John. She has promised to do this with Ruth's help—and Richard's support. If the worst comes to the worst—if he keeps his promise and sees that the child is provided for—the boy will lack for nothing—except his mother. I do not have the strength to strive for my life any more, though I know I should go on trying to recover—for little John's sake, but I am just too tired, too tired to think, to do anything any more, to care any more. I just want to sleep.

Richard, Appleby Hall, Northamptonshire, January 1472

'You say that she is probably dying? Never! Now that I am here, she will rally, I am sure of it. Has she told you what happened to her? The wickedness of these men is beyond belief, and they think nothing of it, have probably forgotten her by now. The chase and getting their own way was all that was important to them. I pleaded with the king to punish them, but you can imagine he took little notice of me in this matter—to his shame. And the Marquess of Dorset and his brother—both depraved libertines—are the queen's sons, of course, so she protects them. But I will find a way to make them pay, somehow, if not at once, then certainly in the future—make no mistake about that!

Now please, take me to see my poor Kate. I would cheer her, if I can.'

'You may cheer her by your presence, my lord, for which she has longed, but you cannot cure her—nobody can. It is in God's hands now and probably only a matter of time before . . .' sobs Lady Appleby.

'Come, come, my dear. Have faith. She has youth on her side, after all. If her spirit could be awakened again and her wish to live, then perhaps our constant prayers will be answered. My lord, I was so angry with you at first, but I see now that you loved each other truly. She still loves you, but how can you give her the determination to live, even if you still love her? She knows you are to wed soon to a great lady and she has just given up.'

'Sir Mortimer, I will never desert her, even if I am married to another. She always knew it would be impossible for me to wed her, ever, and accepted that, long before this terrible trouble afflicted her. Let us go up to her, now—I would try to comfort her.'

'Kate, my dear one, it is I. I have come to you, as I said I would. Now you will get well, you must get well! Think of the boy. He needs you so much, his own mother—as I do. Do you hear me? I will never desert you. Or John.'

'It is no good, my lord. She is quite unconscious, I think, and knows nothing of what is happening any more or who is with her. You are too late. The last thing she said to me this morning was that she just wanted to sleep now—to die peacefully. She begged me to take charge of her son and be his nurse until he is grown. And I promised her that I would,' Ruth says, between barely stifled sobs.

'You are a good woman, Ruth, and have stood by her through everything. But surely this cannot be the end? There must be something more that we can do? She still breathes and her pulse can be felt clearly, though it is thready. I will get the best doctors up from London to her. Even the king's own doctor, Hobbes.'

'I fear it will be to no avail, my lord. She has lost too much blood and has gone beyond all human help. Her body has no more strength left to recover, even if she had the will to, which I doubt now.'

'I will not give up. I will not! I cannot accept that one so young and blameless of sin should be cut off like this remorselessly. Her whole life is ahead of her!'

'When there is nothing more to be done that might help, one can only accept God's will. I helped bring Kate into the world and she has been my dear charge always. But I accept now that she is in God's hands—only he can save her—and I do not think that will happen, sadly.'

Richard, Fotheringhay Castle, Northamptonshire, February 1472

'You must not blame yourself, my son. It was not of your doing and not your fault in any way. You did all you could for Kate. Even the king's own doctor you called, who rode post-haste from London, could do nothing. She had gone beyond all help.'

'She lingered on for another week in that state, just fading away. It is not to be borne! If I could have given her my own blood in some way, I would! A precious young life lost all because of those devils!'

'What they did to her was very terrible, but they did not make her have the abortion which killed her, Richard. She chose that way herself. Many girls in her situation do. They would rather risk death than bear the shame of giving birth to rapists' spawn!'

'You are right, I know, Mother, but it breaks my heart, the terrible unfairness of it all!'

'Life is utterly unfair, my son. Surely you have learnt that by now? And it is completely arbitrary. Death comes too early for many innocent souls. Did you not lose friends on the battlefield who were younger than you?'

'Yes, but I did not love them in the way I loved Kate.'

'Human beings just do not get their desserts—even the good ones. The innocent suffer and the wicked seem to thrive, frequently! It is one of life's mysteries, why God allows such things to happen. But we have to accept his will or his non-intervention, I think.

Now you must try to forget and look to your future and your coming marriage! Eastertide will be a time of joy for you! It should banish these sad happenings from your mind! You will be married to a woman you have always loved dearly. And you will have your whole life together to look forward to! And, of course, you have Kate's boy. She will live in him for you always!'

'That is true—I have John. But I loved Kate dearly too, Mother. It was a most passionate and wonderful love we shared! I shall never forget her—how could I?'

'What will you do with the boy and his nurse, Ruth, isn't it? Where will he be brought up? I know you promised Kate he would later be given a title and estates. But what about now? He is but two years old!'

'I will take him to Middleham, where we are to live, Anne and I. He belongs near me. I must oversee his care and development, later his education and training.'

'But what will Anne think of that? You will have to tell her who he is.'

'Yes, I know that. But she will understand, I am sure. She will realise that I knew other women before I decided to marry her.'

'But another woman's child? A bastard? Will she accept him, do you think, in her home? And what about when she gets children of her own?'

'She is a kind and good-hearted woman and loves children. I do not see there will be any real problem. And if she does object, then I will have to persuade her that it is the right thing to do. She must accept him. The boy stays near me from now on.'

The Duchess Cecily, Fotheringhay Castle, 1472

My Dear Richard,

I was so very sorry to hear about the fate of poor Kate. But it was a foolish thing she did, having that village abortion. They very often go wrong and the girls die. Now I realise what she was referring to when she told me she wanted to go home 'to get the help she needed'. I thought she was referring to her mother's care when her time came. If she had told me what was in her mind, I know of doctors skilled in that kind of thing—not that I have ever used one—whose hands she would have been safe in, I am sure. Still, she was probably too ashamed to admit to me that she wished such a thing—after all, it is a mortal sin, according to the Church's teachings. But desperate people do desperate things. If the baby had been conceived by someone she cared for, the outcome would probably have been very different.

But now you have a very happy time ahead! Your wedding at Eastertime on 22 April!

It is a pity that it is in London, as I will be unable to attend it, owing to my present poor health and the journey is too long for me now, even in good spring weather, I am afraid. But my thoughts and prayers will be with you, you know that.

You must bring your new bride to see me as soon as you can after the wedding. I would like to get to know her. And the little boy John. I miss him a lot. It is good to have young ones round the place! I hope he is happy at Pontefract with his nurse to care for him. You tell me Anne has agreed to have him with you at Middleham when you go there to live after the wedding. As you said, she is very good to accept another woman's child, particularly as she knows you loved Kate dearly too.

I was very angry to hear how implacable George has been about the Neville lands. I agree that he is of an avaricious and difficult nature. It is a pity, but he has always relied on his charm to get him through everything! But he must not be allowed to get his way in this matter. You and Anne deserve your share—it is her inheritance after all. I pity her poor mother, the Countess of Warwick. It is surely unfair that she has been stripped of all her inheritance because her husband was attainted! I can understand she cannot be very happy having to live in sanctuary at Beaulieu Abbey with no one but ascetic monks to converse with, especially after being used to living a life of luxury. But I can see why Edward sent her there, even if none of what her husband did was her fault. He had to be seen to make an example, to deter others from turning traitor!

Well, I will write again soon, and meanwhile, may God go with you, my dear son.

Your loving mother,
Cecily, Duchess of York

Anne, Middleham Castle, Yorkshire, Summer, 1472

At last I can breathe fresh air again! My chest feels better for it already, and my annoying cough has lessened since arriving here. Thank God I am away from that fetid heat in London and that dreadful, perpetual stink from the Thames! Plague is rife there too, as it usually is in summer. I am more than glad to leave London and the court behind, even though I had only been there a short time since our wedding at Easter. I am worried for Richard, who has to stay there for the moment, being caught up against his will in this eternal wrangling with his greedy brother, George of Clarence, for the Neville inheritance. It is really my mother's—at least until her death—when Isabel and I should inherit jointly, but my mother was stripped of all her estates when my father was attainted as a traitor, and then George appropriated everything. She still resides quietly at Beaulieu Abbey, dependent on charity.

George will not release even part of what he holds without a terrible struggle, I know, if at all. He argues interminably on so-called points of law in his defence in the king's court. Richard is hard put to it to fight his side of it in my defence. George holds on tooth and nail! Richard is only trying to get from him my rightful portion of the huge inheritance—half of what my father owned.

The King is sick of George and his never-ending importuning—he seems to present a new reason to back up his claim for rightful ownership every day, it seems! He can afford to pay the top lawyers in the country to fight on his side too! We are all sick of it equally—except George, of course! I feel Edward will say, 'Enough is enough!' any moment now and make an arbitrary decision, just to end it! The lawyers are becoming richer while this goes on, and the king objects to that. It pays them to keep it all continuing—so they do not mind. Whether George is satisfied has become irrelevant any more to the king—he just wants it to stop! So does Richard, so he can come home to me at Middleham. Far too much precious time has been wasted on this matter.

George really has the most avaricious, unpleasant nature, yet on the surface, he is so utterly charming and can get away with anything. And he hates Richard now, mainly out of jealousy, I think, as he has always been Edward's favourite brother. So he carries on this litigation, not only for what he can get out of it, but for the sake of it—to get one better over Richard, if he can. What George wants, George gets—has always got! But not this time, if Richard has anything to do with it. He has an infinitely better mind than George and will match every point of law he may present!

It is not as if George needs any more riches or lands—he has enormous possessions already—far more than Richard. The king has always been far too generous to him.

I pray it all ends soon and Richard can come home to me. I miss him so, and I have some exciting and joyous news to impart to him!

I was only certain of it a short while ago, so have told no one yet, not even my ladies. I want Richard to be the first to hear that he is to be a father next spring!

I have longed for the moment when I can make him happy with this news. Like most men, he desires a son most dearly as his first-born, to be his heir, and I pray to God every day now, most earnestly, that the child will be a boy.

I already try to be a mother, as well as I can, to this poor little child, John, brought to me by a very distressed Richard from Pontefract Castle, where he had been lodging with his good nurse, Ruth, since his mother died in such tragic circumstances. I felt nothing but sorrow at Kate's sad tale, when Richard recounted it to me and understood entirely why Richard wanted him to live with us, now that we at last have a real home of our own here at Middleham. I always realised that there must have been other women for Richard before he decided he wanted to marry me. That was inevitable. A man has his needs. And the child is an innocent victim of terrible circumstances. Richard has nicknamed him John of Pomfret and loves him dearly. I am growing to love him also. He is a beautiful, healthy child and seems to have taken to me too!

I am glad I am away from the court, so full of degeneracy and excess, where that vicious Hastings dominates the king so completely, as do the queen's equally degenerate sons, who brought about poor Kate's downfall.

Women suffer so for the casual wickedness of men such as these—it has always been so. It is a sad fact of life.

Henry Tudor, Hammes Castle, Brittany, Late Autumn, 1472

My Uncle Jasper has always been my mainstay and supporter, and he still is. Without him, I would, no doubt, long since have been dead. Since I was a small boy, he has made sure of my safety, whether near or far.

We have stayed together at Duke Francis's Court in Brittany and now in Hammes Castle, but things have changed. Imperceptibly at first, but now, quite inexplicably, the duke has separated us. No explanation has been given to me. But I suspect it is as a direct result of King Edward's constant demands to have me returned to England.

Perhaps Duke Francis thinks that without Uncle Jasper, I am in safer custody here? For in custody, I certainly am. I realised that long since. Without my uncle, I cannot escape and the duke has a better hold on each of us. Also, my own servants and bodyguards have been taken away and replaced by surly Breton men who hardly speak a word of English. It is almost impossible to communicate with them, and if I try to question them, they just turn away.

It is an unpleasant and worrying development. I no longer feel at all secure here. In fact, I feel very disturbed—even afraid. And very lonely. Perhaps Francis intends to send me back to Edward very soon?

Perhaps he has been persuaded at last—with bribes which he could not ignore? I try to think what the king could have offered him for letting me go now? Up to now, he has resisted all attempts—and I know there have been many—to give me up to the English king. Uncle Jasper has always kept me up to date on Edward's efforts. Maybe they have made a pact of some kind? Who knows? No one tells me anything. I can only guess at what is going on.

I am still allowed to go out hunting sometimes and to exercise in the gardens or to ride—but never without these unpleasant Bretons. I have the freedom of the castle, but there are guards on all the doors, so I cannot leave alone. I have asked to see Duke Francis, but to no avail. The duke used to visit me regularly until recently, when Uncle Jasper was here. But not any more. I do not even know where they have taken my uncle.

Daily, I grow more afraid. For—in effect—I am a prisoner—I do not even get the regular letters from my Lady mother any more. I could rely on those, whatever else happened. In fact, I began to grow tired of them, with their constant exhortations to look to my so-called wonderful future and put up with the present with that in mind! Now, I would give anything to get one. They are obviously keeping them from me. Nor have I heard from Uncle Jasper. Everything has come to a standstill.

I cannot sleep, worrying what the morrow will bring. Any day, I expect to be taken in custody by force to the coast and there put on a ship to England.

Margaret Beaufort, Woking Old Hall, Christmas, 1472

My Dear Henry,

At last, Duke Francis has relented and allowed us to communicate once more. I complained bitterly to him about his ban on us sending letters to each other! When I received no answers from you from several of my previous regular letters, I realised something was wrong and wrote to him most forcefully on the matter—particularly objecting to what is your virtual imprisonment. I am glad he kept them and let you have them at last. Your Uncle Jasper told me how he had been separated from you and that your own men and servants were also taken away and replaced by Bretons. You must have felt very isolated indeed. I think the duke wishes to ensure that you cannot escape, as you are such a valuable bargaining tool to him. I know that King Edward continues to pester him to have you released and sent back to England. I am not so sure that is such a good thing now. I do not trust his motives at all. Perhaps you are better where you are for the moment, though I know you long to be free. At least you are safe from Edward's possible underhand plans. If you were sent back to England, I would not be at all surprised if he had you killed. He realises that you could be a definite threat to him!

Uncle Jasper continues to work on your behalf. There are many of your supporters in Brittany now too, far more than Edward likes. But he can do nothing about it, thank goodness! I still feel there will come a time in the not so distant future, when you will come into your own, with their help, even if things look far from hopeful at present. I have faith that things will work out for you in the end. You are the rightful heir to the English throne! God in his mercy will surely punish the usurper in some way! 'He works in mysterious ways his wonders to perform!' as the saying goes.

Your fortunes seem bleak now, but when one is down, the only way out is by going up!

Duke Francis tells me he has let you join his court for the Christmas feast and New Year revels. That should cheer you up somewhat. At least you will have some company, and some fun! As he seems to be relenting in his attitude to you, who knows but the new year may see you released and reunited with Uncle Jasper and your friends. I hope so. I pray that 1473 will be a year in which we of the Lancastrian persuasion can begin to hope again!

God's blessings upon you, my beloved son. I pray for your welfare and happiness daily.

Margaret Beaufort,
Countess of Richmond

Westminster Palace, Early Spring 1474

'Duke Francis has become more obdurate than ever about releasing Henry Tudor to me! I will have that boy! He is the last sprig of Henry VI's Lancastrians. Francis tells me he has him safely where he can do no damage, has even separated him from his resourceful Uncle Jasper. He is guarded now by Francis's own men. No plotting against me can possibly go on, he says, but he will not let him go, whatever I say, whatever bribes I offer. He knows the boy's worth as a bargaining tool! Hastings, my good friend, what should I do?'

'My lord, there is very little more you can do, at present! Stop worrying about Henry Tudor! Duke Francis will do as he says and keep him well guarded so that he is harmless—even with all those adherents nearby! As you say, the boy is too precious to him!

'Francis really may need your help soon against Louis in his fight for Brittany's independence—and you are the one he will call upon for that help!'

'Then why doesn't he give in to my demands?'

'He is treading a very fine line, I agree, Sire, in keeping his hands on the boy and trying not to offend you too much.'

'I wish Richard were here! He would know what to do. But he is so busy now establishing himself as Lord of the North. I did send him there to do just that, so I can hardly recall him so soon!'

'If things reach crisis point, Sire, and the Lancastrians do use the boy Tudor as a figurehead for yet another uprising, then Richard will come quickly enough. His wife is soon to give birth, I believe, so he will not leave Middleham unless forced to when her time comes.'

'He will have to if I order him to! She has plenty of women to attend her, I am sure. And he has prevailed upon me to let her mother leave sanctuary at Bealieu Abbey to attend her also. Men are not wanted at birthings, anyway. Their job is done in the first stages of conception only.'

'True, Sire, but Anne Neville is apparently ailing—she was never strong. He would want to be there to support her if there are any problems at the birth. Her delivery is expected sometime at the beginning of June, it is rumoured.'

'Well, we will see how things go. Meanwhile, George is up to his tricks again! That man is never satisfied with his lot. He is still stating flatly that he will give up no part of the Neville estates granted to him without a fight! What am I to do with him? I have given him far too much leeway in the past, I am afraid. Now he thinks he can twist me round his little finger.'

'True, Sire, you must take him in hand, for your own peace of mind! He is a constant worry to you.'

'Like a buzzing wasp that, however many times one tries to swat it, keeps coming back to bother one! And yet I cannot help loving him, in spite of his many faults!'

'He is your brother, Sire. One should love one's close family, whatever they do.'

'Yes, I suppose so. Yet I know I am too soft with him—always have been! I must make a final decision about how he and Richard share Warwick's enormous holdings. By the general law of inheritance, the mother, Ann of

Warwick, should have inherited everything when the earl was killed, but I am not having that, as the rogue was attainted for being a traitor! As things stand, she is being regarded as if she were dead—in the circumstances—and will get nothing. She did support her husband. She ought to be grateful for escaping any worse punishment!'

'It is known that she is not grateful for her lot. She apparently rails constantly at what she regards as her incarceration with the kind monks at Beaulieu. Yet she has comfortable quarters there and free board and lodging. What more can she expect?'

'Richard has put in a token plea to me to release her, probably at the instigation of his wife. But I think he agrees she is better out of the way at Beaulieu, where she can cause no trouble. Once Anne Neville has produced an heir, she will go back there. I will make sure of that!'

Richard. Middleham Castle, Yorks. Late Summer, 1474

Thank God it is all settled at last—this wretched land struggle with George! Edward thinks I came out of it badly and is surprised I accepted his decisions without any more demur! But I had had enough of it all—everyone had—except George of course! The king most particularly, I think!

Edward ruled that I had to give up all those lands to George which I had acquired through Earl Warwick's death—namely the Beauchamp estates and the whole of the Countess of Warwick's estates, including Warwick Castle and the Earldom of Warwick. George was not satisfied until he had also received the Earldom of Salisbury, even Earl Warwick's great house in London, the Herber—which he had appropriated long ago and has been living in as his own ever since! He did not want much, only everything it seems! He even persuaded Edward to ask me to relinquish my post of Great Chamberlain to him. The king thought I would never agree to these outrageous requests!

But when it came to the choice—be barred from marriage to my Anne or lose the estates—there was no choice really. I have lost one woman I loved, and still mourn. There was no way I would also lose the other dear one who had agreed to be my wife. We love each other, I realise now how much, and in the end, it was a right easy decision! I did not care about the lands if it meant getting George off my back! I have enough and I have retained my beloved Middleham, also Sheriff Hutton, Pontefract, and Penrith. I would probably never have visited any of the other lands much if I had kept them. I have never even felt any desire to visit my Gloucester holdings, which I inherited from my father, so why would I care about these new ones? George is far more acquisitive than I am, always has been. I care more about people than lands.

And the people of the north are my concern now. In the end, I think the king threatened George that he would take all his lands away if he did not capitulate and agree to my marriage to Anne. Edward did not say as much, but I believe that is what must have happened, as George suddenly caved in after months and months of resistance and demands. The thought of losing everything he had gained on Warwick's death would have been too much for him!

Now I must do something about Anne's mother! She is becoming a real burden, as a guest who shows no signs of wishing to leave. She has to be got rid of somehow! Apart from the fact that she constantly bewails her lost lands and the king's cruelty at stripping her of everything, her extended stay at Middleham has gone on far too long. I will find her a small estate I do not particularly want, somewhere far away so that she cannot bother us with frequent visits. I know Anne feels the same—her mother's presence somewhat overwhelms her and she would rather have her gone now. She has been here since June. Anne and her mother do get on better now, though, and Anne has told her she forgives her for not intervening when her father bundled her off at only fourteen to a strange court in a strange land—France—to marry the obnoxious Edouard, only son of the equally obnoxious Margaret d'Anjou, Henry VI's wife in exile!

The countess flatly refuses to return to Beaulieu Abbey. She is angry that she was ever put there by the king but particularly that Edward did not release her from the abbey in time to get here for the birth—which was early anyway, as Anne produced the child prematurely. Anne had called for her and did need her—then.

She was so frightened of the actual birth after what happened to Isabel on board ship in the Channel, and I was far away. But she does not really need her mother any more. The countess is such a difficult and overbearing woman. I cannot stand her, I must admit!

I have two possible small estates I think she may like in Suffolk: Braxhall or Burwash. She can choose which one she prefers, then I will send her there with an escort as soon as possible. She will also get an allowance which will allow her to live comfortably. I think an estate in Suffolk will do very well.

Now all the King talks of is his proposed war with France next year. He has wanted to take armies there for months to try and win back the lands lost last century which he—and a lot of others in high places—feel still belong to England. I am ambivalent on the subject. I believe there are better things to do here. And Edward has not got adequate funds yet to equip and pay an army sizeable enough. He is trying various ways to squeeze more money out of those who can afford it. He did promise not to bring back benevolences, though I fear what he is doing to get money for his plans is the same in all but name. For instance, he butters up rich nobles; city merchants, and their wives. One wife offered him a small amount, but then, when he caught hold of her and kissed her lingeringly on the lips, she pledged a great amount of money to him. What it is to be popular!

Edward could charm the birds off the trees into his hands!

And then there is Henry Tudor, of course. I have a feeling Edward is going to try to extricate him personally from Duke Francis's custody while he is in France. I am not sure how he plans to do it, but he has grown so impatient with Francis's refusal to hand the boy over that he is determined to try a more direct approach—perhaps send a small army detachment into Brittany to Francis's Court to demand his compliance while we are in France with the main army? There are no definite plans yet—only suggestions as to how the boy might be released to Edward without causing too much friction between Edward and Francis. He has tried money bribes—they have not worked. Perhaps we can think up something else to persuade Francis before we embark? But I think Edward will have enough on his plate with the main invasion, without bothering about Tudor! My brother has big ideas, and though I support him out of loyalty, this does not mean I think he will bring them all off. Actually, I feel quite sorry for the boy and certainly wish him no harm myself. I don't think Edward does either, not really. He just wants him back in England, away from all his supporters, where he can cause no trouble. Lady Margaret Beaufort is continually pleading with the king to get Henry back to England, and I think this is probably the best place for him, if it can be done without too much hassle. Surely he would be better off here with his mother and her husband Lord Stafford—a strong and committed Yorkist—than imprisoned in a foreign castle? She has always had big plans for him, that is true, but would be impotent to carry anything out with the boy safe in England away from those who may cause an uprising in his name in the future!

I have helped as much as I could in preparation for this war which Edward is so set upon, mainly by getting ships fitted out for the transport of men, arms, and horses, which is my particular responsibility in my post as Lord High Admiral. Also, I have promised to supply the king with thirteen hundred expert archers, apart from as many knights, squires, and war horses as I can muster. I have also guaranteed to personally supervise the fletchers and boyers so that no archer can possibly run out of arrows at crucial times—they will probably have a good surplus rather than a deficiency!

Preparations continue apace. The invasion is planned for next summer. We should be ready by then. The French certainly know what we are planning. King Louis, known as 'The Universal Spider', because of his devious and unpleasant nature, will no doubt be ready for us too.

Meanwhile, apart from all these preparations, I continue with the consolidation of my authority in the north and sorting out all judicial disputes brought to my notice to the best of my ability. It has been easier than I thought it would be to win over the Neville supporters. For centuries, they have loyally supported the earls of Warwick. I was an unknown quantity to them and expected much resistance and sullen compliance to my wishes. I have tried to be sincere, open, and just with them, and I feel it is working. One can only do one's best! I know I have a natural ability in commanding men. I thank God for it!

Henry Tudor, Brittany, June 1475

'And you are going to help Edward, the English king, in this war against France and King Louis, my lord? I hear his forces have mustered and have already crossed the Channel? The king and his brother, the Duke of Gloucester, will surely follow them soon, and all the other Yorkist nobles!'

'Oui, if he calls me to his aid, I will provide an army. I did promise him long ago. We made a pact that if I helped him to try and win back some—or all—of the lands lost to France last century, he would help me when I am ready to fight for Brittany's independence from France! Duke Charles of Burgundy has already arrayed his host in preparation, I believe. He will have to help too—his wife, Margaret, is Edward's sister. However, he is quite an erratic and rash man, given to strange decisions and actions. I think Edward should not trust him overmuch!'

'And when you go, will you take me with you and give me up to Edward? I am fearful that if I return to England, he will have me done away with when I get there, whatever promises he makes about my safety and security. My mother is very wary of him too. She does not trust his motives!'

'Mais non, young Henri, you will remain safely here. Have no fear!'

'But he may try and take me by force while he is in France. He could always send a small contingent of soldiers into Brittany secretly. Especially if you are away fighting and I am here alone!'

'You will not be alone. Have I not returned your bodyguards to you? And allowed your Uncle Jasper to visit you? Your mother, the Lady for-mid-able, Margaret Beaufort, prevailed upon me to do that! You should be safe enough, even if King Edward does take it into his head to try and abduct you. But I do not think it is likely. He knows how angry that would make me, and he does need my support against King Louis, now and in the future! You are precious to me, mon fils, so I shall safeguard you! And do not think that while I am away, your Uncle Jasper will have any success in taking you from here, even with all your followers nearby. I shall make sure that will not be possible! And now, I must go. There is a herald waiting to see me with a message from King Edward, no doubt pressing me to fulfil my promise to him.'

Richard Picquigny, Near Amiens, France. August, 1475

'No, Edward, in this matter I will *not* support you! It is not what I came here for—not what *you* came here for! You came, ostensibly, to reclaim English lands lost last century. Not to end all in such a tame way! Think of all that money you amassed by hook or by crook over the past few years, for what was to be a glorious recovery of English land rights in France. Think how it has now all been spent on soldiers, horses, and equipment—pointlessly, it seems!

This treaty, or settlement, with King Louis, without ever coming to blows, without even one tiny skirmish, is not worthy of you, Edward. You were always one for a good fight to settle things. And very successful at it too!'

'We may not have got the lands back, Dickon, but think of it—we are assured of plentiful funds for the rest of Louis's life. This agreement is most advantageous to England!'

'To you, you mean, Edward! Everyone else feels cheated—even the common soldiers. I have heard them talking when they did not realise I was near! They came for a fight; were ready for it, fired with a nationalistic fervour! They did not come to turn back without even lifting a sword! And think of this terrible weather they have endured for weeks—endless rain and wind and mud. Surely they deserve some honour and glory after their misery and privations? Some have grown surly already and will be difficult to control on our retreat—for a retreat it is. Many will expect to do what they usually do after a battle, unless constrained not to—steal from and lay waste the country—if not worse.'

'Then those must be severely punished if they disobey orders to make for the coast in an orderly fashion. And as long as they get paid for doing very little in the end except march—which they will, I have guaranteed—what have they to grumble about? They are all going home alive, by God's bones, when many would be dead now if they had had to fight!

I regard the whole thing as a coup—a triumph of good sense! Surely it is better to treaty than to kill and maim? I think Louis agrees, even if he will be much the poorer in terms of gold because of it. As far as we are concerned, it is easy money for doing very little except issuing threats. And there was quite a lot of diplomacy involved too!

Think of it! Louis is to give me seventy-five thousand crowns within the next two weeks, and thereafter fifty thousand crowns a year! And there is to be an agreed seven-year truce! Added to that, to bind the agreement, my young Bess, who is now nine years old, is to be betrothed to Louis's five-year-old son, the heir to the French throne. One day, my favourite little one will be Queen of France! It is all most satisfactory.

Everyone is pleased—except you, Dickon. That upsets me. My favourite and most-favoured brother, the only one not to support me. What will people think? That we have fallen out. We, who have always been so close?

Apart from your disagreement with me, I am very satisfied!'

'Well I am not! The whole thing is a shameful fiasco. It reflects very badly on the English as a whole—apart from you as their king! The French must be laughing up their sleeves at us, especially Louis.

Expediency has taken the place of what should have been a glorious return home if we had fought. For I am sure we would have won!'

'I would not be laughing if the tables had been turned and I was constrained to hand over so much gold to Louis each year. I do not care what the French—especially Louis—think as long as he comes up with the promised bounty on the due dates!

But I *do* care what you think, Dickon. Will you not reconsider and be there by my side tomorrow when we shake hands, Louis and I, and put our signatures to this treaty?'

'I have never, in my whole life, wavered from my vow of loyalty to you, Edward, as my king and as my dear brother, but my sense of honour is involved here and will not allow me to condone what you are doing. I am sorry for it, but there it is. I cannot be there with you when you sign this wretched treaty and shake hands with that despicable Louis. He will renege on you, you know. He is not to be trusted one inch! He is known by all to be devious and his word cannot be accepted. In a year or two, he will find some clever way to wriggle out of all his promises to you. He is not known as "The Spider King" for nothing!'

'So you put honour—a somewhat nebulous concept in this day and age, belonging with chivalry in the last century—before brotherly love? You have hurt me deeply, Richard. I have done a lot for you and given you so much of my love too! What a way to return it! If you were anyone but my beloved brother, you could be termed a turncoat. But I know it is only your youthful and idealistic beliefs that make you behave so. At twenty-two, you have not yet realised perhaps, my little brother, that in worldly matters, expediency and pragmatism are better in the end as ways to settle differences when it is possible to employ them!'

'Well, you may be right. You are ten years older than me, after all. But I still feel I have a right to my opinion. I shall go to Amiens Cathedral and pray for you—and for England—while you are meeting Louis.

You have changed a lot, you know, Edward, in the past few years. You seem to want to get things done with the least possible effort now. I must admit I do not like the changes in you! I am sure you were idealistic once too?'

'I expect I was. I cannot remember, to be honest. But we all change with time, Dickon—you too. There was a time, until recently, when you would have concurred with everything I said or did without thought. Ah well, the boy is grown up now and has a mind of his own!

You have always been most mature for your age. That is why I gave you commands and opportunities which I denied George. I felt you could deal with them far better. But this time, George is with me all the way and sadly you are not! Such is life!'

Richard, Westminster Palace, London, Late 1475

'Richard, I am writing most strongly to Duke Francis of Brittany, complaining that he never turned up with his host as promised when we went to fight Louis in France!'

'As it turned out, he was hardly missed at the time, you must admit! Perhaps he was on his way after all, but late and when he heard about your so-called treaty, decided to turn back home, knowing he would not be needed?' Richard answers somewhat dryly.

'That is not the point. We made a pact long ago. And he broke it. Whether he was needed or not, he should have come!

Now I want that Tudor boy back here safe in my keeping. I shall order Francis to release the boy. He must comply at once! I no longer need Francis's goodwill. I have King Louis as an ally instead. But Francis needs mine! No doubt about it! Henry Tudor must be sent to England forthwith. I shall send not one, but several ambassadors to "persuade" this obstinate duke. He can hardly refuse now!'

'And have you thought what you will actually do with Henry when—if—he returns?'

'Well, I shall tell the duke that I am to marry the boy to one of my other daughters, to join the Houses of York and Lancaster so there will be no more wars. It would be a good thing. And that would be two daughters married off well. And this country does need peace now, more than anything. I may well do it too or—I may find another solution! It all depends!'

'Incarcerate him in the Tower, perhaps, then have him quietly done away with, as you did Henry VI? It must have been you that ordered that, I have realised. He was in the way, after all, and I suppose it was expedient to rid the country of the old man, though he was harmless enough?'

'I do not like your tone, Richard! You have become rather cynical of late! It was what he stood for that was dangerous—something had to be done about him. He could not go on lingering there for God knew how long as a rallying icon for those Lancastrians who wished to cause me further trouble—though his ghastly wife was safely incarcerated at last, thank God, and could do no more harm! But there would be no reason—at present anyway—to do away with the boy—I think.'

'I hope not. As I told you before, he is not ambitious at all. I do not see how he could be a real threat to you! Not at the moment, anyway.'

'No, not on his own—as I have told *you* before—but that Uncle Jasper of his and more to the point, his powerful mother, Lady Margaret Beaufort, could do a lot of harm in his name! Her second name is ambition, I think!'

Henry Tudor, Brittany, Early 1476

'Henry, mon fils, I have good news! At least, I believe you will find it so! It is surely an answer to the vexed question of your stay here as my unwilling guest.'

'What do you mean, my lord?'

'Why, you are to be married! In England, to one of King Edward's daughters. It is a fitting answer to everything and will unite the Houses of Lancaster and York—which will mean no more wars! You need not fear for your life any longer. Everything is settled!'

'And who has arranged this?' Henry asks fearfully.

'Why, King Edward himself, of course! He instructs me to release you at once into the care of his ambassadors, four of whom, he says, will shortly be arriving to escort you home to England!'

'England is not my home! My homeland is Wales, as you well know, my lord.'

'Anyway, they will take you to Calais, thence across the Channel to London. Think how exciting that will be for you! The wedding will take place almost at once, he says. But of course, your little bride is too young for the marriage to be a full one yet—you understand?'

'Yes, of course. But I do not wish to marry an English princess! It is Maude, daughter of Earl Herbert at Raglan Castle, where my home was, to whom I am affianced and whom I care for. Surely I have some say about whom I want to marry?'

'Not any more! The king's wishes take precedence! Are you not pleased? You will be marrying into the royal family and living with the highest in the land. And above all, you will no longer be in danger!'

'No, I am anything but pleased. Because I fear it is just another of the king's ploys to get hold of me in any way he can! Why can you not resist this request or order, you say—as you have all the others?'

'Because things have changed radically. And I am bound to obey. I still need Edward's support, but he is now allied with France and that creature, King Louis. What am I to do? The future of my realm may depend on keeping King Edward happy!'

'And not me? Does my happiness—and safety—mean nothing to you? I thought we had become friends—of a sort—during my long exile in Brittany. And you have certainly done much for me. Are you to abandon me now?'

'I have no choice. Edward's new treaty with Louis—in which a great deal of gold is involved—has changed everything drastically. And there was no fighting, not a blow struck. Edward has won hands down! I do not know how he manages it. I never get anywhere with Louis!'

'So gold is more important than my life? Has he offered you a large portion of this gold, now he is rich, to let me go then?'

'No, no. Not at all! He has offered me substantial bribes before to send you back to England. But I have always resisted!'

'Then why do you give in now? I do not believe you. Ah—I understand—I am no longer useful to you as a bargaining tool. That is the truth of it, isn't it? I am easily expendable now!'

'I wish I could deny it. But I cannot. I am sorry. I do this for my country, try to understand! If it was just my choice, I would say no again. But Brittany will be better off with you gone now, rather than sheltering you here. That is a plain fact! Also, there is the matter of my breaking my promise to come with soldiers to fight for him when he invaded France in July. I did actually go with a force, but we were late in departing, because of the atrocious weather, and three-quarters of the way to Amiens, we heard that Edward and Louis had come to this agreement and there was to be no fighting. We just came home again. But Edward seems to think I should have carried on and joined him anyway, to show good faith, as it were. I do not think he believes I actually set out! I now have to placate him somehow, or he will never keep his promise to help me when the time comes for Brittany to rise up and claim complete independence from France! You can see how I am fixed?'

I can see clearly how I am fixed! Once more, I am a puppet on a string, pulled hither and thither—and usually where I do not want to go! I did not want to leave Wales, but Uncle Jasper insisted it was for my safety. And I had to believe him, though I would willingly have taken my chances and stayed there. I have found refuge, of sorts, here, though it was, in effect, as a prisoner. Now I am to be uprooted yet again and thrown to the English Lion as a sacrifice! And all for expediency and other people's needs and desires! When will my needs and desires ever be given any thought?'

'It is a hard world, and a hard life, even for those in high places! You must just accept your lot, I am afraid. There is nothing else to be done. I believe that Edward truly means to do what he says and that you will be in no real danger. In fact, you could come out of all this very well. From an exiled, hopeless situation, you will go into a life of wealth and privilege, living your life in palaces and married to a princess. Many would be glad of the prospect ahead of you!'

'Well, I am not. I don't believe any of it! And you choose to believe it, for it is convenient for you to do so! If you send me from here to England, I think you will be sending me to my death! Do you want that on your conscience? As soon as he has me in his clutches, he will either imprison me in the Tower or some awful castle hidden away where I can be forgotten—or, more likely, he will have me quietly killed, just like poor Henry VI! No one believes that he died of melancholy, as they say. He was murdered! And by Edward! Who else could have ordered it?'

'I believe you are right there, mon fils! But kings often do dreadful things for the good of their countries. It is in the nature of the job. He has accepted Louis's gold, so Louis is now his ally and Edward is no longer mine, so I must do as he says. It is a chain of circumstance, like a game of dominoes!'

'This is no game! My life is at stake. I know it. I do not care what you say. Please, I beg you, keep me here. Defy him once more! Otherwise, you will shortly hear of my death in England. I will be the sacrifice!'

'Nonsense! You are letting your imagination run away with you now! Put on a brave face, go to England, and hope for the best—that is all you can do!'

Westminster Palace, London. Early Autumn, 1476

'Yes! Success at last! Duke Francis of Brittany has now agreed to release Henry Tudor from his protection. He will let the ambassadors I am sending bring the boy back to England, via St Malo. But then, of course, there is the problem of what exactly I am to do with him?!'

'Did you not promise Francis that you would marry Tudor to one of your daughters—though of course none of them are old enough yet for a marriage in more than name?'

'That was what I said, Will, but of course we have to think of a way to make sure that he cannot cause any trouble here! To remove him from his many Lancastrian followers and supporters now congregated in Brittany is my main purpose, so they cannot use him in any way as a figurehead to foment plots around.

'But while he lives, there is no real guarantee of my safety. His wretched Uncle Jasper will be allowed to accompany him, no doubt. He has been the boy's protector from birth and is the real threat! I will have to make sure he is kept from the boy here. He will be imprisoned somewhere far away. His influence on Tudor has always been substantial, whether actually with him or not. What would you advise me to do with the boy?'

'While you decide his fate—if you really have not decided it already—the only secure place for him is the Tower of London. You know that, Sire!'

'Husband, while he lives, he will always be a threat. You must do away with him as soon as you have him in your hands!'

'Yes, Elizabeth, my dear, I know that would be the easiest way out of this dilemma, but I did make a promise.'

'An expediency, my lord, that is all. You had tried every other way of getting Francis to release Tudor. He seemed utterly impervious to bribes! Is he so rich he does not care for gold? They say he is obsessed with beautiful jewels. Why did you not offer him diamonds instead of gold?'

'Would you have had me send your most precious jewels to him then, Bess? They are even better than those in the Royal Treasury!'

'No, Edward, of course not. Those I treasure most—as gifts from you!'

'Well then, hold your peace! We know that that way has not worked, so let us forget it. We have persuaded Francis—that is all that matters. The problem now is how to deal with Henry when he gets here.

What say you, Richard? I always value your judgement and clear thinking. Should I carry out my promise or have him got rid of privily?'

'A promise is a promise, Brother! And a king's promise is surely more sacred than most? I have told you many times that the boy is no threat on his own. Surely he will no longer be a loose cannon if you do marry him off to one of the princesses? And some good could come out of it all in the end—the Houses of York and Lancaster would be united, and that could only be a good thing for the country. The people would applaud the marriage wholeheartedly—they are sick unto death of fighting and wars. In one fell swoop, you could bring a continual peace for a long time to come!'

'You are right there, Richard! People would no doubt admire my judgement? Eh? But is peace at any price always a good thing? I still feel he would be better out of the way for good and all. Then we could forget about him!'

'But if you have him killed, it will only stir up even more trouble among his supporters, Sire. I agree with Hastings in this matter. If you need more time to make up your mind what to do with him, then the only place for him when he arrives is the Tower!'

Henry Tudor, Brittany, Late Autumn, 1476

'My lord, we must make haste! The ship will have been waiting at St Malo for days now. King Edward is not a patient man. We must reach the coast and embark before another day is out!'

'I tell you I must rest! I have had a fever for days and I can struggle no more against it. I must rest to recover. Do you want to take me back to the king in a coffin?'

I am swaying in the saddle—I can hardly keep upright. But they think I am shamming. They know I was terrified of going back to England—and they know why—I feel so ill with this fever and cough that I fear I will die if I cannot lay down on a bed for a while. The sweat is pouring off me, and yet the weather is very cold. Perhaps I have the sweating sickness? Then that will be the end of me and all my troubles.

They would not even let my Uncle Jasper accompany me. Why? What can he do? I am a prisoner—a very sick prisoner. They must want me back in England very badly to rush me like this when they can see I am so ill. I have not one friend here. Even their doctor was very peremptory with me and more or less told me to pull myself together.

Everything is going black and I am falling—falling. If someone does not help me, I will fall from my horse any moment.'

'My lord, you are safe! Duke Francis has relented and has sent me to get you back to safety. He has been persuaded by his favourite councillor, John Chenlet, that you are indeed in mortal danger from King Edward and that his wily promises are not to be trusted. As soon as you have recovered a little, my men and I will secrete you away to a place of safe sanctuary in St Malo, where you can have the best doctors and recover fully before making the journey back to Duke Francis's Court. There, he will guard you even better than before, after this suspicious episode! Do not fear—you will not be going to England and the king just yet—and not at all if the duke and I can help it. I will make some excuse to the English ambassadors who placed you here when you collapsed several days ago!'

'Who—are you?'

'I am the duke's treasurer, Peter Landois, and I was sent post-haste by Duke Francis to rescue you, when he was made to see your danger! Your Uncle Jasper accompanied me and will be caring for you soon. My mission is to distract the English ambassadors while my men and Jasper spirit you away!'

'How did you get in here? Were there not guards at my door?' I gasp out, still breathless and racked by a relentless cough.

'They have already been surprised, set upon, and removed. There were only two of them. I expect the English ambassadors thought that, as you were so sick, two would be enough if you did find the strength to attempt to get away. But they did not think that help would come for you!'

'I thank you, Monsieur Landois, it is more than I hoped for. My spirits are raised—a little. But I fear this sickness will keep me laid up for a while yet.'

'Then you will be transported in a litter, if needs be. You can then have the best of care back at the court to recover. Duke Francis feels very remorseful that he ever believed the lies told him and let you go, believe me. He does not want your death on his conscience!'

'I will put myself in your safe hands, and thank God and the duke, of course, for my safe delivery!'

Henry Tudor, Vannes Castle, Brittany, Late November 1476

My Dear Mother,

As you can see, I am back in the custody of Duke Francis again. But at least I am not dead!

And the duke is disposed to be kinder to me now. I am allowed more freedom and I can meet with Uncle Jasper. Though he is held elsewhere at the moment, Duke Francis has promised me he can join me here in November. If King Edward had got his way, I would be in my grave by now or forgotten in the fearsome Tower, perhaps in some ghastly oubliette! My life so far has taught me to be fearful of men. Caution will now be my watchword! I am now become so suspicious by nature that, however safe I may be now or in the future, I will never be able to feel truly secure. Had it not been for your warnings, I am sure that my life would have been forfeit!

I do not think now that Francis will ever give way to King Edward's pleas, even threats. If he were going to, he would have done so by now. I must just bide my time, I suppose, until Edward dies and it is safe to return. But he is a young man. He may live another forty years. I may live—and die—an exile here. It does not bear thinking about!

I know that you will continue to work for my safety and well-being and for my future—if I have one—in England. Surely you have given up your previous idea of me becoming king there one day? It is ludicrous! I am convinced of it. I never did give it much credence, anyway!

My spirits are higher than they were, in spite of what happened recently and my bad bout of ill health. I feel somewhat safer, but, as I said earlier in this letter, I will never be able to feel totally secure, even if the rest of my life is happy and full of good things and people I can trust!

I look forward to your next letter. Your letters are always so forward-looking and optimistic whatever is happening.

Your dutiful and loving son,
Henry Tudor

Westminster Palace, London. Autumn, 1476

'God's bones, Hastings, the young whelp has escaped! I do not believe it! That wretched turncoat Duke Francis was persuaded to change his mind and sent rescuers to pluck Tudor from the inn in St Malo, where he was lying sick—so it is said—under guard. Methinks they did not guard him very well, sick or no! My ambassadors were duped—I shall have something strong to say to them about their stupidity!'

'You have tried everything, Sire, to get this Henry Tudor back. This time, it seemed to have worked. But Francis is really too wily and very aware of the bargaining power the boy gives him. I am sure he did not arrange his rescue out of kindness. Short of storming the Court of Brittany and wresting him away by force, which would cause another war, I think you have done everything you can humanly do over the years to get hold of him! And his so-called importance is surely outweighed now by other, more serious matters? You should put him from your mind, at least for the time being, I feel.'

'Maybe you are right, my good friend. There is my dear but troublesome brother, George of Clarence, to consider—again. He is a constant worry! One wonders what he will do next. His wife Isabel has given birth once more—and to a boy. Surely getting another son will focus his mind away from trouble-making for a time? If he is safe at home, he cannot get up to so much mischief!'

'True, my liege! And I hear the fair Isabel is grievous sick since the birth in October. Worry about her will surely keep him at home. He loves her well, that is certain.'

'That is sad to hear. My Bess has never had trouble producing healthy children or remaining healthy herself after the births. She is just as strong and beautiful now as before her first. She still has the figure of a girl!'

'The Neville family, for all their wealth and prestige, are obviously not so strong physically as the Woodvilles. Lady Anne is a delicate flower too. I do not think your brother Richard will get many sons on her!'

'And yet his bastard, John, grows and thrives lustily! Ah well, God's ways are mysterious, so they say.'

'Indeed, Sire, they are. But the queen and yourself have done your duty for the succession. Two healthy boys and daughters too. You need not worry overmuch now about producing more!'

'It is a good thing. I have many other worries and problems to deal with. But the main one is George. We keep on coming back to him!'

'Because he continues to be a cause for concern!'

'Even when he seems quiet at home, as now, one wonders what he is plotting? No one could have a more easy-going and forgiving brother than I. And I could not have been more lenient with him. But because I am king, I will have to put a stop to him finally, soon, I feel, as his actions threaten the whole nation, not just me. What do you think I should do about him, Will? I am at my wits' end!'

'Soon, he will finally overstep the mark completely, go just that little bit too far! In his arrogance, he is convinced he can continue to do just what he likes and you will always forgive and overlook his behaviour!'

'Then I must finally harden my heart towards him and put a stop to him once and for all. I hate the thought of it, because I believe he does not realise what he is doing or saying half the time. I have even considered he may be mentally unbalanced! He is certainly like a naughty child that cannot see the error of its ways however many times it is told, or even punished! But George has never been punished—up to now.'

'Perhaps that is the answer then, Sire. The very next unacceptable thing he does, have him arrested and put in the Tower of London for a few months. That will cool his heels and give him plenty of time to think on his many sins!'

'Will, you have hit the nail on the head, as always. That is what I shall do!'

Richard, Middleham, Late Spring, 1477

At Christmas, I pitied George greatly, in spite of our many past differences, as he lost his poor wife Isobel three days before the Holy Feast with complications from childbirth in October. Everyone knew it was the dreaded childbed fever. She had been ill for weeks, slowly fading away. And then, of course, the baby died too, just twenty-six days after birth. Poor George, we all thought. He was going around like a ghost, with wild eyes and nothing to say to anyone. I believe he truly loved Isabel; swore he was faithful to her always.

Anne was devastated about her sister's death too. They were always very close as children, though they had grown apart since Isabel married George.

Now, I think George is teetering on the verge of madness. His behaviour, always erratic and unpredictable, has become outrageous.

First, he decided, in his obviously sick mind, that his wife had been murdered. Poisoned, no less. And by the last person, surely, who would have harmed Isobel? Ankarette Twynyho, her old nurse, who had cared for her and the child through her last illness. Grief is a terrible thing, but what George did went far beyond that.

His hatred of the Woodvilles tipped his reason, I am sure. He had obviously convinced himself that they had coerced the poor nurse into administering poison to kill Isabel to get back at him for all his hatred of them—which was mutual—and his high-handed attitude to them over the years. He openly despised them for their low birth—particularly the queen—dismissing them as upstarts.

Now he has had the Twynyho woman dragged off and summarily hanged without trial! It is surely the act of a badly unbalanced mind! He has always been arrogant, but taking the King's Justice into his own hands is beyond forgiveness. The king is furious about it.

Many actions of George's lately make the king angry. I think his days of forgiving our charming brother have run out at last!

And there are other things, very strange things. When he comes to court, which is very infrequently now, he is ominously silent; glowers at the Woodvilles, particularly the queen, and even Edward sometimes. And he ostentatiously refuses all meat and drink when it is offered. Why? Does he think that someone is trying to poison him too?

He has always been one to brood on grievances, or supposed grievances. Now he is in a furious mood constantly. He says little, but we all know why it is. With poor Isabel scarce cold in her grave, his ever-vaunting ambition led him to ask for the hand in marriage of someone far and away above his grasp! None other than Mary of Burgundy, the greatest heiress in Europe, now that her father the duke has lately died. And she, even more arrogant perhaps than her suitor, turned him down flat! Also, as king, Edward forbade the marriage, even if Mary had accepted George's proposal. George will have hated him for that. Perhaps he convinced himself Mary would have taken him for husband if Edward had not scotched the plan roundly? He has such a high opinion of himself! But all Europe knows of George's past indiscretions and his open treachery to Edward when he sided against the king with Warwick. Burgundy would not want such a troublemaker in its midst. But what is even more shocking to the king and I is the fact that our own sister, Margaret, Duchess of Burgundy, supported him in this! What can she have been thinking of? She always loved George best of all of us, her handsome, charming brother who protected her as a child. They were like two peas in a pod. Worst of all, it has come to light, through letters to each other which have gone astray, that he feels himself more suited to be king than Edward; that he also has more right to be king, as Edward was proclaimed a bastard all those years ago by his own mother. That nonsense concerning the archer Blaybourne and our proud Lady Mother Cecily again! Will that silly story never get laid to rest? And according to her reply, Margaret believes he has the rightful claim too!

This is tantamount to treason on George's part, and surely her foolish fondness for George has persuaded Margaret into such an indiscretion as actually writing her support for him down in an answering letter? It is hardly believable! Edward feels very upset, as well as angry, about all this, I know. Surely he must do something about George now. Things cannot go on like this. George has gone too far—even for the king's forgiving nature.

I expect to hear very soon that Edward will take some action, for this is a very serious matter. It is the second time that George has, in effect, turned traitor to the king! Edward cannot ignore it.

And I suppose I will have to leave the peace and quiet of Middleham and travel to London to support the king in whatever decision he makes. I dread it, for I feel I know what the outcome must be. And despite his foolish stupidity and falseness, George is still my brother—and I dread what may happen to him now.

George of Clarence, the Tower of London, Summer 1477

I have gone too far this time. I know it. I will be lucky to escape with my life. I do not think I will. I have never seen Edward so angry with me. He has always forgiven me my waywardness before. All my life, I have depended on his clemency and natural generosity of heart. But not this time. This time I could see he is inflexible. He has made up his mind about me. Something tells me he will never relent again—and that death stares me in the face. A traitor's death.

Surely he will not condemn me to that terrible, brutal death, his own brother? Whatever I have done?

I knew somehow, while I was saying and doing some of these things of which I am accused, where it might lead me. I have been on the downward slope for years, but it has turned into a landslide since Christmas. I have always been weak and easily led, I admit. From boyhood, I've been prey to bad influences. And I do not think before I act. I have had endless time to reflect on my behaviour over the years whilst incarcerated in here, and I see things clearly now, where I have constantly gone wrong. I was warned, many times, that my behaviour was not acceptable as the king's brother, but I ignored all the warnings. And now it is too late.

Of course, it is the drink that is largely responsible for my behaviour since my poor, dear Isabel died just before Christmas. I have always been a heavy drinker, but since that terrible time, I have never been sober. Her death broke my heart. My poor children have lost their mother—and soon they will be orphans! The drink has made me do things I am sure I never would have otherwise done. It has made me very incautious with my tongue—careless too. The brother of the king cannot speak so. I realise that now. It is too dangerous. I have gone well beyond the pale of reasonable behaviour.

This necromancy business, for instance. I have accused Edward of dabbling in the black arts with the aid of Jane Shore, his favourite mistress, and with the queen. These Woodvilles will be the death of me! They have always hated me and persistently tried to persuade the king to see the worst in me. And he has always held out against them and their vicious tongues. Until now. It is the end of the line for me, I am sure.

Of course, the queen has hated me even more venomously ever since I had her father, Lord Rivers, and her brother, John, executed. But that was necessary at the time and I did it on Warwick's orders anyway. She has spread wicked stories, which are mostly quite untrue, about plots against the king I am supposed to have hatched, about injuries I am supposed to have done to her Woodville relatives, and she has complained of evil ambitions I am supposed to have had, and even that she feared her eldest boy will never become king when Edward dies, if I live—as I will have him done away with! My own nephew! I may be a lot of things which are not good—I admit—but I am no child-killer!

Most of it is nonsense. I do hate the Woodvilles, that is true, but I have not done a quarter of what she vehemently alleges, what they all, as a tribe, accuse me of. She has the king's ear constantly, and he believes everything she says, as he is besotted with her. She bombards him with tales of my supposed infamy. I do not hate the king. I am just envious of his position—which a quirk of fate decided, that is all. I admit, I always have been. But envy is a common sin, especially among siblings. But here it is interpreted as treason!

It does not mean I wanted his death!

But he wishes mine now. At last, this hated, evil family has broken through Edward's defences of brotherly affection and family loyalty. The love he has always borne me, despite all my admitted faults, has been dissipated by their constant accusations.

I feel I will not be long here. Edward will either release me soon or have me executed. And something tells me it will be the latter. Even Richard has been pleading for my life constantly, I hear; Richard, whom I have envied all my life too because he came first in Edward's heart. Apparently, he even travelled all the way down from Yorkshire to plead with the king to forgive me—just once more. I must admit it humbles me a little.

I am lost and adrift here, like a piece of driftwood at the mercy of wild waves. Stronger forces than I can control will decide my fate. Will Richard persuade the king to let me live? He is an able and persuasive man. And Edward loves him well and has always listened to him. But I think the king will be adamant. He is afraid of me, you see, afraid of what he suspects I know.

He is doing this because I have a secret about him that I found out by accident! If revealed, it would blow his world apart and that of his vicious wife, the queen—who is no queen in truth and that of his children. The whole succession would be put in jeopardy; would be destroyed! He is terrified that I will open my mouth and tell what I know. So he cannot let me live, fearing what I could do with this knowledge! I am to die, not for my indiscretions, my jealousy of him, or my past treachery in plotting with Lord Warwick against him—he forgave me that—but because of what I know and could reveal any time—I could destroy them all!

And the future of the Yorkist dynasty! I could reveal it now to try and save myself! But who would believe me in here? I am allowed no visitors of importance who might take me seriously. My gaolers would just laugh at me and say it was the ramblings of a drunken man terrified for his life and clutching at any straw to try and save himself. They would dismiss it as lies—but it is all true—all true. Why did I not speak up before?

Because I thought Edward would relent, forgive me again—until I realised that he knew about this secret that I hold! That signed my death warrant, I know it!

How will they put me to death, if the worst comes to the worst? Will Edward commute the terrible sentence for treason? Will he take some pity on me as his brother? Will I be told when it is to happen or just be done away with in the night like old Henry VI?! I cannot bear to think of it, and yet it obsesses me constantly, what is to come—soon, I feel.

I am given every luxury in here, far more than most prisoners, even noble ones, get, I am sure. I have even been given a large barrel of my favourite Canary malmsey. I drink it like water—it is the only comfort I have now; the only resort to blot out what seems inevitable—the only way to forgetfulness.

If it is to happen, my death as a traitor to my brother the king, the supposed king—who rules where I should have ruled—let it happen soon—preferably when I am heavily drunk.

If I am given one last request, then it would be for them to allow me to drink myself into an oblivious stupor before they carry out the deed—perhaps, for past brotherly love, Edward will allow me at least that last favour.

Henry Tudor, Brittany, January 1478

> Woking Old Hall,
> Surrey,
> England

My Dear Henry,

I am sending you the warmest greetings for your twenty-first birthday on 28 January. This is a big milestone in your life, and I am so sad that we cannot be together to celebrate it. I hope that Duke Francis will see fit to arrange a celebration for you, where you can meet with some, at least, of your supporters, especially Uncle Jasper. That would be a kind thing for him to do—and he does seem kindly disposed towards you, I think. He did not let you fall into the hands of crafty King Edward after all last year. Let me know later on how you spent your special day!

Here, in England, King Edward's great displeasure with his brother George of Clarence continues. So much so that he has finally lost patience with his actions. Clarence has shown in more than one way over the years that he has traitorous intentions towards the king. But he also took the king's law into his own hands, having tried and condemned to hanging a servant he was convinced poisoned his wife, Isabel, who of course died from the effects of child-bed fever and perhaps, say some—a lung disease brought on by her weakness after the birth. Anyway, George had this woman hung without trial, and the king was outraged! It was just the end of a long line of George's transgressions. He was forgiven by the king again and again, but never learnt his lesson and changed his ways! He has been imprisoned in the Tower of London for a long time, and perhaps he thought that would be his only punishment.

But now, he has been indicted in a court of law by the king himself, who conducted the trial and expounded all the charges against his foolish brother. It very much looks as if the death sentence for treason will be served on him. One cannot say he does not deserve it! Whether the king will actually have it carried out is another matter, as he has always been close to his brothers, and it may go against his conscience, even though Clarence is patently guilty of so much plotting against Edward. We shall see.

But think, my son. If he is executed for treason, that will be one less contender for the throne between you and your rightful place as the future king. I have always been convinced, as you know, of your destiny! Fate works itself out in strange ways. George of Clarence has many times stated that he should be king and that Edward has no right to the throne. He may be right! There have been many rumours circulating for years that Edward was born a bastard in France, the son of a common archer whom the proud Duchess Cecily committed an indiscretion with while her soldier husband was away at the wars. It may be true. There is no smoke without fire, as they say—and if so, it would mean that Edward's children would have no right of inheritance after him. Which would leave just Richard of Gloucester—and you!

I keep as well as can be expected, though my health was never good. I hope that you are now fit and well again and that this winter has brought you no more agues? Last winter, you had a bad attack of the sweating sickness, I know, which many do not recover from at all. You, being young and strong, were able to fight it off, but still, my son, be careful. Do not take chances with your health. Your presence will be needed for great things in the future! Enjoy your birthday, my dear son! I am always thinking of you and praying for your health and well-being!

Your loving mother,
Margaret Beaufort,
Countess of Richmond

Richard, Westminster, 16 February 1478

'Edward, how could you do this? George is our own brother. He is of our blood. You cannot have him put to death. He is no common criminal. And to actually indict him yourself in a court of law—that is unheard of!

Was it not enough to let him rot in the Tower all those months last year? What was the purpose of that if you intended to have him executed in the end? Why not get it over with straightaway?'

'I wished to punish him and frighten some sense into him, that is all. To make him think, while he was imprisoned, on all the wrongs he has done against me and this realm of ours over the years! Can you not see that?'

'So why decide at this precise moment that he has to die, if you intended to let him go after a salutary lesson? What has hardened your heart so now?'

'I have been persuaded—by circumstances and by many advisors—that it is for the best. After all, while he lives, he will continue to cause trouble. He never learns from his mistakes. It is necessary for him to die. He is a traitor to me and a murderer of the innocent. He spreads sedition, and I believe he hates me and is determined to take arms against me and mine if I do not act now. He has always had a strong ambition to be king, you know!'

'He is an ambitious fool, I grant you that. He has been false to you—even a traitor—when he sided with Warwick against you, but why did you not have him executed then for his actions? You publicly forgave him! Surely you cannot punish him now for deeds committed years ago which you forgave at the time?'

'George intends to oust me from the throne if he can. He will plan uprisings against me. He will be a constant threat and worry. And I have had enough of him. It is best to do away with him, as he will never change his ways!'

'There is more to this than meets the eye. Something you are not telling me. We have always been so close, Edward, as close as brothers could be. We have trusted each other implicitly. I have looked up to you and supported you all my life. I have been as loyal as anyone could be! Can you not explain to me why, in a few days, you have given up all thoughts of pardoning him and are now intent on his execution?'

'I signed the death warrant on the 7 February. It is too late to retract now, even if I wanted to. The Lords and the Commons are demanding that the sentence be carried out without any more delay. Ten days are allowed between my signature and the execution. And the tenth day is tomorrow—the seventeenth! George dies on the eighteenth. I can do nothing now!'

'You could if you wanted to—you are the king. You make the law! Who is pushing you into this? I do not believe you really want to kill your own brother, whatever he has done, or may do. It is the Woodvilles, isn't it? The queen is behind this! She has always hated George.'

'It is true she fears him and what he may do—as I fear him. But mainly she fears for our children.'

'What could he do to them, if he lives? Tell me, Edward. What could he do?'

'He knows too much . . .'

'About what? Do you not trust me enough to tell me?'

'Well—for a start, I have discovered that he believes my children, as well as I, are bastards.'

'How could he possibly come to that conclusion? And even if he did, in his twisted mind, how could he seek to prove such a thing? Everyone has discounted that stupid story that has been going the rounds for years about our proud Lady mother and the archer in Rouen. I suppose George—if he really believes that you are the son of a commoner and a bastard, could seek to prove it, though how, I cannot imagine! But as for the children . . . ?'

'There is more—but I cannot tell you, Richard. I dare not. It is more than my life is worth!'

'If you cannot trust me with your confidence, who can you trust? Whatever it is, I am sure you would feel better telling me of it. I am your friend as well as your loyal subject. I would never disclose to anyone anything you told me in confidence. I can see that, whatever it is, it is making you ill. Lately, you have looked so tired and drawn, so unlike your usual self!'

'I am not myself, Richard, far from it. And I do appreciate your loyalty and love, you know that, but there are some things best kept to myself, that even a loving brother should not know. Be patient, Richard. One day, I may tell you what eats at my soul, but not today. Today, I am the king, not just your brother. I have to keep resolute and do what has to be done. And I have to protect others whom I love!'

'So, whatever this is which weighs so heavily on your heart, you cannot, or will not, tell me? You will not share the pain of it with me? That is unlike you, Edward. It grieves me deeply that you do not trust me enough to confide in me. I can only pray, along with our mother, our sister Margaret in Burgundy, and all the family, that you do the right thing in the next twenty-four hours and lift this terrible shadow of a traitor's death from George!'

'I have no intention of carrying out the ultimate penalty on him, Richard. There will be no hanging, drawing, and quartering. He will die by a method of his own choice. I have already conveyed that message to him. The Constable of the Tower will shortly let me know how he has chosen to die!'

'It is horrible. Horrible! I do not believe you will carry this terrible thing to its ultimate conclusion. I am sure you will rescind the sentence. I am going now, for my heart is breaking. But if George is executed tomorrow, you will have lost not just one brother, but two, for I will never trust you again. It is clear to me that you intend George's death not for what he has done, but for whatever it is you fear he will do—which you will not trust me enough to tell me of! I must now visit our Lady mother at Baynard's Castle. She is inconsolable, I hear. She loves George still, in spite of what he has done. She bore him, remember, in pain and tribulation. I suggest you pray most earnestly, Edward, as she is doing and I will later do. Now I have one last plea to make of you. I wish to visit George this evening in the Bowyer Tower. Surely, he needs to know that we have not all forgotten him in his hour of need?'

'No, I forbid it. He is to have no visitors! I have banned them for weeks. I will not change my mind now. He will have a priest to give him absolution, that is all. I had in mind to send his old friend, Bishop Stillington—he is in the Tower too, as he has incurred my displeasure.'

'Are you afraid George will divulge to me whatever it is he knows which terrifies you so? Surely, if he meant to do it, he would have done so by now? He has had plenty of opportunity, in public, as well as privately! He is in extremis of mind at the moment, I am sure! I must go to him, whatever you say. He needs some comfort from his kin.'

'If you do, you will find yourself barred from the Tower. I am implacable on this. Do not even try to gain entry. The constable has had specific orders not to let anyone—anyone—in to see him!'

'And that is your last word, Edward? I pity you. To deny a man who faces execution a sop of comfort? I shall never forgive you for this, never!'

Dowager Duchess Cecily, Fotheringhay Castle, Northampton, Summer, 1478

My Dear Richard,

I am only just beginning to come to terms with the terrible thing that Edward has done in having George put to death. My grief has been unutterable. And I shall never forgive Edward. He knows that. I have told him so many times since that terrible February day. It is the act of a coward, I believe! For I think I know what it is that he was so afraid George would reveal! You say he would not confide to you why he gave in to that awful Woodville woman's urgings to carry out the death sentence—even though he was disposed to forgive George again until she started pressurising him. Well, George was many things that were not good, I acknowledge that, but it did not give Edward, even as king, the right to behave like Cain and murder his brother. For murder it was, no less!

I know you agree with me. Your letters express the same desolate grief that I have felt these last months. I can understand how you do not want to be at court any more—though you never did like it much, nor did I. That is one reason I have kept myself quiet here all these years. I do not approve of the appalling immorality and licentiousness one sees there, led by Edward himself, the queen's degenerate sons, the Marquess of Dorset and Lord Richard Grey, and particularly that rake Hastings. I have come to the conclusion that Edward is weak in many respects and has been easily led into wrong ways of living and behaviour. I told you before that, in my opinion, he was not fit to be king and that I wished that one day you could claim the throne, as I know you would do a much better job as the monarch. You are far more upright and principled. Perhaps this could be construed as treason that I write, but I no longer care!

When I heard that Edward had married that low-born woman, Grey, in 1464, I wrote to him privily not to commit bigamy and to admit that he was not—and never could be—lawfully married to her, before it was too late!

I urged him to put her away and find a fitting bride from the courts of Europe. But he ignored me! You know that, at the time, I also admitted publicly that Edward was born of an extramarital relationship I had in Rouen while my husband, the duke, was constantly away fighting? That made Edward a bastard in reality. I did not think any of the family—including you—believed me then. But it was true. I was very angry when I heard what Edward proposed to do and, at the time, wanted to punish him by revealing his illegitimacy. I have been a pious and religious woman all my life, but this was my one fall from grace. My husband never got to know of it from me—though I think he may have guessed. Because he loved me dearly and he did not want to compromise me, I think he turned a blind eye to my indiscretion and accepted its consequences. I have always been thankful to him for that! He was a good man and would have made a fine king! He never spoke of my affair or questioned me but accepted Edward as his own unequivocally. And no one but I, and now you, because I have chosen to tell you, knows that. Though Edward's birth and christening were noted in the register of Rouen Cathedral, it was a very small christening only, in a side chapel, not a huge one in the main cathedral like your eldest brother Edmund had. It was deliberately kept low key. Blaybourne, an archer at the Rouen English garrison, was my lover, and I am sure he was Edward's father because the dates fit, from the time I became pregnant to Edward's birth! It was he who comforted me in my loneliness in 1441 when my husband was away for a particularly long period. Now, you may be wondering what all that has to do with George's secret? Well, I will tell you!

Edward was not free to marry, even if the woman he had chosen as his queen was suitable! He had already undergone a ceremony where he agreed to be plight-troth to a high-born girl, widow of Lord Sudely's son for some years, to whom she had been married at thirteen. And she herself was the Earl of Shrewsbury's daughter, and in English law, plight-troth is considered as binding as actual marriage.

Her name was Eleanor Butler, and after Edward married Elizabeth Grey, she retired to a convent in Norwich and took the veil. She died there only four years later. Of course, Edward had had no intention of marrying the girl! He was twenty years old, a lusty boy, used to getting his own way with women—as he still is—and she was a virginal, pious girl. He was determined to have her; he was besotted with her. So he had this farce enacted to persuade her, which of course he did. She loved him truly and believed in his good intentions, foolish girl! But he never honoured the plight-troth. When he became enamoured of Elizabeth, he conveniently forgot it and sought to keep it quiet all his life!

The poor girl never said a word about it but retired to the convent as I have said. But when she was dying, four years later, she confided her secret to a priest, who gave her absolution on her deathbed. The priest also kept the silence of the confessional until he too was about to die, when he wrote a letter to George, his liege-lord, and told all. The knowledge had hung heavy on his mind for years and he wanted to do the right thing by making it known before he died.

You may ask how I know all this? George had always hankered after the throne, and when he discovered that Edward was unlawfully married to Elizabeth and that therefore his many children were bastards as well as Edward—for George did believe my confession, it suited him to—he had now realised he had a chance of realising his dream of attaining the throne, as he was next in line! He confided in me. I too have kept quiet—up to now. But after what Edward has done, I have been very tempted to reveal all. It has hung on my conscience too. But Edward is also my son, whatever his many faults. I am telling you, because I think you have a right to know. If Edward should die, you are the next rightful king! Think on that! But while he lives, to reveal this would cause so much trouble for so many people—particularly those many innocent children of Edward's, who are of course, bastards in effect. I cannot bring myself to do it.

What you do with this knowledge is your affair. If it can help you in the future—then use it! I am sure Edward discovered that George knew this secret and was terrified he would reveal it in order to bring down the whole royal family and achieve his greatest ambition—to become king—which he believed he should have been all along! That is why Edward felt he had to do away with him. I am convinced of it.

But George had known this fact for a long time. If he were going to reveal it, I know he would have done so long since. He dare not speak about it! So Edward need not have worried. Edward knows, of course, that his mother is also privy to his secret—so perhaps he may soon seek to have me done away with too?

And now you know it too, my dear Richard, perhaps you will decide to face Edward with it? He loves you well, and I know you have always loved him well too, so I do not think you would be in any danger from him, particularly as you do not publicly hanker after his throne, as foolish George did! But, who knows? Edward has changed so in the last few years, I would not be surprised at anything he did now!

I advise you to keep the knowledge to yourself, for a time when it may prove very useful to you. That time may come sooner than you think! Edward is not in good physical health, after his many excesses. His allotted span may not be long.

Your loving mother,
Cicely, Dowager Duchess of York

Richard, Middleham Castle, Yorks, Late Summer, 1478

'There is another letter from the king. He is coming to York on Progress and wants to meet up with me. I am not at all sure I want to see him.'

'But you can hardly refuse. He is the king and can command your presence!'

'Anne, you know how I feel, still, about what he did! I know I cannot forgive him. It is all still very raw. I lost faith in him when he had George killed, in spite of my pleading, also that of my mother, Margaret, our sister in Burgundy, and many others. And because he just would not reveal to me the real reason for his decision—me, the closest one to him—apart from the queen. It was she who precipitated him into it. I know! I discovered that she had pressurised the Speaker of the Commons, Sir William Allington, a dependent of the Woodvilles and therefore beholden to them, to go to the Lords to insist the sentence be carried out forthwith! And they supported his request wholeheartedly. No doubt the queen's brother, Sir Anthony Rivers, and many other lords who had reason to hate George or envy him and looked to profit by his death by perhaps getting their hands on some of his great estates and titles the king had granted him, coerced the others into agreement.

She is an evil, vicious woman and she has Edward in the palm of her hand. He has grown to be the one that takes orders from her! She and her many obnoxious, grasping Woodville relatives control him completely now. It is not to be borne. I shall not go to court again in London, unless forced to. He knows how I feel. I made that very clear to him just before George's execution, when he still had an opportunity to commute the sentence!'

'And he didn't.'

'No, he went ahead with it, as he—and the queen—were determined to do. All pleas for mercy fell on deaf ears!'

'It was a terrible thing to do—to kill one's own brother—whatever he had done!'

'But, as I told you, I do not think he had George done away with for what he had actually done but for fear of what he might do! He admitted that much to me but would not reveal what he was afraid of. He just stated that George "knew too much" and that the royal children were in danger from him. I could get no real explanation of it. Edward obviously did not trust me enough to confide his fears. That is what hurt me so. We have always been so close.'

'And now there is this awful rift between you! Could you not find it in your heart to forgive Edward? He must have had good reasons for his actions—even if he did not confide them to you. One would have expected him to, I agree, and to trust his favourite and most loyal brother with the real reasons for his adamant stance on George.'

'Well, he didn't. He caused the rift, not I. I am not sure it can ever be healed!'

'Surely you want it to be? It is a big thing for you to have to forgive, I grant, but you are unhappy about your break with him. I know you are. Do you intend it to be permanent? What truly upsets you most—George's death—or Edward's lack of trust in you, honestly?'

'Both, of course. But I must admit, the fact he did not confide his true fears to me cut deep. We have always told each other everything!'

'Well, I think you should meet up with him in York, however bad you are still feeling, for form's sake, if nothing else. It would not be good for the people to guess that you are estranged from him, would it? They all accepted George's execution as a necessary evil, which of course it was. He had done many unforgiveable things. He was a danger to the state, as Edward said.'

'Are you on Edward's side in this, Anne? Surely you support me? I am your husband. A wife should support her husband at all times—in public anyway—however she may disagree with him privately.'

'Of course I agree with you—both privately and in public! You know that. Why ask it? I will come with you and be by your side in York, if you decide you will meet Edward. Do, Richard. I think you will be the happier for it. You have been so morose and distant for months. And I do not think it is only grief for George.'

'You are right, of course, as always, my dear Anne. You know me so well. Very well, I will reply to Edward and agree to meet him when he visits York.

———

It will be a public occasion anyway, so I suppose it will not be so difficult as meeting him in a private session. He says he is coming without the queen, so that will make it easier still. I do not think I would be able to keep my tongue still if she were there—after what I know she forced him to do!'

Richard, York, September 1478

'Well, Dickon, you seem to have won the hearts of your people here in York! Among the cheers for me, I am sure there were equally as many for you! "Gloucester, Gloucester!" is still ringing in my ears! I sent you to be Lord of the North and win over these people, who were Warwick's followers. I expected you to do it by force—if need be—but it seems you have done it by fairness, justice, and sincerity. That is good, very good. I have nothing but praise for your achievements! You were always an excellent commander of men. Now I see you can win their support in more human ways. You understand what makes them tick. You have the ability to make yourself popular. That is a great gift, Dickon, not given to many! I am actually quite envious of what you have achieved in this region. It is good to rule men loyal to you, who want to serve you! You have taught them how to observe your own motto.'

'Loyalty binds me! Yes, I believe if one treats men honourably and with justice, they respect and follow one. I do my best to carry this out.'

'And it works for you! I have always trusted you to be on my side and support me in my endeavours. Can I still count on you for that? Will you be there when I need you?'

'Of course.'

'But you do not trust me unconditionally, as you once did, do you?'

'It is only since—'

'Yes, I know, since February. But what I did, I had to do. There was no other way. I would dearly love you to understand that, Dickon. As king, I had no choice!'

'I do now. But George would not have revealed what he knew—however much he longed for the throne—he could not do it. Otherwise, he would have told all long before! He had known your secret for years! But you—you went in constant fear of what he might say—that is why you had him killed! It was him—or you!'

'How can you know this? You are clever, but without information from another source, you could not possibly have guessed what I was withholding from you—the real reason George had to die!'

'I did learn it from another source—our own mother—the Duchess Cecily! I fear she is estranged from you forever! She cannot forgive you!'

'How did she know?'

'George told her! The priest who attended the Lady Eleanor Butler on her deathbed, to whom she confessed your plight-troth promise to her, learnt it all from her own lips—and then confessed the secret that was burning in his brain to George, as his liege-lord, when he too was dying. The priest sent him a letter!'

'God's bones! How many more are aware of this?'

'Who knows?'

'And can you forgive me, Richard? Or are you estranged from me forever too?'

'I am still your devoted subject, but things are not quite as they were—I do admit that!'

'I pray that you will understand fully one day, Dickon! As your brother, I too am appalled by what I did. But as king, it was necessary! I regret the need for my action every day but not the action itself. It was the right-and only thing to do!'

'But do you admit that your queen had a lot of influence over that decision? That is what I cannot stomach!'

'She sought to persuade me through fear for her children and their futures—as I tried to explain at the time. That is all.'

'I will try to understand, Ned. But you must give me more time. You were always your own man. You made your own decisions based on your own beliefs. But you have allowed yourself to be influenced over many things by the queen and her family over the last few years. To speak bluntly, I feel you have weakened somewhat! The Woodvilles have become the power behind the throne. They seem to convince you that their will is your will!'

'You judge me harshly, Dickon! If you were anyone else but my dearest brother, what you have said could be construed as tantamount to treason! But I know you mean well and speak from the heart. I have grown tired, Dickon. I do not have the energy—physical or mental—which I once had. Sometimes I make mistakes. I am only human. The king is not perfect, I admit. Mea culpa, mea culpa—in many ways! You're still so young, still have a lot of the idealist in you. As I told you once before, years ago, expediency and pragmatism are often the only way, however emotion tells one otherwise. This is how it was with George. I still loved him—believe me—in spite of everything. But it was needful for the good of the realm that he should die!'

Anne, Middleham Castle, Yorks, Early Spring, 1480

I am in terror for Richard's life. He has had to go to London and the dreaded plague is raging there! The king's own small son, George, who is almost two, is very ill with it and his life is despaired of! This terrible disease, which can kill in less than twenty-four hours with some, is no respecter of persons. I pray continually that my dear husband does not succumb. He is with Edward, comforting him and supporting him while the poor child lies so sick at Windsor Castle. His official reason for going was to discuss the Scottish problem with the king, who wants to go to war against King James of Scotland. I am not sure I completely understand the reasons for this impending war, I must admit. Richard will make it clear to me later, I am sure. While he was journeying there, little George fell ill. Richard did let me know by fast messenger that he would now have to stay at Windsor until all danger of infection had passed within the castle, as he did not wish to bring it home to the children and I. For once, I am sorry for the queen. She must be in mortal fear that her other children will fall prey to the plague! Children get ill so easily. Ned is often sick with his weak chest. The slightest cold goes straight to his lungs and he coughs for weeks. And then there are the terrible breathless attacks he gets, often in the middle of the night. I have tried every remedy I know to help, but nothing does really. The doctor says he may grow out of it as he gets older. I pray so, for it is awful to watch, feeling so helpless, and must be quite terrifying for the poor child. Thank God there is no plague around here in the clear, healthy air of Wensleydale. I am sure Ned would go down with it as easily as poor little George has done. Babes stand no chance against so many ills.

No one knows where it comes from, this most terrible of diseases, though some say 'tis rats that carry it.

A comet was observed just before the outbreak started in September last year, a sure foreteller of terrible times to come!

I begged Richard not to go to Windsor, because the plague was already there, but he felt he had to.

Edward needs his support more than ever now with important decisions of state. His health is not good, and he has lost a lot of his determination and strength of mind. Richard says in his letter that Edward is eaten up with guilt because he believes the little child George has fallen ill through his fault—because he had his uncle of the same name, George of Clarence, done to death. That is surely superstitious nonsense, I think. Would God punish a babe for its father's sins? Though it does say in the Bible: 'The sins of the fathers shall be visited upon the children . . .' But surely, in other, less cruel ways?

I look at my little Ned playing here with John and with the other children we have taken in, George's children. Poor mites, they are orphans now, and Richard felt it was the least we could do for them. I am constantly surrounded by the laughter, bustle, and screaming of lively children! I do not mind most of the time, though it is very wearing when I am not well—which is often, unfortunately. I am frequently sad too, wishing they were all mine. Bella and I were close, so I can regard them as almost mine, I suppose. They are my niece and nephew. I cannot seem to get with child again. I have had a very painful miscarriage recently and fear that I am unable to bring a child to full term once more. With only one son, I long to give Richard more legitimate heirs. It is necessary for a man in his position.

Richard is away so often I hardly see him for weeks at a time sometimes, but he holds so many important positions which the king has made him responsible for, that it is inevitable, I suppose. He does try to fulfil all his various responsibilities to the best of his ability. He goes from town to town and village to village with his group of magistrates holding courts at which any man, rich or poor, can bring him grievances, and he will do his utmost to settle things to their satisfaction. He has become noted for his fair-mindedness and determination to give all men the same chance of justice, whoever they be. He has also become loved for it in these regions. People have got to know that he is above self-interest and is fair-minded and honest.

When he is not engaged in this work, he is visiting his various castles and estates, particularly Sherriff Hutton, Barnard Castle, and Pontefract Castle and making sure that all is well and that the estate managers are doing their job properly. He has appointed completely trustworthy men in each case, thank goodness. Sometimes I travel with him, for a change of scene, but not often. I find I do not have the energy for long days' riding. And I prefer to sleep in my own bed at night.

When he does make time to visit us, he finds it so hard to relax, being forever at his account books and writing important letters, that I have to beg him to take breaks, or the children and I would never see him at all. I worry about him, that he stretches himself too much and works far too hard. He does get very tired, and that is why I fear the plague may get him now, God forefend! I know what I am talking about; my own delicate health has often been made worse by exhaustion.

Sometimes, we entertain here, though not often, as neither Richard nor I like crowds of people in our home. We come here for its quiet. After years at court, which he hated and still hates, only going there when he has to, Richard prefers peace, like me.

Francis Lovell is a frequent visitor and Rob Percy, both old and very close friends of Richard's. They all go off hunting and hawking for days at a time together. Little Ned longs to join them, but he's such a delicate child he can only ride short distances without getting breathless with the effort. John has been promised that he will be allowed to go on the next hunting expedition. He is now ten years old and strong and vigorous. I cannot help comparing his blooming health with the frailty of my own poor little one. But Ned makes up for it by having an excellent mind like his father and enjoys books and quiet pursuits, thank goodness. But I see him looking at John sometimes with resentment in his eyes when he is playing some rough and tumble game, which Ned cannot join in. I suppose it is only natural for him to feel like this. All boys enjoy physical pursuits, and I know Ned would—if he could, but he is secure in our love, so I am sure feels no envy of the other boy in that respect.

Little Meg, George's eldest child, who is seven, misses her mother greatly still, but she took to me straight away as her new mother, and we are very close. I do not think she misses my sister as much as her little brother Edward does, though, and has adapted to her new life here very well. He is often a sad little boy and will rarely talk about George and Isabel, though. I encourage this, as it will help him to grieve for them. What can a child of his age understand about why his father was put to death or his mother was taken to God so young? I try to be a mother to him also as much as I can, but there is a certain guardedness in him; he never opens fully to one. I suppose it is understandable. He remembers his parents well, though he is only five. He tends to fear Richard somewhat, which is a pity. Perhaps it is because he so rarely sees this very important uncle. I must encourage Richard to give him some special attention when he comes home from London. The child is not as quick or bright as my Ned either, so they do not have much in common, though he is quiet like Ned and prefers quiet pursuits too. They get along well on the whole and play together happily enough. The tutors say he is a slow learner and easily distracted. Maybe this is because of all the traumas he has endured in his young life?

Oh god, I pray that my Richard does come home—and soon! I do not think I could bear to live if the plague claims him!

Margaret, Dowager Duchess of Burgundy, July 1480 Greenwich Palace

My Dear Mother,

My joy at visiting my beloved England after twelve years is overshadowed by my anxiety and concern for Edward. Have you seen him lately? He looks truly terrible. Really ill. He laughs it off when I express my concern, but there is a lot troubling him, I can sense, as well as his obvious bodily ills. He is now very fat, and any exertion makes him breathless. He never has his hand away from the wine goblet. Yesterday afternoon, I noted him filling it ten times! That is not good. His face has an unhealthy, pasty colour, and at board, he eats far too much—though he assures me that he has cut out certain foods now, especially highly spiced ones, on Dr Hobbes's orders, as his digestion is not what it was and they disagree with him. He has no energy at all, it seems, hardly takes any exercise—when before, as you know, he was forever out in the open air hunting or hawking—and was an excellent and enthusiastic tennis player! Now he just lolls around and hardly leaves the palace unless he has to, though I have persuaded him to take some short walks in the lovely palace gardens here with me each day. It is his favourite palace, after all, but he seems to have very little interest in it any more.

He admits to me that his mind is troubled too. I am not surprised. He says it is worry over the Scots troubles, which Richard has to go up north to take charge of. Edward has appointed him Lieutenant of the North. Edward keeps bewailing the fact that he is not sure he will be able to take charge himself and lead his soldiers into battle. He is patently unfit and he knows it! I believe he should do more to improve his health, but I see little evidence of effort on his part, as he seems depressed.

When we were alone, I asked him outright what depressed him so. He has a happy marriage with a woman he loves well—though I must admit I do not like her—she is too abrasive in manner, too arrogant, and can have a vicious tongue. He has many lovely children whom he loves dearly—and who love him. What could be troubling him so—apart from his health?

But he is evasive and flippant and laughs off my concern. He will not confide to me what is really troubling him inwardly. But I have a good idea what it is. When I mentioned George, his face blanched whiter than ever, and he turned his head away. He will not discuss his reasons for having him executed with me—says it will upset me more, as he knows I was so close to George and I still mourn him deeply. And I think Edward does too, though he will not admit it. He just said, 'It was necessary at the time, what I did. I had to do it. There was no other way.' And that is all I get out of him. Do you know any more about the reasons he took this ultimate, terrible decision? I know you loved George dearly too—he was the apple of your eye, in spite of his many failings.

I hear from Edward that you are thinking of entering the contemplative life and going into a nunnery.

Why, Mother, why ever should you do that? Isn't your present life of strict piety enough? It can't be George's sad end only, I believe. Terrible things have happened to you in life; you have been through many ordeals and lost many relatives and other people whom you loved. Does it all prey on your mind now? I feel you have been too much alone at Fotheringhay and must have dwelt on these things overmuch already. What you need is more company, not less. I am convinced of that! Still, you must have good reasons and I would dearly like to know them. I realise you would never come to court for company, as you hate the obvious licentiousness of the place. There are others who do too. Richard and Anne, his wife, have admitted they cannot wait to get out again whenever they come to court. They bemoan the fact that Edward has deteriorated, not only bodily, but in character—and put it all down to the pernicious influence of the Woodvilles—particularly the queen.

Edward was such a strong man, both in character, personality, and in body. It is sad to see what he has become. How are the mighty fallen! I still love him, I admit, almost against my will. At first, I hated him when I heard what he had done to George, but the hate all melted away when I met him again. One thing he has not lost, and that is his charm—the power to make people like him and side with him! I wish that you and he were not still estranged over the death of George. Please try to forgive him, Mother. He is contrite to a degree over it—I can see this. That does not excuse what he did, whatever his reasons, but he and Richard are your only living sons now and you should try to make your peace with him, I feel. I do not forgive him and never will in my heart, but I can still bear love to him as my brother.

It makes me sad that I am only here in England on a short visit and must return to Burgundy as soon as may be. So I will not have time to come up to Northamptonshire to visit you. Please forgive me for this. If you were at Baynard's Castle, it would have been easy for us to meet while I am in England.

Please write to me soon. I look forward to hearing from you.

Your loving daughter,
Margaret,
Dowager Duchess of Burgundy

Woking Old Hall, Surrey, Late November 1481

My Dear Henry,

I am sorry I have not written to you for a time. I expect you wondered what had happened to my regular letters of encouragement.

Well, I now need encouragement myself, for my good husband, Henry Stafford, who has long been ailing from the serious wounds he got at Tewkesbury, which never really healed in spite of the best doctors' help I could get for him, has finally succumbed and he sadly died a fortnight ago. I have been very busy arranging his funeral and interment, as you will understand.

I am utterly bereft, as he was a kindly and upright man and always treated me well.

I am now alone and facing a prospect I do not relish. The king, who does not trust me, understandably I suppose, is insisting on me remarrying and to Lord Stanley, a brutish, insensitive bull of a man. And one with half my intelligence, I am sure! He is one of King Edward's chief advisers, and I know why the king wants the marriage—he hopes Stanley can keep me in check! I feel very bitter and angry, as Edward has handed over the entire management of my vast estates to Stanley also. How dare he! As if to imply that I am not perfectly capable of overseeing and managing them myself—which I have always done very efficiently. He has only to ask any of my tenants or servants for verification of this, and they will tell him what a hard taskmistress I can be! But the real reason he has done this is because he wishes to punish me for being a Lancastrian and not supporting him. It is sheer spite! He wishes to humiliate me, that is it—but I am not easily bowed. In this man's world, I have always had to fight to get my own way and survive as a woman, in spite of being wealthy. I have learnt a lot about precisely how to do that!

I believe the king has also instructed Stanley to do all in his power to stop me communicating with you and to forbid me to meet with any of your supporters. He is obviously convinced I am forever hatching plots against him. Maybe I am—or not—but he has no proof anyway and will not get any of my men to say a word against me. They are too loyal—and paid too well—not to keep silence on what I do and say!

Do not worry. Even if the usual avenues of communication are cut off by the king's efforts, I will find other ways to get letters to you—and to your Uncle Jasper—who now has a large number of your supporters gathered in Brittany ready to follow him if any chance comes to further your cause. There are also many secret supporters of yours here, in England and in Wales. I am often in communication with their leaders, who keep themselves in readiness for an uprising, when the time comes.

And I feel the time is fast approaching which I have always assured you of! The king is in poor health.

The news spread like wildfire that he had to give up his idea of leading his armies into battle against the Scots! Apparently, he managed to travel as far as Nottingham to join Duke Richard in October, after several months of putting off the expedition, to everyone's puzzlement—and the great annoyance of his leaders.

But, when he arrived there, he was so exhausted and ill he had to hand over the whole command to Duke Richard and retire in humiliation back to London after a good rest! His life of excess and debauchery is no doubt catching up with him at last! He is only thirty-seven, but looks fifty. He is vastly overweight and drinks so heavily I should think he is never sober! He is on the downward slope, as far as his health is concerned.

Maybe he has a hidden mortal illness, though he is still quite young in actual years? Who knows, maybe he will die soon?

And if he does, what then, you may ask? Well, his young son Edward, Prince of Wales, who is but ten years of age, is the heir apparent. He has spent his childhood away from court at Ludlow Castle, on the Welsh borders, being brought up mainly in the care of the queen's brother, Sir Anthony Woodville, Lord Rivers, as his mentor and guardian. He is still but a child and far too young for some years yet to be king! There would probably have to be a Protectorship. And who would be his Protector—and Protector of the Realm? That is debatable. But it would probably be between the Duke of Gloucester and the queen's brother. She herself, even if she wanted to, could not undertake this most important position with the new young king still in his minority. She would be barred by reason of her sex. It would have to be a man. As I pointed out, somewhat bitterly before, women are not deemed capable of important tasks, particularly in administration, even if they have proved themselves—as I have—very capable! And there has to be an adult in charge of the realm. There is an old saying, 'Woe unto the land where a child is king!' That has happened twice already this century and was partly to blame for this endless fighting for supremacy which has gone on since. I anticipate a great deal more strife if all this happens.

I know I am speculating, perhaps far into the future. But somehow I feel it will not be long before all this comes to pass!

And then the stage may be set for the Lancastrian cause to re-emerge—with you as its figurehead! Your supporters, here and in Brittany, would not be slow to see the window of opportunity.

King Edward's shaky truce with France could also collapse at any time! Louis is in poor health too, having had two strokes recently. When he dies, the truce of 1475 will die with him—and the enormous amount of gold Edward gets every year from France! He has been tempted to aid Duke Maximilian, who married the Duchess Mary of Burgundy. The duke has been fighting a losing battle against France for Burgundy's sovereignty and begged for Edward's help. But I expect Edward cannot bear to risk losing all that precious gold! So he has refused help and his own sister Margaret may be in danger if Burgundy is over-run by French occupying troops—as seems likely. The king is very avaricious and obviously cares more for money than human life.

That is a common sin amongst men, I am afraid, in all walks of life!

Well, my dear son, I have given you much to think about. Ponder well my speculations on the possible near future, and write to me when you can.

Your loving mother,
Margaret, Countess of Richmond

Richard, Edinburgh Castle, 4 August 1482

My Dear Edward,

Well, here I am, occupying Edinburgh, and it has all been surprisingly easy! Considering it is their capital, I had expected a fight with the Scots to capture it.

I can hardly believe that we have more or less just walked into this city and taken it over, lock, stock, and barrel, with little or no resistance whatsoever from King James's men!

And the king himself is already a captive in the great castle. But not put there by me, but by his own disaffected barons! Would you believe it? They had grown tired, it seems, of his ineffectual rule and his preference for consorting with his favourites, mostly low-born men, such as artists, musicians, architects, and the like. He refused to listen to their counsel, so they staged a coup when he had marched as far as Lauder with his army to fight us. He was angry, no doubt, at our sacking and burning of Dumfries. They took several of his favourites and executed them summarily, then imprisoned him—to show that they meant business.

What a turn-up for the books! By the end of July, we had entered this city without the loss of a single man, and I have made it my business to rule that my men do not touch a hair on the head of any man, woman, or child here nor plunder their goods. So far, I am being obeyed implicitly. The city is completely under our control.

Now, I am sending you word of this by the same most effective courier system which you set up earlier, using a relay of riders, so you should have knowledge of what has happened here in only a day or two. But that is not the end of it. I am determined to press on, now that Edinburgh has been secured, and return to Berwick, where I left Lord Stanley continuing the siege while I came to Edinburgh with my remaining army. I can only afford to pay the army for another two weeks, so I must dismiss all but those men needed to resume the siege of the citadel of Berwick. Pray we are successful this time. Stanley must have worn them down somewhat if he has kept up the offensive in my absence, as instructed. The actual town gave in easily to us last time around, but that strong castle is another matter! Being on the coast, the sea is its main defence and it is impossible to approach from that side. The landward approaches are always very well defended, but I am determined to take the citadel this time. It will finish off a most successful Scottish campaign—where, to be honest—we have hardly had to do any real fighting at all!

The Duke of Albany is still proving very troublesome. Now he has changed his mind and decided he does not want to continue trying to become King of Scotland in place of his brother. He has decided he will be happy if we can just get him back his lands and titles. That is good news as far as I am concerned, as I do not think the Scots will welcome him as their new king. He is so erratic and untrustworthy that they would rather stick with the devil they know than the one they don't!

But, of course, there is one sticking point here. You had half-promised your daughter, Princess Cecily, in marriage to the Duke of Albany when he became King of Scotland, instead of King James's heir. Now he is not to be king, all that money you have already paid towards Cecily's dower should be returned. And

I intend to get it back, all £5000 of it, from the ruling lords, before I leave Edinburgh. Also, I intend to insist that they leave Berwick Castle to its fate. They must not resist our new attempt to take it back into English hands—where it belongs. With just the actual defenders in the castle to deal with, I am sure we can bring it off!

I am permitting Albany to seal a bargain with the Chancellor of Scotland, whereby, if he agrees to swear allegiance to his brother James for good and all and cause no future trouble, he will receive a full pardon and restitution of his estates, which he is so anxious to get back. I do not hold out much hope that he will keep to the agreement, but that is not my problem after I have returned to England. I am afraid he is another rather like Clarence—if not worse. He has been nicknamed Clarence in a kilt, I have heard. He is fickle and faithless to his own kin and will probably remain so, whatever oaths he swears now, so I intend to get him to swear an oath to keep faith with you, Edward, before I leave here!

A message has just come in to me while I am writing this—it is from the magistrates of Edinburgh. It states that if, as their conqueror, I will withdraw peaceably from their city with my men, they promise that, if you no longer wish to marry Cecily to James's heir in the circumstances, they themselves will refund every last penny of the dowry money to you in yearly instalments. So I do not have to go a begging or threatening, after all, before I leave. Another problem off my back!

I will write again and let you know the outcome at Berwick, which I hope may be a successful one this time!

Then, I pray that I will at last be able to go back to a bit of peace at Middleham with dear Anne and the children. You have no idea how I long for that blessed day!

I hope that you are now looking after yourself more and taking real steps to safeguard your health. It shocked and saddened me that you were not fit enough to command our troops in this Scottish enterprise, and I know you were very disappointed yourself to have to give over the command to me. I have done my best, as always, to carry out your wishes here and will continue to do so. I thank God that he has given me the strength to command effectively and pray I may remain strong and healthy to continue my work until the campaign is over.

Your affectionate brother,
Richard

Westminster Palace, Late August 1482

My Dear Dickon,

I am amazed at how much you have achieved in such a short time! You are truly my rock—my trusty and able brother. To have occupied Edinburgh without a fight was incredible enough (where were King James's soldiers while you carried off this feat?), but now to have regained Berwick at last—permanently this time, I hope. After thirteen changes of ownership between us and the Scots over the years, it is about time our right to regard the town as English was settled once and all!

I only wish that I could have been with you to witness your victories! I had fully intended to take charge of the army, as you know, when we began this wretched Scottish War, but I had to concede defeat—not to the enemy, but to my own diminished bodily capabilities. I realise—too late—that I have overdone the feasting, wine, and women over the years, and my health has suffered badly in consequence. I am far too overweight and tire easily. I have to admit it is all my own fault. I am determined to take myself in hand, diet, and drink a smaller amount. I already seem to participate far less in my recreational activities with the ladies. I do not have the energy any more! It will be hard for me to accept the changes I must make in my lifestyle, I know, but otherwise I can achieve far less physically when it comes to things I should do—such as lead my armies into battle. Thank God I have you as my strong right arm! I will reward you handsomely when you return home, you know that.

I seem to have become much weaker in so many ways since George's death, not just physically. Having to make that decision to have him executed killed something inside me. I have lost much of my strong will, and, I admit, I let others guide me when I cannot decide what to do—perhaps not always the right counsellors or the right council. You were right when you said the Woodvilles have too much influence over me. I would not admit it then, but I freely do now! When you are by me, it is fine. You always seem to know exactly what to do when problems strike. You are most decisive and energetic. But I feel somewhat lost without your presence these days, even though I know you are achieving great things elsewhere in my name—as you have lately been doing in Scotland. It takes a lot for me to admit all this, and I have done so to no one else—not even the queen. Although I still love her, I find I cannot always trust her now, or her motives. I admit she is most self-seeking, like all her family, and can be venomous at times to those who oppose her. A pity. But you are as honest as the day and have always been my greatest friend and confidante, as well as my dear brother!

I hope that the Scots will settle down now that you have given them something to think about. They must realise that you are an opponent to be taken on at their peril!

The king's younger brother, the Duke of Albany, has been a particular problem, acting towards his brother in much the same way—if not worse—as George did to me.

I hope the fighting will come to an end soon, Dickon, and that you will come home safely to your dear wife, Anne, and your boy, Edward, whom I know miss you greatly, and to me. I need you by me, now more than ever!

Your affectionate brother,
Edward, Rex

Anne, Westminster Palace, Christmas, 1482

All the bells of London are ringing, it seems, to welcome us into Westminster. I am almost deafened by them. They are mainly for Richard, of course. He is the hero of the hour!

The king ordered a wonderful reception for us at the city gates. We rode in escorted by the Lord Mayor himself and his aldermen, resplendent in all their finery, who were waiting there to greet us and welcome us to the capital!

I was a little embarrassed, really, as I know it is all for Richard, not me. I am just his wife.

We are cold, stiff, and very wet from our long journey down from Middleham, which has taken nearly a week, in unrelieved, miserable December weather. It was mostly raining, but we also had to contend with fog and several icy mornings. I am so thankful it is over. I am coughing again, probably from a chill I caught sleeping on damp linen in one of the inns we stayed at. I hope it gets no worse. Richard is concerned for me, but I assured him it is nothing.

Now, all the misery of our long journey and my indisposition fall away as we reach the gates of Westminster Palace itself. For Edward, the king, is here himself to greet us! Richard's most beloved brother is welcoming him with open arms and tears of joy streaming down his ruddy face. He kisses Richard heartily on both cheeks, then bows to me and kisses my cold hand, which he has withdrawn from my sheepskin muff. Then he hands me down from my grey himself, like any groom. Richard has gone down on one knee to kiss the king's ring, but now he rises, smiles directly into my eyes, and kisses my hand too. Then he takes my arm to escort me into the palace. He includes me in this great welcome. I am his beloved wife, and he is proud to acknowledge me as such in front of all! He wants the whole court to see it. I begin to feel warm inside, in spite of the damp cold which still envelops me from the journey and a burning sensation in my throat and chest. The servants, grooms, and equerries, the whole castle population, it seems, are cheering and clapping us as we enter the palace, the nobles of the court lining the corridors and thronging the anterooms we pass through. Only the queen is noticeable by her absence. But then she never did like Richard, and the feeling is mutual. He sees right through her. And she has always feared and hated his popularity with, and influence on, her husband.

Edward claps his hands, and hot mulled wine appears as if by magic and is served to us on golden trays in golden goblets. I drink deeply, then cradle my goblet in my frozen hands and feel the welcome warmth surge through my veins.

'My Lady Anne, I pray your cold little hands will warm quickly now you are here. We cannot have you ill! I have ordered hot water to be brought for both of you so that you may take long, hot baths and banish the December chill. Then we will eat and talk for a long time in my privy chamber. I cannot wait! But first things first.'

So the king did notice how cold my hand was when he kissed it.

Now we are in the Great Hall, with roaring log fires on both sides and the pageantry of Edward's Court all around us, like I imagine an exotic tropical jungle would be—though I have only seen pictures in books of such places. The strong colours, and stronger smells of hot bodies and perfumes, envelop us in their pulsating life.

They are almost overwhelming, almost too much a contrast to the long days' travelling in the raw December cold. I have always hated this court, as Richard does, but today I must admit, I welcome its warmth, if nothing else, and am grateful for Edward's hearty welcome.

Now, I take a closer look at the king and am truly shocked by what I see.

His bonhomie is sincere and unforced, but his face is flushed unhealthily, not only from the heat. His eyes have a feverish brightness, it seems to me. I can see that Richard is concerned too. But he does not comment on his elder brother's unhealthy appearance; he says nothing at Edward's endless goblets of wine—brandy—wine too, until the hectic flush on his genial face becomes really worrying.

The king is obviously no longer in control of himself, I think. He is grossly fat and obviously dependent on the huge amounts he drinks. I catch Richard's eye when Edward is pouring himself yet another goblet-full and shake my head. He acknowledges my concern for his brother by a slight nod, followed by a frown as he watches Edward down it in one gulp. It is a worrying sight, as he seems to drink continually. What a sad state of affairs that this splendid man, with his erstwhile splendid physique, should be reduced to this sickly looking alcoholic! He seems so pathetically grateful to have Richard back by his side. He is even reluctant to let him out of his sight when we go to our rooms.

Later, bathed and dressed in clean clothes more suited to the court, we attend the special feast Edward has had prepared for us. I am almost too tired to eat and my chest hurts. But I make a show of enjoying myself for Richard's sake.

The king drinks copiously throughout—his capacity is incredible. Richard drinks and eats most sparingly—he always has. Seeing what has happened to his much-loved brother through overindulgence is enough to put him off his meal altogether, I should think.

After the feast, I am nodding with tiredness and plead the excuse of exhaustion to the king and Richard to retire to my bed. But it is more. I feel now that I am ill, though I say nothing of this in front of Edward. Later, I suppose, I will have to admit to Richard that I seem to be going down with a lung affliction again. I have had a weakness in my chest all my life, and I think I am in for a bout of bronchitis. The only cure is bed and rest and keeping in an even temperature. Then I must be patient as it runs its course. Even so, I can see it will be sure to ruin Christmas for Richard if I make a fuss. But I will not.

And I think Edward wants Richard to himself anyway. Even if I were not exhausted and ill, I would have felt it right to withdraw and leave them to talk together without interruption. They must have so much to say to each other—so much to catch up on. My ladies will mix me horehound from my herb box, which I always carry with me for just such a time. It is good for coughs and lung-congestion. Also, I think, a little poppy juice will help me to sleep.

Richard, Westminster Palace, Christmas, 1482

I fear that my poor Lady wife, Anne, is sick. The journey in that damp cold was surely too much for her. I should have realised that her delicate constitution could not stand the rigours of the journey in winter and ordered her to stay at Middleham with our son. But she insisted on coming, in her quiet way. She wanted to be with me at Christmas, as she knows how much I hate the court, even though I was longing to see Edward again. I am used to travelling in all weathers, in all seasons, and the weather has no effect on me. I am hardened to it, I suppose. But Anne is a different matter. She is now confined to her bed and missing all the Christmas celebrations, not that I think she minds too much. Even well she is of a retiring nature and hates this court, as I do, normally.

But I did look forward to coming this time, as I wanted so desperately to see my brother. I was so worried about him. And I had reason to be. I realise now that there must be something seriously wrong with him. It is not just the heavy drinking, though that is bad enough. He is in a physical lethargy most of the time, and he was always such an active man.

Things are preying on his mind, apart from his obvious ill health. Last night, we had a long conversation when he poured out a lot of his worries.

'That wretched Louis! He is involved in so many machinations all over the place that it is no wonder he got the nickname of "The Universal Spider". He spins his web over his unwitting victims, then sucks them dry! Now it is this impoverished Maximilian of Burgundy! Louis is backing him into a corner with his demands for Burgundy to be handed over to France and lose its independence for ever. Maximilian has held out well up to now, but he has run out of money and resources to continue his fight against the wily Louis. He has begged me again, and again, to help him. But what can I do? If I go against Louis, we will lose that precious grant of £50,000 crowns a year, which we have been receiving since Picquigny! The money from the last seven years has built up into a sizeable sum now in the treasury, along with the profits from my wool-trading, especially with Burgundy. If Maximilian has to give in to Louis, then all future trading with Burgundy will lose its profitability when Burgundy becomes part of France. If I go against Louis, I lose the £50,000 crowns every year! The wily old frog has even tried to seduce me with a further offer recently to extend the truce made in 1475 for another whole year beyond whichever of us dies first. He knows how to tempt a man!

I must admit, I am at my wit's end what to do I am just too tired to deal with it. I am in between a rock and a hard place. How do I extricate myself? Tell me that. Whatever I decide to do will hit us hard!'

'You have always been an excellent diplomat as well as a capable soldier and statesman. There will be a way forward. Just let it ride for a bit and stop worrying. After all, Louis is in such poor health after those two strokes recently he may just die soon. Then this problem will resolve itself without you having to do a thing. But then, of course, you will probably have to face losing the yearly grant from France if he does die. I think you must realise that that is inevitable. After he is dead, I doubt if the new rulers will continue handing you cash for nothing every year! You have done very well up to now out of that treaty I disapproved of at the time, I must admit! So just resign yourself to the inevitable. Money is not everything—though I know you set great store by it. I think you must concentrate on getting fit again, so that you can deal with these international problems easily when they arise, without undue worry, as you have always done!'

'I am sure you are right, Dickon. You usually are! My mind is not as clear as it was. I cannot be decisive over important matters like I could before.'

'You are only forty, Edward, still a young man. I feel the problem is clear for all to see—except you, it seems. Though I thought you had realised your own main personal problem when you wrote to me in Edinburgh.'

'What do you mean?'

'Why, your heavy drinking, of course. And your constant overeating. You vowed you would do something about them, not to mention your overindulgence in the charms of Mistress Shore—and others. You must take yourself in hand. Only you can do it. You are the king. No one can order you to indulge yourself less!'

'But when one is stressed—and a king has more stresses than most with all these wretched international problems to deal with—they are my comforts, I suppose, my escapes! But I know you are right, Dickon. If you were here all the time to keep me on the straight and narrow, I might succeed. But you are so often away in your beloved north.'

'You appointed me Lord of the North! And, like everything I undertake, I have tried to carry out my responsibilities there to the best of my ability. And I cannot do it sitting around at court here, you know that.'

'I know, Richard. Of course you must be on the spot to deal with problems there. But I hardly see you now. Just when I need you most!'

'I will come and visit you as often as possible, you know that. I seem to spend my whole life on the trot. But I will find the time for you somehow. Never fear.'

'I feel I have been handing over my responsibilities to you lately rather too much. But you are so able! What I would do without you I do not know! You have always been indispensable to me—especially now.'

'I have a strong back, though small in stature. I can take it! I have always been only too pleased to carry out your wishes. Though, I must admit, I'd like a rest sometimes!'

'I have taken you too much from Anne and the boy, I know it! You deserve a holiday. When Christmastide is past, I give you permission to return to Middleham and stay there as long as you wish. You must try to relax, Richard. You are a workaholic, truly! Even when not fighting or administering on my behalf, I know you rarely rest. Anne has told me of this.'

Richard, Westminster, New Year's Day, 1483

Thank goodness that my Anne seems to be almost recovered after spending several days in bed over the Christmas period. But she still has a persistent cough. She passes it off lightly, but it is still very worrying. She never seems quite well, really. I have told her to take care of herself and stay in the warm. There is no question of her accompanying Edward and me on the New Year Hunt.

This is the one physical activity that the king is still capable of, as he is seated most of the time on horseback. He needs a huge, strong horse now, capable of taking his weight. But it is not to be an all-day affair any more, just a morning one. We will return for lunch, and in the evening, the spoils of the hunt will no doubt be served up for the special New Year Dinner.

As we ride in about one of the clock, tired, hungry, and dirty, after starting out just before dawn, which is so late at this time of year, but with a fine stag and several pheasants, pigeons, and hare, there is an anxious messenger waiting for the king. He, like us, is dishevelled and exhausted, but for very different reasons. He has ridden post-haste from Dover with bad news—news that the king has dreaded for weeks but hoped would never come. Duke Maximilian of Burgundy has capitulated. He has made peace with Louis on December 23rd. He has given up the unequal fight against Louis and his overwhelmingly stronger military force. Burgundy will now become annexed to France, under Louis's rule. It will never be an independent state now. A new treaty has been agreed upon between Louis and Maximilian, called the Treaty of Arras.

And even worse, perhaps, even more humiliating for Edward and his elder daughter, Bess, Louis has reneged on his long-standing agreement with the king that Bess would one day marry the Dauphin and become Queen of France. He plans to marry his son to Maximilian's daughter Margaret instead, and she will bring, as her marriage portion, the counties of Artois and Burgundy to Louis!

And already, French warships are sailing into the Channel aggressively!

It is a deliberate kick in England's—and Edward's—face. And Edward reacts predictably.

'How dare he! The little weasel! I always knew he was untrustworthy!'

'Did you? What about the Treaty of Picquigny? You trusted him then!'

'Yes, well the terms he agreed to were very favourable to us!'

'The enormous yearly grant, you mean? I told you then that he would change his mind and break his promises whenever it suited him. But you would not listen!'

'No, Dickon, as usual, you were right! But I wanted—I needed—that money so badly. And it seemed such an easy and profitable way out at the time! Better than fighting!'

'You should have taken a longer view, knowing Louis's character and unpredictability!'

'I do not know which is worse, losing the money now Louis and I will be at loggerheads again, losing the high profits on the wool trade with Burgundy, or seeing one's favourite child humiliated in front of the whole world! Oh, why didn't Louis die? He is hanging on by a thread to life by all accounts! Then none of this would have happened! He is too bloody-minded to die, of course! It is too much! I just cannot cope with it! But I know that what Louis has done deserves punishing! We must not take this lying down. I depend on you to do something about it all, Dickon.'

'Declare war on France, you mean? And I thought I was due for some time off. You promised me that over Christmas—remember?!'

'I am sorry, Dickon. But we cannot ignore Louis's actions. He must be made to pay, somehow! I am sure you will think of a way! Now I have to find my poor daughter and tell her the bad news. I just hope we can find a new marriage partner for her of equal standing, but I doubt it. And I am in no mood for starting negotiations with other countries now. And I am too tired. What shall I do, Dickon?'

'Well, at this moment, the best thing you can do is have your bath and some lunch! And then we will sit later, with Will Hastings as your advisor and closest friend, and thrash out a course of action, as, unfortunately, one seems to be needed!'

Henry Tudor, Rennes Castle, Brittany, Late January 1483

'But, Uncle Jasper, Richard of Gloucester is only five years older than me, and look what he has achieved!

'And now even more honours, estates, and positions have been heaped on his head because of his spectacular success in the Scottish Wars. The King's Parliament has passed new laws to raise taxes and to honour him further because he deserves it!

He has been given permanent possession of the Welsh Marches. And Lordship over all of Cumberland and even those parts of Scotland he has conquered. If he manages to conquer any more, he is to be lord over them too—for life. And this will be passed on to his successors in perpetuity!

It makes me feel very inadequate. What have I achieved? What have I had a chance to achieve, stuck here since I was fourteen—and before that, in the backwaters of Wales all my childhood! He was leading men into battle at fourteen, commanding them!

I fear my Lady mother was wildly wrong in her predictions about my so-called glorious future. And old King Henry. Nothing will dim her vaunting ambitions for me!'

'You are still young, lad. There is still plenty of time for you to achieve much! Richard is unusual in that he started his achievements so young, but then, remember, boyo, he is the favourite brother of the king. He has had everything going for him from the start. You have had everything against you. But things will change soon, I am sure of it!'

'How? Tell me that! Just how?'

'The king is sick, for one thing. Everyone knows he is going downhill. And he has lost his grip as a ruler. He depends on Richard of Gloucester a great deal to carry out his wishes. He may die soon. Then, everything will change. George of Clarence is dead, who was next in line to the throne and Edward's eldest son is but eleven years old. He is far too young for kingship! As your mother told you, there would have to be a Protectorate until he is at least sixteen. And, in the meanwhile—who knows? Something may happen to him!'

'Why should it? He is heavily protected, along with his younger brother, Richard, in Ludlow Castle on the Welsh borders! His guardian and mentor is Earl Rivers, Sir Anthony Woodville, the queen's brother. What could happen to him? And, if King Edward should die soon, he would be even more carefully guarded!'

'But perhaps they would move him to London to prepare for his coronation? He would be crowned quite quickly, even if he could not rule for several years yet. It would be more possible for anyone wishing him harm to get at him there!'

'Even in the Tower of London, where kings-to-be spend the last night before their coronation, by tradition?! It is the most impregnable place.'

'Even there. Anyone really determined to do the Crown Prince harm would find a way somehow to breach even those formidable walls!'

'Anyway, what has all this to do with me? We have gone off the subject rather.'

'Not at all. If the king and the Prince of Wales were both dead—don't you see? It would be your chance to make a play for the kingship! You have just as much right to the Throne by virtue of your ancestry as this boy prince. And I have heard rumours—word gets around—that he may not be so blue-blooded as one would think . . .'

'Are you mad, Uncle? Where would I start? And what do you mean—rumours?'

'You have hundreds of Lancastrian supporters now. They have been gathering quietly here and in England for a long time, waiting for the right moment to rise up and challenge the Yorkists. That would be it! And even if the prince is a bastard, as some think, then it would be easier still. He would have no real rights at all!'

'But all this is based on wishful thinking and hearsay, Uncle. King Edward may live for many years yet, after all. And the Prince of Wales would still have to be killed. Who would kill a young child to succeed in his ambitions?'

'Many, boyo, many! Ambition is a powerful incentive to carry out necessary deeds—evil or not!'

'Well, I would never do such a thing, and I hope none of my supporters would kill the child in my name. I would never condone the deed!'

'You would not have to. You would have nothing to do with it! And there are many people in high places in England and here, remember. They would arrange all that was necessary. You would have to lead an invading army against England—that would be your part!'

'Where would the money come from—the soldiers, the horses, the arms, the ships? And I have no experience of active warfare in the field. Only the theory—which you have taught me. In my head, I know all about tactics and such, but I am a complete novice! How could I command men?'

'Many nobles in high positions, famous soldiers, such as the Earl of Oxford, de Vere, would aid you. The necessary money would be obtained somehow. All you have to do is wait!'

'More waiting. That is all I have ever done, wait!'

'Let us hope the waiting will not be long, now! Preparations for an uprising are well in hand. A little more patience, boyo, and you may yet triumph!'

Anne, Middleham Castle, Yorkshire, Early March 1483

'Thank God we have arrived home safely at last! The journey was another nightmare of snow, wind, and sleet, but at least I am not ill this time!'

'Amen to that! I was really worried about you over Christmas. In many ways, it was a good thing that we had to stay at court longer than I had anticipated for me to attend the King's Parliament, because it meant you were forced to rest while you waited for me. Or I know you would have insisted on coming home before you were properly better. But you still have that cough sometimes, so you must take care. No more riding on horseback and getting soaked through when we have to travel! I know you hate the litter I made you come home in, but at least you were protected in there!'

'You are right, I do hate the litter! Have you any idea how uncomfortable it is? One feels every bump and shake. I swear my bones are all bruised. I much prefer a horse's back!'

'Never mind. At least you seem all in one piece!' Richard squeezes my arm as if to test its soundness, and I catch his hand and raise it to my lips.

'My dear lord! At last we will have some time alone together and time for Edward and John. When all these important personages who have accompanied you home go soon, what bliss it will be! The king promised you a holiday from your duties and cares. How long do you think he will leave you alone to live your own life now, after fighting his battles for him all this time?'

'Who knows? Hopefully until Eastertide, when I expect he will want us back at court.'

'Oh dear. You do need rest, my love. But, if I know you, as soon as these guests have departed, you will be just as busy riding around administering your estates here and doing the accounts. You are so restless and energetic, I swear that, even if there were no work to do, you would make some!'

'There is much to catch up on here, Anne. I have been away for a long time. But I promise that you and I and the children will find time to be together. I want that as much as you do, you know that. Now we must rejoin our guests. The laws of hospitality still have to be observed, however tired one is! Later, we will be alone, my love!'

The promise in Richard's voice washes away the bodily exhaustion I feel. Maybe I will be fortunate now that we can forget the king and his constant needs and demands for a while. Maybe my husband will get another son on me! That is what I desire most, apart from my dear lord's presence by me . . .

Edward IV, Westminster Palace, London, 9 April 1483

I can hardly believe that a dip in the river after a simple fishing trip has brought me to this. It was the first really beautiful spring day—I could not stay in—I longed to be outside. But the weather changed in the afternoon, and it poured. I was already wet when I tried to get out of the boat at the landing stage and missed my footing.

I got very cold after the day's heat. I had been drinking heavily in the boat—as it was such a warm day. I had a hot bath and went to bed, as advised, but the next day I had a fever, which has worsened steadily. Dr Hobbes's remedies are useless—I have grown weaker each day.

Now there is a bad pain in my side. I can scarcely catch my breath. I am coughing up disgusting brown phlegm streaked with blood.

I see those around my bed shake their heads—I know I must be dying. I must somehow order my affairs.

If only Richard were here—I need him so. He would help me—he always has.

Dear Will Hastings is on one side of my bed, all concern. He truly cares for my welfare, the best friend a man could have.

Who is that on the other side? Ah yes, Thomas Grey, Marquess of Dorset, the queen's son. He dissembles concern.

I am terrified for my son, little Edward, only eleven, away in Ludlow—the Crown Prince. He will be king soon, when I am gone. But I must make sure that everything is settled for his welfare.

Richard—yes. Richard—he will do the right thing. He will make sure little Edward is safe and these two warring court factions, the Woodvilles and the old nobility must swear—yes, swear—over their dying king—to cease their enmity and become dedicated to the new king's welfare.

The Woodvilles—a self-seeking, venomous tribe, I realised this too late—I have not asked for the queen. She will want to be in charge of the boy—of the country—but this cannot be. Richard—it must be Richard. He must be Edward's Protector now that I am about to quit this world.

I will make him Protector of the Realm—I can trust him utterly to do the right thing. He has always been completely loyal to me in life. He will continue to be after I am dead. I do not have long, I know it. My eyes are covered by a thick, shifting mist. I see faces of others long gone—whom I loved and lost.

George, forgive me. I am sorry, so sorry. I regretted signing your death warrant, believe me. I have never ceased to be melancholy since that dreadful day you died in the Tower—forgive me, forgive.

Richard, I need you, my dear brother. Where are you?

I must call for my confessor now. I have done all I can to make sure things are settled for the future of the realm and young Edward. Now I must make my peace with God. I have so many sins to confess. Oh, mea culpa, mea culpa.

Anne, Middleham Castle, Yorks, Mid-April 1483

If I did not know how strong-minded and level-headed Richard is, I would have feared for his sanity the last few days. His soul is torn asunder with overwhelming grief for Edward. Never did a man love his brother more dearly, I think. He seems lost, yet he has always been the truly strong one. And he knows it.

For Edward was weak in many ways. Where ruling the kingdom was concerned and as a soldier, he was very strong in will, but as a man, he was weak-willed—often, and easily led, especially in his last years, mostly by the Woodvilles. He admitted as much.

Richard is his own man. He could never be led into anything, whether personal or in the interests of the country, which he did not believe was right or needful. He is like a firm rock in a raging sea; completely steadfast; a calm and dependable support—to me always—and to his friends and followers. Edward depended on him utterly. Richard knew that too. But, at the moment, the rock is almost torn from its moorings. But I know that however many torments of soul beset him at this dreadful time, he will survive, as strong and determined as ever.

It is a terrible burden to bear. First the loss of George, foolish George. And now this.

So unexpected, out of the blue! Edward was not very ill, at first. Just a chill, they said. But he deteriorated rapidly. His profound melancholy contributed to his death, the doctors vowed. He seemed to just give up. And in only one week, he was dead.

I pity the Duchess Cecily, his mother. What torments must she be feeling, poor woman? All her sons dead now, except Richard. How she despised him for his physical frailty as a boy! He has told me of it, and I saw it for myself, but not for years now. She came to realise his true worth and admires his strength of spirit and courage in the face of adversity, for he takes after her in this. She has had a terrible life, full of tragedy and loss and has survived it all by her indomitability!

Richard was not told at once about the king's illness—not even about his death! No one bothered to inform him, until the lying-in-state and the funeral were all over and Edward joined his ancestors in the crypt at Windsor. Richard never had a chance to say goodbye to his beloved brother, let alone attend the funeral. This must be a terrible source of extra sadness to him. They were so close.

A messenger eventually arrived with the devastating news. Richard was felled like a lightning-struck bough. For two days, he shut himself away and would speak to no one, not even me. He left his food and drink untouched; would not unlock the door to let the servants bring it to him. I begged him to let me in, to offer comfort where I could. But he ignored me.

Eventually he emerged, looking like a ghost, so white and drawn was his dear face. I longed to run to him, hold him in my arms, kiss him, and enfold him close, giving him comfort in the only way I know, but something held me back. My own husband—and he was unapproachable—even to me!

Then the second messenger came. And Richard was galvanised into action. It was as if he had awoken from a deep sleep or had emerged from a dreadful prison of the soul no one else could enter. He is normally a man of action and few words, but now words rushed from his lips in torrents. Instructions—endless instructions to his men! And then came the letters he must write. At last, he stopped long enough to talk to me.

'I must go to London as soon as possible! The king appointed me Protector of the Realm before he died. Hastings wrote post-haste to tell me. Otherwise, I would not have known! That Woodville woman has deliberately prevaricated.

I know why. She does not want me there. She wants to get the Crown Prince safely to Westminster before I can arrive and oversee his swift coronation! Once that is done, I would not be officially needed, and the Woodvilles would be in complete charge. Apparently, they have set a date for the coronation already, 4 May. And the reason for this haste is most apparent to me. And to Hastings. That is why he has sent me these instructions: "I advise you to secure the person of the prince as quickly as you can, then get you to London!"'

'Will you have to go to Ludlow to get him?' I ask uncertainly.

'No, I have written to him already concerning his father, the king's death and offering him my deep condolences. I have also sworn my deep allegiance to him. Now I must gather my men and try to meet the new king and his retinue on the road, long before he reaches London. According to Hastings, he will set out almost at once with his guardian, Lord Rivers, also Vaughan. It is the only way!'

'The only way? To do what?'

'To save him from the queen's clutches and her overweening ambition for her wretched family!'

'But she is his mother. Surely she will do the right thing by him. What harm can he come to in her care?'

'She hardly knows him, remember. He has spent his entire life at Ludlow. What she really wants is to get him into her care so that she and her family can assume authority and be the real power in the land now that Edward is gone. Not if I can help it! If I can get to the boy quickly, I can take him into my care at once—as Edward wanted—and forestall her plans. Now there is a great deal to do, for I must be away as soon as may be. I must leave you, my dear Anne!'

'How long for? Will you stay in Westminster once you have the prince secure?'

'I will have to. But, for how long? Who knows? It all depends on what happens then!'

Richard, Northampton, 29 April 1483

I am moving into very dangerous waters now, I know it. My plan to secure the boy king here and put him under my protection, as my poor brother Edward desired, is fraught with many difficulties.

I had arranged to meet Earl Rivers, the boy's uncle and governor with his charge at Northampton, but reaching here, I found the wily Rivers had sent the boy ahead with Lord Richard Grey and Vaughan to Stoney Stratford. This is fourteen miles nearer to London!

Earl Rivers came to me very nonchalantly at my inn here in Northampton and explained that the only reason his nephew had been sent on to Stoney Stratford was because there was not enough accommodation for his large retinue in Northampton. It all sounded innocent and convincing enough, I suppose, but I am naturally cautious and something about it made me suspicious, so that I smelt a rat. Something was not quite right—I sensed that strongly.

The Duke of Buckingham was of the same mind. He had ridden post-haste from Brecon Castle in Wales to join me in my endeavours, after promising to do so in his earlier letter to me at Middleham. He has already become a tower of strength. I am grateful for his enthusiastic support in the difficult course of action I have started. Now there is no going back. I am determined to see it through, for Edward's sake. He may be dead, but I am still utterly loyal in my intentions towards him and his son. I will carry out his wishes as well as I am able.

I invited Lord Anthony to dine with us at our inn and he accepted with eagerness. The landlord provided us with excellent meat and wine and the evening grew very convivial. But I was always on my guard, and at last, when Rivers departed to his own lodgings, completely won over, I think by our seeming acceptance of his good faith, Buckingham and I got down to the real business in hand. Both of us were clear-headed enough, having managed to actually drink very little, while Rivers had partaken deeply.

'Rivers is but a Woodville pawn. He is obeying the queen's instructions, I am sure of it. There is more to all this than meets the eye. Rivers is too affable, by half!' I asserted.

'To be sure, Stoney Stratford is that much nearer to London. They are desperate to convey the boy there as soon as humanly possible. It is a race against time. With him in their hands, they are in power. Perhaps they had hoped to avoid you altogether, my lord, by making such haste,' declared Buckingham.

'Well, they have failed. I have never trusted the queen. And now she is showing her hand most decidedly! We must get the young king away from Rivers. Also, we must arrest the queen's son, Lord Richard Grey and old Vaughan. They guard him too closely. I will have them taken into custody and decide what to do with them later, when we have secured the king. Earl Rivers must never get to Stoney Stratford to claim his charge. We must get there first and take the boy into my protection.'

'Will you have Rivers done away with then, my lord?'

'Not yet. All must be kept as well-ordered as possible. This will be a bloodless coup. We must not terrify the young king. That is the last thing I wish to do. I will send an escort of armed soldiers now to surround Rivers's inn and have him locked in his quarters. In the morning, we will set out for Stoney Stratford while he remains in custody here with an armed guard. Later, we can decide what to do with him, also Grey and Vaughan. Richard Grey in particular will not escape me, as I have an old and bitter score to settle with him!'

'It is a clever plan, my lord, but will it work, do you think?'

'It has to. My life, your life, in fact the lives of anyone who is not a Woodville supporter, will be worth nothing if we fail. I am certain of that! While I will carry out my dead brother's wishes to the best of my ability, I must not forget that this Woodville family is very devious—and dangerous. Once they get into power, with the boy king as their figurehead, our lives would be forfeit!'

Richard, Stoney Stratford, Early morning, 30 April 1483

I must admit Anthony Rivers was very convincing in his feigned bewilderment at his arrest and committal into my custody earlier at Northampton.

'My Lord of Gloucester, I confess myself at a loss to understand your actions. Do you imagine that I take the young king into danger? He has been in my care practically all his life. Naturally, I was requested to bring him to London by the queen, my sister. Where is the harm?'

'By the queen! By the mother who has hardly set eyes on him or shown much interest in his welfare since his birth! Why the undue haste now to bring him into her care?'

'To prepare him for his coronation, my lord, on 4 May!'

'So soon? Is not all this somewhat precipitate, Lord Rivers?'

'It has been thought best—'

'By the Woodvilles no doubt, acting on the queen's instructions? Well, I am officially young Edward's Protector and guardian now, at the late king's express wish—made on his deathbed! So I will make the decisions concerning his welfare, along with my chosen council, when we reach the capital. As I plan to reinstate most of the men who were my brother's trusted councillors, we shall manage very well. You are therefore relieved of your custody of the child forthwith!'

He continued to protest, but I had him taken away and put under secure lock and key, where he will be completely impotent to thwart my will. He will be confined indefinitely at Stoney Stratford, then at Pontefract Castle, one of my most secure strongholds, until I have decided what shall be done with him.

The young king was, perhaps, much less pleasant towards me as I approached him here a short while ago. We had ridden fast at dawn, Harry Buckingham and I, from Northampton.

Edward was ready to move out on the road to London and was already mounted, surrounded by his ranked escort of armed soldiers. He did not take kindly to my news that I was his new Protector and that I had confined Lord Anthony Rivers. I assured him I would explain my actions simply, when he haughtily enquired where Lord Rivers was, for he is but a child, after all, and complicated political reasons were not appropriate, though it is known he is a highly intelligent boy and mature for his age.

I saw him looking hopefully along the ranks of my men, hoping to see him there, no doubt. When he failed to do so, I saw him blanch a little, but he remained completely in control of himself, nevertheless. His two other companions, Lord Richard Grey, the queen's son, and Thomas Vaughan, his old retainer, looked puzzled also.

I knew I must offer a complete explanation to them as well as I could. It was only fair on the boy.

'Please to re-enter the inn, Your Majesty, and also your chief attendants!'

I nodded at Grey and Vaughan, who at once dismounted, as the boy king reluctantly did so too.

The Duke of Buckingham and I ushered the three of them into the hostelry, and when we were alone, I tried honestly to explain my actions.

'Firstly, I offer my deepest condolences at the loss of your father, the king, who could not have been more dear to me in life. Now that he is gone, sadly, I am determined to carry out his last wishes, made on his deathbed, to the letter. This is for your safety and the future safety of your realm!'

'My safety? Surely I was quite safe with my dear guardian, Lord Rivers? He has cared for me and instructed me since I was but two years old. He is like a second father to me!'

'Circumstances have changed drastically, Your Majesty! And there are many things you know nothing about, which you have never been told. You have been brought up quietly and led a most sheltered existence, away from the hub of events, so could not understand what has been going on. You have only ever been instructed in one side of things—that of your mother's family, the Woodvilles!'

'And what, my lord Uncle, has been going on that I am in ignorance of? Kindly explain!'

'I will do my utmost to. And to make my purpose with regard to you clear. Certain ministers about the late king have helped to ruin his health by encouraging him in his excesses! Indulging in too much drink, food, and women, he was abusing his body dangerously, which therefore became weak and unable to withstand a serious illness when it attacked him. These men must be removed from power, forthwith, in order that they might not play the same game with you, his son, as with your father.'

"I suppose you include my brother, the Marquess of Dorset and myself in this incrimination my lord?" interposed Richard Grey indignantly. 'The king needed no urging to indulge himself easily, you know! You cannot blame my brother or I!'

'Be silent and hear out the Lord Protector!' shouted Harry Buckingham. And Grey, purple in the face with suppressed anger, shut his mouth reluctantly. Never a brave one, as I had noticed on the battlefield, he had no desire to risk Buckingham's considerable ire further.

'And now, these very men have openly conspired, not only to deprive me of my lawful Protectorship, but have laid a trap for my life. I narrowly escaped assassination last night in Northampton when going but a short distance from my inn to talk to some of my soldiers. If it had not been for the presence of mind of my bodyguard, I would be dead now!

And I know who was behind it! Earl Rivers, the Marquess of Dorset, and Lord Richard Grey here—whom you say you trust so implicitly! There are dark forces commanding them, Sire! They were obeying instructions!'

'Who instructed them?'

'I know they carried out the wishes of the queen, who has been my implacable enemy always! For my own safety—and ultimately for yours—I was forced to arrest Earl Rivers at Northampton. He is now in my custody and will be charged with attempted murder shortly! Then I will decide what shall be done with him. He will be punished, never doubt it!'

'Please, do not harm him! He has been my good friend and kind mentor always.'

'You may be king now, Edward, but you are still a child in years. You must accept that, whatever I do, will be done for the best!'

The young king's head drooped visibly at that, but he did not let his emotions overwhelm him, showing resolve and control well beyond his age, for which I could not help but admire him.

'I have always trusted the earl, the marquess, and Lord Grey. I have had no reason not to. They are my friends. I would not lose them! Surely, as the new king, I can command that they be not harmed? They have shown no ill will to me ever! And as for the governing of my realm, I am certain that my mother, the queen, and my chief nobles—'

'No longer the queen, lad! And the ruling of the land is for men, not women. Your mother has no rightful authority in law, though she dares to assume it!' Buckingham roared angrily. 'The Duke is correct, Your Majesty! I agree. You have been deceived; the truth hidden from you! Now listen, and he will try to explain in detail what you should now know.'

'Everything has happened so fast, my Uncle of Gloucester, that I can hardly take it in! But I must admit, I have been deceived in one thing—I was never informed by my guardian when news of my father, the king's death came to Ludlow, that you had been given Protectorship of my realm and person. I should have been told!'

'Indeed you should, Your Highness, indeed you should. What your father, the king, did as he lay dying in appointing me—the one he trusted most in the world—was the best he could do in the circumstances, for the good of his kingdom and his heir! He knew himself to be surrounded by those who, though making promises to work together after his death for the good of the country and yourself, would soon forget those deathbed promises after he had gone! The Woodvilles and the nobles are at loggerheads. They always have been and probably always will be! Your father may not have seen you very often, but I assure you, he loved you well!'

'Then why was I sent away to Ludlow as an infant? Why did he not keep me by his side at court?'

'He wished he could, but he also wished to protect you from the many evil influences there. It has been a place of depravity. I have always avoided it as much as possible, even though I often missed my brother too and longed to be with him! He often talked about you to me. He kept you well away from court in Ludlow so that you might avoid the bad things there, which he himself had often fallen prey to! He wanted your mind kept clear and unsullied. If you do not understand this now, you perhaps will when you are older. Your father was in a web, mainly of the Woodvilles' making, and could do little to extricate himself, especially as his health worsened. I saw it all, and feared for him. I also hated it and prayed he could be delivered from their influences. But it was not to be. But you, he wished to keep safe! Now I will undertake that task, most heartily!

For many years, since I was not much older than you, I served your father faithfully in council and in battle. He trusted me utterly, more than anyone else, as his most loyal brother, because I kept to my motto 'Loyalty binds me', where he was concerned, as I loved him dearly and admired him greatly. I tried never to let him down.

Now, because of my experience, my good reputation, and my nearness in blood to your father as his favourite brother, indeed, his only brother now, he chose to appoint me as Protector of the Realm and of his heir—you, Edward.

Will Your Highness accept me now as your new guardian? And will you be content with your father's decision? I understand it will be hard for you to accept all these changes in your life, but it is necessary, and right, for you to do so.'

'It seems I have little choice. And as I respected my father, though I hardly knew him, I will be content with the government he arranged for me. But I cannot help feeling the loss of my friends.'

'That is understandable, especially in one so young, but you will make many new ones, I am sure.'

Edward nodded miserably. I could not help being somewhat sorry for him. He had spoken falteringly, with no enthusiasm, in accepting his new lot, but with a quiet dignity.

After all, in a moment, his whole world had collapsed around him in effect, and though he had a glittering future, his mind must have been a turmoil of confusion and resentment. It was inevitable. I understood that. I tried to speak kindly to the boy.

'Your Highness, it is necessary, for safety's sake, to return to Northampton until word comes to me from London concerning the effect my actions have had upon affairs there. If all is well, then it will be safe to take you there soon. Lord Hastings, your late father's dearest friend and Lord Chancellor, will contact me as soon as he can. He is loyal to you also, Sire, as he was to your father for many years. Together, we will make sure that no harm can befall you.'

The young king nodded mutely again and allowed himself to be escorted back to his chamber in the inn. He seemed to have accepted the situation. In truth, what else could he do, though surrounded by a large armed guard? He would be looked after well and guarded securely until I could take him to London safely.

He broke down a little at last and cried eventually, as children will, even older ones, when faced with situations they cannot understand, still less control. This was when he was informed that his personal attendants, most of whom had been with him all his life, were to be replaced with men of my choosing. I saw him shoot a glance of pure hatred at me through his tears at that point, possibly because he had given in to his feelings in front of me, the instigator of all his misery that day, as much as for the loss of his trusted servants. But it was necessary, like all else I have carried out. Who knows but that the old body servants may have tried to get him away at his pleading in the night and take him to the queen? They are, after all, loyal to him, not me. They had to go.

That seemed to be the last straw for the boy after an eventful and traumatic day.

I grieved to disturb him so, but I had no choice in the situation. Perhaps he will understand later on, when he sees it is all for his own good. I hope so.

As soon as he was safely lodged, I had Richard Grey and Vaughan promptly arrested. They had made no attempt to ride off when they saw what was happening. They would not have got far. They would be imprisoned in one of my northern castles, possibly Sheriff Hutton, or even Middleham, until they could be brought for trial.

Then I told the young king's servants and considerable armed guard that they were no longer needed in the circumstances, as the late king's wishes had now been carried out, and the boy king was delivered safely into the hands of my Protectorship.

I half-expected some dissension, or resistance, but they did not demur, accepting the situation and my authority unquestioningly. After all, their leaders had been arrested, and they were only too happy to drift away to their various homes in small groups, muttering quietly.

Then, I felt little anxiety, as all seemed to have been achieved quite painlessly, with no blood-letting or loss of life, as I wished, thank goodness.

After all, I had done no more than to assume the office of Protector, as my poor dear brother wished.

Fast messengers had been dispatched to Hastings and others, informing them of the last two days' events and the successful outcome. I awaited the answers quite calmly. I had done what Edward wanted; what he expected of me, as always.

What would happen when we eventually reached London was in God's hands.

Edward V, the Young King, Stoney Stratford, 30 April 1483

I knew I would become king one day, but I had not given it any real thought yet, believing it would be many years off. My father was but forty, after all, far too young to die.

Now I am torn away from all I have known, even the people I know and trust. Uncle Richard of Gloucester is an unknown quantity to me. I have heard that he is an upright, honourable man, a great soldier, fair-minded, and certainly very loyal to my father. But I do not know him.

And he is to be my new guardian and Protector and order my life in all things from now on. His aspect seems rather grim to me. He does not often smile or say much. I do not find him approachable, as I did my dear Uncle Rivers, now taken from me, I do not know where? I think he has been arrested, but everyone is so evasive and will not answer my questions about his whereabouts, although I am now the king and they should surely obey me in all things?

Why is Uncle Richard doing any of this anyway? I do not understand his actions at all. He told me that it is needful to put me under his protection at once, before we reach London and that a plot is afoot! It seems I am in some kind of danger, but I do not know exactly what.

He says he will give me a full explanation soon and that I must trust him, as he is only carrying out the last express wishes of my late father.

Although I am the new king, it seems I am still just a child to Uncle Richard and the Duke of Buckingham, his chief supporter. I have no powers yet. I just have to do as I am told and accept their authority until I am crowned. The date of 4 May is not long off, my coronation day. Then perhaps things will change for me. Surely I can then order things the way I want them, not the way Uncle Gloucester wants them?

I must bide my time, be patient, and put my fears aside. But I am frightened, very frightened, by what has happened today. I feel cast adrift on a dark sea, with no land in sight.

Princess Elizabeth of York, Westminster Palace, Evening, 30 April 1483

'Quickly, quickly! Haste is of the essence! We must go into sanctuary at once! When Richard of Gloucester arrives, our lives will not be worth a fig. And we must secure Edward's treasure! It must be taken from the Tower and come with us into the sanctuary. Once Gloucester gets his hands on it, we will never see it again, and it represents all my poor dear husband's hard work over the years! Surely I, as his wife, have first right to it, to secure my children's futures?

And my favourite pieces of furniture and those lovely tapestries that cost so much must come too. Hasten to get them into the sanctuary, before Gloucester arrives! Oh my god, that it has come to this. We are all undone!'

'But, Mother, why do you fear Uncle Richard so? He was devoted to our poor dead father and has little Eddie in his protection—as father wished. What do you think he will do to us? He is now the Lord Protector! And father willed it so. So why all this haste into sanctuary? Is it really necessary?'

You stupid girl, Bess. Where are your brains? Think about it! Don't you realise that Gloucester hates me and mine—always has done? And the feeling has been mutual from the minute I arrived at court in 1464. I do not trust him an inch. With Edward gone, we will see his true colours. He has always reminded me of a snake about to strike. And now he will. I am sure of it!

Quickly, girl, get your things together! Pack your jewellery and most precious possessions. The servants can do the rest.'

'You are beside yourself, Mother! All will be well, I am sure of it.'

'I think not. Now, do as you are told and do not argue the point. I think I know men better than a mere inexperienced slip of a girl!'

I just do not understand why Mother is making all this fuss. Of course, I know she is angry and upset that she has lost control over Eddie to Uncle Richard. She does like to be the controlling force—in everything. She controlled Father completely, though he was king. He was butter in her hands. He gave into her every whim. That was not good. Though she is my mother, I know her faults—only too well!

She is a hard woman, self-willed, overbearing, and most determined. She makes life difficult for anyone who dares to cross her—her own family included. I am often the victim of her vicious tongue. Her will has to be our will.

I know one's duty is to love one's mother. But I cannot. I have tried, God knows. She is too brittle, avaricious, and self-seeking. One does not make an enemy of her. Those who have, have paid the price. One does not go against her without expecting dire consequences. She will pursue revenge to the bitter end!

I adored my dear father, the king. He was a lovely, kind, and loving man. All of us children loved him dearly—and he us! But Mother—she is another matter. She even envied us his love, I know.

I miss my father unbearably. What my life will be like now that he has gone—and having to bear the brunt of all Mother's moods and tantrums as the eldest—I hate to think. I am now of marriageable age. If Father were here, he would be searching for another suitable husband for me after Louis, the King of France, rejected me last year for his son, the Dauphin, after an understanding of many years. Father was furious about it. And I was very upset. I had expected to be Queen of France one day!

Father promised me he would do it soon, just before his last illness. I was his favourite child always. And he always did what he promised me.

What will become of me now? I will be nothing but a mere nursemaid in the sanctuary to my young brother and sisters. And I will be at the beck and call of Mother continually. I will not be able to escape her constant demands. She has no patience with the little ones. She has always left their care to others. It will be hateful—though I do love them, because I want to spread my wings now, and I will be imprisoned against my will. I want my freedom and I want to have some fun now I am grown up. I looked forward to the court balls and meeting lots of young men who would make much of me. Now I will see no one but Mother, the children, and the servants. It is awful to think of. I want to be free more than anything now.

I do not fear Uncle Richard. I have always liked him a lot on the occasions he has come to court to see my father, which were few and far between in recent years, as he has been living in the north, where he has been ruling virtually as a king in his own right. They call him the Lord of the North, and the people there trust and love him.

He has a quiet, gentle manner. He says little, but what he does say is always to the point. He has kind eyes that crinkle at the corners when he smiles, which is rarely enough, though he has smiled at me many times. I am sure he likes me, as much as I do him. But when Father and he were together! Then there were many smiles and laughs! They were devoted to each other and loved each other's company.

I look forward to his coming! I do not care what Mother thinks or says. Surely he can mean us no harm? Father appointed him as Protector because he trusted him so. We must trust him too, I am sure.

I confess I find him attractive as a man. If he were not married to Aunt Anne, a gentle soul, whom I respect and care for, I might dare to tell him so. Sadly, I can only do it with my eyes and show him how I like him in my manner, as things stand. But it would be hopeless anyway. Girls in my position get little choice in a marriage partner. It is all political. I have been brought up to realise and accept that.

But it does not stop me dreaming of what might have been, if things were different. I know that I am beautiful, not with such beauty as my mother had—like a porcelain doll and very delicate, but I have my mother's hair and I see men stare at me. But I am not really interested in their stares. The only one I am interested in is out of my reach.

William Hastings, Lord Chamberlain, Westminster, 1 May 1483

My Dear Lord of Gloucester,

The news for which you have eagerly awaited is good, very good!

Your clever coup at Stoney Stratford, with no bloodlet, filled me with joy and admiration when the news reached me very late last night. It was a clever and most adroit manoeuvre you carried out on Anthony Woodville and the others in young Edward's party, Lord Richard Grey and old Thomas Vaughan. You managed to turn the tables, evidently with no real problems!

Here, all is in confusion at the court! The erstwhile queen and her son, the Marquess of Dorset, ever my enemies both, and yours, desperately had all the queen's most precious possessions moved into Westminster Sanctuary in great haste.

This includes the late king's treasure from the Tower. Unfortunately, it had already been moved there before I had knowledge, or I would have stopped the transfer, if I could.

So eager was she to get herself and her goods into the abbot's lodgings that she had a huge hole broken through the wall from

Westminster Palace, so that all might be done more easily and quickly. She was ever avaricious, with an eye to the main chance. Poor Edward must be turning in his grave! She plans to lock herself and her children away inside the sanctuary, terrified, it seems, now she has lost control of the situation, of what you will do when you arrive! The marquess has disappeared—none knows where. I have men searching for him now. I believe he has taken a portion of the treasure with him.

No one seems willing to help her cause, you will be glad to hear!

The queen and the marquess sent messengers far and wide during the night, I have been informed, to those whom they assumed were Woodville supporters, beseeching them to raise an army to wrest the young king away from you by force, but no one has so far responded. Her so-called friends are both evasive and non-cooperative, thank goodness! Perhaps the queen realises now how truly hated she was. She was only tolerated because Edward was so much loved by the people. So now she has her back literally up against the wall and does nothing but weep and bemoan her lot. It is about time she was brought down and her haughty arrogance received a damaging blow, which, I assure you, it now has!

The Woodville cause has collapsed completely!

The chancellor, Thomas Rotherham, the Archbishop of York, when he heard the news from me this morning, at once seized the Great Seal, his precious charge, and rushed to the queen at Westminster Sanctuary, pressing it into her hands personally. He has always been a supporter of the Woodvilles, God knows why!

But this afternoon, being informed of the illegality of his action, he went back quickly to the sanctuary and demanded its return. He is obviously too old and indecisive to hold such an important position any more! The Lords have at last recognised this and taken the Great Seal off him permanently. It is now in a place of safety, you will be relieved to know!

I was up at crack of dawn, sending messages and notes here and there, greeting all the lords and gentlemen who have flocked to my standard. I hope it is to offer you support, but I expect a lot have just come to seek counsel or gain my protection in the changed circumstances. As the late king's dearest friend, people seem to trust me in these conflicting and confusing times. They must believe that, in your absence, I know exactly what the late king, Edward, wished for the good of the country and the Crown Prince.

I today gathered the Lords in an informal assembly and warmly defended your actions as right and proper in the circumstances. When your letter arrived, they were further reassured, as it was read out to them and your good intentions revealed. Your explanation satisfied them when you vowed that you had not captured the young king, but had rescued him and the realm, both of which had fallen into the hands of those who, having ruined the honour and health of your father, would not be expected to show any more respect for his son!

They agreed that you were right to do this for your own safety, also for the safety of the kingdom and young Edward, and to arrest Rivers, Grey, and Vaughan.

They actually cheered when you wrote that you would soon bring the new king to London for his coronation, though that event would now be some time further off than 4 May, which the Woodvilles had worked towards, to ensure they got into power quickly.

Everything you have done has been approved wholeheartedly by the Lords, and they eagerly await your entrance to London with Edward, as indeed I do, my lord.

There are only two bad things to report to you.

On 29 April, the Woodville fleet, commanded by Edward Woodville, sailed with a portion of the late king's treasure on board, which the Marquess of Dorset had pilfered and was obviously determined to get away from England as soon as possible to feather his own nest! Perhaps he forsaw the outcome of his family's attempts to take power. He deserted the queen and her children fast enough in the sanctuary. These self-seeking Woodvilles! They are not even loyal to each other! You would think he would have stayed and supported his mother in the circumstances!

I will acquaint you at once of any more developments here as soon as they occur.

I await your arrival with alacrity.

I remain your trusted friend and supporter,
William Hastings,
Lord Chamberlain

Edward V, Westminster Palace of the Bishop of London, 4 May 1483

My uncle Richard of Gloucester has take great pains, I must admit, to put me at my ease and comfort and reassure me, though I find it very hard to relax in his presence, as I still feel very uneasy and resentful at what his actions, lawful or not—though he assures me they are wholly lawful—have meant for me personally.

I understand that my late father's wishes are paramount to his actions, but what about my wishes? I am King now, after all. Am I to have no say in who my companions are to be? I do not like the men appointed to care for my personal needs, though they are respectful and not unkind. I miss my familiar body servants so. Most had been with me all my life. I feel all at sea, as if on a leaky boat which may sink at any moment. I have no idea whether I am really safe now, as Uncle Richard insists I am, or whether I am being deceived. It will have to be proved to me that all is for the best, before I really begin to relax and trust this stranger uncle and the Duke of Buckingham, his close companion and supporter.

I enquired today where Lord Rivers, my dear guardian, Lord Richard Grey, and Thomas Vaughan, my old retainer, were. I feared the worst, but have been assured they have been sent away to places of safety in Yorkshire, to different castles owned by Uncle Richard, I believe. They are not together, that was made clear. It was not spelt out, but I know that imprisonment was implied.

I am trying to come to terms with all that has happened to me so quickly. After all, as soon as I am crowned, I will be king indeed, even though my uncle will be my Protector until I am sixteen, and, in effect, the real ruler of the realm until then.

But I will have some powers, surely?

Today, we travelled from St Albans at dawn, where we had spent the night, to London and entered my capital city with crowds cheering and waving banners to welcome me. All the church bells seemed to be pealing at once. The noise was overwhelming. But somehow, none of it touched me. It all passed over me. I did not feel happy inside. I have not felt happy at all since leaving Ludlow.

And I cannot forget that this should have been my coronation day.

They dressed me very grandly in blue velvet for my entrance on horseback, with my new Protector riding on my right and Harry Buckingham on my left, both attired in black. Perhaps this was deliberate to make me stand out? I do not know.

I was feted and applauded all the way from the city gates to the palace of the Bishop of London, where I am now lodged. I am assured that these are only temporary lodgings, until my coronation, which will be soon, Uncle Gloucester says, but no actual date has been conveyed to me yet.

From my effusive greeting at the city gates by the Lord Mayor of London and his aldermen and a train of leading citizens to my arrival here, where all the great lords of the realm waited to greet me, to kneel and pay homage to their new king, it has been a dazzling feast of colour and sound. Everyone has been in high spirits and in their most splendid clothes, and the streets have been lined with elaborate welcome banners, while multicoloured streamers have rained down from the upper windows of all the buildings we passed.

But strangely, none of it touched me. I felt nothing, just numb inside. It was like a dream, unreal somehow.

I have lost all those I loved and depended on. And I am not even going to be allowed to see my mother or sisters and brothers, who are shut up in the sanctuary at Westminster. True, I hardly know any of them, but they are my family and I would like to be able to visit them at least.

But it is not to be at present, apparently. Why? Could my family hear all the bells clanging and the people cheering as I passed by earlier? They must have been able to and know it was all for me. Do they wish they could be reunited with me, as I do with them?

I just do not understand what is going on really. Why is my mother in sanctuary with my brother and sisters? What is she afraid of? Is she afraid of Uncle Richard? She must be, or she would surely have come out to greet me, with everyone else. But why is she afraid? Should I be also? Am I safe or really in great danger? I can only hope it is the former and that God will protect me as the new king by divine right, soon to be anointed.

Surely no one means to do me harm? It is treason to even speak against a king, let alone do violence against his person, with the most appalling punishments.

I must pray most earnestly that God will keep me safe from any enemies—if they exist—and I somehow feel that they do. Somewhere among the cheering crowds, or even closer to me, an assassin may be waiting. I feel vulnerable and exposed. But I must not dwell on that, but on more cheerful things and trust all will be well. God help me!

Crosby Place, Richard of Gloucester's Town House, 5 June 1483

'My dearest Anne! Right glad I am to see you and to have you with me once more! Affairs of state weigh heavily on my mind, and I have been closeted all morning with my chief councillors. Knowing you would be here soon, I managed to extricate myself a short while ago with Francis here, and we have been attempting to relax over lunch with a few beakers of best Yorkshire ale. I had some barrels brought down to me from Middleham last week. The London ale is not a patch on it, is it Francis?'

'Nay, my lord, you are right there. Lady Anne, your coming is like a breath of fresh moorland air from Richard's beloved county!'

'How is the boy? You did not bring him? I was so looking forward to having you both here with me. Is he unwell again?'

'A nasty spring cold, Richard, which hung on for weeks and left him with a persistent cough, which will not shift, however he is physicked. And with his usual shortness of breath, I did not wish to risk his health more travelling all this way, especially as the London air is so bad. You know how delicate the child is.'

'Sadly, I do. It is something we just have to accept. Little seems possible to make him stronger. As a boy, you know that I was delicate too, but somehow grew out of it. Perhaps it will be the same for little Edward?'

'Maybe, but I often despair of his ever becoming strong like other boys his age. John is such a picture of health and strength and I know Edward envies him.'

'But yourself, my dear. Are you well?'

'Well enough. And I was determined to come to you, heat or not! You have lines of worry on your brow, Husband, which you did not have before. Francis, what has been worrying him so much lately? I thought that all was well here now in the capital and all you had to worry about was preparing for the Coronation, a joyful occasion!'

'Lady Anne, much has happened. But I think it would be better if Richard tells you in his own way and in his own time.'

'Yes, all I will say now is that there are seething undercurrents of unrest which I can feel and do not like.'

'Where, my dear lord?'

'As yet, I cannot quite place my finger on what exactly is wrong, but I fear there is disaffection and plotting afoot against my Protectorship!'

'By whom? Is it the Woodvilles again?'

'They are probably at the bottom of it! There are still many in high places loyal to the queen, unfortunately.'

'What can you do?'

'Watch and wait for one of them to put a foot wrong. I have my watchers, listeners, and spies. So has Harry Buckingham, and he tells me everything he finds out!'

'You have a good council to help you govern? Do they not take some of the weight off your shoulders?'

'I welcomed the same men to my council board who had served as advisers and ministers to my brother. It seemed best. And they ratified my position as Protector at once when I arrived with the young king. There were no problems then. My power depends on their goodwill.'

'So the problems have appeared lately, then?'

'It would seem so. But I will flush out any who go against me behind my back, never fear!'

'How is the little king? Has he accepted you yet?'

'He is a withdrawn child, very studious and learned for his age. I am afraid he still regards me with obvious suspicion. I know he does not trust me. I have tried my best to be kind and understanding to him, but he does not respond. He is malleable enough though, I suppose, in spite of his quiet arrogance, which he must inherit from the Woodvilles and does as he is bid. We moved him to the chambers of state in the Tower, the most fitting place for him to stay until he is crowned.'

'When is that to be? Have you decided yet?'

'The coronation date is tentatively set for 24 June, with Parliament convening the day after, but it may be moved forward a bit, depending on whether all arrangements have been made. There is so much to do in preparation for it, you have no idea! For example, there are many tailors fashioning satin, velvet, and cloth of silver and gold into ceremonial costumes for the young king, his household, and the many lords who will attend. It takes a long time if it is done properly. And Master Peter Curteys, keeper of the king's wardrobe, likes things done exactly so!'

'And Edward's mother, the Dowager Queen?'

'Steadfastly refusing to come out of sanctuary, though I have given her many promises that no harm will come to her or her children. All I am met with is tears, scorn, and indignation. She is her own worst enemy! It would be better for her—certainly for the children—to come out. Then she could take her place as Dowager Queen and live quietly somewhere. I would provide her with adequate means to live comfortably. This I have also promised, but she just sneers at my suggestions, calls me thief for removing the treasure she purloined from the sanctuary to a place of safety where the Woodvilles cannot get their hands on it! She seems to think she has a right to it, because Edward amassed it. I have told her categorically it actually belongs to the state now, not to her.'

'It must be most unpleasant, cooped up in those small airless chambers in the bishop's palace in this very hot and humid June weather!'

'It is her choice to be uncomfortable. She is not a prisoner. She can come out any time she likes. Princess Elizabeth has told me she begs her mother every day to reconsider, for the children's sake and relent, but that woman thinks only of herself. She cares naught for the health of her little ones. She is inordinately proud and obviously sees giving in to everyone's pleading as a slur on that pride! It is more important to her than anything else. How Edward stood her, let alone loved her, I do not know. And the princess is desperate to be free. She longs for fresh air and new companions. But her mother has a will of steel and prefers to let her children suffer, and herself, rather than capitulate to me and accept the present situation.'

'That is a great pity. And King Edward, does he go to visit his family in sanctuary?'

'He has been only once, as far as I know. He now realises it is his mother's choice to remain there and not of my doing, thank goodness!'

'My lord.'

'Yes, Francis?'

'Is there any other news? I confess that Woodville woman and her ways weary me!'

'And I! I dread going to the sanctuary, though I have to. But as little as I can. I do have more to tell you, Francis, but first, I really must insist that my dear Anne here rests and refreshes herself after her long journey. Then I will acquaint you with other matters. Anne, please do not think that I am trying to bar you from knowing about what is going on, but you look so tired, fit to drop, and I can tell you later on. You should not be concerned with these burdening matters at the moment, which, after all, only I can deal with. Go now then, my dear one, and later on when Francis has gone, we will rediscover each other after so many weeks apart!'

'Very well. I suppose I should be grateful that you acquaint me at all with affairs of state. Many men tell their wives nothing of their work, thinking it is none of their business and beyond their understanding!'

'Well, I am not one of those, am I? We have always trusted each other with every confidence. You are more than a wife to me. You are my dearest companion and friend, as Francis here has been my close companion since boyhood. I trust you two more than anyone else in this world.'

'Thank you, my lord. I have always been proud to be your friend and confidant. Now, what were these other matters you would tell me?'

'Well, I have dealt with the Navy, which was disloyal under Sir Edward Woodville. It was simple enough. I made it known that a free pardon was offered to all soldiers and sailors who deserted their ships and declared for the Protectorate! There were a few hardliners, but most came over straightaway. But Edward Woodville managed to get one of the ships away to Brittany with a large portion of the stolen treasure from Edward's treasury in the Tower! Apparently, the Marquess of Dorset had it put on board at once when he purloined it, at the time Elizabeth, the Dowager Queen took the rest of it into sanctuary. After that, he disappeared and cannot be found anywhere. It has probably gone to promote the cause of that Henry Tudor, calling himself the Earl of Richmond!'

'Could Tudor stir up any real trouble for you? He must be twenty-five years old now, and his supporters have been growing there in Brittany over the years, especially since Tewkesbury!'

'Edward did his best to get hold of him, without success, as you know. But Duke Francis of Brittany was obdurate and devious. Perhaps I should try, when my present worries here have been solved. But I have more pressing matters to deal with here at home. And I remain unconvinced that he poses any real threat to the Crown. Splits are appearing in the council I appointed. After the coronation, any competing interests could become a bitter struggle to gain the young king's ear, as he will soon be powerful in his own right, when he comes of age at sixteen. It is essential that the Protectorship is continued until that time!'

'Splits? You mean it has divided into opposing factions?'

'Not exactly opposing, but there is rivalry, certainly. One cannot help but be aware of it. Buckingham's swift rise to power as my stalwart supporter since Stoney Stratford and his continued pre-eminence in the council is resented by many, particularly by Hastings, Stanley, Morton, and the Earl of Northumberland. Their noses have been pushed out of joint somewhat, I suppose! Some private meetings have taken place with this group, which I was not invited to. I only found out about them by chance, from Harry Buckingham. That does not bode well.'

'You mean you think they are plotting against you?'

'I do not know. I hope not. But be assured, I will find out, by fair means or foul, Francis!'

'Hastings? Surely not? I can hardly believe he would be implicated in plotting against you. Look how he has supported you ever since Edward's death!'

'One would hardly think so, especially as it was he who was so anxious to get word to me at Northampton of the Woodvilles' attempt to secure the young king quickly, before I could do anything about it! But Hastings and his group have also met several times already with the boy privily in his Tower apartments, according to Buckingham's spies. What has been said and done there I have yet to find out, but I will.'

'Maybe they just visited him in a kindly fashion, taking pity on the lonely, sad boy? Could that not be a more innocent explanation? After all, you visit him, so do many others, I believe. And these men were at the heart of the late king's government, and hope, no doubt, to be at the heart of the new king's. Perhaps they just want to get to know him, and he them?'

'True, but why this particular group altogether? I am suspicious by nature, you well know. Life has taught me to be so! I do not like what the meetings might infer. They want to assure themselves of continued power under the new king, I am sure, as you say. At the moment, they have rivals for power in my Protectorate and have had to take more of a back seat lately, which they probably do not like! Anyway, I have instructed Buckingham to find out what they are up to by chatting with them in a friendly fashion out of the Council Chambers. In this way, he may discover their true intentions and then tell me about them!'

'I pray all will be well and that your suspicions are unfounded, my lord.'

'So do I, Francis, but I must confess that it is not so much Hastings alone whom I worry about, but the fact that I have had reason to distrust the other men in his group, at other times. Stanley, in particular! I cannot be certain of them, unfortunately. Bishop Morton is another one—devious in the extreme, I would say!

'That Hastings should mix with them so much and show that he resents Buckingham—and my trust in Buckingham—is what disturbs me most! Buckingham has proved his loyalty and goes on doing so. He is a steadfast rock to me at this difficult time—as you have always been, as my dearest friend. I have to trust someone, and I trust him! And, as you know, I have always believed that loyalty, once declared, should be maintained. Buckingham has given me no reason to doubt his, so I must maintain mine towards him also! If Hastings resents that, so be it!

'And now, my dear Francis, I must go to Anne. I shall be glad to throw off these weighty problems for a few hours in her calming company!'

Francis Lovell, Crosby Place, London, 18 June 1483

'My Lady Anne, I fear Lord Richard has become possessed. I have never seen him in such a great rage. He was beside himself. He seemed to lose all control! He has done a terrible thing! I would never have believed it possible of him. I am still shaking from the horror of it!'

'Dear Francis, you terrify me! What has he done?'

'If I had not witnessed it, I would not believe it!'

'What? Tell me!'

'Lord Hastings. He is dead! Richard had him summarily beheaded, no trial, no chance to defend himself, hardly a moment to make peace with his Maker! Just bundled straight out of the White Tower on to Tower Green and executed! The executioner did not even have a proper block for him. They used an old piece of wood left lying around there from some recent building works.'

'How dreadful! And Richard ordered this?'

'Yes.'

'Why, by all the saints?'

'Because Hastings was a traitor to Richard and the Protectorate. Richard accused him bluntly in the middle of the council meeting, then had him dragged out. There were soldiers waiting behind the door. Richard must have planned it!'

'He was driven to it, I'm sure! He did tell us that he suspected Hastings. And the others of his group—Bishop Morton, Stanley, Bishop Rotherham. I liked Hastings. Everyone did. I am amazed at his duplicity! But I know Richard would not have done this without real proof and good cause. I trust his motives, though the deed itself is horrific. He believed Hastings to be his friend!'

'I trust Richard too, but it is so unlike him. I have never known him to do anything like this without careful thought. He seemed to be a slave to an overwhelming passion!'

'Betrayal is a terrible thing. Especially in one's friends or in those one believes to be one's friends! What happened to the others?'

'All arrested and imprisoned!'

'Then they were all plotting against Richard!'

'It would seem so. Though I confess, I do not really know all the ins and outs of it. Richard did not tell me any more than you beforehand and certainly nothing of what he felt compelled to do to Hastings if he were proved disloyal. Apparently, he and his group joined up with the Woodvilles, and they planned to overthrow Richard and take the boy king Edward back into their protection by force! Hastings was to be his new Protector! Buckingham obtained irrefutable proof of this plot for Richard.'

'So, what else could Richard do? I am sure he was driven to it, could see no other solution.'

'And with the rest of the council and Parliament agreeing to Richard's continued Protectorship, the plotters would have had to act quickly. But Richard struck a blow against them first. He was always one for making pre-emptive strikes! He often did against enemies in battle, and avoided endless trouble later. I can see his reasoning, Anne, but I could not have done it. Not to Hastings anyway. He seemed to be everyone's friend, such a genial fellow! And all the time . . .'

'He was plotting Richard's downfall!'

'And the others—I am not surprised! Stanley, he was never one to know which side he was on—unless it was on the winning side. Bishop Rotherham had openly professed for the queen all along, but had seemed to acquiesce to Richard's rule. Bishop Morton is a deep one. No one can fathom his mind! He is extremely clever, but also very unscrupulous!'

'Poor Richard! What he has done is so out of character. To be forced to execute his dear brother's closest friend! Where is Richard now?'

'I do not know. He went off by himself after the execution. I could only think to come and tell you what had happened, so it would be less of a shock to you later. Richard will need your support, I am sure of it.'

'He will have it, though I liked Hastings. It is a wife's duty to support her husband, whatever he does, even if she is unhappy inside about it. And I am.'

'There is more on his mind too, my lady, I know it. Something to do with the Bishop of Bath and Wells, Bishop Stillington. The old man came to see Richard a day or two since and was closeted privily with him for a long time. When they emerged, the bishop was visibly shaking, and when Richard came out to the rest of us in the anteroom, he was so white-faced and drawn and as strung-up as a bowstring. He said nothing then but was obviously under a terrible strain. What it can have been that caused this he has not divulged yet, even to his closest friends and supporters. But he has clearly many troubles weighing him down!

Also, he suddenly sent away to the north by special messenger—one Richard Ratcliffe—commissions of array. He obviously expects trouble and wants the soldiers of the north to come down to London as soon as possible to be on hand for it. He trusts them. They are utterly loyal to him. Richard was always a close one, keeping his own counsel and often betraying little of his plans and thoughts even to me, his closest friend! I long to know what is going on in his head.'

'I am sure we will both find out soon enough. Now, try to forget the terrible events of the morning, Francis! Come and drink a cup of wine with me. We must both try to relax, to prepare for Richard's homecoming.'

Richard, Crosby Place, London, Night, 15 June 1483

'My dear lord, you have slept but ill these past two nights. Does the death of Hastings still weigh heavily on your spirits?'

'Aye, I regret my actions, in spite of his obvious treachery! And I am right weighed down with many other troubling thoughts besides.'

'Can you not confide in me and ease your mind? If not me, your loving wife, then who can you confide in?'

'Anne, if you only knew how I long to unburden it all. But my mind is such a maze of indecision and unsolved problems. I have to decide what to do. There is so little time!'

'Do? I thought that you had dealt with the biggest problem—the plot against you? Surely now you can go ahead with the young king's coronation on 22 June, and when Parliament convenes immediately after and ratifies you officially as the boy's Protector until he comes of age, then will not all be plain sailing again for you?'

'If only that were true! No. My Anne, something has reared its ugly head, which I had knowledge of years ago, and which I ignored for Edward's sake, as it concerned him so intimately. It has to be dealt with urgently, for the sake of the realm! Or all may be plunged into chaos again!'

'Whatever can that be? Pray tell me. Maybe I can help you decide for the best?'

'Only I can make the ultimate decision, unfortunately. It is possible that the boy's coronation will not be able to take place at all now, if I make known what the Bishop of Bath and Wells, Robert Stillington, lately told me!'

'The Bishop of Bath and Wells? Francis did tell me you were closeted with him for a long time recently.'

'Yes, and what he had to reveal could rend the bedrock of the whole Yorkist succession! His secret is out at last. And I feel I should reveal it to the nation. It was this secret that led to poor George's death! Edward discovered that he had knowledge of it when he was imprisoned in the Tower and so felt compelled to sign George's death warrant, for the sake of this. George could have revealed all at any time.'

'What is this terrible secret?'

'Well, Bishop Stillington was a close friend of George and must have told him—though he swears he did not—about the plight-troth ceremony he carried out many years ago between Edward, then twenty, and a high-born lady, Eleanor Butler. In this, he promised her marriage. She would not bed with him else. And Edward was young and lustful and did not consider the consequences. She gave in, of course—Edward always got what he wanted—then he deserted her. She died only a few years later in a nunnery near Norwich.'

'Poor lady!'

'Yes. When Edward met Elizabeth Grey and married her in 1464, he actually committed bigamy, according to the law. He had no right to marry her, but he chose to ignore this inconvenient fact! I don't suppose he even told Elizabeth about it at the time, knowing him, though he might have told her later.'

'This is appalling! Do you think the bishop is telling the truth? Has he any proof?'

'If one cannot trust the word of a man who has dedicated his whole life to the service of God, then who can one trust? And why would he lie about such a thing? He said it had burnt in his brain for years, and he was grateful to be rid of the burden of it now. Apparently, proof did exist—a parchment signed by all three parties at the time and witnessed by one of Stillington's priests, but Edward insisted on keeping it—a mistake, obviously. I expect he destroyed it when he married Elizabeth or maybe straightaway? Who knows?

I loved my brother dearly and looked up to him in all things all his life, but now I must admit he could forget about morality when it suited him, or got in his way!'

'What a dreadful story. And what a dreadful situation it must put you in! Does it not mean that all Edward's children are bastards because of this, and that the little king is not king at all and has no right to be crowned?'

'Exactly. That is the nub of the matter. And his coronation is exactly one week off! All is nearly prepared; hundreds have been invited to attend. The Lords are travelling from all parts of the country now to attend both the Coronation and the Parliament immediately after. Am I to blow it all apart with this bombshell news? Am I to go to this poor lad and tell him that he is not to be king after all? How can he possibly understand? How could I do this to my dear brother's child? It seems like an unforgivable betrayal of the loyalty I always swore to Edward! That is what is causing me this terrible indecision! Anyway, I have called a meeting of the Council tomorrow morning. But if I tell them what I have learnt from the Bishop, though I myself heard something of it years ago from my mother, but kept it to myself then for Edward's sake, as I did not really believe it anyway—then I feel I will be set upon a course of action from which there is no turning back!'

'Dear Husband, you frighten me!'

'I am afraid of the terrible consequences myself! And what a viper's nest Edward's marriage to that awful woman Elizabeth caused at the time too: Warwick's anger and his disaffection; George's disaffection—and much more! Stillington swears that he never revealed the plight-troth secret to George, ever. But nevertheless, George had apparently known of it for years, according to the bishop. But he does not know from whom.'

'Could it have been from the priest who was a witness, think you? He was the only other one there.'

'Possibly, I suppose. Who knows? Perhaps we shall never find out exactly how the secret got to George. But it did. And he lost his life because of it!'

'Oh, Richard, none of this dreadful situation is your fault! "The sins of the fathers shall be visited upon the children" it does say in the Bible, and this is a terrible example of that. Edward was to blame and no one else.'

'I know. But I am the one who has to deal with it. I still have to sort out Edward's problems, even though he is dead—which I always did for him in life. Whatever I do will cause endless repercussions and complications. If I decide to ignore Stillington's revelations and let the coronation go ahead, then I am remaining loyal to my dead brother but not to the realm. I have never broken a trust in my life, knowingly. I have always tried to keep to my motto "Loyalty binds me!" Am I to abandon my principles now for expediency, to avoid trouble?

I believe Stillington. I feel he has spoken nothing but the truth, as compelled to by his unquiet conscience! Knowing Edward through and through as I did, this was typical of his thoughtless, selfish ways, unfortunately.

Stillington's conscience is clear now, after unburdening himself to me, but he has unloaded the unwanted burden of knowledge on to me!

I have written to my mother to ask her advice. I expect an answer tomorrow, as I have stressed the urgency of it. Then I will make my decision—the hardest one of my life!'

'I know that you will do the right thing, my dear lord. I trust you to do that.'

'Yes, but what is the right thing to do in these terrible circumstances? Am I to let the coronation take place? Or bring all down like a pack of cards? Whatever I do, it must be done quickly!'

Richard, Baynard's Castle, London, 16 June 1483

Today, I met my privy council at the Tower, and we were rowed upstream to Westminster. My armed men surrounded the sanctuary. We had determined to get the erstwhile queen's youngest son, Richard of York, removed from her care and out of the sanctuary. It was vital to get her consent this time, by one means or another, if not for herself and the girls, at least for young Richard.

As Buckingham had most eloquently asserted to the council, if the queen herself still could not be persuaded to leave the sanctuary, the little prince must be secured anyway. No more refusals were to be allowed.

The arguments he gave were persuasive: the young King Edward needed his brother with him as a companion; the child could not be absent from the coronation ceremony, and he neither needed or wanted sanctuary. Surely he could be removed in these circumstances without violating the sacred law of sanctuary?

The duke eventually won them all round, even the Archbishop of Canterbury, who had held out to the end of the discussion, but gave in uneasily at last. Frankly, he had to be coerced into it, I know, but occasionally political necessity overrides even the rules of the Church.

And so we entered the abbot's lodgings in Westminster, where the queen and her children had taken sanctuary, determined to do what must be done. Buckingham and myself waited in The Star Chamber at first, knowing the queen would never respond to us. She had made that patently clear on numerous occasions already that she scorned and despised us and would never come out herself at our request. So why would she release her son to us?

Instead, Lord Howard, accompanied by the old Archbishop of Canterbury, went in to plead with her to release little Richard. I think the kindly archbishop's sincere, quiet assurances that her son would be treated kindly, gently, and respectfully brought her round, or maybe it was the sight of Lord Howard's grim and determined face and the fact that he was well-armed; also the sight of his large group of armed men outside the doors. Who knows?

But a short while later, the lad was brought to me in The Star Chamber, led out hand in hand with the archbishop, with Buckingham on his other side, who had gone forward to meet them in Westminster Hall. I talked reassuringly to little Richard, who was only nine years old, for a short while. Then the archbishop took him to his brother in the Tower, where they could get to know each other after so long apart. I am sure they will both be the happier for this meeting.

I pray that all will be well with them and that Edward will be less miserable and withdrawn, now that he has been joined by his younger brother. They will be good for each other, surely?

Richard, Baynard's Castle, London, 21 June 1483

After much prayer to try and calm my troubled mind, I decided to call a council meeting again and tell my chief councillors, Buckingham, Francis Lovell, and Northumberland, also my chief supporters, about Bishop Stillington's revelations and the quandary I feel this has put me in.

I still await my mother's reply to my urgent letter. It is a pity that she is so far away at Fotheringhay. She had not planned to attend the coronation for health reasons anyway; otherwise, she would be here, as this is her London house that I have removed to, leaving Anne at Crosby Place for the moment. It is more suitable for urgent meetings without disturbing her peace. I would have appreciated my mother's advice now, but I had to make my decision today, alone.

I truly did not know how my councillors and supporters would react to this earth-shattering news, but had put the outcome in the hands of God. What will be, will be . . .

To my astonishment, they have responded to me quickly, advising me that I should reveal all to the Lord Mayor and chief citizens of London at once and see their reaction too. If, like the councillors, they are then against the coronation tomorrow, in these unprecedented circumstances, would I consider, as the next in bloodline living to my brother Edward, taking the throne myself?

Most men, it seems, would support me or agree to my taking power, now that it can be justified.

I am amazed and overcome at their suggestion! I can see that it would make sense, though. George would have been next in line, had he lived. But he is dead. And there is no one else! And my father had a good claim to the throne years ago.

I am not at all sure that I want this advancement. I had not looked for it. But what is the alternative? If the boy king were crowned tomorrow and Bishop

Stillington's confession should come to light generally to the Commons and the country as a whole at a future time, all hell would be let loose!

It seems I have little choice. If it is for the commonweal of the realm, then I should step in and accept.

But the burdens of kingship are heavy. Edward knew that only too well, and I often tried to share them with him when he felt overwhelmed. Who would help me? Francis certainly. Buckingham? He has lately become a most enthusiastic supporter. Stanley? He is a dark horse and difficult to trust entirely. Lord Howard never wavers. He is a rock. It is so difficult to decide. I must think, and quickly!

The councillors have assured me that I am the right man for the job. They say my experience as my brother's right-hand man in council and war ideally suit me for it. But it is a huge step to take, one I fear, and yet which excites me greatly with its endless possibilities at the same time!

Several thousands of my stalwart men of the north will arrive in London shortly, also many of Buckingham's sturdy Welsh soldiers. They will support me if there is an outcry from the Woodville supporters, which I anticipate, even if I do not become king.

It is best to stop the doubts, speculations, and rumours which I know grip London, as soon as possible. People naturally wonder what is going on in high places and hate uncertainty. It affects their futures. To be decisive has always been my best defence. I think the people will be glad to know that the safety of the realm is assured and that good order will be maintained, whether I remain Protector or become king.

Perhaps the revelation of the pre-contract is establishing a rightful opportunity for me? For I would not take such a step unless I felt it was the right, the only thing to do in the circumstances!

Child kings have always guaranteed endless trouble and warring factions. The people want—they need—an experienced man as king! If I can do some good and realise my lifelong dreams of equal justice for all men and women, which I have always wanted, then maybe I should accept their proposal?

God help me! I pray for his guidance in making this second, most sacred decision, the most important of my life. On it rests so much!

Cecily, Dowager Duchess of York, Fotheringhay Castle, 20 June 1483

My Dear Richard,
    This news is most disturbing, but not surprising. Knowing how Edward always lusted after practically every attractive woman he

ever met and how he was used to getting his own way with them, the fact that he made a plight-troth to a young high-born girl who had kept her chastity up to then in order to get her into bed does not amaze me in the least. Nor the fact that he then let her down and abandoned her later. She probably intrigued him with her purity. It was something he did not often come across, as most women fell willingly at his feet! That Woodville woman must have had great strength of will to persuade him to marry her before giving in to him. One has to admire her determination to get what she wanted—marriage—before giving in to his charm—if nothing else about her!

If he had known the terrible consequences his shameful act would cause all these years later, would it have made him think again? I doubt it. Edward was always one for instant gratification in all things, whatever the cost. I deplored his lack of morals in life, as I do now. One should not speak ill of the dead, I know, yet I only speak the plain truth, after all.

But the other side of the coin—it has opened the window of opportunity for you. I always knew your time would come; your chance to take power and the throne! You used to ask me how I knew this, but I just felt it would come to pass. I felt it deep within me, that my most able and upright son would one day get his chance. It was always your destiny! And you have!

The situation clears the way for you to take the throne now as you deserve. Take your opportunity at once. Do not think of refusing the offer made to you. You will be a great and good king. All you needed was the chance!

My dear husband should have been king, but lost his chance and his life. Now the son most like him in appearance, character, and achievements, will ascend to his proper place! I urge you to decide at once. Agree to the councillors' proposition!

You are the man of the moment and the right man for this high office! I will be the proudest mother in all Christendom on the day you are crowned. And somehow, in spite of my poor health, I will journey to London to be at your coronation!

Your loving mother,
Cecily,
Dowager Duchess of York

Prince Edward, The Tower of London, Evening, 22 June 1483

Today has been the worst day of my life. It should have been the happiest—my coronation day! I awoke this morning at dawn, excited and full of anticipation. I felt lighter in spirits than for weeks. I had just become more settled in my new circumstances and was actually looking forward to my great day. I expected my servants to come early to robe me for the great event, but to my puzzlement and mystification, I was told that my Uncle of Gloucester had come to see me and wished for an audience at once. With him was the Duke of Buckingham.

Thinking it was some last-minute details of the coronation they had to discuss with me, I received them pleasantly enough. But they brought terrible news. Unbelievable news. My joy and anticipation were turned to dust. Uncle Gloucester's visit put paid to all that!

I had heard rumours, of course, was aware of my servants whispering in corners who immediately became silent when I approached. That in itself was strange enough. But now the reality hit me. Surely my uncle would not—could not—do this? Surely he could not take my throne, inherited from the king, my father, for himself?

But it is true. His visit confirmed this.

I am no longer to be king!

He began to explain the complicated reasons to me. They both did, but I was so full of resentment, misery, and anger that I hardly listened. Something to do with my father not being properly married to my mother, making me a bastard, making all King Edward's children bastards. And bastards cannot inherit thrones!

My blood is not pure enough, it seems. And his is. And he is next in line. So he has decided to be king in my place!

I can hardly understand how this could be lawful. I am at a complete loss. It is not to be borne! I was right not to trust him. I am sure he planned this all along. That is why he stopped Uncle Rivers taking me to London for my coronation, which my family had planned for 4 May. That is why he abducted me—yes, abducted me—for his own ends!

I see it all now. My Protector? He is nothing but a vile, ambitious, and devious usurper! I hate him! I shall always hate him—as my mother does! I see now that she has had good reason. He has deprived me of my birthright—my rightful place as king! I am sure he must have achieved this through clever lies and political manipulation. I shall never forgive him, never!

And when he had gone, there was more dreadful news. Unbelievable news! A messenger from Pontefract Castle came to the Tower. My dear uncle Rivers,

Lord Richard Grey, and Thomas Vaughan, my old retainer, my devoted friends all my childhood are no more. They were executed out of hand, by orders of that devil, Gloucester! Perhaps he knew of it this morning but did not mention it to me. Is it something so trivial to him then? Does he have good men killed without compunction, as one would tread on an ant or swat a fly?

To me it is an outrage; a terrible blow! These good men loved me, protected me; were devoted to my care, particularly Lord Rivers, my guardian and mentor. And I loved them.

Why did he do it? What did he think they would do, could do, imprisoned in three separate Yorkshire castles? Plot against him? How could they make plots, let alone carry them out? He is just clearing the way for himself, getting rid of anyone in high position who may object to him taking the throne in my place!

Will it be my mother next? Gloucester knows she hates him; is his implacable enemy. And he has always hated her—she told me so. That is why she fears what he may do if she leaves sanctuary! She was forced to let Richard out, to be with me; Buckingham said. It was because they felt I needed a companion, and who better than my brother? But we hardly know each other. I suspect another reason, though I do not know what.

I must write to my mother or go and visit her—if they will allow it. I am not sure what my position is at present—maybe my brother and I are both prisoners now? I asked to go to her this afternoon but was refused. Why? They let me go before, when I was the king.

I need to ask her about Gloucester's allegations concerning her marriage to my father. Ask her to her face. Surely she can tell me the truth? I am her son, now deprived of his rightful inheritance. It is my right to know the truth! Surely she must know all about it? She was married to my father for many years and she bore him many children. Surely he must have eventually told her if he had once made a plight-troth promise to another woman? It is a mystery which I want, I need, to get to the bottom of. If true, the consequences have ruined my chances.

But I still think it is all lies and hearsay, brought up so that Uncle Gloucester can benefit from it! Will I be deprived of my life too soon because I get in Gloucester's way? Will he find reasons to have my whole family killed? It seems he has the power to do anything he likes. Power which should be mine! I would not put it past him. He has got the throne. Now he must want us dead!

Anne, Crosby Place, London, 26 June 1483

I am completely bewildered and utterly appalled by what has happened. I could not believe it. What has Richard done? My good, upright husband has surely committed a terrible deed? An unlawful deed?

He insists that the council persuaded him to take the throne. But surely he has usurped it? He told them about Bishop Stillington's revelations and at first they wanted proof. There was none forthcoming, except the sworn word of the bishop that he himself had carried out the plight-troth ceremony with Edward and Lady Eleanor Butler, and that there had originally been a dated deed signed by all three parties, which Edward, as king, had insisted on taking possession of at the time. Where it is now, even if Edward did not destroy it when he married Elizabeth Grey and made her his queen, is anybody's guess.

But if the sworn statement of a bishop cannot be trusted, whose can? They accepted it as true, anyway. Harry, Duke of Buckingham, made an impassioned speech on Richard's behalf in the Guildhall a day or so ago to a large assembly of lords and gentry. Lately, he has become Richard's strongest and most outspoken supporter. He speaks very eloquently and persuasively. He obviously influenced his audience strongly, for they at once drew up a petition requesting Richard to take the throne, and Buckingham, the assembly, the Mayor and Aldermen of London presented it to him this morning at Baynard's Castle.

The day before, Ralph Shaw, the cleric, had made a long sermon to the people at St Paul's Cross, with the theme 'bastard slips shall not take root' referring to the poor little ousted King Edward and his siblings, no doubt. He explained that they were all bastards, because of what Bishop Stillington had revealed and this was the reason Edward could never be king now. I am sure his audience was very confused and unhappy afterwards. They had expected a wonderful coronation ceremony on that day, and all they got was this strange and disturbing justification for the boy being put aside, as he no longer qualified for kingship!

Richard tells me that he is really very reluctant to take the throne, but in the circumstances feels he has no other choice, if the good of the realm is to be his main consideration. He assures me that it had never occurred to him that the situation might arise where it seemed the only thing for him to do, to stabilise the country. But now he is taking the throne and becoming king, he is regarding it as a challenge to do some good. I can see that. He is an able man, well regarded and respected, and I am sure he will rule wisely and well.

If he is in charge, it will avoid much endless political upheavals, for, with a boy as king, this would be inevitable. But I do not like it. It still seems wrong, whatever the reasons for Richard's acceptance of the throne. That poor little prince in the Tower! I cannot help thinking how he must feel. He cannot possibly understand the political reasons behind Richard's decision. He must feel very bitter and unhappy. He must surely hate Richard!

And I have no wish whatsoever to be queen! All the heavy duties and responsibilities that entails fill me with dread. But the main thing is the need to stay in London, as it is the centre of power. I hate the place. It is so dirty and polluted, full of disease and too crowded. We shall be able to get up to Yorkshire only rarely. And my boy is there, my little delicate child who has been left too long already. He has a good nurse and is well cared for, but it is not the same as a mother's care!

I shall miss Middleham dreadfully. I was looking forward to going home soon after little Edward's coronation. Now that is cancelled, God alone knows when a visit home will be possible. I prefer the quiet life in the country. And my sick child needs me. John too. But London is the capital and Richard has to stay here. I must be by his side, so my sick child is deprived of the mother he needs so badly. I cannot be in two places at once. But I am torn, so torn emotionally.

Ned has to stay at Middleham. He cannot live here with us. His health would not stand it. He needs the clean, unpolluted air of Wensleydale with his weak lungs. His nurse tells me, in her most recent letter, that he is still coughing and has frequent breathless attacks which are very worrying to see. And the doctors say that nothing can be done to help the poor child. It is heartbreaking. I cannot bear it. If Ned is like this in summer, what will his health be like next winter? I hardly dare to think about it. Ironically, I have another little child here with me now, Edward, George of Clarence's eight-year-old son, my nephew, recently brought to me to look after again, as Richard discovered he was very unhappy where he was. He is also in much need of care and attention, and though I give it willingly enough, it makes it even harder to bear the separation from my own Ned. The boy has always been backward for his age, but perhaps this is because he is an orphan and has not been nurtured lovingly lately. Being an orphan he is a sad child too. He has never had much to say for himself. My heart goes out to him, even though it is torn with longing for my own son.

My own health is not good. I have never been strong, but now I tire so very easily. I wonder how I will be able to find the stamina to keep up with all the demands on a queen's time? I have a persistent cough too. I try to hide it from Richard so that he will not worry over me. He has enough worries on his shoulders already.

With Richard now to be crowned king on 6 July, I shall have to be crowned too at the coronation ceremony. I dread it. It does not bear thinking about! How will I cope with the endless hours of religious ceremony in the July heat, wearing all those heavy ceremonial robes, let alone the processions and the great feast that will go on and on late into the night? It will be a nightmare. I hope I do not faint and let Richard down. I will have to use every bit of my will power! Never was there a more reluctant queen!

Margaret Beaufort, Countess of Richmond, Woking Old Hall, 26 June 1483

My Dear Henry,

There is amazing, astonishing news to impart to you! I can hardly believe it myself, and it fills me with deep concern. And yet, what has happened in the last few days gives you, in the long term, if not in the short, more of a real opportunity to take your rightful place as King of England. If this is not immediately apparent to you when you have read this letter, just think about it!

Prince Edward is not to be king after all! His coronation was set for 4 May, then postponed to 22 June, when his uncle, Richard of Gloucester, took over the post of his Protector and Protector of the Realm, which was according to the deathbed wishes of King Edward. But now, Richard has usurped the young king and is to become king in his place! Some story has been given out to explain the sudden upheaval in events—not that I believe a word of it. It is something dredged up to suit the Duke of Gloucester's purposes, so that he can make himself king, I am sure of it!

Briefly, a bishop called Stillington has confessed to some long-ago plight-troth that King Edward made to another woman before he married Elizabeth Grey. As this is regarded in English Law as binding, he was apparently in no position to remarry. So now, they are saying that all the king's children are bastards. And bastards cannot inherit money, property, or estates, let alone the throne!

Duke Richard is not well-liked in the south of England or among your many supporters in Brittany. He only has a really loyal support base in the north, where he has ruled for years as Lord of the North. Now that he has usurped the throne from his nephew, you will suddenly become the focus of attention of everyone who deplores his action and will want to get rid of him quickly. Quite simply, there is no one else to turn to. More and more influential people are sure to see you now as the potential king!

My son, the time is imminent when what I always predicted will come to pass. I know it!

So you must prepare yourself to take arms against this usurper. Duke Francis will surely help you or the King of France? Especially the latter—the French have no love for Richard. They remember his stubborn refusal to endorse the Treaty of Picquigny. Also, his refusal to accept their presents afterwards!

You will need much money for ships, horses, and arms. I will help you too. I can send you a goodly amount of gold to help in your enterprises, but it is up to you now to take advantage of the situation and prepare for an invasion. I have communicated with your Uncle Jasper regularly and he and your other friends there, and here, are at the ready to support you!

Richard of Gloucester has had his two nephews, the young princes, locked away in the Tower of London, that dark and threatening place, ostensibly for their own safety, but who knows what he plans? They are in the way, after all!

The queen remains in sanctuary with her daughters. She knows better than to risk all their lives by emerging, in spite of many assurances as to their safety. She and I share the same doctor, who visits her in Westminster Sanctuary, and he is easily prompted to reveal her thoughts and desires to me and, I expect, mine to her. I plan to visit her soon. Also, I plan to visit her boys in the Tower. Edward, the eldest, is quite sick with an abscess in his jaw from a rotten tooth, I hear. I shall take in some of my soothing pain-killing remedies to help him, which my doctor supplied me with. I shall reassure Elizabeth that I, at least, am taking pity on the young prince in his situation! I am able to go in and out of the Tower freely if I so desire, as my husband, Lord Stanley, is acting Constable of the Tower. The younger prince, Richard, is not well either. I am not surprised, being cooped up in that place all the time. The only recreation they both get is a little shooting at the butts in the small garden by the walls outside their tower. They are sometimes observed there playing at their games too. But they do not have their freedom, any more than you have yours!

But all that will soon change! My friend, Bishop Morton, an implacable enemy of Gloucester and a very clever and resourceful man, has assured me that he is also working industriously on your behalf. Though a member of the Yorkist council until Lord Hastings was accused of treachery and summarily executed, when Morton was sent to Brecon Castle as a prisoner of the Duke of Buckingham, being suspected of collusion with Hastings, he has always supported the Lancastrian cause privately and is just waiting for the right time to oppose Richard openly! He is very devious and, though a prisoner, he will know exactly how to go about stirring things up and headhunting influential men to rise up against Richard when the time is ripe and all is prepared! He is very persuasive and always gets his own way, I believe. He is a most useful ally to have on our side. And he loves money. I have plenty of that to assist him to make the right decisions in our favour and to work on our behalf to influence others in high places! I would not put it past him to persuade Buckingham to change sides. He could offer him many tempting possibilities if he does, I am sure!

So, now do you see that what seems a setback is actually going to boost your claim?

I will be in constant communication now through my agents.

Until you hear from me again soon, please reply and let me know that you are ready in your mind for the coming confrontation. You have had plenty of time to think about it over the years, with my constant exhortations for you to have faith in your ultimate destiny!

Your loving mother,
Margaret Beaufort,
Countess of Richmond

Henry Tudor, Vannes Castle, Brittany, 30 June 1483

My Dear Mother,

I am replying to your last letter at once, as I am in communication with Uncle Jasper, who has also heard the news of Richard of Gloucester's usurpation and is making all haste to join me here to discuss the situation. My other chief councillors are nearby, ready for the Council of War we shall soon have.

I have spoken to Duke Francis, and he has agreed to advance me enough gold to equip ourselves well with ships, horses, and armaments. He has no love for Richard and is scandalised by his treatment of young Edward, who should have been crowned king, but if he had, this window of opportunity for me would hardly have come now! I would have had to wait patiently even longer. I have spent my entire life waiting for something or someone, it seems!

I am very sorry for him. In many ways, his experience recently has been like mine: dragged away from all he knew and loved and was familiar with in Ludlow, as I had to leave my beloved Wales at short notice and come here, leaving behind my home, Maude, my dearest friend and the girl I loved, and Owen, my horse, whom I missed so dreadfully. And he is much younger than I was when it happened to me. At least I was taken by friends and looked after since by them, though I have been in exile. He is locked in that dark Tower, surrounded by potential enemies, the chief of whom must be his Uncle of Gloucester, I should think, who was appointed his Protector. How afraid he must feel! And he is ill too. It is kind of you to visit him with your herbal potions to ease his pain. At least he has a companion now in his little brother, Richard of York.

I do understand, Mother, what you mean about the time to strike a blow for my own claim being almost here! As soon as we are ready, I will sail for England. But it may take a few weeks before we can set out. There is so much to do! Richard is a great soldier. I have no experience of fighting battles whatsoever, though I have studied tactics and do have good men who can advise me in this. If I am to have any hope of taking him on in battle—and winning—I must listen carefully to their advice, and we must make detailed plans for the invasion and what happens after!

I am filled with trepidation and exhilaration at the same time! It is very strange.

All these years, I have been in limbo, as it were, and now suddenly, I am called upon to take extreme action! Can I do it successfully? Can I win and oust Richard? And become king myself? It still seems an impossible dream!

But I am prepared to take my chances anyway! You have always had great faith in me and urged me on to realise my destiny when the chance came. Now it has! And I welcome it with open arms!

I once met Richard, you know, when I was at Raglan Castle, in Gwent, and he came to visit Lady Herbert. We got on, and I liked him a lot. It will be strange to be forced to fight him. I would rather have been his friend. I admired him as a man and as a soldier. His achievements were awesome, even then. I was always sorry we were on opposing sides. So was he, I think.

But I realise I cannot harbour any sentiment now when it comes to fighting for the Lancastrian cause. I have been a pawn all my life, but now it is my chance to assert myself and see what I can achieve, not only for the cause, but for myself! I have achieved little in my life up to now—unlike Richard. I have always envied him.

The gold that Edward Woodville brought me from King Edward's treasure is safely stowed away in Duke Francis's strongroom. I thank the Marquess of Dorset for arranging to have it sent to me.

It will aid greatly in paying for equipment. Strange that English gold should be used to pay for an invasion of England!

I look forward to your next letter. Events are moving so fast now, I wish that I had you by my side, along with my dear Uncle Jasper, to advise and support me!

Your loving son,
Henry Tudor

Margaret Beaufort, Woking Old Hall, 15 July 1483

My Dear Henry,

Thank you for your letter in reply to my news about the usurpation, which I received today. I am pleased that you are now so excited by the possibilities opening up for you and that you have started preparations for your great adventure! The sooner it can be accomplished, the better. Uncle Jasper will be a great help to you in this, I know.

On 6 July, I had the questionable honour of being the new queen's train-bearer at the Coronation. Poor lady, I could not help being sorry for her. None of this is her doing, that is evident. She looked very ill at ease and so white I am sure she is physically ill too. At one point, her other ladies and I had to support her during the never-ending ceremonies, or I think she might have collapsed. At the feast afterwards, she hardly ate or drank a thing. I think it was all too much for her. She is obviously most reluctant to take on her new position. But she is bound to support her husband in this. There is no way out for her. I have heard that she is desperately worried about the poor health of her only son, now the Prince of Wales, little Edward, but eight years old, and, if reports be true, unlikely to live into his teenage years. Again, I am very sorry for him, but if he does die young, which seems likely, then that is one more obstacle removed from your ascent to kingship!

The coronation was the grandest and most expensive that has ever taken place, at least in my lifetime. It was far grander and more elaborate than either Henry VI's or Edward IV's, both of which I attended. The cost must have been enormous! This Gloucester does not skimp or economise on himself. He is obviously determined to make a statement. But when you come into your own, my son, your coronation will be the grandest ever, I will see to that. You will outshine even this usurper's glory! And you will have a right to it, unlike him.

I am in communication with Bishop Morton, in Brecknock Castle, as I told you I would be. He is working hard on your behalf, believe me. He knows my determined aspirations for you, and, as a loyal Lancastrian, will do all in his power—which is considerable still, though he be Buckingham's prisoner—to bring them into being!

I shall be visiting the erstwhile queen in Westminster Sanctuary tomorrow. I have an idea in my head which is most persistent and will not go away, and I plan to discuss it with her. There is no love lost between her and the new king, and I feel sure she will acquiesce to my proposition that you and her eldest daughter Elizabeth wed when you become king and bring the Houses of York and Lancaster together. Think about this—would it not be the perfect answer to everything—especially the chance it would offer to heal forever the dissension between Lancastrians and Yorkists which has torn this country apart for so long? I am sure you will agree that it could be a very good thing for all!

Meanwhile, my son, I send you my love as always. I will let you know the reaction of Elizabeth Grey to my proposition when I next write. I am almost certain that she will agree to the marriage—as I am sure you will also wish to do!

Your loving mother,
Margaret Beaufort,
Countess of Richmond

Anne, Queen of England, Westminster Palace, Late July 1483

My Dear Edward,

How I long to see you and be with you! Your father and I would have come home to Middleham weeks ago if he had not decided to take the throne, when it was pressed on him, which he felt was necessary at the time, though I was not happy about it and still am not. But he made me understand that it was the only course of action open to him if the good of the realm was to be considered above all else and the future of its people. As far as I am concerned, I must now support your father in all things, as being a king is a very difficult job, and you must too, my son!

And because of this happening, it means that you too will one day be king! A long time in the future, I hope, but you are now the Prince of Wales and will be given a great ceremony by your father soon to mark that and to install you in your new high estate.

Your father has decided that we must go on a king's Progress through the country, especially to parts where the people do not know him, so that he can meet them and persuade them of his good intentions for the country. But we will visit York, where people know him and have always loved him, and there, in York Minster, you will be made Prince of Wales! I am not sure of the date set yet, but it will be soon.

It is a pity that you were not well enough to come down to London for the coronation on 6 July, which was an incredibly grand affair. It went on for hours and hours and was almost too much for me, so I know the day would have proved too much for you too. The children who were there were falling asleep in their seats at the great banquet afterwards, which went on late into the night! Still, I expect you were very disappointed that we would not let you travel so far, as you were unwell. I hope you understand that it was only for your own good, and all we were trying to do was protect your health, not deprive you of anything?

I do hope you are feeling better now and that your nasty cough has gone? You must try to keep well for your great day at York soon! Get plenty of fresh air, and if you go out on wet days, make sure you are well wrapped and never get soaked. It is not good to let wet clothes dry on one. I know, for this happened to me on my December journey to London, and I had a bad chest for weeks afterwards.

Your father is incredibly busy and works all day and often far into the night on important state papers and at meetings with his councillors. Some days, I hardly see him at all!

It will be good to get away from London, which I hate, and get some fresh air when we go on Progress, though all the travelling will be tiring, I know, especially for me. Your father is used to it. I hope John is well too and that you enjoy playing together? It is good that you have a companion, even if he is a little older than you. We are also sending Edward Warwick to live at Middleham with you soon, as he is your father's ward, being the son of his brother, the Duke of Clarence, who is dead. With both his parents dead, he and his elder sister Margaret are orphans unhappily. He is rather a sad boy. I hope you and John will try to cheer him up. He has been staying in London for a short while, but it is more healthy at Middleham for children, so he will soon be with you. What fun that will be for you—a new cousin to get to know! I am sure you will like him. He is quiet like you and does not like very boisterous games.

I know you will be a good boy until we come, your father and I, and do as your nurse tells you. She is there to guard you, after all, so knows best what is good for you and what is not!

I look forward to seeing you soon, my darling child. I think of you every day. I hope you miss me too?

Your loving mother,
Anne of Gloucester,
Queen of England! (I can hardly believe I must sign myself so now.
It still seems very strange and unbelievable!)

Henry, Duke of Buckingham, London, Late July 1483

I do not want to do this. But I see it makes good sense. My aunt, Lady Margaret Beaufort, has assured me that she will make it easy by drugging the boys heavily so that they are fast asleep and are unaware of anything when I come with my henchmen. They will pass easily into perpetual sleep when the pillows are placed over their faces.

Afterwards, my men will bury them quickly within the Tower precincts. It will be late in the evening. No one will think anything of my being there, as I can gain access any time. Being Lord High Constable of England, I have a right to enter any fortress in the country without let or hindrance. And, as the king is away, as second in command to him, I am in charge of the capital. No one dare gainsay me. After all, many visit the boys: Richard, the king, and Anne, his wife, before they went on Progress; various members of the king's council. Also, my aunt has been a lot lately with her potions for the boys, as they are sick and, of course, her doctor, Lewis.

I am not sure whether he or she will give them the heavy dose of opium which will make them sleep so deeply that they do not know when they pass into the next world. I do not want to know. It is bad enough to have this awful task placed upon me.

But I know I must do it. My aunt assures me that the Woodvilles are stirring insurrection against the king again, determined to wrest power once more while the king and queen are away and set young Prince Edward on the throne after all. That cannot be allowed to happen in any circumstances. My life, and the lives of the king and queen and many others would soon be forfeit! Those hated Woodvilles must never rule this country!

King Richard will thank me for this. It is another great service I am prepared to do for him. I was the one who supported him most strongly from the first and argued his case for taking the throne most vehemently, even eloquently, people said. I am his chief supporter and chief minister. He has rewarded me handsomely, I must admit. Who knows what honours he will heap upon me now? Maybe he will bypass the act of Parliament needed to reinstate my inheritance of the entire Bohun estates, which were ceded to the Crown when I was a teenager by King Edward after my father was attainted? They do belong to me by the laws of inheritance. Even the king has admitted that, though he has not reinstated me yet.

When the unpleasant deed is done, which is costing me dear too—my two henchmen have demanded incredibly high rewards for their work and their silence afterwards and will probably blackmail me for more later if they get the chance—I will to horse at once and ride to Gloucester to meet the king there and inform him that he is at last safe in his new position and that it is all down to me—my loyalty and concern for his person! He will be told nothing of Lady Margaret Beaufort's hand in it and the underlying reason why she wants the princes dead—the claim of her son, Henry Tudor, to the throne. She has promised me very high office and many more estates if and when he becomes king, for my help in clearing the way for Henry now.

After informing the king that the princes are no more, I will continue with him on his triumphal Progress; take my honoured part in the Prince of Wales' investiture at York. There is even the possibility that Richard will have another coronation in York for the benefit of his beloved Northerners. They are his most loyal followers, always have been.

And now I must prepare myself for the night's work. I must set my mind to it. And it is hard. I have killed in battle. All men must or be killed themselves. But this is different. It is repugnant and I just want to forget I ever agreed to it and ride for Wales and the wide open spaces. Will I ever erase it from my mind afterwards or will it haunt me forever?

Francis Lovell, With King Richard's Progress, Gloucester, 29 July 1483

A day or so ago, we came into Gloucester on my Lord King Richard's Progress. Many other lords and I have accompanied him from Windsor, from which we set out on 20 July, among them the Earl of Northumberland and of course Lord Stanley. Richard is never happy about him unless he is close by, as he has shown himself to be untrustworthy more than once. There is something about the man which makes one uneasy, though he is ostensibly loyal to the new king. A great train of lords, bishops, justices, and officers of the royal household came too. The queen will join him later on, as she begged him to let her visit their sick little son Edward at Middleham first. A mother's pleas have been listened to! Probably, she will join him with Edward before they arrive at York, where a great reception is sure to await them. It has ever been Richard's favourite city, and the people of York love their master greatly too. I know he intends to have Edward invested as Prince of Wales in the Great Minster there.

On 13 July, he honoured me with one of the greatest posts in England, that of Lord Chamberlain. I was humbled by being raised so high, but Richard insists I deserve it as his loyal and loving friend and supporter since we were children together. Many great positions were poured upon the head of Harry, Earl of Buckingham too. He is now even stronger than the Earl of Warwick was. Another kingmaker, in effect!

I understand that Richard is deeply grateful to him for his zealous and enthusiastic support in helping him to become king, especially the eloquent speeches he made in Richard's defence when he decided to take the throne. But I admit I have never liked the man and cannot understand what Richard sees in him. His high-vaunting arrogance and grandiose attitude, also his immense charm—which has completely won over Richard—leave me cold. He is too much like George of Clarence—and he was never to be trusted! So much about Harry Buckingham reminds me of that traitorous brother to King Edward and Richard that I am always uneasy and on my guard in his presence, but Richard is completely won over by him and trusts his loyalty completely. But I am not so sure. The man makes too many protestations of loyalty somehow. He works too hard at it.

He also arrived here in Gloucester today, on his way home to Brecon Castle in Wales, he said, where he holds Bishop Morton prisoner. For some reason, he did not accompany Richard when we set out on Progress on 20 July. I wonder why. What can have detained him in London that was so much more important than being with his king, as his chief and most powerful minister, as Richard goes to present himself to his people? He offered no explanation publicly why nor the reason he is not joining us now, at this late stage, for the Progress onwards, but chooses to return to Wales instead. What is the urgency for him to do that, I ask myself. Richard and he met only briefly today, I know, but I was not there. Richard met him privily, so I do not know what passed between them and whether Richard asked him for an explanation of his actions. Perhaps Richard will confide in me later what was said? I hope so. I cannot press him to tell me. Richard is a deep one and a man of few words. Even though I am his closest friend, I know that he will tell me if he chooses to, or not. But he usually takes me into his confidence about important matters.

So far in the Progress, we have been welcomed in every town and city we have visited. We have stayed a day or so in each one, starting with Reading, then Oxford, where Richard enjoyed some lectures and some earnest theological discussions, which would have bored me rigid, but Richard is very religious and reads deeply on theological matters.

Then we arrived at Gloucester. Tomorrow, we will set out for Tewkesbury, travelling along the side of the Severn River. There, I know Richard plans to pray quietly at the tomb of his brother George, which is behind the high altar of Tewkesbury Abbey. He still feels George's death deeply. He loved him and cannot help himself. I do not think he ever forgave King Edward for having George put to death, whatever the provocation.

After Tewkesbury, we will go to Worcester and then spend a week or so in Warwick, where Richard tells me the queen will go first to Warwick Castle, the place of her birth, after visiting Middleham to see her son. Then they travel on together. The people wish to see their new queen too, though I hardly think her delicate health will stand up to the constant travelling very well.

Then, I am hazy as to our route, but I think it includes Coventry, Leicester, and Nottingham, where we will stay, of course, at the great castle on the hill overlooking the town. He will meet up with his son, so he tells me, at Pontefract, about the third week in August, before the royal family's triumphal entrance into York! I know a great welcome has been planned for Richard there.

At every place we have visited, great gifts of money have been presented to Richard, but he has always refused them. He tells the people that he would rather have their love and loyalty than their money. I think this has made a big impression!

At Nottingham, Richard has summoned in advance seventy knights and gentlemen of the north to meet him, and he will read out the powerful speech again that he made in London after his accession, in which he promises to administer true justice and to rule fairly. That made a strong impact in London, and he hopes it will in Nottingham too. And he means what he says. I know Richard so well, and all his life he has felt the need for justice to be equal for all, rich or poor. Now he has the chance to carry out his wishes, which I know he will, to the best of his ability!

York will be the highlight of this great Progress. The travelling is very tiring, but it will all be worth it!

I heard that the Mayor of York and four of his chief aldermen, on hearing of Richard's coronation on 6 July, rode to Middleham about 10 July to pay homage to the little Edward, who will be invested as Prince of Wales in their city soon after the king arrives. They presented the boy with many gifts, including demain bread—the very best—a barrel of red and a barrel of white wine, six cygnets, six herons, and twenty-four rabbits! I wonder about the birds and the rabbits. Is he expected to eat them or, more likely, to let them loose on the estate so that they may grow and breed? The latter, I expect. Soon, Middleham will be overrun with rabbits!

The York worthies are busy planning a triumphal reception too, we have been informed, for when Richard, Anne, and Edward enter York. He will look forward to that, as they obviously do. We shall soon see what entertainments, receptions, and feasts they lay on for his pleasure!

Now, I go to see Richard, in the hope that he will welcome me into his confidence about what passed between him and Harry Buckingham. He is always pleased to see me, but I never presume on his company, especially now he is king! I hope it is about Buckingham. The man looked very agitated and exhausted when he arrived, as if he had ridden post-haste from London with very urgent news for the king. Perhaps Richard is somewhat suspicious of his rather strange behaviour, as I am, and wants to discuss it?

I am often the first to be told important news, as his closest friend.

I shall soon know!

Richard, King of England, Gloucester, 29 July 1483

'Francis, I am beside myself. I cannot believe my stupidity. I have been blinkered like a very horse, blinded by his charm and vivacity, by his silver tongue and protestations of loyalty! What can I have been thinking of, not to see the other side of him—the avariciousness, the foolishness, the stupidity—the rashness?

Underneath the charm, he is only thinking of himself. He is just like George, too much like George! And I loved him, so I tried to ignore his bad traits! But he was my brother—perhaps I could be forgiven for that? But this young fool has hoodwinked me completely. Why do I go for these charming but unstable men? I prefer the down-to-earth, rather taciturn Northerners in theory. What you see is what you get. But somehow, I let myself be taken in by the Harry Buckinghams of this world!

And look how I have heaped honours, estates, and positions upon him! Mistakenly, I see that now. But I was flattered by his open-heartedness, his unfailing support of me from the first, by his willingness to speak most eloquently on my behalf! I needed this loyalty and support so very badly to justify what I was doing in breaking my dear brother's trust and ignoring his dying wishes in putting his son Edward aside and taking the throne for myself. I felt out on a limb, as if I were hanging over a precipice! And Buckingham provided me with the confidence, the determination, to take that final step! He is so self-confident and arrogant, so sure of himself! He acts without a moment's hesitation or thought, as now. But I am deeper thinking. I ponder long over my actions, as you know. I have ever been cautious. I see both sides of a situation, which makes it hard for me to take decisions. In the end, I always have to take a chance and hope my decision is the right one, as decisiveness is all in effective rule! I found that as a soldier commanding men, and I find it now, as a king. It was out of my nature to take the throne, Francis! I did not want to do it. I felt it to be wrong. But I seemed to have no other choice at the time with the situation as it was!

I know that you and dear Anne have not been happy about my decision, have even deplored it. Although neither of you have said anything, I feel your uncertainty. But you have supported me unfailingly, of course, without demur.

I wanted to have Buckingham arrested at once for his contemptible and precipitate action, tried and executed without delay, as Hastings was. My anger was great and I let him know it! He was scandalised by my reaction to what he thought would be wonderful news, welcome news! He had not the understanding to see the baseness of what he had done, could not comprehend my grief and repulsion. I told him to get out of my sight and say nothing of what had occurred. I will deal with him later, as he should be dealt with, but not now, not in the middle of this Progress, in which I wish to show my people my sincere desire to rule them well!

Think what the reaction would be from the whole country! I would be inevitably linked in culpability. People would think that I had ordered him privily to carry out this dreadful deed! I will not be tarred with the same brush; blackened by another's evil! I still have Hastings's death on my conscience. Who knows whether that plot was all that Buckingham assured me it was? Hastings had been a loyal and stalwart supporter up to then, first of Edward, his king and dearest friend, then of me. Why should he suddenly turn against me, as Buckingham assured me at the time? Maybe Buckingham manoeuvred events then to his own advantage?

Who knows? But I will find out! Buckingham will be questioned before he is executed for this present vile deed. Maybe another, deeper chain of events will come to light? The truth will out!

And now, I must somehow put my grief and horror to the back of my mind and carry on with the Progress! I have learnt how to dissemble, thank goodness. It is part of a king's stock-in-trade. But it will be difficult, so difficult! To have to smile and pretend that one is happy, when one is torn apart inside!

Soon, my dear Anne will meet me at Warwick. Then we will travel on to Pontefract, where my little son will join us. And so to York and his investiture. I must try to think of happier things. Our great reception at my favourite city, my northern capital. I know they have spent weeks preparing it!

And you will also be at my side, my dear Francis. The most loyal friend ever! What you must have thought of my foolish attachment to Buckingham, I cannot imagine. Now, after he has been shown up for what he is, you are the only one I can confide the truth in. Not even Anne will be told who killed the princes—though she, like everyone else, will soon suspect that something has happened to them, when they are no longer seen at the Tower!

I am sick at heart, Francis! The world and its evil ways are a heavy burden on me!'

Bishop Morton, Brecknock Castle, South Wales, Early August 1483

My Dear Lady Beaufort,

It is done. It was surprisingly easy really. The angry and rebellious mood which Buckingham was in when he arrived back here after his stormy interview with the king at Gloucester made him a prime target for my suggestions. I hardly needed to persuade him. He was ready to get his revenge on the king, whom he feels has mistreated and berated him very harshly, after all the good service he has done him! He believes a wrong has been done to him; a base injustice!

I am sending this letter by your trusty steward Reginald Bray, who came post-haste after my brief and urgent note to you. Through him, I will also convey to you by word of mouth only, which is safer, more details of the course of action which, I believe, the Duke of Buckingham will now begin to pursue. His mind is set on revenge, that is certain! I have let him know that the Woodvilles are planning an uprising soon in the southern and western counties, which are already rebellious to the king, and I suggested that you, his aunt, would be very eager to take this golden opportunity and call on your son, Henry Tudor, to bring a great army from France and Brittany to join in this rebellion against King Richard and that you had agreed to a marriage between your son Henry and Queen Elizabeth's elder daughter, Bess. I told him you had been visiting Queen Elizabeth in Westminster Sanctuary and that she had agreed to this marriage as long as the Woodvilles were given considerable help in rising against Richard. I pointed out that it would unite the warring factions of York and Lancaster forever and make sure that there was no more dissension. Buckingham's reward for helping bring this about would assure him the highest office in the new regime!

His eyes glowed with anticipation of his glittering future if this were achieved! He knows that King Richard is now his enemy and will soon find a way to get rid of him. The alternative is far better, though he has always hated the Woodvilles for forcing him into marriage as a young boy, when a ward of Queen Elizabeth, with one of the queen's sisters, who is a commoner, like them all. He considered her not worthy of marriage with one of the highest rank such as he! But now he must put his aversion aside to assure his own survival.

He was worried about the Woodvilles finding out before they started the uprising that, in fact, their young figurehead was already dead, but I pointed out that there was no way they could discover this. After all, Richard was unlikely to inform them or be accused of the deed, and Buckingham himself would certainly not make public his involvement.

He fell into the trap beautifully, as he did into yours with regard to Edward and Richard and was all for riding out that minute and raising his troops. He is rather foolish and gullible and easily led, thank goodness. It makes our task simpler!

If he only knew that he was not in fact responsible for the young princes' deaths, but that they were already dead when he entered their chamber in the Tower late that night! But who is to tell him? Neither you nor I and no one else knows, except your trusty doctor! And he will certainly not incriminate himself. What some men will do for a great deal of gold! And I am sure the price you paid for his continued silence was very heavy? Would it not be better to assure yourself of his permanent silence? Surely that could be easily arranged by yourself, without employing others? Slip in a great overdose of the poppy into his wine glass, say, when he visits you next? That would surely be one weight off your mind!

Do you plan to ever tell your son about the boys' elimination and your part in it? Better not, I would think. Keep it between ourselves! But of course, you will have to tell Lord Stanley, your good husband, about Buckingham's planned insurrection. There is no need to reveal more to him. It is best he keeps himself completely aloof from the plot and stays with Richard. He must keep a foot in the king's camp for the safety of you both. I am sure he is as good at dissembling, when the need arises, as his Lady wife!

I expect you will visit Queen Elizabeth in sanctuary at once when you receive this to tell her the good news about her change in fortunes and to impress on her that the rising planned by her family and their supporters must be timed to coincide exactly with Buckingham's rebellion in the west!

Meanwhile, I suggest that you inform Henry at once of the planned uprising, so that a date can be set for the armies to synchronise their hosts' movements.

I look forward to the visits of your well-trusted steward, Reginald Bray. I now have plenty to discuss with him and much to say for him to convey to you privily.

Your faithful servant, Madam.

John Morton,

Bishop of Bath and Wells

Edward, Prince of Wales, York, 8 September 1483

Today has been a wonderful but very tiring day for me. I tried to forget how ill and exhausted I felt, especially in the great Minster of York, where my investiture as Prince of Wales took place, to make me officially the next in line to the throne to my father, the king. But it was difficult, very difficult. I did not want to let my father down by giving way to my persistent cough, so I tried hard to stifle it. This often made things worse, and I felt so faint and breathless that I had to pray for strength to get through the endless ceremonials, prayers, and music without falling down. I was determined not to give in to my bodily weakness and somehow managed to keep upright, though at times I was very glad of my father's encouraging smile to keep me going and my mother's loving touch on my shoulder. She too is unwell. She has a troubling cough like me, but she has kept it from my father. He has enough to worry him now he is king.

If only I were well, like other boys my age! Here am I, the most important prince in the land, and I have a weak and sickly body like the runt of a litter! Will I ever get well? Father told me he was delicate as a boy too and look at him now: a strong soldier and able to stay in the saddle on his many travels for days on end without trouble! He grew out of his delicate childhood health. Maybe I will too one day? I try to be cheerful and put up with not being able to do much. Mother says it is God's will when ill health strikes, and one must pray for deliverance. I do, every day. But I seem to get worse, not better, especially in winter and spring. I feel healthier in the summer and can breathe better then. The sun seems to help me. But we do not get a lot of sun in Yorkshire, even in summer.

I could not even ride here from Middleham. I had to come in a horse litter. I felt humiliated and angry. I have no patience with my constant illness. I do my best to cope with what I have to do, such as getting through today, but I know that others pity me, particularly John, my bastard brother. I envy him his rude health and strength. He never gets ill—never even a cold. And I am constantly coughing and wheezing; always catching chills and infections, however much care I take, however well I am looked after. I hate the fuss they make of me, my mother, the servants, and my nurse. But without it, I know I should probably be dead by now. So I have to put up with it.

One day, I may be king—if I live long enough. I cannot imagine how I would cope with it. My father never stops work; never relaxes. He has enormous responsibilities. He is driven by a constant desire to prove that he is a good king and loves his people. He plans to do all kinds of good works during his reign, which I hope is long. For I do not want to take his place. The very thought of it terrifies me, though I have never admitted it, and will not. I admire him greatly for that. All this travelling he has done in his Progress, to show himself to his people and prove that he really cares for their welfare, proves that he is a good man. I am lucky to have him as my father.

When the mayor and Aldermen of York came to visit me at Middleham after they heard my father had become king, I was very proud. I knew I was now Prince of Wales and the heir to the throne. They brought me presents, and I was grateful.

But all I really want is good health: to run and play like other boys; to go hunting with my father; to be a knight when I grow up, and fight in battles as he has.

Will God be good to me and grant my wish one day? I have so much in many ways, I know, far more than other boys. I try not to feel resentful. Most boys would envy me. But not if they knew my fine clothes, possessions, riches, and position come at a price—a very high price. I think they would choose to be poor and healthy, rather than rich and sick.

But God does not give us a choice. We have to accept whatever he gives us—or chooses not to give us—in life.

Francis Lovell, Lord Chamberlain, Lincoln, 11 October 1483

It is a nasty shock for King Richard, for us all, after such a successful and happy September. The wonderful welcome Richard and his family met on entry to York from the ecstatic townspeople; the pageantry and grandeur of little Edward's official investiture as Prince of Wales in York Minster; the feasts, the plays; then the continued, heady atmosphere of joy as town after town opened its arms to the new king, his queen, and Edward! It was a golden month—like an incredible dream—but one wakes up from dreams to reality.

And now reality has become a nightmare for Richard, with this terrible, this unbelievable news! It has come out of the blue.

Henry, Duke of Buckingham, has raised a rebellion against Richard and is joining with Henry Tudor, who has taken this chance to launch an invasion he has apparently been planning for months, with ships, arms, and men financed by Duke Francis of Brittany and, of course, his very wealthy, formidable, and highly ambitious mother, Lady Margaret Beaufort!

It is a terrible blow for Richard, an unlooked-for turn in affairs.

He knew that Buckingham had been upset and angry at Gloucester by his reaction to his news about the princes in the Tower. But this—this from a man who was Richard's chief minister; whom he had given so much to; had raised so high above all others in the country, next to the king only in importance. This from a man who, only three months ago, was the chief supporter and mover behind Richard taking the throne; who made great and persuasive speeches in his support, with impressive eloquence and determination! Who became, in effect, another kingmaker, like Warwick before him was to Edward IV.

And this is how he repays his king!

'The most untrue creature living!' is how Richard described him today, in disbelief and loathing. Richard should have had him arrested and executed there and then at Gloucester, to show the world what kind of man his new second-in-command was.

But I can understand the reasons he did not do this; why he shelved the problem until the great Progress was over. It would have shown Richard up as a bad judge of men and ruined his growing popularity. But it has surely made things worse now? If Richard accuses him of the deed in addition to raising a rebellion against him, who will believe Richard? Who will believe that he was not originally implicated? It is a terrible situation for the king to unravel. I do not envy him, but I support him wholeheartedly in whatever he decides to do. I know he is a good man, who only tries to do his best for the commonweal and that he had nothing to do with the princes' murder. Under his dissembling happiness of the last month in public, I know he has grieved greatly for those boys.

Henry Tudor, of course, has been a thorn in the side of the Yorkists for many a year, but, it seemed, one which caused little trouble and was not to be worried about overmuch. King Edward tried for years to get him back to England, without success. I know Richard did have him on his agenda to deal with in the future. Now it has caused a sudden and disturbing upflare, combined with the unexpected rising of the south and south-west against Richard, stirred up no doubt by the same hand which aided Henry Tudor, for Lady Margaret Beaufort owns vast tracts of land in those areas and can call upon the support of her knights and vassals to aid her in any endeavour at a moment's notice.

The whole thing has been cleverly planned and engineered, it seems, while poor Richard was enjoying the adulation and fervent support of his loyal Northerners. Now he has come down to earth with a great jolt!

What will he do? How will he deal with the situation? He is a great and successful soldier. He will come up with an effective plan soon, I know it. At present, he sits alone in his room, allowing no one to disturb him while he works out the situation and how to deal with it. That is his way. And none dare disturb him, even Anne, his wife, or I, his closest friend. He will not emerge until he has his plan of action all worked out. Then, there will be a fever of activity as he issues orders, sends messages, and commissions of array all over the country. There is not one soldier or man-at-arms here with him on Progress, only a few personal bodyguards. Now he will have to get together the greatest army possible in a short time to meet this formidable threat!

Henry, Duke of Buckingham, Shropshire, Mid-October 1483

How did I come to this pass? How did I get into this dreadful situation where my very life is now forfeit if I am caught? And it is most likely that I will be caught soon, for there is none willing, or able, to help me here.

I am uncomfortably sure now that I have been played for a fool, used as a pawn in some clever political game engineered by that wily fox Bishop Morton, whom I thought of as my friend and by Lady Margaret Beaufort, the chief instigators. They worked on my ambition and dreams of greatness when Henry Tudor came to power; told me trumped-up lies of plots the Woodvilles were planning. After that terrible interview with the king at Gloucester, I felt forced to throw in my lot with that hated family; I could see no other course! I just thought that the king had me marked for harsh treatment later, when he returned to London from the Progress. The cold look in his eyes told me that. I was not willing to wait to be publicly humiliated and maybe meet a terrible death for my deed in the Tower later at the king's pleasure! I would not allow myself to be dangled like a rat in a cat's mouth until it chooses to go in for the kill! But I was hasty, and I admit it. My action in embracing the uprising was very ill-judged. I see that now, when it is too late!

And it has brought me to this—reduced to wearing a farm worker's rags in order to disguise myself and avoid capture; to beg shelter and a hiding place from one who was my servant years ago, Ralph Bannaster, who works a small farm in Shropshire; throwing myself on his mercy in my desperation. I hoped for help. And what has he done? He has deceived me! I suspect, in fact I am pretty sure, that he has made my presence here known to the authorities—for the reward the king has offered for my capture! One thousand pounds is a fortune to him,

I suppose! Faced with the possibility of all his money troubles disappearing forever, loyalty to his old master came a poor second! I do not blame him really. In the end, most men put their own well-being and hope of gain first. What did he care for my skin? Now I must leave this poor place somehow and get away before I am apprehended. Where I will go I know not.

The appalling weather was the main problem. That and the absence of any real loyalty to the cause by my hastily gathered tatterdemalion army.

Week after week of drenching rain, chilling us to the bone, high winds, lack of shelter, poor food, and then the Severn floods which effectively cut us off from our goal—all contributed to the outcome—complete failure.

My poorly motivated soldiers, whose morale had plunged to the lowest depths, now slipped away, bit by bit, whatever I said or did to re-energise them. I begged, I even pleaded with the remnants to go on with me but was ignored. I, who but a few short weeks ago, was the highest in the land, bar one—lowering myself to this rabble! They just slipped away to their homes whenever they had the chance, mainly in the night. We never fought a single skirmish with Richard's soldiers, let alone a full battle! It was just one long, disillusioning, and depressing trek through endless muddy—often impossible-to-negotiate tracks, achieving nothing but the complete collapse of the enterprise—and my sure downfall. For unless I can escape abroad somehow, I am done for. Bishop Morton has already done this. I discovered, to my horror, when I returned in despair to the manor house at Weobley where I had left him earlier hoping for further help, which perhaps his clever mind could conjure up—that he had fled to the fen country of Cambridgeshire, his See, and thence to Flanders, no doubt, to hide out. Little did I guess, when I rode away from my castle at Brecknock on 18 October, with Morton as my companion, leaving him later in Shropshire, that I would be reduced to such a poor state within the space of a week or so! My army was smaller than I had hoped—a mere few hundred men—and I could sense a definite sullenness in the Welsh contingent, who seemed less than willing to leave their homes with autumn fast approaching. But Morton laughed off my misgivings; spurred me on with his talk of great victories to come, calming my fears. He assured me my army would surely grow in leaps and bounds as men flocked to the cause. It would be their chance to get rid of the usurper! The Kentish men were already up—so keen they had started the uprising a whole week early! The south-west and south were blazing with rebellion! What had I to be unsure about?! And soon, Henry Tudor's 5,000 Bretons would land and join in the insurrection. King Richard would be routed in no time at all and dead before Christmas. I would be at the new King Henry's side in the place of honour at the Christmas Feast at Westminster!

I believed him, every word. My star had risen so high already earlier in the year, raising me from virtual obscurity, in spite of my noble birth—to the highest position in the country as King Richard's right-hand man—surely it was still in the ascendancy? Surely nothing could stop my success? I was on a winning streak!

How wrong, how utterly wrong I was! And now, it seems, I am likely to pay for it—mayhap with my life! How the wheel of fortune can turn so fast, raising men high, then plunging them into the lowest pit in a twinkling of the eye is beyond my comprehension.

Richard, King of England, Salisbury, 29 October 1483

'Sire, my Lord King! The Duke of Buckingham has been brought in, in shackles! He is here, in the town prison, and begs leave most urgently to see Your Grace. He has confessed his rebellion against you, his lawful king, and has already been sentenced to death by Sir Ralph Assheton, the Vice-Constable of England, whom you appointed to lead the commission which put the duke on trial. But Buckingham would speak to you one more time, before his execution!'

'That wretched traitor? That faithless dog? Given so much and giving nothing but treachery in return! I will never set eyes on him again willingly, Francis, let alone speak with him. The sound of his honeyed voice and the sight of his smiling, villainous face would have me retching!'

'But, Sire, he swears that none of this rebellion was his doing. That he neither conceived it nor planned it. That he was a pawn in a deeper plot, that he was drawn into it by the clever machinations of powerful ones whom he would name to you, if you will but grant him audience! He says that they are so dangerous that they may still do you great harm—even after he himself has met the headsman's axe!'

'I do not want to know! It is all lies, lies! It is just a ploy to persuade me to see him. It is enough that he raised an army against me, that he set himself against me. None could force him against his will to become my enemy! He merely hopes to win me over with his charm and persuasiveness. I rue the day that I ever listened to him in the first place. I must have lost my reason!

But I will not be made a fool of a second time. He can keep his excuses for his Maker. For soon, he will meet him—if the wicked can be granted audience with God before descending into hell—where Buckingham belongs! Perhaps he can pour out his so-called confession to him. Perhaps God will listen to him, for I will not. I disdain him and all he stands for!

Prepare for his execution on the morrow. I will brook no delay. He has done so much other evil too that none knows of, save you and I. I can never say a word of that other dreadful deed of his, which he confessed to me at

Gloucester—rue the day! I would have found a way to punish him for that before long anyway! Now he will die for it all! I am sick to my soul by the very thought of him!'

Henry Tudor, At Sea, off Brittany, 4 November 1483

My Dear Mother,

As you may already have heard—bad news travels fast—the recent great storm completely dashed any hopes I may have had of succeeding in my endeavour!

Having set out rather later than planned from Paimpol on 31 October, with fifteen ships, five thousand Bretons, arms and horses, prepared to land on English soil and coordinate my invasion with the Duke of Buckingham's great rebellion, this tempest blew away, God knows where, thirteen ships of my fleet on the very first night! I hope they are not dashed to pieces on the rocks of Lands End, but have reached safe haven somewhere by now in Normandy harbours or Breton ports. But I fear there must have been casualties. It is inevitable. And when I think how much they all cost and how I have had to beg, borrow, and steal every piece of gold to pay for them—just to see them blown away out of sight before we had even reached British shores!

But we have not encountered any floating wreckage either, so maybe they are safe.

There is no way of knowing what may have happened to them at the moment. There is certainly no sign of them. We too are limping back to Vannes with half our sails blown away and several men lost overboard. I am not a good sailor, I discovered, and never want to experience such a storm at sea again. They are bad enough on land, but at least one can find shelter there. At sea, it is as if all the elements have been let loose in determination to destroy one!

We found ourselves the next morning off the coast of Dorset. I could see that the shores around Poole were lined with troops, but we were too far off to ascertain their identity. I sent out a small boat with one or two men to inquire who they were. The soldiers shouted that the rebellion had succeeded and that they were sent there by the Duke of Buckingham himself to conduct us to his camp.

But I was not fooled by all this. My life has taught me to be cautious and suspicious and to put my trust in very few. The fact that there were no banners and no colours visible first put me on my guard. Something was just not right. And I acted accordingly. We withdrew well out into the Channel, away from the obvious danger.

We sailed on to Plymouth and learnt that the king had already reached Exeter in unopposed triumph, so I decided to abandon my enterprise and sail back to Brittany. There was no way we could achieve anything now, with the situation as it was.

I heard also that the Duke of Buckingham had been caught like a rat in a trap, taken to Salisbury, where the king was then, and summarily executed. It does not do to get on the wrong side of this king—he does not wait for trials but makes his own judgement then and there! Remember Lord Hastings? So Buckingham achieved no more than I and has lost his head for his pains. At least I have escaped the king's clutches!

I just pray that your part in all this will not be discovered, or you could face terrible punishment too. Just because Richard has never had a woman executed, there is no guaranteeing he will not if made angry enough! My stepfather, Lord Stanley, has been with the king the whole time, I believe, so maybe this fact will guard you? He could hardly be shown to have helped with the plot, as he kept such a low profile—though he did, of course.

Bishop Morton, whom I know was the real brains behind it all, got away safely to Flanders, I expect? That one knows how to look after himself!

I plan now to travel to Nantes, when we reach Brittany, and find out what happened to my ships and men. There I will petition Duke Francis for a further 10,000 crowns, by means of which I may maintain myself and my exiled supporters while we begin to plan another venture as soon as may be. This time, I am determined it will be in late spring or summer, when the weather will not ruin our chances before we have even begun!

As soon as I reach a Breton safe haven, I will have this letter conveyed to you quickly, as you must be worried about my fate since news of the great storm must have reached you by now.

It was simply not the right time! God made it abundantly clear by sending that terrible weather—on land as well as at sea—at just that very moment. It also ruined the uprising I believe?

I must be patient now I suppose, again. I have spent my entire life waiting and being patient!

Please let me know as soon as possible that you are safe from the king's fury?

Buckingham was his right-hand man and chief supporter until the rebellion, but that did nothing to save him from the headman.

Your loving son,
Henry Tudor

Margaret Beaufort, Countess of Richmond, Woking Old Hall, Late November 1483

My Dear Henry,

At last, I have a chance to write an answer to your letter, written to me at sea off Brittany, at the beginning of November. I expect you wonder why it has taken me so long to answer you. Well, the king has forbidden all communication between us from now on. But of course, I shall completely ignore his command! I have ways and means of sending and receiving letters, in spite of being spied on constantly, I know, by the king's men. I have loyal servants who can travel incognito, quietly and unobtrusively, often in disguise. They are paid very well, so they make sure they do not get caught! They risk their lives willingly in my service. I do not flatter myself that it is through love for me that they do this. I am a wealthy woman, and they do it for what they can squeeze out of my purse. It does not matter to me, as long as the job gets done. You have a cynic for a mother! But life has taught me to be one.

The king discovered my part in planning the rebellion, of course, and your involvement at what seemed the opportune time for an invasion. He also found out about my collusion with Bishop Morton, that sly and clever old fox, who has now fled to the Low Countries and keeps his head down, out of harm's way!

What the king does not know is the fact that that arrogant fool, the Duke of Buckingham, was guided and directed by Morton and I, and my husband, Lord Stanley, was in the know too, though he remained always by the king's side and was ostensibly one of his most loyal supporters. If only Richard knew the whole truth.

But we must make sure he never finds out! We were very lucky that the king refused outright to see Buckingham one last time when the duke beseeched him to, before his summary execution in Salisbury. He sent word that he had important news about the other conspirators which he must tell Richard. He even sent a letter by one of his gaolers to the king, I heard, which probably contained my name and that of my husband and Bishop Morton. But the king tore it up without reading it in a great rage. Thank goodness! Luck has certainly been on our side. If Lord Stanley had been named, he would most certainly have lost his head. As it is, his secret collusion has remained hidden!

I have escaped very lightly really. The king could easily have had me executed. If I were a man, there is no doubt I would have received the death penalty. But this king is of a squeamish nature, it seems, with regard to hurting women. Lucky for me!

But he has stripped me of all my estates and put me under the care of my husband, in semi-imprisonment. Lord Stanley must guarantee my good behaviour. And he is to administer my estates from now on. I am to have no hand in it. Well, we will see about that! I am not worried. Stanley has little influence over me. I have three times his intelligence and can circumvent any ideas he may have about controlling my actions! He is my husband in name only. There is no love lost between us. It was a marriage of convenience, after all. A woman must have a husband, society says. But I have always been of a most independent nature, and no man will control me and decide what I should do or not do!

It is lucky for me the king is disposed to be lenient, I suppose. But I do not respect him for it. A king must be strong—and seen to be strong! Any action like this can only be interpreted as weakness. When you are king, I will teach you that you must be ruthless whenever your enemies step out of line. It is the only way. Perhaps Richard will learn that yet—to his cost!

Your patience will be rewarded—and soon, Henry. I know it! Go on waiting and planning. Gather as many men as you can to your cause. Many of the highest nobility have fled from England after the failed rebellion to join you in Brittany!

I have been to see the erstwhile Queen Elizabeth several times. She is still in sanctuary with her daughters. She is very fearful about the fate of her two sons in the Tower, as rumours have been flying around for months that they are dead, as they have not been seen since the summer. I did not enlighten her, nor did I reveal to her that I know a great deal more about that matter than it is politic to reveal! I need her on our side. If she also knew that her doctor—who is also my doctor—had a lot to do with administering the overdose to her precious sons, she would have him killed, no doubt. She is known to have a most vicious nature. If she knew of my involvement, God knows what would happen. I think that King Richard would soon forget his aversion to hurting women and I would be for the executioner's block!

I have persuaded her to agree to her Woodville family supporting you wholeheartedly in another uprising, when the time is ripe, in return for your promise to marry her daughter Bess and make her your queen when you become King of England. Elizabeth Grey is extremely ambitious; always has been. Any chance to raise her family is irresistible to her! If Bess becomes your queen, her mother will then hold another most important position as Dowager Queen. The Marquess of Dorset has already joined you, I believe—her beloved eldest son by her first marriage?

I played her like a fish on a line! It was like taking comfits from a baby!

Now Christmas approaches, I am going to give you another piece of advice. I hear you groan and think, what now? I know that I urge you to many things, but it is only your ultimate good that inspires me. If I give advice, it is that I know, with experience, that it will surely benefit you!

I suggest that you make a proclamation to all your supporters in a public place soon, regarding your willingness to make Elizabeth of York your queen when you ascend the throne of England. Stress that this will unite the Houses of Lancaster and York forever, and that will mean no more strife, no more wars. What everyone wants is peace now, after all! Your promise will be welcomed with great joy, not only in Brittany, but here, by your many secret supporters, in fact, by the country as a whole, which is sick unto death of the killing and bloodletting of civil war!

And now I must send for my most trusted messenger to convey this missive to you. I suggest that you destroy it as soon as you have read it—it is too incriminating for too many people to get into the wrong hands.

Remember, my son, I work constantly in your interest. It is my mission in life—and obsession, if you like. What other mission should a mother have than the good of her son? I neglected you in the past, as a small child—not deliberately, you know that. Now I try to make up for that by dedicating myself to your future!

Your loving mother,
Margaret Beaufort,
Countess of Richmond

Elizabeth Grey, to the Marquess of Dorset, London, 8 March 1484

My Dear Son,

I have news of great import to convey to you.

I have at last been persuaded to leave the wearisome confines of Westminster Sanctuary with my five daughters, by none other than Richard, the king!

I can imagine you gasping in surprise now as you read this, for you know how determined I have been not to give in to his many persuasive approaches. I let poor little Richard out with many assurances that he would be treated kindly and well in the Tower and that he would be a playmate and companion for Prince Edward, who was too much on his own there—and look what has happened to them! They have not been seen for months, and a heartbroken mother now knows for sure that they are dead, as everyone says. The Archbishop of Canterbury himself took Richard from me by the hand into his own charge. I had little choice but to trust this high churchman. If one could not trust an archbishop, I thought, who could one trust? I have learnt not to trust anyone now though, except myself.

But things have changed greatly, and the king made me an offer which I felt I could not refuse. He also made it clear that it was the last time he would ever attempt to change my mind on the subject. I think that, as far as he was concerned, we could all rot in there for the rest of our lives, if I ignored this last request.

His terms were not exactly generous, but I felt I could not turn them down. My life in sanctuary had become utterly intolerable, and the poor girls' lives were not lives at all, but an endless succession of dull days in which nothing ever happened and they never met any new people. I could not continue to impose it on them. They need fresh air and other young people, balls and parties, the chance to spread their wings!

Those few musty rooms could offer them nothing. Elizabeth, the eldest, was getting positively ill with the perpetual confinement of our self-imposed imprisonment and had learnt to hate me for keeping her a prisoner, I know, even though she had been informed about the proposed marriage with Henry Tudor when he becomes king, which I had agreed with her mother, Lady Margaret Beaufort, who sometimes visited me there. We became quite friendly, though she is a deep and devious person, I feel, and I certainly would never put any real trust in her. But she seemed honest and sincere in her wish for her son and Bess to be united for the good of the country, and I had no reason to distrust her motives, at least over that. Her husband, Lord Stanley, is one of the king's most stalwart supporters—supposedly. But I think he is one of those who give their allegiance to whoever it is politic to at the time. Lady Margaret has assured me that he supports her completely in this proposed marriage—so what does that tell one about his shifting loyalties? Her son, Henry Tudor, made a solemn vow in Rennes Cathedral on Christmas Day to marry Bess, as you know (I expect you were there?) and unite The Houses of Lancaster and York. As he did this in front of a great congregation of all his noble supporters, surely he is in earnest? You know him. What do you believe? I have never met the man. Do you think Bess will like him as a proposed husband? She was to have married the Dauphin of France until 1483, when Louis reneged on the agreement with my husband. It upset her greatly. I do not want her upset again.

In the light of new information, I have come to believe that Richard offers no real threat to us. I am now sure that he had nothing to do with the death of my poor boys in the Tower last summer or disposed of them expediently.

But I have so many other reasons to hate Richard, and I still do, in spite of this new knowledge which has come to me lately, which I think exonerates him, at least in this terrible deed. For all anyone knew at first, my boys could just have been taken away and be held imprisoned where they could not be a motivation for more uprisings. I prayed constantly that they were safe somewhere, but in my heart of hearts, I admit that I had to believe the poor little souls must be dead. And now I know for certain that they are. Someone had them smothered in their sleep, after they had been heavily drugged. I pray they knew little about it and passed over into heaven, where the innocent go, unaware of the terrible wickedness of their murderer.

I suppose my hatred for Richard started when I felt him a rival for my husband's love—he was so obviously the favourite brother, the one Edward listened to and whose advice he followed in all things. I could not bear it, knowing that this beloved brother had hated and despised me from the first. He did not think me good enough for Edward—and he made it very obvious. So I retaliated in kind! And he has such a clever and able mind—he was far cleverer than Edward! If we were both in the room, Edward would ignore me, pass over my remarks and advice—so intent was he on listening to Richard's! I felt humiliated and angered by that, even though I knew Edward loved me more than any other woman. He had many women, but he always came back to me. In all things, I was the closest one to him, but not in matters of state. There, Richard influenced him completely and I did not even have a look in—the king's own wife!

Richard's chief councillors first assured me that he had some proof that he did not kill my sons or arrange for others to murder them. Someone else in a very high position had, apparently, more real motive: burning personal ambition to become king himself—and a real opportunity to kill my little sons, being the Lord Chamberlain, with access to any castle or fortress whenever he desired, by virtue of his position!

And that someone was the man who came to me and first told me of the rumours going around that the boys were both dead and that King Richard had killed them or had them killed! That was the one who urged me to stir up rebellion against Richard with the aid of my large Woodville family, in retribution for his murderous deed. And all the while, he had committed the deed himself already! That foul creature was the Duke of Buckingham! I actually entertained my little ones' murderer unknowingly. How he smiled and dissembled so to the mother of his innocent victims, I know not. Surely this was the evil one in disguise?

Lord Francis Lovell then came to me alone and told me in confidence that he had been instructed by King Richard to tell me of what passed between himself and the Duke of Buckingham at Gloucester during his Progress. No one else but the king, Francis Lovell, and now myself, knows of it, and I was only told to allay my fears. Francis told me of the king's terrible anger with Buckingham; how he shouted abuse at him violently and cursed him to hell, for committing this appalling deed. He told me also of Richard's great grief for my sons, as he had loved them as the children of his beloved brother, Edward. Francis was the first one to be taken into Richard's confidence the same day, as his best and closest friend, after Buckingham had been sent away with the king's curses ringing in his ears and promises of retribution which would catch up with him soon! And then, of course, not long after, Buckingham raised his great rebellion against the king to remove him—not to help put Henry Tudor on the throne, as he had promised Lady Margaret Beaufort, his mother, who was also implicated in the uprising—but to elevate himself to the highest position in the land! He had planned it all along. Even King Richard had been taken in by his flamboyant and frequent gestures of loyalty and had rewarded him extravagantly!

Why would Francis make this up? I believed him. He had no reason to lie. He had more reason to keep completely quiet on the king's behalf; to tell no one, least of all myself, whom he knows has hated Richard always. But Richard had actually instructed him to tell me of it, because I needed to know what had happened to my little sons and not be kept in torture of mind any longer. I was devastated to hear the truth, but at least I can begin to grieve for them now. Richard also wanted me to know what really happened, to allay my fears for myself and my daughters and to bring about our speedy release. Somehow, this confidence rang true to me. I knew it was time to emerge at last from my self-imposed imprisonment. I have to admit, against my will really, that Richard must have a streak of good in him, after all! He had no need to do this for my children and I. Something of common decency motivated him to it. But I have been instructed never to divulge a word of it to anyone else, so I have broken that promise already by telling you, my eldest son. Unless you want your mother's death on your conscience, you must never breathe a word of it to another living soul! Richard would not show kindness to me a second time, if this became common knowledge!

Since 2 May, I have been living quietly in a house on the outskirts of London, where it is peaceful and my girls have freedom again. I think we will be able to live fairly easily on the 700 marks a year Richard has granted me. But I do have a sort of guardian, appointed by Richard, to keep an eye on me, a man named John Nesfield, one of the squires of his body. Ostensibly, he is my attendant, but I know he is really a spy to make sure I do not get out of line. If I do, I will lose my stipend. I cannot afford to get on the wrong side of Richard any more. If I am tempted, I will remind myself that my girls' lives depend on my good behaviour.

Now, my son, I urge you to abandon your support of Henry Tudor in Brittany and come home to England.

The king has promised you a pardon! He made this long proclamation in which he promised to keep me and mine in safety, and that surely includes you. I urge you to put yourself in Richard's hands, as I have. I think that will better serve your future prospects. After all, it is best to be on the side of a king in office—which

Richard most certainly is, than on that of one who only may or may not achieve that high status!

I know you will find it hard to understand really, in spite of what I have told you, that I have decided to come to terms with the man who has done me so much wrong, who declared my little sons bastards for his own ends, then deposed them, drove you into exile, and executed your brother Richard, Lord Grey, and my much-loved brother Earl Rivers. I have lost three of my beloved sons. You are the only one left. And I need you near me. I need your support.

What else could I do? I am a woman alone now and I had had enough of my miserable existence in sanctuary. I put my pride, my hurt, and my anger aside. I had no choice.

Please come home soon, my dear son! If you cannot leave the Welsh prince openly, then find a quiet and secret way to do it! I am sure it will be to your future advantage.

Your loving mother,
Elizabeth, Dowager Queen

Duchess Cecily, Fotheringhay Castle, Northants, April 1484

My Dear Richard,

This is a blow, a terrible blow! It is unbelievable, yet only too real for you and for poor Anne. I know that little Edward was not a strong child, but this is still so unexpected. However, I did wonder that he had not the strength to attend your coronation in London, even if transported down by horse litter. Then I could see that he was barely able to get through the day of his investiture at York in September when he was officially made Prince of Wales, and your successor, in that grand ceremony. But he bravely did his duty and did not give in to his bodily ills. He showed great courage and maturity for one so young. I thought it was just another of his heavy colds. He tried so hard to control his persistent cough. I did not think that it was a really serious condition. Children are always ill with something or other. They go down fast with chills and infections but usually recover just as quickly. But you tell me that he had a very bad winter again? It is sad, so very sad. At least Anne was with him for part of that time, even if neither of you were there when he at last succumbed to his illness on 9 April, so she must not feel this terrible guilt you say has overwhelmed her. As the king's wife, her place was by your side. She did not know how seriously ill little

Edward was—none of us did. Her role as a mother came second to her role as the queen. Those in high places often feel this awful guilt when they have to leave their children in other's hands; when duty frequently calls them away—even if the children are well. I did, frequently, when I felt constrained to support your father by accompanying him on his many expeditions—even when I was heavily pregnant at times—so the depth of despair that Anne is in is very understandable. But it will pass. God will give you both the strength to bear this terrible loss somehow.

And the doctors tell you now that they think he was actually suffering from the consumption, but because he did not cough blood until a month or so ago, it was not diagnosed? Even if it had been, I am sure there was little more that they could have done for him. Everything that could be done was done, I am sure. As the king's son, I am sure he had every possible care.

Once more, as so often is the case when appalling things happen, we must say that it is God's will. But God's ways are quite inscrutable at times. As it states in the Bible so truly, they 'passeth all understanding'. But we are not meant to fully understand, I suppose, but just accept whatever he sends us in life, both good and ill. It is very hard, almost impossible at times—such as now.

And you surely did not deserve such as this. Ever since taking the throne, you have gone out of your way to be a good king! You have worked unremittingly for the commonweal—which was your stated intention—and I know you allow yourself little rest but are involved in continual schemes and plans to improve the lot of the ordinary folk of this great country.

Your recent great Parliament after Christmas and the new laws you had passed there for the benefit of true justice for all men, both rich and poor, have proved that you have the best of intentions, my son. You have even risked alienating those nobles who would support you in times of need, as these new laws do not benefit them—indeed, often go against their interests in some cases! And this is how you are rewarded for the care and concern you have shown for your people. It is a cruel injustice! But the world is full of injustice.

What God gives with one hand, he often seems to take with the other. You have so much in many ways: the highest office in the land; great riches and estates; a loving and faithful wife; an excellent mind and the strength and determination to carry out your will successfully, as men respond to your leadership with respect and loyalty. But I expect you feel the one thing you valued most of all—your dear son—has been torn from you cruelly and inexplicably. And of course, Anne is not a strong woman, and I expect you fear there will be no more sons. But there is still time! She is young yet. Who knows but in a few months she may bring forth another male babe! I know that that would not compensate for Edward's loss, but you must try to look forward now, both of you. What else can you do?

I am with you in mind and heart, Richard, if not in body. I understand and feel your pain. As your mother, how could I not? Try to gain some comfort from prayer, even if you feel God has used you harshly. I find it helps greatly to calm my mind and spirit, so I devote a good part of every day to prayer. I will pray most earnestly now for your peace of mind, and also for Anne's.

God be with you, my dear son.
Your loving mother,
Cecily,
Dowager Duchess of York

Richard, King of England, Nottingham Castle, Late April 1484

My Dear Mother,

I thank you for your long letter and your loving words of comfort. Anne and I need all the comfort we can get at this dreadful time. She has been utterly felled by what has happened. She has taken to her bed, will hardly eat or drink, refuses to speak—even to me. She seems to have cut herself off from the world. I cannot get near her in spirit. We are cut off from each other. I want to comfort her, but I do not know how, as she even rejects my physical presence. I cannot understand it. I need her so much. If she would at least allow me to hold her in my arms, perhaps we would both begin to heal? Surely she could begin to accept our little son's death if she would allow herself to be comforted. She does not even cry now—just lies there like one dead to the world, uncaring and unresponsive. We are all at our wits' end as to what to do to help her.

I have called the best doctors in to see her, but they can do nothing for maladies of the spirit, they tell me. Only time will perhaps heal her. All they can say is let her rest and give her time. Am I to lose my dear wife's companionship at this time when we surely need each other most, as well as my poor son's life? It is unbearable.

And affairs of state still have to be dealt with somehow, though I have not the heart to do anything. I have to force myself to read and sign papers about things which now seem to have no relevance to my life, which I honestly could not care less about at the moment. Things which concerned me most intensely until a fortnight or so ago are now meaningless. I have to concentrate hard to listen, to understand, to get the meaning from the words in front of me, when all the time, I just want to tear them up, throw them to the four winds, tell my councillors to go away and leave me alone. I can only keep going by an effort of will.

This is my punishment. God's punishment for doing what I should never have done, for taking the throne. For breaking faith with my dear brother Edward and overriding his deathbed wishes by superseding his son! I know that many call me a wicked usurper and hate me for wresting the throne from that poor boy, who could not defend himself against my decision. I am a usurper—even if I became one for the best of reasons! At the time, it seemed the best, the only thing to do. But I must have been wrong. And now is the time of retribution! My retribution.

Anne blames herself for Edward's death. I know she does, for not being there with him. She does not seem to understand that it would surely have made little difference to his condition. He would have died anyway. I know that. There is no cure for the consumption—especially not the fast kind my little son was afflicted with, which is also so infectious. I pray to God that Anne was not infected when she was with him recently. She has a hollow, dry cough. She has had it for some time. I know she has tried to suppress it when I am near and pretend it is nothing. But I know better. It is not her fault. Of course it is not. It is mine, if it is anybody's. Mea culpa.

You are right, and I should pray, not only for comfort, but for forgiveness!

I am being exhorted by my ministers to carry on with my public duties; to leave Anne in the hands of the good doctors. There is much to do, and they say I cannot help her recovery, but would be better out and about, dealing with the problems a king should deal with. They say I would be better in myself too, that I should try to get my mind off Edward now with other pressing matters. Maybe they are right. The world goes on, though we feel at such times it should not. And I have to deal with the living.

But I am so loath to leave Anne. She is the heart of my heart. I am lost without her, and before this, she was lost without me. Supposing she should come out of this terrible lethargy and depression of spirit and call for me? And I would not be here. I now call this place 'The Castle of Care', and in truth would be glad to leave it and get out into the fresh air again—if it were not for my wife's state.

I have poured out all to you, my dear mother. I have admitted to you things I would not speak of even to Francis Lovell, my dearest and closest friend, not even to Anne.

My son died on the exact anniversary of Edward's death last year. Does that not prove something? That God is speaking to me in a very strange way? That he is telling me my little boy's sudden death is a direct retribution for my many sins, the worst being when I usurped the throne? I have never been one for superstition. But this fact alone makes me very uneasy and half inclined to believe there is something in it.

I hope that when I write to you again, I can tell you that things are better, especially for Anne. Until then, I am always,

Your loving son,
Richard

Margaret Beaufort, Woking Old Hall, Surrey, Late April 1484

My Dear Henry,

You have no doubt heard already of the sudden death of Edward, Prince of Wales, in Yorkshire on 9 April? The king and queen are utterly devastated by it, as one would expect. He was their sole son, their only child, and Anne is a delicate flower and unlikely to produce another heir for them. So the succession lies wide open! No doubt Richard will name Edward of Warwick, the great Kingmaker's son, as his successor soon, though he is somewhat tardy about it. One wonders why? The boy is known to be mentally backward. Maybe the king is uncertain that he is the right one to name? A king should be intelligent, surely?

Although one cannot help being sorry for the king's son—he suffered all his life with such poor health—his passing means another obstruction removed from your path to the throne! It is surely fate? Certainly, I feel, some Higher Force is clearing the way for you. Events have moved in such mysterious ways to your advantage over the past year, have they not?

Firstly, Edward IV died young. Then his two sons died. Now, the usurping king's only son, the Prince of Wales, has died.

Richard is trying his best to make himself popular with the people. He is going all out to get their loyalty and support by promising them justice for everyone, rich and poor, without fear or favour. But unfortunately, he favours the people of the north openly, and this does not bode well for him, especially as he has replaced the local jurisdiction of the many nobles and lords of the south who have joined you in exile after the rebellion, with Northerners, whose speech cannot be understood by Southerners, and who are regarded as interlopers. I suppose it is because he knows and trusts these men well, but has he thought that the ordinary people of the south might feel exactly the opposite way?

He is trying hard to become a well-regarded king, but I do not think it is really working. And even the great Yorkist nobles resent his tampering with the laws as they stand and making new ones in his recent Parliament which do not favour them at all! He will need their support to supply men and arms if he has to fight more battles, but they may not be so happy to help him, as he has depleted their personal powers.

All in all, he is not doing as well as he would hope, in spite of his efforts! This means that the general atmosphere is fraught with distrust and resentment.

You did well to take my advice and make that proclamation at Christmas in Rennes Cathedral in which you vowed to marry Elizabeth of York if you became King of England, to unite the Houses of Lancaster and York for the lasting good of England! English people would definitely welcome that. Everyone is heartily sick of war, after these endless years of dissension!

How are your preparations going for your next invasion? The good weather will be here soon, which will surely aid you greatly, if you decide it will be this summer! Watch out that your plans are kept secret, as King Richard, for certain, will have his spies in your camp, though they may be hard to discern!

I live quietly now, in my semi-imprisonment here imposed by the king. But it has not restricted my ability to communicate with those with whom I need to keep in contact, such as you, my son. He expressly forbad me to contact you in any way. It is a good thing I have my secret ways and means, which even my husband knows nothing of! For example, my good confessor, Christopher Urswick, undertakes many secret missions for me, as well as his official duties.

The king could hardly take away my personal priest, could he? Little does he know how resourceful a priest this one is!

Even my husband has not the slightest suspicion what I am up to. Even if he did, I think he may turn a blind eye to my doings. As long as he is not involved in any way, I do not think he really cares! He never questions me. I do not think he really wants to know. What he knows nothing of he cannot be blamed for by the king!

I will write again as soon as it is possible. It cannot be as often as before—for obvious reasons! Let me have your news as soon as you can.

Your loving mother,
Margaret Beaufort,
Countess of Richmond

Henry Tudor, Vannes Castle, Brittany, June 1484

My Dear Mother,

I am sending this letter to you through the good offices of your faithful servant and confessor, Christopher Urswick. He brought me an urgent warning letter two days ago from your friend John Morton, the Bishop of Ely, who has been taking refuge in Flanders since the Duke of Buckingham's uprising, to escape the wrath of King Richard for his part in organising it.

He warns me that I am no longer safe here at the Court of Brittany, as Richard has made an agreement with Pierre Landois, the Duke of Brittany's treasurer and chief officer, to have all my freedom here taken from me forthwith. Duke Francis has been ailing for some time now, and his frequent bouts of insanity are getting worse. It is very sad and disturbing to witness. When he is in one of these strange states, he speaks to no one, and spends all day examining and admiring his many jewels. He keeps these in a huge coffer, which goes everywhere with him. He is obsessed by their beauty and radiance, particularly the diamonds and the rubies. He is always spending huge sums acquiring more. One would think this would be a woman's obsession, but they seem to comfort him when his mind is disturbed. Many say that he is in no fit state to rule any more! Landois has taken over all state business from him, without his knowledge, I am sure.

I must say Francis has been more of a friend to me over the years than a gaoler, but I now fear for my life here, without his support.

I have been advised by Bishop Morton to slip unobtrusively away from Brittany, into France, as soon as possible, and to present myself at the court, where I am sure to be given support and sanctuary from now on, until my invasion plans are complete. I am sorry for Francis. I know that when he is well, he would never authorise this, but his power is being taken out of his hands by the cunning and devious Landois, and I must distance myself from this dangerous man as soon as I can.

It is a great shock to me to hear that Landois plans to give me up to King Richard soon. I have been safe enough here at the Court of Brittany for years, but of course, the king now regards me as a real threat after my attempted invasion last autumn and is obviously trying to put a stop to any future invasion plans I may have, by getting his hands on me as soon as possible. He has apparently made a treaty with Landois for there to be a truce with no more war until at least 25 April next, after the recent sea battles between the Bretons and the English, which Richard is anxious to bring to an end. There was a secret codicil to this treaty however—regarding me! In return for a thousand archers to help Brittany fight against the French—who now see another good chance of overwhelming Brittany and annexing it, as they have long wanted to do, because of Duke Francis's indisposition—Landois apparently promised Richard to have me put into the same close custody as when I first came to Brittany all those years ago, so that I can no longer organise any invasions against England! Then King Richard could have me taken to England as a prisoner whenever he wishes! Morton also thinks that he was bribed by Richard with promises of estates and possessions which belonged to the attainted noble rebels, who have now joined me in Brittany after the Great Uprising of last October.

So, as you can imagine, I am in a fever of quiet activity, trying to work out a way to get out of Brittany unobserved before Landois carries out his intention! However I go about this, it must be done quickly, before anyone even has an inkling of what I plan to do. I think Uncle Jasper has actually thought of a good way of escape for me already—one which should work!

Briefly, Uncle Jasper and my chief supporters will set out from Vannes, ostensibly on a consultation visit to Duke Francis, who happens to be staying, while he is sick, in one of his castles, which is very close to the French border and Anjou. As they approach the frontier, they will suddenly turn south and gallop into Anjou! I shall go out two days after with a very small group of bodyguards and one or two servants, saying that I am just going hunting and also visiting Duke Francis with the present of a fine boar—if we can find and kill one. He is known to prefer this meat above all others, and I will say that it is a gift to cheer him up. All know that we have more or less become friends over the years—so it should not cause any comment. What could be more natural than to visit a sick friend?

Soon after we enter the forest, I will change clothes with one of my servants. Then I will ride hard for the border with just two bodyguards, frequently altering our route in order to throw off any possible pursuers. We will only halt when really necessary to feed and rest the horses. We will make for Anjou. As soon as we have crossed the frontier, we will meet up with Uncle Jasper and the rest of the embassy and continue on in safety to the Court of France! There is no reason why it should not all go according to plan, I feel, unless we are betrayed by anyone. When the main body of my men find themselves deserted by me, I hope that none will feel so bitter as to betray me, if any knowledge of my actions has somehow leaked out. Hunting trips can often take two or three days, so we should be well away and safe in France before anyone could guess what I have done! Later, when they join me in France, I am sure they will understand, when informed of the very real danger I was in from Landois! I hope so.

I beg you not to worry over me, as I have learnt how to look after myself! I am always very careful and cautious as, in truth, I trust only Uncle Jasper. I will not do anything headstrong or foolhardy, I assure you. My actions will be well-planned and thought out before I make any move!

As soon as I reach France safely, I will let you know.

I sent Urswick on into France at once, to the court of the boy king Charles and his elder sister, the Lady of Beaulieu, who is really in charge there in an official regency, until he comes of age. I informed them that I am coming and requested permission for my chief noble English exiles, who will accompany me, to take refuge in France also. I stressed the need for a speedy reply. As soon as it comes, in a day or so—and I do not anticipate a refusal, as it will be a political advantage for the French to have me there, after all—I shall leave, with a picked group only. The rest, I hope, will follow soon after and will also be welcomed.

I feel bad about the necessity of sneaking off and leaving the main body of my men behind to take their chances. But I am sure Landois will be only too glad to let them all go when he finds out what I have done—feeding and housing them costs a lot of money, after all! They have all been so loyal to a man, except that rogue, the Marqess of Dorset. As you probably heard, his mother Elizabeth influenced him to desert me and go back to England to make his peace with King Richard! Luckily, some of my soldiers were soon on his tail before he reached the coast and took ship. They easily managed to 'persuade' him to return to us! I was grateful to him initially for bringing over that large portion of King Edward's treasure he appropriated to help my cause, but this action shows him to be a vacillating fool! His mother obviously exerts a strong power over him. Surely he is safer with me?

But then, of course, for some strange reason which none can fathom, the woman has come out of sanctuary with her daughters at last and put her trust in the king—surely her sworn enemy and the instigator of so much of her personal tragedy? It is very strange, this. How can she trust him now after he has caused her so much heartache? I will never understand women!

Pray for my safety, my dear mother!

I remain your devoted son,

Henry Tudor

Anne, Westminster Palace, Autumn, 1484

Richard has been so busy all summer dealing with many pressing problems that I have hardly seen him.

He stayed with me in Nottingham as long as he could, but grief was a luxury he could not afford to indulge in for very long. He has been away for weeks now—and there will be a great shock awaiting him when he does return.

More Scottish wars; trouble with Burgundy and Brittany, on land and at sea, have occupied his time greatly. Also, he has spent much time setting up his Council of the North, which will prove a very good thing for all people there, I am sure. I know he would prefer to be with me, but he has no choice as king but to deal with these endless problems and important affairs.

I have done my best to pull myself out of my lethargy of mind and spirit which assailed me after my little son died, but it has been almost impossible, as my body has already given way under the terrible strain of my grief, and this life of endlessly being on show and of having to attend all kinds of functions; of meeting dozens of people in whom one has not the slightest interest, but which it is necessary to do to keep good diplomatic relations with. It utterly wears me out. I hate my life as queen. I knew that I would—even if I had not become ill. I have not complained to Richard, but he must know.

Richard seems to thrive on it—the more work there is to do, the more he likes it. Perhaps it is because it keeps his mind off darker things, being busily occupied. He is lucky that he can be distracted in such ways.

My mind goes round and round on the same subject—my inability to give him another heir. All women like to give their husbands a boy. Being queen, it is a necessity to ensure the succession. But I clearly cannot do it. I have come to the conclusion that I am now utterly barren. I dread the childbirth ordeal—I nearly died giving Edward life—but I would be completely willing to subject myself to it again for Richard's sake. We make love frequently—when he is with me. But nothing happens. I despair more and more and have grown to hate my weak, sickly, and infertile body.

I have not told Richard yet, though he must surely guess by my constant cough, which was bad enough when I last saw him—and which is well-nigh uncontrollable now—that I am surely in the grip of a mortal sickness, such as killed my poor sister Isabel. My doctors have confirmed this and tell me that Richard must be informed at once when he comes back—as his health will be at stake living with me. I am reluctant to do this, as I know what it will mean for our marriage. With Isabel, this illness followed on quickly from her child-bed ordeal and the fever after, and she was dead in less than three months. George stayed by her and was inconsolable when she died. The doctors could not keep him away, but he was not the king.

Is it to be the same for me? Perhaps I caught the infection when I was last with poor little Edward, who also had an incessant cough? My doctors tell me that this disease is called the consumption, because it consumes the sufferer, destroying the lungs and taking bodily flesh away so rapidly that it kills very quickly. Some call it the wasting sickness. It is very common. Whole families die of it—one by one. There is little to be done to alleviate it, let alone cure it. And I do not have the strength to fight it. There is no more hope for my recovery—I accept that.

I have resigned myself to the fact that I am not long for this life The doctors give me months—no more. With some, it can even kill in weeks, they reluctantly informed me. I needed to know—to prepare myself, to prepare Richard for being alone when I am gone—I am but twenty-eight years old. I have always attempted to live a good, Christian life. I have not hurt anybody if I could help it; I have tried to be kind and think of other's needs, but God has decided, in his wisdom, to afflict me with this sickness anyway. There is no justice in the world. I would rather be a poor cottar's wife and be well and strong for my husband than Queen of England, with every privilege and endless riches, but weighed down with this dreadful illness and my inability to bear more children. But we do not have a choice about what trials God sends us in life. He gives with one hand and takes with the other.

For myself, I care not. It is Richard I worry about. How will he cope without me? He has recently lost his only beloved son. He has been bereft—we both have.

He is very strong, but he depends on me for his emotional health. I know that.

Very soon, I must let the doctors tell him the truth about my condition. I fear that it will break his heart when they inform him that he must no longer share my bed for fear of becoming infected himself. I am already beyond tears at the thought of what this final, irrevocable separation will mean to both of us. I need his arms about me; I need his kisses and caresses to comfort me. He needs me just as much in his own way.

We will never embrace closely again or be as one in the body. He is the heart of my heart and I know he feels the same way about me. Our love is deep and enduring.

I will see that he does not ignore the doctors' orders, though it will break my heart too. I would not have him ill. He has great work to do. He is a good king and will be a great one. I know that, given the chance. I see now that it was God's will that he should take the throne, though at the time I was very unhappy about it.

I shall still have my dear husband's companionship, I suppose, but even that the doctors may prohibit. It is dangerous for his health to be too near me.

I have lost that which was the centre of my life, which can never be replaced—my darling child. Now I am to lose the physical love—even the presence—of my beloved husband. How will I stand it? I pray to God daily to give me the strength to bear not only my illness, but the loss of Richard's nearness.

I am nothing but a useless burden to Richard now. In the end, he will be better off without me. So I hope my dying is not too protracted. I will not be able to cope with the terrible despair in his eyes when he looks at my poor, wasted body. I have seen it already, only too well, after our little son died.

I hope that he will find happiness with another, after I am gone, though I know he has sworn to me that I am the real love of his life and that there will never be anyone else for him. But who knows? He deserves to be loved, and if I am not here to love him, then I hope he may accept another woman's love—in time.

I have seen that certain look in the eyes of Princess Elizabeth. I know Richard has always been her favourite uncle, even before the death of George and her father, King Edward. I believe she loves him. She has not shown him overtly, at least in public. That I know. She is fond of me and would not deliberately hurt me. She knows that Richard is my life. And he would hardly have realised how she feels anyway, would not be even slightly aware of it, would not care. While I live, his thoughts and devotion are for me alone.

But I know what is in her heart. It takes another woman to see it.

Perhaps when I am gone, she will come to his attention. He will need to remarry. He will need an heir urgently. His ministers will urge him to do it—and quickly. She is young, beautiful, and strong. She will bear many healthy children, I am sure.

I feel no envy that I am leaving my Richard to the certainty of another woman's embraces. It is inevitable. Whether he desires to remarry or not is not the issue. He will have to. As king, he will not be given the choice.

And maybe the Princess Elizabeth will be the one? Who knows? She would certainly have him, there is no doubt about that, I am sure. But the question is—would he be willing to marry her—his own niece? That is all in the future, when I am long gone and not for me to worry about, after all. For now, I must bear my lot as best I can from day to day—for Richard's sake.

Richard, Westminster Palace, Christmas Day, 1484

I decided we should have a really grand and spectacular Christmas this year, with no expense spared—the kind that Edward, my brother, was wont to have every Yuletide. He never counted the cost as long as everyone enjoyed themselves—he certainly always did! The royal treasurer would be wincing for weeks after as the numerous bills came in.

A king needs to make a show, I have discovered—it is what people expect, extravagance in clothes and in living. For myself, I would not care, as I have always tended towards simple pleasures, and I am not a hearty eater or drinker as Edward was. Neither do I over-spend regularly on rich materials and the latest fashions, as he did. When the occasion dictates it—such as for my coronation and little Edward's investiture, I will forget the cost. Edward, as king, indulged so much in rich food and wine. I am sure it weakened his body and hastened his end.

But Christmas is special after all, and Anne and I badly need cheering up after our sad loss in the spring. And Anne's illness has progressed so fast. I do not think she has long to live—the doctors do not think she will survive to the spring even. It is unbearable. She is far more philosophical about her fast-approaching end than I am. She has accepted that it is the will of God. She is not afraid, only sad to leave me alone. I try to accept his will, also, but it is almost impossible. What has she done to deserve this? And I am hardly allowed to keep her company for fear of infection, let alone share her bed.

Safeguarding the king's body has to come first, I am told. I belong to the people, not just to my wife. If I can help to make what is certain to be her last Christmas a really enjoyable one, perhaps it will serve to take her out of herself for at least a short while? I do not think she can forget how ill she is for a moment, but I pray it might help to lift her spirits a little perhaps, and mine. Always we must smile and put on a show. Never can we reveal the true state of our feelings in public. That is the lot of royalty. Only those closest to me know my great despair, my indifference to what is going on around me. My mind dwells only on the loved one I have already lost and the most beloved one I am cruelly soon to lose. God gives us terrible burdens to bear. Being king does not exempt one.

I have arranged for some incredible entertainments to divert us, as well as the great feast. We have brought in tumblers and jesters from Italy, dancers from France, even a troupe of performing monkeys and dogs with their trainers. Anne loves dogs and so do I. Maybe we might have a laugh or two from watching their clever tricks and antics.

There is a wonderful minstrel coming to court tomorrow for the Boxing Day revels, whose fame has been spread through all the courts of Europe. His fee is exorbitant, but apparently his singing and playing on the harp and several other instruments are extraordinary, so he is worth it. He composes all his own songs also.

Normally, he brings his trained performing bear with him too, but I did not want this form of entertainment, as I believe it to be cruel. A wild creature should not be poked and prodded into performing unnatural acts. Even more do I detest bear-baiting and have tried to ban it in my kingdom where I can—though it is almost impossible to do this, it is so popular, unfortunately. I love music—it has always been the art closest to my heart—and it can act like balm on the troubled mind. I play for Anne often, to try and calm her spirit. Music has a healing influence. I can do nothing to heal her body, but there are ways to lift the spirit certainly and music is one of them.

Already, on Christmas Eve, that most holy day, the boys of the Royal Household Chapel sang to us in the morning, in their most heavenly voices, directed by Master Gilbert Banister, that clever musician who manages to get the boys to sing so superlatively. At Midnight Mass, which Anne insisted on coming to, though she was in no fit state—and the chapel is very cold—they sang again of course, frequently. Their singing moved both Anne and I to tears. The beauty of the music brought forth the wellsprings of our hearts' sadness.

Today, while we were feasting earlier, the Westminster Waits entertained us with their cheerful songs and instruments. For a town band, they play very well on their fifes, tabors, and trumpets. Afterwards, my court minstrels, chiefly William Davy and Thomas Freeman, helped by several others brought in for the occasion by Master John Crowland, my Marshal of the King's Minstrels, and directed by him, played for everyone to dance.

With gaiety and happy smiles all round us, it was very difficult for both of us to enter into the spirit of it all. People understood why Anne could not dance, though she enjoyed the caroles before her illness, but I was not allowed to sit out, like her. All the court ladies wished to dance with me, it seemed. There was one lady who kept pressing me to dance with her, smiling up into my face enticingly. If she hoped to attract me in that way, she had no success. I have never been a one for indulging in women's charms, as Edward was—especially now. Anne, my wife, has always been the one—the only one since I married her—whom I will take to my bed. But this girl was my niece, and I know I am her favourite uncle, so maybe I misinterpreted her intimate looks? I really do not know, and I care less. After a while, I made the excuse to all the ladies that I must keep Anne company now, and that I had had enough dancing, anyway.

Earlier, this lovely lady, the Princess Elizabeth, eldest daughter of my brother Edward, and now in the full bloom of her beauty at eighteen, caused everyone a big shock when she appeared dressed exactly the same way as the queen. She had on a gorgeous new dress made of turquoise cloth of gold brocade, streaked with silver, and when she came to curtsy to us, the whole court drew in its breath and stared, silent at her indiscretion. The girl merely looked around, puzzled and uncomprehending at their reaction, and then I realised that her sin was not deliberately provocative, especially when Anne whispered in my ear that she had actually given some spare material to Elizabeth about a month before, as she had ordered too much for her new Christmas Day gown. But, of course, she had no idea the girl would break the laws of etiquette so stupidly in this way. On reflection, it is rather odd that Elizabeth, who had spent all her life up to her father's death at his Court, did not know about such things. I can hardly believe it was deliberate. She has such an open, sunny nature. It never occurred to me she could be devious. Why should she be so now?

Anne quickly defused the situation by taking Elizabeth's hand as she curtsied to her and commenting on how beautiful she looked. It must have taken a great deal of courage for Anne to do that—the girl could not have drawn attention more compellingly to the sad contrast between her healthy young body, sparkling with youth and beauty, and my poor, sick queen, so wraith-like thin and pallid—except for the hectic flush on her high cheekbones, a feature of this disease, which gives a false impression of health at a distance. When Elizabeth at last realised what she had unwittingly done, she apologised profusely to Anne. But, of course, the damage could not be undone. This enforced gaiety will go on for twelve days, including the New Year revels. I can hardly bear to think of the strain it will impose on Anne. I will try to persuade her to rest all the time she is not constrained to be on show—as now. If she will listen to me, that is. She has a will of iron in her frail body. But I fear she will collapse if she does not do this. I will get Dr Hobbes, the chief court doctor, to point out to her that this might happen, that she must do as she is told at this stage in her illness. Otherwise, she will be confined to bed permanently, which I know she would hate.

And when the Christmas Season is over—what then? At that time of year, in the dark and miserable January and February days, I normally look forward with great anticipation to the coming of spring, like most people.

But spring now has a dreadful association in my mind, not with new life, as it should, but with death. I lost my dear brother Edward when the buds were breaking; the daffodils blooming in all their annual glory as the heralding trumpets of spring on April, the ninth—in the midst of nature's most glorious reawakening. My little son died the following year on exactly the same date.

Am I to lose my dearest wife in spring too? Though, looking at her, I do not think it will be that long before she leaves me. Winter will take her, as it takes so many. Spring will again be a time of deep mourning, I am certain.

As I have asked myself before—many times—is this God's retribution on me? Is my mental suffering a direct result of my decision to take the throne? But would he inflict worse suffering—and ultimate death—on two innocent souls because of my actions? If so, he is not a God of love and compassion, as we are led to believe from our first prayers at our mother's knee. My mother has always been a most devout woman and she brought me up in her beliefs. Are we hoodwinked completely in the Christian faith? Is he really a God of unbounded anger, bent on punishment, as in the Old Testament?

For the first time in a life of unquestioning faith, I begin to doubt. I know God puts the faithful to the test. Witness the lives of the saints and their horrible deaths as martyrs, in many cases. I have been loyal and faithful to him, as to all those I have loved in my life or given my allegiance to. I pray I do not lose my faith in him, as I surely feel its foundations have already been shaken to the bedrock.

Elizabeth of York, Sherriff Hutton Castle, Yorkshire, April 1484

They called the day that poor Queen Anne died, the day of the black sun. And so it was—for at the very moment she was drawing her last agonised breaths, the earth grew dark; the sun was blotted out in an ominous gloom. It was a complete eclipse of the sun by the moon, of course, but, that it should happen just then seemed like a sign from God.

It certainly portended the end of all my slender hopes and dreams, as it brought to a finish all the happiness that my dear Uncle Richard had known in life. He had lost the three people he loved more than anyone else in the world in the space of only two years. First, his brother, King Edward, the year before last on 9 April. Then, on exactly the same date last year—strange mischance—his only son Edward, the little Prince of Wales. And now his much-loved wife, Anne. These terrible events seemed like God's punishment to many because he took the throne from his nephew. I did not feel that way. I pitied him deeply. But I loved him deeply too. I shall always love him, whatever they do to me; whoever they force me to marry.

And I could have given him more happiness—and myself, if they had only let me. I know I could. I was never given the slightest chance to prove that. I had done nothing to be ashamed of, openly. I had my dreams of course, but they were cruelly dashed, within a few days of my poor mistress's passing.

I had been at Westminster as one of her ladies-in-waiting with my sister Cecily for several months. I saw how the poor queen suffered, both in body and in mind. I pitied her too, truly; I loved her and would never have caused her deliberate hurt, however I felt about her husband, the king. I would never have admitted it to anyone, let alone him—while she lived. She was so brave. She even sat through the entire Christmas and New Year court celebrations stoically, though visibly hard-pressed at times to keep from fainting right away in her exhaustion and illness. She coughed incessantly and held herself upright by sheer will power, I am sure, so as not to let Richard down.

She gave me a lovely pre-Christmas present of turquoise cloth of gold, streaked with silver, which I had made into a special court dress for Christmas Day. I realised, when I caught all eyes upon me, that it was exactly the same material as Anne's dress! She had given me the material out of the goodness of her heart, because she had purchased too much. But people, seeing us together that day, could not help but contrast my health and strength with her pallor and wasted body, I realise, in retrospect. I am sure it was interpreted as deliberate on my part. I had no such intention. How naive I was! How I blundered unintentionally! No wonder the wagging tongues never stopped! It was the filthy suspicions and even filthier insinuations which brought about my expulsion from court and had Richard send me post-haste here with my sister Cecily, to have me safely out of the way—out of his way.

He did not even guess, before they told him in that horrible manner, about the rumours which had been flying about the court and the capital—how I felt about him; how I loved him. I never crossed the line with him. I was simply the affectionate niece-in public and in private. I kept my real feelings to myself. It was the others who saw in my every glance and action near him some signs of intimacy between us that did not exist! Did my eyes betray, like words, what I was feeling when I looked upon him? I did not intend them to. I am innocent of all deliberate seduction. I never even flirted with him—I would not dare!

People convinced themselves that we were lovers! They felt that an illicit relationship had been going on for months between us—ever since Anne became so ill that the doctors forbade him her bed for fear he would be infected with her deadly disease! Most men would probably seek comfort with another woman at a time like this—indeed at any time—given the opportunity. But Richard is not like most men. He is honest and upright and has led a most moral life. That is why my admiration for him as a king—and as a man—turned to love.

I suppose I could have tried to tempt him, if I had wanted to. I know I am very attractive in appearance and in personality. People are always telling me so. But I respected him too much, and I knew he would have given me short shrift, as he loved his wife so dearly and had never been unfaithful to her. All who knew him well were sure of that.

I waited, hoping that I might perhaps dare to voice my feelings tentatively when a decent period of mourning had passed and he had recovered from her inevitable and harrowing death. I knew that he would be pressed to remarry very quickly. A king must have an heir, and his son was dead. Anne could never give him more children. She had not the strength, even before her illness. She was delicate all her life, like her sister Isabel, who died of the same disease, like her little son, who carried the seeds of the disease in him too from birth, no doubt. That the great Earl of Warwick—the mighty Kingmaker—should have produced such sickly offspring!

But I am strong and healthy. My mother bore many children with no trouble. I am physically like her. I could have done the same—for Richard. I would have put the idea into his mind so gently. I would never have pushed myself forward until I felt the time was right—when he could bear to envisage being married again and bedding another. But political considerations have ruined all that; have trampled on my tenderest feelings! I am a bastard named and too close in blood to Richard.

Apart from the horrid insinuations and downright certainty in some quarters that something was going on between us though where they think they got any proof from that Richard and I were having an affair, I do not know—it was pointed out to me by Richard's chief ministers and by Richard himself that, even if had wanted to marry me, he could not. It would have been regarded as incest! The consanguinity is too close! I did not realise that. I had no knowledge of the laws of both Church and state which would apparently forbid such a marriage. As I said, I am an innocent; an innocent who simply loves the wrong man, who is well out of my reach.

He does not love me. He has not the slightest interest in me that way. The very idea seemed to horrify him—I know that now. But given time and the chance, I might have succeeded in making him do so. I am beautiful—everyone remarks on that. I am strong. I would have made him a good wife. But there are too many obstacles in the way, apparently. I could have married the Dauphin, who I neither knew nor cared about, it seems. I have been told that Henry Tudor wishes to marry me. And that will be acceptable too. But the man I love I can never have. It is an unjust world!

But he will have to marry someone—and soon, probably some pock-marked foreign princess who cannot speak English and cares nothing for him, but who is suitable in ways which I am not. As long as she can bear him an heir and bring a large dowry, that is all that matters, it seems. And who is not related by blood, as I am. But that is my misfortune.

All those miserable months as a prisoner in the sanctuary with my awful mother—then a few months of happiness at court, with some hope, if only slim, for my future. And now this. Back in virtual imprisonment again in a cold northern castle, away from my friends, my relatives—except Cecily—and away from the one I love best in the world, but will probably never be allowed near again—Richard.

Life is so unfair. And I am only eighteen. Too young to be in despair, I know that. But I am. All I have to look forward to now is the possible marriage with Henry Tudor. The pictures of him I have seen do not look very appetising. They say he has bad teeth and bad breath. What a lovely prospect! All princesses and princes are simply pawns. Our wishes are the last to be considered in the political game. I feel I shall never be happy again.

Lady Margaret Beaufort, Northumberland, Early May 1485

My Dear Son,

You have no doubt heard already of the sad demise of the king's sick wife—the Lady Anne of Warwick, my poor niece?

What you may not have become aware of yet are the rumours that abound that Richard actually hastened her death by the privy use of poison, though she was already dying of the dreaded lung-rot, consumption, and would not have lived much longer anyway. But he could not wait, apparently, such is his lust for another!

Poor Anne had probably become too much of a burden to a king unsure of his position and anxious to put it on a firmer footing by producing a son and heir as quickly as possible. And he can only do that by marrying another! And the chosen lady is, for certes, the Lady Elizabeth of York. She has been looking on him—and he her—with much suppressed lust—even in public, so the story goes around the court. People have noted her frequent smiles and coquettish glances in his direction, and he has been observed following her around the room with eyes betraying his obvious interest!

It is not surprising, I suppose. She is a beautiful, young, and healthy girl—the very opposite of his sick wife. He is a man barred from his wife's bed for months for fear of infection, and men have their needs! If they cannot satisfy them in ways sanctioned by Holy Church, then they will find relief elsewhere. And she has been an open invitation to him, it is said. If their behaviour is so overt in public, one can imagine what they get up to in the privacy of the bedchamber!

On Christmas Day, he danced with her several times openly, though there were many ladies who did not even get one chance to do so. What does that say about his preferences? And this in front of his desperately sick wife, who could hardly keep herself upright on the throne from sheer exhaustion! How dreadful she must have felt, poor slighted Queen, not only in body but in spirit, seeing that brazen girl flaunt herself in public and make up to her husband. It does not take much imagination to realise that! I pity her greatly.

Elizabeth was noted by many as she gazed adoringly into the king's face whilst they danced. She made her feelings very plain. There was definitely a secret intimacy between them—it was plain for all to see. She made no efforts to hide her lust for him!

Richard has denied it all most vociferously, of course—but then, he would! He even went to the trouble of making a humiliating public statement to an enormous crowd in the Great Hall of the Knights of St John at Clerkenwell, in which he stated categorically that he had no intentions whatsoever of marrying his niece, that he had loved his wife most deeply, and mourned her passing greatly, and that he had certainly had nothing to do with hastening her death by poison, which came all too quickly from her mortal illness. My husband, Thomas Stanley, who was there, stated that Richard was most convincing. He is obviously a great dissembler—God rot him!

If he does marry her, it is the end of your chances as her marriage partner. But perhaps that is part of his plan—to outmanoeuvre you?! And she does not know you and cares for her uncle. So he is certainly a good few steps ahead of you in this matter!

But what a completely unacceptable marriage this would be—if he dared to make it a reality. It would be incest in the first degree! The Church—and the people—would certainly never accept it without great protest. But then, kings are most adept at getting their own way and bypassing any obstacles and problems which stand in the path of achieving their ends!! Richard is no exception—everyone knows he can be completely ruthless. He acts very quickly and with determination when confronted with difficulties. I would not be surprised if he had systematically poisoned his wife, nor would I be surprised if a royal wedding were not announced immediately the official mourning period is up—if not before.

He must have an heir, and quickly, to ensure the succession—there is no gainsaying that. They will make him marry another as soon as possible anyway—it is his duty. Whether he truly mourns for Anne or not is beside the point. She could never have given him another son anyway, even if she had lived. She was too delicate. He may have been forced to divorce her, even if he did love her. What he needs is a strong woman to be the future mother of his sons. And Elizabeth is certainly that. Her mother produced children like other women shell peas, and with as much ease! And Bess has the same strong constitution. She would be an ideal wife, in theory.

But the Lady Bess has been earmarked for you, my son, and somehow Richard must be put off the idea of marrying her. It will not do—for a multitude of reasons! Will not the people say that she is a bastard? Of course, he could get an act of Parliament to reverse that, but then, what about the two princes? Their bastardy could have been reversed in a like manner—if Richard, as Protector, had really wanted it. But no, he desired to be king himself, and used the fact that they were supposed bastards as an excuse to take the throne!

Could he now reverse all that for his own ends again? Would Parliament do his bidding? I doubt it. No, Henry, I think that even Richard may be checkmated in this one. I feel the marriage will never happen—cannot happen! There are too many inconvenient obstacles ranged against it for even Richard to unravel. And his poor reputation is such already that it can take no more blackening. It would be the straw that broke the camel's back, as the old proverb goes!

I must admit to you, Henry, that I saw an opportunity to blacken Richard's reputation even more with the general public and helped spread the story of the possible poisoning, when it began to appear—as if it is not black enough already with the little princes' disappearance, and possible murder still unexplained—and never even referred to now by the king! I make no apologies for being completely ruthless myself, when it might aid you. If the poisoning accusation becomes generally put about in the north especially, where he has been very popular and where his main power base is still, he will find that the many adherents of the Nevilles will turn against him utterly! They are still faithful to the old House of Warwick! Then what will become of him?

He is hated in many quarters. All the better for you, my son. His supporters leave him daily and come over to you in Brittany! I do not think he knows whom to trust now. My husband is one of his chief councillors—and supposed chief allies—but if I know Thomas, he will take sides where the best advantage may be at the time he is called upon to fight! He gives his allegiance at the very last moment. Saving his own skin is what has directed his lifelong actions. I do not blame him for this extreme caution, especially with a man like Richard as king, who acts first and thinks about the consequences after, witness Hasting's death!

Buckingham could have trumped up all the charges he made against the man—he was proved to be a traitor himself shortly after!

Well, my son, I hope that you have almost completed your plans for your great invasion? Have you enough ships, horses, arms, and men yet? If you need more money, I can get some to you—but I cannot use my good messenger Reginald Bray again. He has begun to cause comments by his frequent absences from England, and I would not have him thrown in prison on our account, or worse. He has been a very faithful servant.

At present, Christopher Urswick seems to have remained undetected. I shall go on sending you letters through his good offices as long as possible. Soon, though, my son, there will be no more need for letters—you will be in England! You will be king and I will be at your side, at court, to guide and help you—as I have always sought to do!

Your loving mother,

Margaret Beaufort (You will have noticed that I no longer sign myself as Countess of Richmond, as the king—in his great generosity—has withdrawn that title from me for my part in Buckingham's rebellion. But it will be returned to me, along with my estates and my freedom—by you, my son, when you ascend to the throne—so I am not unduly worried!)

Richard, Nottingham Castle, June 1485

'Francis, I have gone out of my way to prove to the people that I am determined to work for their good! I have worked non-stop, since taking the throne, at revising the law; bringing in many new laws to ensure proper justice and have instigated many other reforms generally to help different causes. Why is it I now feel on shaky ground, in spite of all my efforts? I certainly do not feel secure, and, except for a few long-time friends, such as you, am uncertain who are my truly loyal supporters. Loyalty has always been of the first importance to me, as you know. How is it I do not trust others to give it to me unstintingly when I give it to them? With war looming at any time with Henry Tudor, I need to know whom I can depend upon to fight with me and for me!'

'You are unusual, Richard, in that you never waver from your affiliations. I am afraid most men support the side they think will bring about the best result in their interests! Witness the past-master at this game, Lord Thomas Stanley! He always manages to land on the winning side without embroiling himself in trouble! I would not trust him an inch, my friend, or depend on him for anything, but I think you can trust your other main supporters, the Duke of Norfolk, his son, the Earl of Surrey, and probably the Duke of Northumberland, Lord Percy, though he has always been a law unto himself, oftentimes acting as if he were above the law! You have said so yourself. They can all array large armies to fight in a short time, when it is necessary to do so.

Unfortunately, you have unwittingly alienated many lords with your amendments to laws which do not work in their favour any more, as they used to! You did it with the best intentions, for the good of all. But these men do not care about others as you do, only about their own interests—these will always come first in their minds, and resentment has built against you because of it.'

'Surely a king must care about all his subjects, not just a special few?'

'Agreed, but these nobles can't, or won't, see it the same way. They do not care for the common man, as you do, Sire. They are usually indifferent to his needs and will only help him if forced to and if it does not compromise themselves, or cost too much!

Also, you have brought in Northerners to take charge of whole areas in the south which have lost their overlords to Henry's cause and who fled to Brittany after Buckingham's rebellion. That is causing great resentment, I am afraid.'

'But I know these men. They are good administrators—and loyal to me! They will do what needs doing without fear or favour! Does it matter where a man comes from as long as he can do the job he is appointed to do?'

'One would think not. But folk prefer someone they know, and—to be frank—one who speaks their language! There are complaints that the northern accents are often incomprehensible to the men of the south and that their vocabulary contains many words foreign to them. You must admit that, Richard! You were brought up with Yorkshire folk, so it presents no problems for you. Try to put yourself in the shoes of many who do find great difficulty in even understanding the orders of their new overlords. People tend to like what they know and know what they like!'

'I would have thought that is a problem easily overcome, with some give and take on both sides? I do understand what you mean about putting complete strangers into positions of authority though. But it is done now. I had no choice. I do not plan to spend ages reappointing new men to these posts. There are too many other pressing needs for me to deal with! The Southerners will just have to learn to accept their new masters with a good grace!'

'I know you mean well, my lord—and I hope all will come to realise that. Those who know you realise your heart is in the right place! But there is another thing you have done which has caused a lot of bitterness, if you don't mind me being frank with you.'

'Francis, I know that whatever you say is said with the best intentions! So go on.'

'Well, this business of raising war loans. I know it has been absolutely necessary to gather money in a short space of time to pay for the looming war, but people say these are nothing more than the hated benevolences, or forced loans to the Crown, in another guise! Of course, Edward was so fond of getting money quickly in this way—with him, they were always a necessary evil! But they were generally loathed. And you abolished them categorically in your great Parliament last year, saying you would never resort to them again!'

'I know. I hated them myself and wanted them abolished permanently—truly I did. What I was forced to do to raise money quickly does prey on my conscience, I must admit. But what am I to do to acquire enough money for the defence of the realm otherwise? Edward's treasure, or the remains of it, after Dorset had filched a great portion of it and sent it to Tudor, who had no right to any of it, is now gone. There is no money in the Exchequer to pay for anything, let alone this costly war—which is now inevitable and imminent. Tudor could invade any time! And he has plenty of French money to aid him too!'

'It is a tricky business, agreed. You want to do the right thing, but the consequences are often unforeseen. Unfortunately, the people do not understand your reasons. They just feel it is nothing more than theft! They are sick to death of fighting anyway and do not see why they should be made to pay for more!'

'A great pity, Francis. But it is done now. Am I to give it all back? How will the war be paid for then? Soldiers have to be paid. Horses, arms, and equipment have to be bought.'

'No, of course not, but perhaps some kind of proclamation may help, concerning the money—an explanation of your dire need for it in the circumstances!'

'I will think about that, though I doubt it will help unless I actually make a promise to reimburse those who paid out! And when would I be able to do that? It may cause even more unrest and resentment if I made another promise I could not keep. They would think me a liar as well as an extortioner then! And anyway, an amount way below what we had hoped for—£30,000—has actually been raised. They have shown their objections to my request for money by just not responding adequately.'

'In some situations, one cannot win, Sire, I agree! I do not envy many hard decisions you have to make.'

'But apart from the reasons we have discussed, which may partly be to blame for the general distrust in me which I feel most strongly, except in the north, where they know me and trust my motives, I am very aware that I am murmured against and that vile accusations about me continue to circulate! It seems people would rather believe in rumour, speculation, and hearsay and ignore my explanations and honest efforts to do right by them! Look at that business recently with Bess Woodville. I am sure my proclamation fell on deaf ears. They believe I slept with her because they want to believe it! They enjoy bandying around scurrilous rumours about those in high places. They believe these more readily than the real truth! And those wicked lies about poor Anne. They still believe I poisoned her, I am sure! Even though the doctors must have let it be known that she had been ill for months with consumption. They would twist even evidence of the symptoms of her suffering in her last months into evidence of slow poisoning—instigated by me!'

'All those who know you well, my lord, would never have countenanced such an accusation for a moment! But then, there is the continuing mystery of the disappearance of Edward's sons from the Tower, I am afraid. Speculation about that will not go away until some real information about them is forthcoming, you know.'

'I realise that—too late. Ever since that appalling deed of Buckingham's, I see the questioning looks thrown at me in public; I feel the general distrust, even sheer dislike. I hope there is not general hatred there too, though I fear in some quarters—certainly among the Woodville supporters—it definitely exists. Especially in London. The hatred there is palpable! That is one reason I am here at this time, while we await news of Tudor's movements, though the main reason is, of course, that we can move easily to anywhere necessary very quickly from here, as it is the virtual centre of the realm. What can I do about it all? I sometimes feel I am hitting my head against a brick wall when I try to communicate my honest intentions; my sincerity.

Everything I do seems to backfire or work in the opposite way to that which I intended! The people mutter more and more about me under their breaths, and every day, dozens more slip away to Brittany and Tudor.

And all I ever wanted was their good opinion and their commonweal and have tried to work for it in every way I can!'

'Is it not possible for you to announce something about the princes? Let it be supposed that they have been removed to a place of safety—up north, for instance? You need to mollify the general suspicions against you. It may be a lie, but it is better than this continued silence and will keep them quiet for a while at least. Be honest—you have not uttered one word either to confirm or deny the fact that all believe them dead!'

'How can I? I hoped that all the speculations would just die down. What could I say about their disappearance now? The general public believe me guilty of murder anyway. What good to deny it—without revealing the truth about Buckingham?'

'Why not do it? He is dead and cannot deny his actions!'

'But I would need proof or the country would just think it all a tissue of lies to vindicate myself. I think the public prefer to believe me guilty. After all, they need a scapegoat to pin their suspicions on, and I am the obvious choice. They would not believe me if I swore on the Bible to my innocence in Westminster Abbey! It is too late to do anything about it, Francis. Maybe if I had told the truth at once . . . ?'

'If only you had not peremptorily destroyed that letter he sent you on the morning of his execution without opening it! Mayhap it did contain the names of his fellow conspirators? Apparently, he swore that it did! And they may still be at liberty—plotting against you again! You would not be in this situation now, with no proof to back you up.'

'True, but I was so furiously angry and disgusted with him. I wanted nothing more to do with him, ever. I just wanted him wiped off the face of the earth at that moment!'

'One you knew of—the Lady Margaret Beaufort. Why did you let her off so lightly? Surely she should have been severely punished, even beheaded for her part in it? Especially as she is the mother of Henry Tudor! She is known to have insatiable ambitions on his behalf, always has had. Do you think merely being put under house arrest by Stanley will have stopped her plotting? All you did was put her in her husband's custody in a castle up north. I am sure she has gone on actively communicating with her son Tudor, in spite of your orders to her husband Stanley. Knowing him, I expect he turns a blind eye to such a strong-willed woman. He is said to have a soft spot for her, though she repudiates him as a true husband. And he must be away from her a lot. I am sure she would take every opportunity then to disobey his instructions and yours!'

'I have never believed in the beheading of women. And I must trust Stanley to keep her in order. I cannot do it myself. He is a strong man. Most men can control their wives!'

'Not this wife! And what if a woman's crime be treason, as hers surely is? Mayhap you should consider it—if it is proved she has gone on helping Tudor and conniving with his supporters?'

'Never! Some other way will have to be found to punish her. But not the block!'

'You are too kind, Richard. Women can be every bit as clever and devious when it comes to protecting their own and working for their advancement—completely ruthless too. I believe she is such a one!'

'You are probably right, Francis. I will have Stanley questioned closely. If anything is proved against her and his supervision of her shown to have been lax, I will have them both incarcerated—but after the battle. I need him on my side now, remember—as one of my chief councillors. He is in the Privy Council for God's sake! And he will lead a goodly number of soldiers into battle on my side. I cannot do without his help!'

'Oh, Richard, I dare to say that with the best will and the best intentions in the world, you have made some dire mistakes!'

'And I would agree with you, my friend! It is easy enough in hindsight to perceive where one went wrong—the hard part is knowing what to do to put things right!'

Henry Tudor, The Welsh Borders, Near Shrewsbury, Shropshire, 11 August 1485

My Dear Mother,

You will no doubt have heard already that we landed at last on 7 August in Pembrokeshire, at Dale, near Milford Haven. I was so overcome with emotion to be back in my beloved homeland after all these years that I went down on my knees and kissed the ground—to all my companions' amazement, I am sure! I implored the favour of heaven by saying the psalm: 'Judica me Deus, et discerne causum meam . . .' Then, making the sign of the cross, I prayed fervently to God to aid my just cause in the coming fray! The next day, we marched ten miles to Haverfordwest. There, we received some very good news from Pembroke. A delegation was there—the mayor and several of his aldermen—to promise that the town would serve my Uncle Jasper Tudor, and therefore me. He is its natural lord, after all.

I was eagerly on the look-out then for the host of Rhys ap Thomas, the greatest landowner of the area, who had sent oaths that he would support us as soon as we arrived. It was a terrible blow—and not a good omen—to be told that he had decided to uphold Richard's cause after all with his considerable force. We had counted on him. It had not occurred to me that that he would renege on his promise, and I did not understand why he had deserted us.

Later, we found ourselves a short distance from Cardigan, when my scouts reported that Rhys was just a few miles ahead of us to the north. I humbled my pride and decided to petition him to change his mind and join us. I promised him that he would be given the Lieutenantship of all Wales for life, if he would reconsider. It was not pleasant to have to offer bribes, especially at this early stage, to one whose loyalty had been counted on as a fellow countryman. But I need him. I await his answer in trepidation. I wonder what King Richard offered him to secure his loyalty? Perhaps he just needs time to think about his options? I hope he decides in our favour. It is crucial.

It made me very uneasy too, as we marched along, to realise that we were not being constantly joined by Welshmen eager to fight against Richard. I had believed that this would happen also because of the old hatred of the Welsh for the English, going right back to Llewelyn Fawr's time. One would had thought them eager to take any opportunity to cause trouble for their ancient enemy, but not so, it seems. A steady trickle have joined us, but not the eager hosts I was expecting.

It seems I have assumed too much about the reactions of my countrymen to my bid for the throne! The people of Wales have not swarmed to my banner, as I had hoped and expected!

We march proudly under the Red Dragon Banner of Cadwallader! If anything is guaranteed to inspire men to join us, surely the sight of that ancient symbol of the desire for freedom will do it! And I am the great Cadwallader's heir. Surely that stirs something nationalistic in Welshmen's hearts? I can only pray that it does!

Good news has come in, as I write this! Having reached the outskirts of Shrewsbury, on the borders of England this evening, after a most arduous trek across the mountains, a messenger has just arrived from Rhys ap Thomas—he has thought better of his earlier decision and will be joining us soon after all! I wonder whether it was the large bribe I offered him which suddenly seemed more important than his fear of Richard and whether his estates would be attainted if I lost the battle?

I have also sent messages to all who have pledged me their support and hope they will join us soon, as we march towards London. I have been advised most strongly not to make for London directly, but to aim at meeting Richard at a more northerly point. I will see how things go. Maybe I will change my mind later about our direction, depending on where I hear Richard is. Hopefully, we can take him by surprise—he may not even know we have landed yet! I believe he is at Nottingham Castle, waiting for news.

One of my most hoped-for supporters, is, of course, your husband, my uncle by marriage—Sir Thomas Stanley. I pray his brother William will also be on our side. Both can amass huge forces at very short notice! I have written urgently to Sir Thomas, as I need to know as soon as possible whether we can count on his support!

It is all very stressful, not knowing whom I can really count on! I need all my battle commanders, as I have had no practical experience of fighting. I am utterly dependent on their superior knowledge and feel very vulnerable at the moment, wondering if they will be there for me at the crucial time—I am sure you can understand that!

Thank God, my most experienced commander, the Earl of Oxford, Lord de Vere, is utterly loyal! He is already attainted for his part in Buckingham's rebellion, so regards Richard as a bitter enemy! And, of course, my dear, battle-scarred and trusty Uncle Jasper Tudor is with me always. He has been my mainstay since early childhood!

Now I must sleep. I must restore my energies, which are badly needed, for tomorrow, we enter England! I pray that Lord Stanley and I will meet very soon and that he will confirm his support! Do what you can, Mother—if you have any influence at all with him—plead my cause most forcefully!

Your loving and apprehensive son,

Henry Tudor

Richard, Beskwood Hunting Lodge, Near Nottingham, 16 August 1485

'My lord, there is news at last! Henry Tudor, whom, as you know, landed near Milford Haven in Pembrokeshire on Sunday, 7 August, has been marching with his host ever since and has now reached Lichfield completely unopposed, it seems. They were on the direct route to Nottingham at first, but your scouts have reported he suddenly changed his mind and started marching south-east instead!'

'Strange, but thank God there will be action soon! This endless waiting and not knowing which route he would approach us by has been most wearing. But it is very worrying that he has met no opposition along the way. That does not bode well! Now I will see who will obey my call to arms at once and who else will find excuses to prevaricate!'

'What mean you, Sire? Do you not expect all your supporters to come immediately and march to your chosen rallying point?'

'I truly do not know with some, Francis. They are unknown quantities, especially the Stanleys. I can only hope they see sense and do what they pledged to do when the time came! I have already instructed the Earl of Northumberland, Lord Percy; the Duke of Norfolk and his son, the Earl of Surrey, and faithful Brackenbury to make for Leicester, with their considerable forces—whither we go now, in the hopes that they will have reached there already. You, of course, were the first to arrive, my friend. I am glad that you are with me at this crucial planning stage. I have tried to get my mind off the situation, until I could do something about it, by indulging in a little hunting—it is better than sitting in that wretched, miserable castle at Nottingham completely inactive!'

'I know you hate the place, Richard, ever since—'

'Yes, ever since poor Anne and I received the terrible news there of little Edward's death at Middleham. From that time, I have called it my Castle of Care! And it was that which precipitated her own illness and death, I am sure—she was so felled by grief she could never recover. Nottingham is an ill-omened place for me.'

'You did not summon Sir William Stanley, why?'

'Because I assumed he would march with the men of North Wales to intercept the invader, which does not seem to have happened, from the news of his easy entry into England! I know that Thomas Stanley is untrustworthy and wayward—it seems his brother is in the same mould. On 11 August, I ordered Thomas Stanley to come immediately with his forces to Nottingham, but is there any sign of him yet? Of course not! He sent a message by a fast scurrier yesterday that he is desperately ill with the sweating sickness which abounds at present and that he cannot come. I do not believe it—it is just an excuse not to obey!'

'It is only five days, my lord, since you sent your orders out. Give him time. He may have been on the northernmost parts of his vast territory when the call to muster came. And if he is indeed as sick as he insists—this illness can kill, Sire! He must needs to rest in his bed until it passes—then, I am sure he will join you.'

'I try to have faith, but his behaviour in the past has made me cynical of his actions.'

'It is not surprising, I suppose. But you do have his son, Lord Strange, in custody in Nottingham Castle, as a hostage for his father's good intentions. Surely Thomas would not deliberately disobey you and risk his firstborn son's very life? Especially as I believe Strange attempted to escape yesterday and is now in closer custody than ever in a deep dungeon?'

'Who knows what he will do? He is a law unto himself, like that awful wife of his, Margaret Beaufort. She will no doubt be rejoicing right now that her precious son has got so far into England unopposed, in such a short time! Perhaps she has persuaded Thomas to go over to the rebels? I would not be surprised at anything either of them did! He may have even urged his son to escape. The lad revealed, when questioned, that his Uncle William had definitely gone over to Henry but insisted that his father was trustworthy. He even begged to be allowed to write a message to his father. I gave him paper and ink—it could not do much harm for him to write, but whether it will do much good remains to be seen. He wrote of his terrible danger and implored his father to come in at once to me with all his forces. We await the answer. I must now send orders to the sheriffs of the realm that Sir William Stanley is to be found and arrested as quickly as may be. If he has definitely defected, then you may count on it that Thomas has too! I definitely smell treason, my friend!

All I need now is for Percy of Northumberland to change sides. Defection is infectious!'

'Let us pray not, Sire. Any news of the Duke of Norfolk, John Howard?'

'No, not yet. But I know he will obey me to the letter. He will have been urging his men-at-arms and yeomen archers from all parts of Essex, Norfolk, and Suffolk to get to Leicester as quickly as may be. I would trust him with my life! And his son is of the same loyal stock. I need not worry over either of them! But I know that there are many whom I hoped would come—but cannot actually order to come—who will not.'

'Who do you mean, Richard?'

'Well, a great many men—lords, gentry, or commoners—are utterly weary to their souls of the constant alarms, marches, and battles of the past years. They just want to stay at home with their families and, administer their estates, farm their lands, work at their crafts, and earn their living quietly. They have had enough and do not want to know about war any more. It is not that they long for my overthrow—they just do not wish to join in any more fighting. Who can blame them? I feel the same—if the truth be known. But I have no choice but to fight! One such whom I know will just ignore my call is the Duke of Suffolk. And his son, John of Lincoln, is my designated heir to the throne!

He has never responded to any call to arms over the years, even for Edward, after 1471! I know Edward was sad that he did not join him at the Battle of Barnet. He is a man who prefers to stay quietly at home, enjoying his estates. I do not suppose he has any burning desire for an unknown exile to be king. He just does not care who is in power so long as he is left alone. This is typical of the mood of many whom I cannot constrain, I am sure!'

'It is a sad sign of the times, Sire, that people are so bone weary of war they will not help their anointed king!'

'It does not matter. I have realised that I have gone out of my way to win the people's hearts, by bestowing justice, which, unfortunately, has alienated powerful interests. I have tried to show my goodwill with many gifts; I have forgiven rebels and been kind to their wives and have tried to help commoners where I could. None of it seems to stand me in good stead now in the hour of my need to muster a strong army! I am fighting indifference, Francis! Half the country no longer cares about loyalty, which has been my own guiding star throughout life, until I broke my own loyalty to Edward's son. That was my undoing! I am only reaping what I have sown. I know it! None of my goodwill seems to matter to a people sickened by war and betrayal. And they see me as the master betrayer, whose hands are stained with the blood of the innocent! Why should they fight for me?'

'Richard, that is not so, I am sure! You are depressed, your spirits are low, which is not surprising after the dreadful two years you have endured. You are letting your own misery cloud everything!'

'Maybe you are right. You do see to the heart of things, Francis. But seeing the situation as it seems to be—though you assure me I am mistaken—does not help me deal with it. The question is will enough men actually come to fight this invader when we meet him on the field of battle? I have really no way of knowing! I am forced to take a chance, not only on the outcome, but on my life!'

Henry Tudor, Tamworth near Lichfield, Staffordshire, 20 August 1485

'You have no idea how pleased I am to see you, Uncle Jasper! Last night was one of the worst of my life!'

'What mean you, Henry? What happened? We began to get very worried, boyo, as you seemed to have disappeared! Even began to wonder if you'd been captured by a contingent of the king's men!'

'No. I am ashamed to tell you that I got lost on the road to here! It was pitch dark and we could not see a welcome light anywhere. Had to spend the night in a wood! Thank God it is summer, for it was uncomfortable enough, I can tell you. I would never admit it to the Earl of Oxford or any of my other commanders, as I feel so foolish.'

'How did you come to lose yourself, whatever?'

'Well, I had at last managed to arrange a meeting with Lord William Stanley at Stafford. You had gone on ahead with Oxford and the main army to Lichfield, while I stayed behind to see William privily. I just had a small band of twenty bodyguards with me. We planned to follow you soon after. You know how anxious I have been to find out whether he and his brother, Lord Thomas, are definitely coming in on our side to fight the king's army? Anyway, I met him at an inn. He was alone. There was no sign of his brother, annoyingly. But he did tell me that Thomas has been very ill the last week or so with this sweating sickness which has broken out everywhere and could not come to see me yet. But he assured me that both of them were sure to support me when it actually came to the battle, but not openly before. I think they are afraid the king will attaint them, and they have much to lose! Also, Lord Thomas's son, Lord Strange, is held as hostage by the king! As an assurance of his father's good faith, I suppose. And where does that leave me? I can understand Thomas does not want Richard to have his son executed, but I told William I would be happier to have both armies immediately. It would assure me an extra 5,000 fighting men. But he did nothing but prevaricate, would make no definite promises, just said that Thomas and he would join us with their armies "when the time was ripe"—whatever he meant by that.

No wonder we lost our way, as we set out after this most unsatisfactory meeting. Darkness had fallen long since. It was very late. Although it is only seventeen miles from Stafford to Lichfield—and we managed that all right—I was not concentrating on the road. It was in the last three-mile stretch to Tamworth we got hopelessly lost after we skirted Lichfield. Stupidly, I decided it would be best to avoid the town in case we were detained by any of Richard's supporters there, and we left the road in the darkness. That was a huge mistake, as I learnt to my cost! I was deep in thought and feeling very frustrated about these Stanleys, who are so difficult to pin down. They promise everything but actually do nothing, it seems to me. Somehow, we found ourselves wandering around in open fields in the pitch dark.'

'They are well known for sitting on the fence, lad. That is nothing new. They have avoided actually fighting in several crucial battles already by taking this stance. No doubt they have told King Richard the same thing as you!'

'What—that they mean to join him if—and when—it is convenient for them?'

'Exactly. Do not count on either of them, Henry. You may be let down badly.'

'But we need their hosts, desperately! Thomas is my uncle by marriage, for God's sake! Surely my strong-willed Lady mother will have made sure he intends to support me?'

'Who knows? He may have lied to her, to keep her happy. A self-willed and ruthless man like that would never give in to a woman's wishes! We will only know the Stanleys' true intentions on the day of the battle, lad—perhaps they do not even know themselves what they plan to do! They will wait to see how things work out and decide at the very last moment, I expect.'

'That is just not good enough, is it? It makes me feel desperately vulnerable! I know I have you and Oxford and several other seasoned commanders to help me plan what to do, but without a lot more soldiers, we cannot hope to win, surely? Richard is a brilliant soldier and commander, and I am a complete novice when it comes to battles. I am beginning to wish we had never set out on this uncertain venture! I was pushed into it for years by my Lady mother and you. Can I really hope to win in the circumstances?'

'Circumstances can change, boyo! In the balance, I would say the Stanleys are more likely to join with us in the end. They have more to gain with you as king. There is no love lost between them and Richard and they have many grievances against him. And what is in it for them in any given circumstances has always been their guiding star!'

'I can only pray that you are right, Uncle. You have more faith than I in the outcome of it all. It is awful to have to depend on such shifting and uncertain loyalties!'

'I expect King Richard is feeling exactly the same way as you at the moment with regard to those two shifty characters, if that can give you a little comfort! It is in the hands of God now, boyo!'

Richard, Leicester, 20 August 1485

My Dear Mother,

Though pressed for time, I made up my mind that I would write to you at Berkhamstead just before the battle which will decide my fate. This is now imminent, and we expect to meet with the rebels soon after tomorrow.

I do not know how all will turn out—that is in God's hands—and I beg you, pray for your son. I can do with as many prayers as I can get. For all I know, this may be the last letter I shall ever write to you, as, for the first time in my life before a battle, I am not entirely confident of winning.

It is not that my army is lacking in skill and determination. I am sure we will have mustered sufficient men to fight and overcome what we have been informed is nothing more than a rag-tag rabble from the gaols of France, let out on the understanding that they fight for Tudor. These are supplemented by mercenaries, who have no real loyalties—except to their pockets! In theory, he has no chance against my well-trained, loyal, and disciplined forces and he is a complete novice in war, after all, though he does have that renegade Earl of Oxford as his main commander, who escaped from Hammes Castle, where I had him in custody for taking part in Buckingham's rebellion.

But there are other worrying factors in the situation. I fear that I am the victim of treachery! And from those who should be my most staunch supporters!

I grow ever more perturbed at the developing situation. On the evening of 16 August, just after I returned to Beskwood from some hunting in Sherwood Forest, aimed at taking my mind off the coming confrontation for a while—a little light relief, as it were—two exhausted messengers arrived from York on urgent business. I barely had time to bathe the day's sweat and dust off me and was about to sit down for supper when they came.

What they had to say filled me with the greatest trepidation, to put it mildly, and made me realise that others, apart from the shifting Stanleys, may plan treachery against me! They were men of York I knew well, John Sponer, the sergeant mace-bearer, and John Nicholson, messenger of York.

The mayor and aldermen were very puzzled. They knew that the rebels had landed on 7 August, but no word had come of any kind with instructions to prepare an armed force to join me in helping to deal with the invasion. They just could not understand it, especially as they knew I regarded this, my favourite city, as full of my most loyal men! Had someone omitted to bring word to them or, more ominous, had it been deliberately decided not to inform them at all? But for what possible reason? Could it be because of the plague which had broken out there that they had not received orders of array?

At once, I saw what could be behind this omission, though I prayed that it was not so, was not deliberate. Lord Percy, Earl of Northumberland, was responsible for sending requests to York on this matter as the Commissioner of Array for the East Riding of Yorkshire. And he patently had not done so! Why? I hardly dared to ask myself the reason; it filled my mind with such ominous fears.

Had Percy decided that he did not want these men in his forces? They are so zealously loyal to me I am sure he realised they could not be relied upon to obey him, like his own personal army directly under his command, if he decided to play me false? It stunk of treachery, the whole thing, though I tried to tell myself that I was now being paranoid and that it was just because of this sweating sickness plague which has broken out there, as well as in many other parts of the country. After all, it only needs one plague-infected man to cause this new dreaded disease to run round the entire army like wildfire and decimate it—meaning disaster! Or maybe he had just not got around to sending the message to York yet. But that was too far-fetched, surely? I had sent out orders far and wide the day I heard that Tudor had landed. Even if Northumberland had been in the northermost parts of his great estates, he would have received my message very quickly, as this system of scurriers I brought in—my brother Edward's idea in war—ensures quick delivery. And he would have used quick messengers himself to do my bidding.

I said nothing of my fears to the two tired men of York but assured them that of course I would be most grateful to receive as many men as their city could muster to support me. They were to make their way to Leicester, where the main rally is taking place. I did not really think their soldiers could be there in time now, but I did not tell them that—what was the point?

Then I instructed them to rest and refresh themselves and start back the next morning with fresh horses—the ones they had were well-nigh dead with exhaustion. John Sponer chose to remain with me to fight, while Nicholson was to take the answer to the mayor on the morrow.

I rode back to Nottingham Castle on the morning of 17 August, my mind full of dark thoughts and forebodings. But in spite of the mounting threat of treason, I still knew it was possible to outwit not only the rebels, but the possible treachery within my own ranks by some careful planning and fast action. I have always been aware that God has given me gifts as a general and commander of men and as a tactician. Now was the time to bring them into play!

If forced to it, I could always arrest Northumberland—even the Stanleys—on the basis of the suspicions of treachery I already had about them. I have not done this as yet. I am loath to do it. I would rather give men the benefit of the doubt. After all, the only thing I have as possible proof for their treachery is assumptions, based on their actions or lack of action. I want to trust them in the end to do the right thing. They swore loyalty to me when I became king. Surely they will not break their pledge?

I have been playing up to this devious and arrogant Percy for nigh on fifteen years. I have had enough of his slippery ways. I know he resented me taking away much of his inherited autonomous power when I set up the Council of the North. Perhaps he hopes that I will be defeated so that he can resume the proud traditional sway of his vast northern lands? Well, he will not find me so easy to overcome. If I act decisively and quickly—as has always been my wont—I can outwit him yet! I must put him to the test—get him to show his hand before the battle! For a start, my armies stand between him and the rebels. Perhaps I can manoeuvre him into taking a definite stand for one or other of us before the day of the battle? Then, if that does not work, take him into custody? Most of his Yorkshiremen would happily follow my banner if it became necessary to deprive Northumberland of his command!

With luck, could I not also force the Stanley brothers to make up their minds and unite openly with the invader at once? At least I would know where I stood then! Many of the men in their armies would take that very ill and refuse to obey orders for a last-minute turncoat attack during the actual battle. They are loyal to me as Northerners, I am sure!

Today, we had a last minute council of war here, at the White Boar Inn, where I lay, as most commanders have arrived here now with their hosts: The Duke of Norfolk, Jockey Howard, and his son, the Earl of Surrey have come. Francis Lovell, my dearest friend, was first to come to me in Nottingham, where he had ridden post-haste from Southampton, after his abortive waiting game for the rebels, who were expected to land in nearby Milford, but landed in Milford Haven in Wales instead. We still await the Stanleys and Northumberland, but that is no surprise! I have been told that they are encamped a few miles off, having approached us from the west.

We have heard that the rebel army is only a short distance away, near a village called Market Bosworth, by a marshy plain called Redmore. There is a hill there called Ambion, which sounds ideal for our purposes. If we can occupy it quickly, we will have the advantage of height over the rebels.

We will wait here one more day to see if the rebels change the direction of their march and to await Northumberland and other captains—and the Stanleys. There is no sign of my faithful men of

York yet. I doubt they will come before we have to engage in battle. I know they will be anxious to catch us up and take part.

Men are still streaming in from all parts, thank goodness, and we are very busy assigning them to their ranks. We have a problem in accommodating them all in quarters in such a small town.

Another shock revelation has just greeted me. My faithful Thomas Brackenbury, Constable of the Tower, who has today arrived from London, informs me that Thomas Bourchier, the Archbishop of Canterbury, and Walter Hungerford—two of my chief councillors—have slipped away to the rebels on the way here at Stoney Stratford—that place which has such bad associations in my memory! It was there that I feel my life took a wrong turning. From that moment, nothing has seemed to go right, however hard I tried. And tragedy has dogged me endlessly too, since that fateful day. I cannot help thinking it is all the judgement of God for my sins! I have no time to write more, my dear mother. I pray that I will be able to meet with you soon when all this is over.

Tomorrow, we march to engage the enemy in battle, which will probably be the day after. This will be the most decisive battle of my life, as I have made up my mind there can only be one of two outcomes—either I win—or die in the attempt! If I meet my Maker in the battle, remember me with affection and know that whatever mistakes I have made—and I have made many—I set out to be king with the best of intentions. If given the chance in the future, I aim to build upon all the good works which I have initiated. No man can do more than that.

Your loving son,
Richard

Henry Tudor, Atherstone, Staffs Evening, 20 August 1485

I had barely caught up with my Uncle Jasper, the Earl of Oxford, and my gathering army at Tamworth, after my unpleasant night spent lost out in the fields, when I had an urgent message to go at once to Atherstone nearby, where both the Stanley brothers, my uncle Thomas and William, were waiting to see me. At last they had come! Surely this boded well now for my venture?

'After all this time, we get to meet at last!! I have heard so much about you from my beloved mother, Uncle Thomas—I may call you Uncle? I hear that you have been grievous sick? I am glad that you seem to have recovered!'

'Aye, well, I was one of the lucky ones! This sweating sickness has proved fatal in many. And, lad, it is good to meet you. I have heard a lot about you too—from Margaret! For months—nay years, I suppose, she has talked of little else!'

I must say, he did not look sick—not at all. Most men, after a near brush with death, would at least have looked pale; would have seemed tired, but not him. He seemed full of energy—very strange. I wondered—though I did not like to ask him outright—if his sickness had been a ploy to keep from joining the king, who had commanded his presence long ago. If it was such, then I suppose I could take heart from it, knowing that he had come to me instead, supposedly just after rising from his sick-bed. Surely that must mean he intended to give me his support?

But my mood of exhilaration did not last long. Neither of them had come to promise me that their hosts would join me at once; both would go no further than to keep reiterating that their intentions towards me were favourable, but there were no concrete promises made of immediate support, none at all. I was only able to assume, from what they said, that they would aid me, but only during the battle.

'Uncle, I am anxious to know that you are both on my side! Is that why you have arranged this meeting—to assure me that you are about to instruct your armies to join mine at once? Without your men, I only have those I brought with me—many of them not trained soldiers at all—and the few picked up along the way! I did not get the overwhelming support I hoped for from the Welsh, and Rhys ap Thomas, whom I had assumed would join me the moment I landed, only came over to me because I bribed him with promises that he should be Lieutenant of All Wales if he did! I have heard that the king has named him traitor already and has issued a warrant for his arrest, if he can be caught—which I doubt! My numbers amount merely to about 5,000 men—not enough to face Richard's mighty hosts! With your men, it would be about 10,000!'

'Stop worrying! There is no basis for this extreme anxiety. As William told you a few days ago, we will join you when the time is ripe. We cannot show our hand at once. For a start, you know that my eldest son, Lord Strange, is in deadly peril in the hands of the king? He tried to escape once, so he is now in one of the deepest dungeons in Nottingham Castle—unless Richard has had him brought along to Leicester. As a hostage for my good intentions, he would be killed immediately if I declared for you before the battle! I have to think of his well-being—surely you can understand that? Have faith! Why do you think I have risked exposure to meet you here? It is an assurance of my future goodwill—our future goodwill—eh, William?'

'Aye, it is that, lad. But we can do no more openly at this moment, as Thomas says. You will have to be content with what we do offer!'

'I understand all you say. I realise the problems you face, especially with regard to the peril of Lord Strange. But it seems to me that what you are trying to say is that you must keep King Richard hanging on in the belief that you are loyal to him, when all the time you plan to defect to my cause at the very last minute?'

'We must keep him happy, yes. In his supposed security lies our safety! He depends on our help too. He must not get an inkling of what we plan or we could lose everything—not only the life of my son, but all our estates, our very lives! He would not wait, but would have us done to death immediately! He has a quick way of dealing with those he sees as his enemies! I cannot forget what happened to the Earl of Buckingham and Lord Hastings, who was only suspected of plotting against him—summary execution! We have to bide our time and say nothing until the battle is joined. Then, we will show our hand!'

'I suppose I will have to accept what you say with a good grace, though it is difficult. I am untried in the ways of war; I only know that to have an army double the size of the one I have at the moment would have made me feel more secure!'

'Never fear, lad. I have told your Lady mother what we plan to do. Margaret is in complete accord with us and asked me to send her assurances that you can trust us. She has spent her entire life working towards this time; towards your taking the throne! Do you think I would dare to lie to you, knowing what a virago she can be when a rage takes her? My life would not be worth living afterwards if I did not come to your aid! Now we must away, back to our camps. There is still much to prepare. Be of good heart, Henry. All will be well on the day!'

Richard, Yorkist Camp, Bosworth, Staffs, Night, 21 August 1485

'Lord Francis! My Lord Lovell! Come quickly, I beseech you. The king—he is ill. He is in most desperate straits!'

'What mean you, Stephen? I left him sleeping, not two hours ago.'

'He sleeps still, my lord, but is beset by the horrors and tortures of nightmares in his sleep! He thrashes and shudders violently! His body twists as if in violent pain! He will do himself a damage! It is as if all the hounds of hell beset him! I cannot bear to look upon it! And he screams out, calling on God to forgive him, over and over! Please come, my lord. He must be woken from these horrors, but I dare not touch him. You are his friend. You must do it!'

Stephen, Richard's body squire, looked to be in bad case himself. I know he loves the king, as I do. I could hear Richard as we approached his tent, calling out as if his elder brother were there. I sent the boy away, as he was shaking like a leaf.

'Edward, Edward, forgive me! I did it for the best of reasons. I did it for the good of the country! I did not want to do it—I have never had a moment's peace since—I betrayed you—betrayed your trust. Loyalty binds me—Loyalty binds me—And now is the time of retribution! God has punished me—goes on punishing me!'

I bent down and shook Richard's arm gently, then more urgently, as he was sunk so deep in this terrible place of torture in his mind. Stephen was right. He must be released from it!

He woke suddenly, sat up, and clutched at my arms, staring with red-rimmed eyes unseeingly at my face. His face was pinched and ghastly white. Then he began to laugh, louder and louder, quite hysterically. I slapped his face to bring him back to reality. He stared again, this time with comprehension and shuddered.

'Francis. Thank God you are here. I tried to make them understand, but they would not listen to me! Edward, then Hastings. George. And those two poor boys in the Tower! Edward just kept saying, "You were my dear brother, my most loyal and devoted friend. And you betrayed me. You killed my best friend, Hastings. You usurped my son and imprisoned him in that dreadful place. People say you killed him and his brother. I shall never forgive you—never! You will burn in hell for your deeds!"

'And most of it is true, though I did not kill those boys—you know that I did not—Then there was George—his face and body all bloated, his eyes red and staring, his mouth loose and dribbling—the face of a drowned man. I saw one once, half-floating in the mud of the Thames shallows outside Baynard's Castle, after the tide had gone out. It was just like that. I loved George. I begged Edward not to have him executed—that was not my fault either. But he was there, with the others! His eyes accused me. Perhaps he believed I was the one who ordered him killed—went to his death believing that—never—never! Young Prince Edward and Richard of York were there, pointing accusing fingers at me. Hastings's bloody head was on a pole—just like my father's at Micklegate—and he accused me from his dead mouth, "Murderer! Murderer! Black-hearted villain! I was your friend!" Then they were at me—slashing and hacking—I was drowning in my own blood—retribution! The vengeance of God! "Vengeance is mine," saith the Lord! My mother's very words! And it has come to me—is claiming me!'

He stopped this crazed torrent of self-accusation for a moment to take breath, and I put my arms around him and held him close, rocking his body as I would a small child, to try and give some comfort to his tortured soul.

'Hush, Your Grace, it is all right now. You were merely dreaming—a dreadful nightmare, that is all! It is gone now and you are here—safe, with me, your friend.'

'My dearest friend—yes. Thank God for you, Francis. I have few friends. So many are against me—determined to see my downfall! Why? Why do they hate me so? I have made so many mistakes, but I did mean well—you know it—I have worked so hard to justify my actions. Why can they not see it?'

'You meant well and you have done well! God can see that clearly, as I do. You are not a wicked man. God is not seeking vengeance—retribution is not hanging over your head! It is all in your mind, the product of too many nights without sleep lately, a natural apprehension about the morrow—which we all feel—too much recent tragedy and too much work! You never let up, never give yourself a chance to relax. No wonder your mind is disturbed. But it will all come right. I believe it and you must also!

Tomorrow you will be your usual capable, assertive self. In the morning, you will vanquish all these nonsensical nightmares—as you will your enemies! They will all melt away like snow in spring. And then, there will be peace—peace and tranquillity for us all—which you must seek now, my lord, in proper rest. I will stay by you until you sleep.'

I held up a beaker of strong hippocras to his lips, made him drink it all, and stayed by him until he slept again, this time peacefully, in my arms.

Bosworth Field, 22 August 1485, 5 a.m.

'They have taken the best position, my Lord Henry! They got here before dawn and have now occupied Ambion Hill! Their armies are spread the entire length of it above us! It gives them a distinct advantage!

'At the bottom of the hill to the south-west is a marsh—impossible to fight there—the horses would sink fetlock-deep in the oozy mud, men too! We are left with the rest of this unprepossessing area—Redmore Plain, they call it—to dispose our armies. I will have to think most carefully about this. And we have little time!'

'I trust you, my Lord Oxford, to make the best use of the place. Just instruct us what to do and where to go and we will obey you in all things! You know what you are doing—and I do not!'

'We have been taken by surprise, Henry, lad! Richard was quick off the mark in his planning—we must give him that. Here, in the open plain, we are at a definite disadvantage unless we stir quickly and move right away from that wretched marsh. Do not want to be caught with that at our backs to blunder into, whatever!'

'Uncle Jasper, I feel that all the theoretical knowledge of battlefield dispositions you drummed into me is of little moment until one actually sees the land available. And I am about as much use here as a babe in arms. It is practical knowledge I need!'

'You will certainly get plenty of that, boyo, in the next few hours!'

'We must move at once! Order the men to advance as quickly as may be! We will move south-west, which will give us the best position we can get now to deal with the Royalists as they gallop down from the western heights. We will be ready, waiting for them! We must try to arrange our ranks with the sun to the side of us. No army can fight effectively facing east and blinded by its August rays. Ideally, it should be directly in the enemy's eyes for our best advantage, but the king has craftily made sure his men are facing west!'

'He stole a march on us with that, Oxford. This side of Ambion Hill faces west, so he assumes we will be forced to face due east!'

'Clever devil, Richard! But then he is known as a supreme tacititian and planner. We should have got here yesterday to outwit him, Jasper!'

'So we start off with half the men he has—only 5,000 to his 10,000? And we risk having the sun directly in our eyes during the fighting! Can we overcome such considerable disadvantages?!'

'Henry, remember the Stanleys! They will be waiting on our flanks, whatever! I have already spied the red coats and horses of William's host away to the north-west. And over on our other south-east flank, I am sure Lord Thomas's infantry will now be massing. They have come and they will be sure to join us later, never fear!'

'Yes, when the time is ripe. Whenever that is! I am sick of waiting for them to commit themselves. They could just as well be waiting there to join Richard when they find the time is ripe!'

'My lord, we must be positive. We can win! And we do not have the disadvantage of possible treachery which the king faces, if the Stanleys decide to abandon him for us—when they are officially on his side! Also, I have heard privily that there may be others in high places who will not support him as they should when he most needs them—so do not worry. My spies have worked hard for such information and have been highly paid to ensure that it is accurate!'

'Thank you, Lord Oxford. You cheer me somewhat. I cannot help my cynical, distrustful nature. Life has made me a pessimist, I am afraid! I am in God's hands now and in your most capable ones, my lords. I must try to believe the day will be ours!'

Bosworth Field on Ambion Hill, 22 August 1485, 6 a.m.

'My liege, you do not really mean to wear that crown into battle?' Lord Howard, Duke of Norfolk, looked appalled as Richard set the small gold circlet, symbol of royal rank, upon his helmet.

'Why not? I am the king and shall live—or die—as such!'

'But it is an open invitation to any rebel to strike you down! Do you want to die?'

'No, of course not. But it will also act as a spur to my men to see me casting my lot as king into the jaws of danger—as they are bound to do! It will make them feel I am one of them in body and spirit. They will be inspired to fight all the better for it!'

'But you are not one of them—you are the king, set apart and anointed by God for a special purpose upon this earth! And you cannot do that if you are killed through what is nothing more than sheer bravado! You must protect yourself. And you must keep yourself apart from the melee. I insist! Especially as you did not choose to take Mass early this morning and invoke God's protection.'

'You can insist all you like, Howard, but I shall do as I think fit! I will wear this crown to identify myself to all—and I will fight if I deem it necessary! I have put all in the hands of God already. I did not feel the need for Mass at that time. He will spare me if my cause is just!'

'Madness! This is madness, Sire! A king should not fight in battle!'

'I have fought in battles all my life and escaped serious injury thus far. I know how to fight effectively and to protect myself. Nothing you can say will change my mind. I am set upon it. Yes, Francis, what is it?'

'Richard, this note has been found fixed to Lord Howard's tent in the camp. I think he—and you—should read it.'

Francis Lovell held up a grubby piece of cheap paper to Norfolk on which was scrawled in large, uneven letters by an obviously illiterate hand, the words: 'Jack of Norfolk, be not too bold, For Dickon, thy maister, is bought and sold!'

Hastily scanning it, Norfolk shrugged and would have screwed the note up dismissively into a ball and thrown it away if the king had not held out his hand for it.

'Let me see, Jack! What is it?'

'Nothing. Some prankster trying to stir things up and worry us—that's all. Not worth bothering about!' His big, ruddy face, tanned to the colour of old leather after many years at sea, took on a laconic look. 'Pay it no heed!'

Richard stared down at the missive for a few moments, then shrugged.

———

'As you say, not worth any consideration. And yet—there is truth in it, I suppose!'

'How so?' Norfolk looked puzzled.

'Well, you know, as well as I, that the Stanleys' devious behaviour can be interpreted by others as treachery. It is not just we who know they will likely play us false and join Tudor! I sent Thomas a note over an hour ago commanding him to join us forthwith and is there any sign of him? Of course not!'

The bitterness in Richard's voice betrayed his inner fury, but his face was quite expressionless.

'Come, bring me White Surrey, and help me mount. I have had enough of waiting for this renegade's pleasure. When I catch up with him, it will be my pleasure to see that both he and his brother pay the extreme penalty! A traitor's death is the most terrible thought up to punish those who choose to desert their king in word or deed. And they both deserve it, most assuredly!'

'But Thomas's son, my lord!' cried Francis. 'We have him under heavy guard in the camp! What is to happen to him? Surely his father will not abandon him?'

'Thomas knows Lord Strange is my hostage—under threat of death if he chooses to betray me!'

'But supposing you get no reply before the battle begins? Is he to be put to death at once for his father's betrayal? The boy is in the last extremity of terror—I have seen him. He has lost all pride and hope now and cries like a child. He cannot believe that his own father should abandon him so. He had no reply to the letter you allowed him to write himself to Thomas, begging him to remain loyal to you, knowing his son was under sentence of death!'

'And I do not expect I will receive an answer either!'

'How a man could abandon his son—his own firstborn son—in this manner, is beyond belief!'

'Well, there you see the true baseness of the man! He puts other considerations, such as assurances of even more future riches and estates—probably promised by Henry—above the duty and love of a father for his son. I despise him!'

'Will you not take pity on the lad, Richard? Surely you did not expect it to come to this? Surely you did not really expect to have to execute him?'

'What kind of a signal would that send out, Francis? That I am weak and vacillating. I shall have to carry out my threat regardless! I will have no choice! And now we must make haste to get ready. I think I hear trumpets in the distance. Tudor's army is anxious to begin the battle, I trow! The men must be arranged in their dispositions. Norfolk, you shall take the vanguard halfway down the hill—a half-moon arrangement is best, I think. I will be on the brow of the hill with the main body of cavalry and archers. And a message must be sent to Percy of Northumberland that, as he has not deigned to appear here to me yet, he should maintain the back-up forces on the ridge over there, as he insisted he wished to do anyway. He can keep an eye open for the Stanleys' movements. Now, my horse has arrived, and I must mount!'

White Surrey, resplendent in his battle array, his chest, sides, and throat protected well by armour and his head encased in his special spiked battle helmet, was whinnying and pawing the ground, eager to be away, as his master was. Just as Richard had been helped to mount by two squires, there was a commotion nearby, and Thomas Brackenbury called out, 'Your Grace, there is a horseman galloping up the hill from the south-east! Perhaps it is the answer from the Stanleys that you crave?'

'I hope so, for our sakes—and for Lord Strange! What news then?' he challenged the rider, who had drawn up alongside White Surrey, his horse practically bursting its chest as it drew in rapid, noisy breaths like a wheezy old bellows in its exhaustion. But the look on the messenger's face told the king all he needed to know before the man even opened his mouth.

'My Lord Stanley says that he is unable to meet up with you at this moment. I am sorry, Your Grace!'

'He will be sorry! And what of his son? Did he mention his son?'

'His answer was . . .' the man paused, as if unable to believe himself what he was about to say, 'Tell the king I have other sons!'

'And that was all?'

'Aye, he turned away then, bidding me to hasten to you, which I have done!'

'I see. Well, when you find your master again, tell him that Lord Strange's life is now forfeit, but that I will wait to have him executed until after the battle be won. Perhaps then, he will regret his decision and come over to us after all!'

The man turned and urged his tired horse down the hill again and away.

'My lord, you give this Stanley endless chances!' Robert Percy challenged! 'Why so? Can you really have any hope that he will fight with us now?'

'Not really. But hope never really dies, as they say. Maybe when he realises my deadly intent to kill his son, he could still change his mind? He is a waverer by nature, after all! But it seems we must fall back upon our own resources only and use them to the best advantage we possibly can! And now, to horse!'

Henry Tudor, Battle of Bosworth, Redmore Plain, 22 August 1485

'You are safe here, lad, on this ridge, with your household knights around you! It is a good observation point. You may learn a lot by just watching what happens on the plain in the next hour or so!'

'But, Uncle Jasper, am I not to fight then? Am I just to stand by and let others decide my fate? I had assumed I would have a hand in it myself?'

'You are too precious to risk on the actual battlefield, boyo! You must keep well behind the battle lines! What would be the point of men fighting—and dying—for your cause if you were killed too? No point at all, whatever! Kings, and kings-to-be, do not fight, ever! I am sure the Yorkists have Richard somewhere safe too, where he can observe without being in actual danger!'

'I see what you mean. But won't I be regarded as cowardly, skulking here?'

'Not at all. The army will be glad to see you kept safe, believe me! Now I must away to my men—they will be wondering if I have deserted them. Any moment, I am sure, we will see Richard's vanguard rushing down that hill, bent on our destruction. I must be there to do my part!'

'Take care of yourself, Uncle. I have depended on you all my life—I could not bear it if you were killed!'

'I will do my best to avoid that, lad. I have had plenty of experience of battles—never fear. I know how to defend myself!'

I watch in much trepidation as my uncle gallops off, wondering if I will ever see him alive again.

The sun is still low in the east, but its brightness already dazzles my eyes and it is hot, even though it is barely seven of the clock. The weather seems set fair to be even hotter than the day before, as hundreds of exhausted men on both sides had trudged through the dust and heat to this place. They had only rested briefly and were up before dawn to prepare for the trials of today. I can only hope that tonight they will rest happy in the knowledge that they have done their duty and been victorious! I pray there will not be too many who will sleep eternally after the battle. And all this is because of me and my indomitable mother's overweening ambition. I hope I am worth it!

The thought of dozens—perhaps hundreds of men—dying for me causes not a few uncomfortable qualms in my mind.

A moment later, there is the shrill bray of trumpets, startling me from my thoughts—the signal for Norfolk's vanguard to move downhill, I suppose. Then I see a huge multitude of at least 4,000 soldiers, well armed and armoured, their weapons and accoutrements glinting in the sun, moving down Ambion Hill to where my entire force waits drawn up in battle lines on Redmore Plain below. My army is a hotchpotch: French mercenaries—professional soldiers who fight merely for money; the dregs of the French gaols; a fair number of Welsh—but not nearly as many as I had hoped for—and a few Scots, in all, not more than 5,000 in total. They look very exposed there, when I can also see Richard's back-up force drawn up on the brow of the hill and Northumberland's on a far ridge, bringing up the rearguard. We are outnumbered by two to one, surely?

And, of course, there are the two forces of the Stanleys, standing immobile on either side in the distance, just staring at what is happening, but making no move, My heart jumps with apprehension. Are they not to join in the battle at all then—for either of us? Without them, Richard's superior forces could mean our utter downfall. And, if the Stanleys choose to join the Yorkists, our fate is sealed!

But then, all thoughts flee in the sudden action! The noise assails me most and the smell of smoke and gunpowder. Bombards erupt from the hill down on to my men, who are surely sitting ducks. Guns flash and boom. Deadly flights of arrows cut through the air, over and over again—and find their marks. My army sways like a field of tall grasses in the wind, then great swathes of it are cut down like new-mown hay! I hear screams and groans which sear my soul. The guns, arrows, and bombards have done terrible damage!

My army regroups itself and moves forward, as Norfolk's force, mainly on horseback, bear down upon it at speed! Surely, it cannot withstand another onslaught?

Then it is vicious fighting, hand to hand, with any weapon available: star-maces, covered in sharp, pointed barbs, swords, daggers, lances—and worst of all—the terrible battle-axes, swung around the head then finding their marks to appalling effect. My stomach churns and almost erupts. The terrible cries of wounded horses added to those of wounded and dying men would have me block my ears, if I dared. But I am surrounded by my seasoned household knights, who have seen it all before many times and are just itching—I know it—to be off, galloping across the plain to join in the fray! If it were not for their duty to me, they would do it. They probably see me as a terrified weakling already. I must stay my ground stolidly, as they do, and not show weakness by such an action.

But I would rather be anywhere but here. I did not imagine it would be like this! The stench of blood carries strongly upward and fills my nostrils and mouth. It is quite sickening.

A messenger is galloping towards me from the thick of the battle. He is smeared with blood on the face, and his arms and hands are thick with it. But it is others' blood—he is uninjured.

'My Lord Henry! King Richard's chief commander, the Duke of Norfolk, is down! He has been killed in the first engagement. His men are in disarray, shocked by their loss. They wander around as if uncertain what to do. We now have the advantage!'

'What about Richard's force? Have they joined in yet to back up Norfolk's men?'

'I last saw him galloping down the hill on his great white charger, White Surrey. He is fighting now in the midst of them all, like a madman! Perhaps he will soon be killed. Then it will all be over in a trice. Men do not have the heart to fight without their leader. There is no point!'

'Send me further word when there are more developments!' I cry, somehow moved by Richard's courage and determination. He is not hiding behind the lines like me.

The man rides off, and I strain my eyes to try and see what is happening through the thick haze of stinking smoke and blinding sunlight. I am sweating heavily, either through heat or horror, I know not. I feel both unbearably. There seems to be a lull. A strange silence has descended on the field. Maybe the king is dead as well as the Duke of Norfolk? Barely half an hour has passed. Surely the battle cannot be over yet?

No. It was just a pause for rest and regrouping. Then I see Richard's reserves pouring down the hill, but Northumberland's force has not moved, neither have the Stanleys. Just what are they playing at? What is their game? Why are they here at all? It is all very strange and terrifying. And quite incomprehensible.

Then Lord Oxford is by my side. He is filthy and covered with blood too but has no injuries, thank God. If he were to be cut down—like Norfolk—I would be utterly lost. He is actually cheerful and encouraging, to my amazement.

'My lord, King Richard has surely been abandoned by Lord Percy of Northumberland. He makes no move to join his king—who is now in desperate straits. Against all odds, we are prevailing! I think Norfolk's men just lost heart when he died and now fight but lamely. The king badly needs reinforcements, but they are not forthcoming—from anywhere!'

'So the Stanleys are not moving to join him after all? I have tried to see what they are doing—or not doing, but the smoke and haze is too thick!'

'No, they still stand, silent and unmoving, I am afraid!'

'So they are not coming over to us either, then? Can we possibly win without them?'

'I did not think so before, but now I think we have a chance, a slim one, I must admit, without the Stanleys, but your army, mixed bunch that it is, fights exceptionally well. Those French mercenaries certainly know their stuff and the Welsh and Scots are indefatigable! I must get back to the lines, but take heart, lad. All is not lost yet, by any means!'

I look around, screwing up my eyes to try and make out what is happening. There is another lull. A space has opened up ahead of me and the smoke has cleared somewhat, so I can see far better across the plain now.

Suddenly, I make out a great cloud of dust ahead. About a hundred Yorkist knights are galloping directly towards my position! I can see the colours of my adversary—the White Boar flag! My own knights move to surround me closer, taking up their weapons in readiness to protect me. Great John Cheyney, my giant chief bodyguard, has his equally giant axe in his right hand and moves his horse to stand between me and the thundering hoofs of horses bearing their riders ever closer! My colour-bearer, William Brandon, is next to him. The Red Dragon of Cadwallader flutters proudly by me.

Then I see him—the king! King Richard! He is at the head of his knights, and he is cutting down all who dare to get in his path quite indiscriminately! My knights go down like scythed corn! I suddenly quail inside, as I know what he plans to do! He is determined to get to me at all costs and finish me! With my death, the battle would be over and he the victor in one fell swoop!

There is nothing I can do but watch him come. I am frozen to the spot! As if in a nightmare, I see him cleave William Brandon's chest open with his axe, and the colours fall with their dead bearer in a dreadful slow-motion dance! Then he raises his dripping axe to strike my giant bodyguard, John Cheyney!

The axe cuts into John's skull, splitting it in two! He is down, dead—falling with a great thump like a sawn tree trunk, and I am defenceless! I am about to die, I know it!

God help me now, for man cannot save me!

Francis Lovell, Leicester, 23 August 1485

To the Dowager Duchess of York, at Berkhampstead Abbey

Dear Lady Cecily,

As Richard's closest friend, I feel it is I who should write to you at once and acquaint you with the saddest news one can imagine.

Yesterday, a great battle was fought near here by the Yorkists, led by King Richard, at Bosworth Field, against Henry Tudor and his renegade Lancastrian rabble. Richard insisted on taking part in the fighting himself, in spite of our advice that, for his own safety, he should merely observe from behind the battle lines, as kings usually do.

After half an hour or so, he saw an opportunity to ride hell-for-leather towards the Welsh upstart, where he could be seen isolated, his Red Dragon colours in front of him, on the right rearguard of his host. Richard was determined to kill Tudor himself and so make an end, once and for all, to the appalling civil strife this country has endured over the last century. He would not be deterred. He had almost reached Henry in his headlong rush, was but a few yards from achieving his goal, when a large detachment of that despicable turncoat, Lord William Stanley, suddenly appeared out of nowhere and confronted Richard, who had just split the skull of Henry's giant bodyguard, John Cheyney, and was going in for the kill, as Henry was completely defenceless. Richard was caught completely off guard; his great war horse, White Surrey, had also become bogged down and injured in the marshy ground there. He was set upon determinedly by Stanley's men and overwhelmed in a few moments. He stood no chance, though he fought bravely and fiercely to the end, calling out with his last breath, 'Treason! Treason!'

This is a tragedy of the worst kind. It should never have happened. Richard was treacherously betrayed by those whom he thought were on his side. My heart breaks to have to bring this terrible news to you, a woman whom I know has had far more than her fair share of tragedy in life.

It was almost as if he had a death wish, though. Even the night before, when we talked of the coming fray, Richard was very depressed and I think he believed, in his heart of hearts, that his end was near. He confessed to a superstitious dread that he was to be punished by God for taking the throne. We tried our best to cheer him up, but then, he had a dreadful night, full of terrifying dreams, in which he slept but little. Apparently, Edward and George appeared to him—Hastings too—then the two little princes in the Tower—accusing him of appalling acts, but he could not make contact with them, could not speak to them in this nightmare, however hard he tried. He kept saying that he just wanted their forgiveness. In the raw dawn light, he appeared ghastly—drawn and pallid, sick at heart. He would not have Mass said, would not eat or drink a morsel. It seared my soul to look upon him.

He was a truly good man and a great king. I admired him as a man and as King and loved him dearly. He had so many plans for the commonweal of his people that he will never have the chance to carry out now. I doubt if this Tudor can do better.

I can write no more. I am so heartsick. I pray for his soul constantly, as I know you will do also.

My deepest condolences on your great loss,

Francis Lovell

King Henry VII, Westminster Palace, September 1485

Last night, that terrible dream came to me again! I have had it frequently of late. I wake drenched in sweat, yet shuddering uncontrollably with cold and fear. My body servants are concerned for me. They say I call out in my sleep and toss and turn in my bed in desperate agitation. I have assured them that it is nothing—just dreams.

But it is almost a living nightmare! The horror of it is so intensely vivid! What happened at Bosworth Field is replayed over and over again in my flinching mind. The reality of it—and the aftermath—never leave me! In my sleep, I am there again. I cannot leave the dreadful place, although I long to forget!

When I am awake, it preys on my mind too, and I do not want to retire to my bedchamber. I dread going to sleep, for this dream comes without fail, every night!

I am sitting on my chestnut horse observing the battle, and just in front of me, the huge figure of John Cheyney sits astride his giant horse next to William Brandon, the colour-bearer, who is proudly holding up my Dragon Banner. Suddenly, there is a cloud of dust ahead, and a white horse appears, galloping directly for me! Surely it will swerve any minute or it will collide with me? But no, it continues on apace, and then I see that it is mounted by none other than King Richard himself, in full armour, but with his visor up and eyes blazing! He wears a golden circlet round his helmet, so it is easy to see who it is. As he approaches me, he raises his mighty battle-axe, already dripping red, from indiscriminately hacking his way to my position. Then I realise what he means to do! He is making an all-out, determined rush to kill me! I am frozen to the spot. I cannot move, as the fury approaches. I have never fought in a pitched battle before. I should turn and flee, but I am unable to. I feel hypnotised by the horror of it!

Then John Cheyney lifts his own battle-axe and intervenes to strike down the king, but Richard is quicker, strikes Brandon to the ground, then splits Cheyney through the skull in one terrible, swift action! John falls with a thud like a clap of thunder! The Dragon Colours, symbol of my homeland, have fluttered down and are torn and trampled in the mud and I am left defenceless! The great white war horse, White Surrey, raises itself up, rearing on its back legs. Richard lifts his axe to finish me too—then I wake!

What is causing it? Is it guilt? Why should I feel guilty, really? I did not kill him. I did not kill Richard! But I saw him die horribly, a few moments later, crying, 'Treason! Treason!' over and over again, when William Stanley's men surrounded him, hacking him down with endless blows until he lay dead, his face in the mud!

He did not deserve to die like that! He did not deserve to be murdered in such a manner by those he believed were his allies and friends! Kings should not die in battle, but his foolhardiness and determination to get to me when he thought he saw his chance to kill me and make an end to the years of civil strife, left him an open target—as I had been a few moments earlier!

And afterwards, I let them take his body away. I will regret that forever! For they mistreated it in the most sickening manner! I did not guess—how could I possibly know what they meant to do—how they would desecrate it? God's anointed, for that is what he was. But a few moments more, and it would have been me dead in the mud instead, hacked to pieces!

I did not realise they would vent their hatred in such obscene ways. They treated him far worse than a dead dog in the street! It preys on my mind—the horror of it! Someone told me later what had happened to his body, when I enquired if it had been given decent burial—as befits a man who had been the king and had once been my friend, even if only for a few days. What they told me made me sick to the stomach. I actually vomited at the news. I certainly did not authorise that—I did not even know of it until later! It brought home to me the vileness of men!

They stripped him naked and threw him backwards across a horse, breaking his body, so that his poor bloody head hung down low and was thrown from side to side. They paraded him through Leicester like that, for all the populace to see, to jeer at and revile, to throw excrement at. They made one of his own squires sit up on the horse to guide it. He apparently cried all the way, being but a lad of fourteen or so. Richard's broken body was covered with so many wounds that it could be seen they had mostly been inflicted after he was dead—in sheer vicious hatred. As the horse crossed the Bow Bridge, his head repeatedly hit the parapet on one side, crushing his face. The people laughed and hurled obscenities. These were the same people surely who, only the day before, had seen Richard at the head of his armies, in full shining armour and the crown upon his helmet, leading the way proudly towards the battlefield? Did they cheer him then? Or did they watch in silence? No one seems able to tell me.

Then they threw him, naked and unshriven, into a ditch. After a few hours, the good Grey Friars, holy men, came quietly by night and removed his body to their abbey, into sanctuary. They buried it, I was told, in an unmarked grave, so it could not be desecrated more. I bless them for their pity and compassion. They at least respected the dead. I would visit his grave if I knew where it was, but they would tell nobody. I hope they shrived him before burial. No one should go to God unshriven. For I am sure he has gone to God. I believed none of the tales spread around during his reign about deeds of great wickedness which he was supposed to have done. I knew him better than that. I think I had got to the heart of the man, even in the few days I was his constant companion and we became friends. He was devout and good-hearted. He cared for people—could never have been responsible for such atrocities! Also, my mother had told me that the worst of them, the murder of the little princes in the Tower, was actually carried out by Buckingham—with her connivance!

And all of it—the bloody realities of the battle—my first; Richard's headlong lunge at me; his terrible death and the inglorious aftermath—lives with me, day and night—especially at night!

I know that if it had not been for the murderous intervention of those treacherous Stanleys, he would have killed me and won the battle! And he was also betrayed by Percy of Northumberland, who never even brought his great army into the fray! This appalling treachery had all been pre-planned and Richard was the victim!

Did he know—did he guess—what they might do? Did he realise it all, but fight bravely anyway? That would have been in keeping with his courageous nature! To win—or die in the attempt—would have been his ultimate decision!

My Uncle, Thomas Stanley, picked up Richard's crown—the circlet of gold he had worn round his helmet—from where it had rolled under a hawthorn bush. He pressed it on to my head then and there. I should have been proud, full of joy! But I was filled with loathing for him and horror at what had just occurred.

And now I am king! By default, I feel! I occupy the highest position in the land, as my Lady mother ever predicted I would. And how she worked for it continually, in her ruthless way! I love her, but I shall never forgive her for some of the things she did on my behalf, especially her dark involvement with Buckingham. I have achieved my destiny, but at what a cost?!

By the death of a good, upright man, committed to justice for his people; eager to reform the law and right wrongs—often personally, when he could! You see, I secretly followed his life; I kept myself informed of his doings; I never ceased to regret that we were on opposite sides by an accident of birth. As a boy, I hero-worshipped him, though I admitted this to none! I admired him tremendously—his achievements even then were amazing! I hardly dared to aspire to emulate them!

His reign was short—too short; his life cut off in its prime by the wickedness and treachery of men. He never had a chance to achieve everything of which he was surely capable! He could have become a truly great king, one of the best the country ever had! Can I do better? I quail at the prospect, as if I were a boy again, years ago, when my Uncle Jasper and my mother continually tried to inspire me to go all out for this throne! How they plotted and planned with this one end in mind!

I have done as they desired, but I did not wish this! When I knew I had to fight him, my whole being rejected the thought, but I had no choice, and neither did he. When he tried to kill me, he was doing it for his country—not for himself. He had to try and consolidate his position, to get rid of the threat, which was me! He was doing his duty. In his heart, I am sure he would rather have been my friend, not my enemy. All those years ago in Wales, he told me as much. We knew that it could not be and both regretted it. It was our destiny to be on opposing sides.

Now I am king of this great country in which I feel an alien as yet. I only hope I can do as well as Richard did in his short time on earth. I feel I have no right to be here, really. I will have to work hard to make my mark, to show that I have the commonweal of the people at heart, like Richard. I will have to justify my new position as king—as he did, most assuredly!

I pray every day for his soul—the soul of a great and good man—who was my friend in spirit, I know, as I was his . . .

The End

4468512R00185

Printed in Great Britain
by Amazon.co.uk, Ltd.,
Marston Gate.